CompTIA Security+:
Get Certified Get Ahead
SY0-201 Study Guide

Darril Gibson

ISBN: 1-4392-3636-4

ISBN-13: 9781439236369

Library of Congress Control Number: 2009903491

Visit *www.booksurge.com* to order additional copies.

Dedication

To my wife, who even after seventeen years of marriage continues to remind me how wonderful life can be if you're in a loving relationship. I'm ready for at least seventeen more.

Acknowledgments

Books of this size and depth can't be done by a single person. I'm grateful for the many people who helped me put this book together. Daniel Mielewski, the technical editor, provided outstanding feedback and superb technical insight. The entire team at BookSurge was easy to work with and provided excellent services from the first contact through the entire editing and layout process. I'm thankful for all the work and support they provided.

About the Author

Darril Gibson is an accomplished author and professional trainer. He has authored five books and coauthored one. He holds many current IT certifications including: CompTIA A+, Network+, Security+, CISSP, MCDST (XP), MCSA, MCSA Messaging (2000, 2003), MCSE (NT 4.0, 2000, 2003), MCDBA (SQL 7.0, 2000), MCITP (Vista, Server 2008, SQL 2005, SQL 2008), MCTS (Server 2008, SQL Server 2008), MCSD (6.0, .NET), and ITIL Foundations v 3.0.

He's the CEO of Security Consulting and Training, LLC and is currently working on an Air Force contract teaching a wide variety of IT topics including CompTIA Security+. He also works as an adjunct professor at ECPI College of Technology.

In addition to the CompTIA and CISSP exams, Darril has passed over thirty Microsoft certification tests. You can view his Microsoft transcript here:

http://www.microsoft.com/learning/mcp/transcripts

Transcript ID: 660310

Access Code: DarrilGibson

Darril lives in Virginia Beach with his wife and two dogs. Whenever possible, they escape to a small cabin in the country on over twenty acres of land that continues to provide peace, tranquility, and balance.

About the Technical Editor

Daniel Mielewski has been engaged in troubleshooting and maintaining computer hardware, software, and network connectivity issues for more than ten years. He holds CompTIA A+, Network+, and Security+ certifications. When he's not working with computers, he enjoys spending time with his family.

Table of Contents

Introduction

Congratulations on your purchase of *CompTIA Security+: Get Certified, Get Ahead*. You are one step closer to becoming CompTIA Security+ certified. This certification has helped a lot of individuals get ahead in their jobs and their careers, and it can help you get ahead too.

You're in good company. Since inception, over 50,000 people have become CompTIA Security+ certified, and it is one of the top ten certifications sought by IT professionals today.

Who This Book Is For

If you're studying for the CompTIA Security+ exam and want to pass it on your first attempt, this book is for you. It covers 100 percent of the objectives identified by CompTIA at enough depth so that you'll be able to easily answer the exam questions.

The first target audience for this book is students in CompTIA Security+ classes, which I teach. My goal is to give students a book they can use to study the relevant and important details of CompTIA Security+ in adequate depth for the topics that are challenging but without the minutia in topics that are clear for most IT professionals.

However, it can certainly be used by other instructors teaching the same class and by those who are able to pick up a book and study the materials on their own.

Additionally, you can keep this book on your shelf (or in your Kindle) to remind yourself of important relevant concepts. These concepts are important for security professionals and IT professionals in the real world.

About This Book

Over the past several years, I've taught literally hundreds of students, helping them to become CompTIA Security+ certified. During that time, I've learned what concepts are easy to grasp and what concepts need more explanation. I've developed handouts and analogies that help students grasp the elusive concepts.

Feedback from students was overwhelmingly positive—both in their comments to me and their successful pass rates when they took the certification exam. As the objectives changed in 2008, I knew that I needed to rewrite my handouts. This book is a result of that work.

On the other hand, I only reach so many students a year. This book allows me to reach a much larger audience and share the information I have on security. Even if you aren't in one of the classes I teach, this book can help you learn the relevant material to successfully pass the exam.

How to Use This Book

When practicing for any certification exam, the following steps are a good recipe for success:

- **Review the objectives.** The objectives for the SY0-201 exam can be found in this introduction.
- **Learn the material related to the objectives.** Material is covered throughout this book, and the introduction includes a map showing which chapter (or chapters) covers the material.
- **Take practice questions.** A key step when preparing for any certification exam is to make sure you can answer the exam questions. Yes, you need the knowledge, but you also must be able to read a question and pick the right answer. This simply takes practice.
- **Read and understand the explanations.** When preparing, you should make sure you know why the correct answers are correct and why the incorrect answers are incorrect. The explanations provide this information and are also worded to help you get other questions correct.

This book has more than 375 practice test questions you can use to test your knowledge and your ability to adequately answer them. Every question has a detailed explanation to help you understand why the correct answers are correct and why the incorrect answers are incorrect.

You can find the questions in the following areas:

- **Assessment exam.** Use these questions to get a feel for what you know and what you need to study more.

- **End-of-chapter practice questions**. Each chapter has practice questions to help you test your comprehension of the material in the chapter.
- **End-of-book practice exam**. Use this as a practice exam to test your comprehension of the subject matter and readiness to take the actual exam.

It's OK if you do the practice questions in a different order. For example, you may tackle all the chapters in the book and then do the pre-assessment and post-assessment questions. That's fine, but make sure you cover all the questions.

Remember

Throughout the book, you'll see text boxes that highlight important information you should remember to successfully pass the exam. The surrounding content provides the additional information needed to adequately understand these key points, and the text boxes summarize the important points.

These text boxes will look like this:

> ### Remember
> I strongly encourage you to repeat the information to yourself in the text boxes as often as possible. The more you repeat the information, the more likely you are to remember it when you take the exam.

A tried-and-true method of repeating key information is to take notes when you're first studying the material and then rewrite the notes later. This will expose you to the material a minimum of three times.

Another method that students have told me has been successful for them is to use an MP3 player. Many MP3 players can record. Start your MP3 recorder and read the information in each text box for a chapter and the information in the Exam Topic Review section of each chapter. Save the MP3 file and regularly listen to it. This allows you to reaffirm the important information in your own voice.

You can play it while exercising, walking, or just about any time when it's not dangerous to listen to any MP3 file. You can even burn the MP3 files to a CD and play them back from a CD player.

If the MP3 method is successful for you, you can also record and listen to exam questions. Read the question, only the correct answer, and the first sentence of the explanation in each practice question.

Vendor Neutral

CompTIA certifications are intended to be vendor neutral. In other words, the certification is not centered on any single vendor such as Microsoft, Apple, or Linux. With that in mind, you don't need significantly deep knowledge of any of the operating systems, but don't be surprised if you see more questions about one OS over another simply because of market share.

In October 2008, Windows had about 90 percent market share of desktop systems. Apple MACs were next with 6 percent and Linux at about 4 percent. A survey in 2004 showed Microsoft also had about 90 percent market share, indicating it's staying relatively stable.

Since approximately 90 percent of systems you'll touch in a corporate environment are Microsoft based, don't be surprised to see some Microsoft-specific questions.

Web Resources

Check out http://sy0-201.com for up-to-date details on the CompTIA Security+ exam. This site was created to provide additional information related to the CompTIA Security+ exam and this book.

Although a lot of people have spent a lot of time and energy trying to ensure that there are no errors in this book, occasionally they slip through. www.sy0-201.com includes an errata page listing any errors we've discovered.

If you discover any errors, please let me know at Darril@sy0-201.com. I'd also love to hear about your success when you pass the exam. I'm constantly getting good news from readers and students who are successfully earning their certifications.

As changes occur to this exam, I'll also post updates to this site. Check back often.

Assumptions

The CompTIA Security+ exam assumes you have at least two years of experience working with computers in a network. It also assumes you have either been certified in A+ and Network+ or at least have the equivalent knowledge. While writing this book, I have largely assumed the same thing.

However, I'm well aware that two years of experience in a network could mean many different things. Your two years of experience may expose you to different technologies than someone else's two years of experience.

When it's critical that you understand an underlying network concept in order to master the relevant exam material, I have often included the concept within the background information.

Set a Goal

Look at a calendar right now and determine the date forty-five days from today; this will be your target date to take this exam. Set this as your goal to complete studying the materials and to take the exam.

This target allows you to master about one and a half chapters per week. It may be that some of the chapters take you less time and some of the chapters take you more time. No problem. If you want to modify your target date, do so, but a recipe for success includes setting a goal.

When I teach CompTIA Security+ at a local college, I often help the students register for the exam on the first night. They pick a date close to the end of the course and register. I've found that when we do this, about 90 percent of the students take and pass the exam within one week after completing the course.

When I didn't help the students register on the first night, more than half of them did not complete the exam in the same time frame. Setting a goal helps.

About the Exam

The CompTIA Security+ exam was first released in 2002 and has quickly grown in popularity. As with other CompTIA certifications, once you become

CompTIA Security+ certified, CompTIA considers you certified for life. You don't need to retake the exam to retain your certification.

The exam objectives were revised in 2008, and the new exam is numbered as SY0-201. SY0-101 (the original version of CompTIA Security+) was retired in July 2009.

A summary of the details of the exam includes:

- **Number of questions:** 100
- **Time to complete questions:** 90 minutes (does not include time to complete pre-test and post-test surveys)
- **Passing score:** 750
- **Grading criteria:** Scale of 100 to 900 (about 83 percent)
- **Recertification requirements:** None—certified for life
- **Question types:** Multiple choice
- **Exam format:** Traditional—can move back and forth to view previous questions
- **Exam prerequisites:** None required; recommended to have Network+ certification
- **Exam test providers:** Prometric and Pearson Vue

Number of Questions and Duration

You have ninety minutes to complete one hundred questions. This gives you about one minute per question. Don't let this scare you; it's actually a good thing. With only about a minute to read and answer a question, you know the questions can't be very long.

Passing Score

A score of 750 is required to pass. This is on a scale of 100 to 900. If the exam is paid for, and you don't get a single question correct, you still get a score of 100. If you get every testable question correct, you get a score of 900.

If all questions are equal, then you need to get eighty-four questions correct—900 maximum divided by a passing score of 750 = 83.333 or 83.33

percent. However, CompTIA does not say if all questions are equally scored or whether harder questions are weighted and worth more.

While you shouldn't underestimate the difficulty of this exam, it has been passed by over 50,000 people, so you can pass it too. With this book, you will be well prepared.

Some questions are beta questions. They aren't graded but instead are used to test the validity of the questions. If everyone gets a beta question correct, it's probably too easy. If everyone gets it incorrect, there's probably something wrong with the question. After enough people have tested a beta question, it's analyzed and may be added to the test bank or rewritten and retested.

You are not graded on beta questions. However, you don't know what questions are beta and what questions are valid, so you need to treat every question equally.

Question Types

Expect the questions on the exam to be straightforward. For example, what's 5 X 5? Either you know the answer is 25 or you don't. The exam questions test your knowledge of the material, not necessarily your ability to dissect the question so that you can figure out what the question is really trying to ask.

I'm not saying the knowledge is simplistic, only that the questions will be worded so that you can easily understand what they are asking.

As a comparative example, Microsoft certification questions can be quite complex. Microsoft questions often aren't just testing your knowledge of the topic but your ability to analyze the material and logically come to the right conclusion.

Here are two examples of questions—the first, the way Microsoft may word the question on a Microsoft certification exam, and the second, the way that CompTIA may word it for the CompTIA Security+ exam.

- **Microsoft.** You are driving a bus from Chicago to Atlanta at 55 mph with twenty-two passengers. The bus is painted blue. At the same time, a train is traveling from Miami to Atlanta at 40 mph. The train has a yellow caboose. What color are the bus driver's eyes?
- **CompTIA Security+.** What color are your eyes?

Notice the first question adds a lot of superfluous information. Two pieces are critical to answering the first question. It starts by saying, "You are driving a bus…" and then ends by asking, "What color are the bus driver's eyes?" You're required to put the two together and weed through the irrelevant information to come to the correct answer.

The second question is straightforward. "What color are your eyes?" There's very little analysis required. Either you know it or you don't. This is what you can expect from most of the CompTIA Security+ questions.

Some of the CompTIA exam questions may have a little more detail than just a single sentence, but overall, expect them to be one- to two-sentence questions. They are only giving you about one minute for each question, and it's not intended to be a reading comprehension exam.

As an example, you may see a question like: "What port does HTTPS use?" In this case, you'd need to know that HTTPS uses port 443.

However, knowledge of expanded material could be tested by rewording it a little, such as: "What port needs to be opened to allow secure web server traffic?" In this case, you'd need to know that a web server uses HTTPS for secure web traffic, and HTTPS uses port 443.

Exam Format

Questions are multiple-choice types where you choose one answer or multiple answers. When you need to choose multiple answers, you may be told to choose two, choose three, or choose all that apply.

You start at question 1 and go to question 100. During the process, you can mark any questions you want to review when you're done. Additionally, you can view previous questions if desired. For example, if you get to question 10 and then remember something that helps you answer question 5, you can go back and redo question 5.

Exam Prerequisites

All that is required for you to take the exam is money. Other than that, there are no enforced prerequisites.

However, to successfully pass the exam, you're expected to have at least two years of experience working with computers in a networking environment. If you have more than that, the exam materials will likely come easier to you. If you have less, the exam may be more difficult.

Exam Test Providers

You can take the exam at either a Pearson Vue or Prometric testing site. Some testing sites do only testing. However, most testing sites are part of another company, such as a training company or college. You can take an exam at the training company's testing site even if you haven't taken a course with them.

Both the Pearson Vue and the Prometric web sites include search tools you can use to find a testing site close to you. Check them out at http://www.vue.com and http://prometric.com.

At this writing, the CompTIA Security+ exam is $258 if you purchase it at full price. However, you can usually purchase discount vouchers for less than the retail price. If you want to pay less for the exam, use Google and enter "Security+ test voucher." You'll get several links to companies that sell vouchers at a discount.

When you purchase the voucher, you get the voucher number, and you can use this number to register at a testing site. A word of caution: make sure you purchase a voucher for the right testing center. If you purchase a Pearson Vue voucher, you won't be able to use it at a Prometric testing center unless they are also a Pearson Vue testing center. Some testing centers support both Vue and Prometric, but you should check first.

Exam Domains

The exam objectives are divided into the following domains, or general topic areas. Additionally, CompTIA publishes the percentage of questions you can anticipate in any of the domains.

- **1.0 Systems Security:** 21 percent of examination content
- **2.0 Network Infrastructure:** 20 percent of examination content
- **3.0 Access Control:** 17 percent of examination content

- **4.0 Assessments & Audits:** 15 percent of examination content
- **5.0 Cryptography:** 15 percent of examination content
- **6.0 Organizational Security:** 12 percent of examination content

CompTIA publishes a listing of the objectives on its web site. At this writing, this listing is accurate, but CompTIA includes the following disclaimers:

- "The lists of examples provided in bulleted format below each objective are not exhaustive lists. Other examples of technologies, processes or tasks pertaining to each objective may also be included on the exam although not listed or covered in this objectives document."
- "The CompTIA Security+ (2008 Edition) Exam Objectives are subject to change without notice."

You can verify that the objectives haven't changed by checking on www.comptia.org. Additionally, you can check this book's companion site at http://sy0-201.com for any up-to-date changes and additional materials to help you take and pass the exam.

Objective to Chapter Map

The objectives that are in *italics* are those that are new in the SY0-201 exam.

This following listing also includes the chapters where the objective is covered.

1.0 Systems Security

1.1 Differentiate among various systems security threats. (Ch 5, 6)

- Privilege escalation (Ch 5)
- Virus (Ch 6)
- Worm (Ch 6)
- Trojan (Ch 6)
- Spyware (Ch 6)
- Spam (Ch 6)
- Adware (Ch 6)
- Rootkits (Ch 6)
- Botnets (Ch 6)
- Logic bomb (Ch 6)

1.2 Explain the security risks pertaining to system hardware and peripherals. (Ch 7)

- BIOS (Ch 7)
- USB devices (Ch 7)
- Cell phones (Ch 7)
- Removable storage (Ch 7)
- Network attached storage (Ch 7)

1.3 Implement OS hardening practices and procedures to achieve workstation and server security. (Ch 5)

- Hotfixes (Ch 5)
- Service packs (Ch 5)
- Patches (Ch 5)
- Patch management (Ch 5)
- Group policies (Ch 5)
- Security templates (Ch 5)
- Configuration baselines (Ch 5)

1.4 Carry out the appropriate procedures to establish application security. (Ch 3, 5)

- ActiveX (Ch 5)
- Java (Ch 5)
- Scripting (Ch 5)
- Browser (Ch 5)
- Buffer overflows (Ch 5)
- Cookies (Ch 5)
- SMTP open relays (Ch 5)
- Instant messaging (Ch 5)
- P2P (Ch 3)
- Input validation (Ch 5)
- Cross-site scripting (XSS) (Ch 5)

1.5 Implement security applications. (Ch 4, 5, 6)

- HIDS (Ch 4)
- Personal software firewalls (Ch 4)
- Antivirus (Ch 5, 6)
- Anti-spam (Ch 5, 6)
- Popup blockers (Ch 5)

1.6 Explain the purpose and application of virtualization technology. (Ch 5)

2.0 Network Infrastructure

2.1 Differentiate between the different ports & protocols, their respective threats and mitigation techniques. (Ch 3, 5, 6)

- Antiquated protocols (Ch 3)
- TCP/IP hijacking (Ch 6)
- Null sessions (Ch 6)
- Spoofing (Ch 6)
- Man-in-the-middle (Ch 6)
- Replay (Ch 6)
- DOS (Ch 6)
- DDOS (Ch 6)
- Domain Name Kiting (Ch 6)
- DNS poisoning (Ch 5)
- ARP poisoning (Ch 6)

2.2 Distinguish between network design elements and components. (Ch 3, 4)

- DMZ (Ch 3)
- VLAN (Ch 3)
- NAT (Ch 3)
- Network interconnections (Ch 3)
- NAC (Ch 4)
- Subnetting (Ch 3)
- Telephony (Ch 4)

2.3 Determine the *appropriate* use of network security tools to facilitate network security. (Ch 3, 4)

- NIDS (Ch 4)
- NIPS (Ch 4)
- Firewalls (Ch 3)
- Proxy servers (Ch 3)
- Honeypot (Ch 4)
- Internet content filters (Ch 3)
- Protocol analyzers (Ch 7)

2.4 Apply the appropriate network tools to facilitate network security. (Ch 3, 4)

- NIDS (Ch 4)
- Firewalls (Ch 3)
- Proxy servers (Ch 3)
- Internet content filters (Ch 3)
- Protocol analyzers (Ch 7)

2.5 Explain the vulnerabilities and mitigations associated with network devices. (Ch 5)

- Privilege escalation (Ch 5)
- Weak passwords (Ch 5)
- Back doors (Ch 5)
- Default accounts (Ch 5)
- DOS (Ch 5)

2.6 Explain the vulnerabilities and mitigations associated with various transmission media. (Ch 3)

- Vampire taps (Ch 3)

2.7 Explain the vulnerabilities and implement mitigations associated with wireless networking. (Ch 4)

- Data emanation (Ch 4)
- War driving (Ch 4)

- SSID broadcast (Ch 4)
- Bluejacking (Ch 4)
- Bluesnarfing (Ch 4)
- Rogue access points (Ch 4)
- Weak encryption (Ch 4)

3.0 Access Control

3.1 Identify and apply industry best practices for access control methods. (Ch1)

- Implicit deny (Ch1)
- Least privilege (Ch 10)
- Separation of duties (Ch 10)
- Job rotation (Ch 10)

3.2 Explain common access control models and the differences between each. (Ch 2)

- MAC (Ch 2)
- DAC (Ch 2)
- Role & Rule based access control (Ch 2)

3.3 Organize users and computers into appropriate security groups and roles while distinguishing between appropriate rights and privileges. (Ch 2)

3.4 Apply appropriate security controls to file and print resources. (Ch 5)

3.5 Compare and implement logical access control methods. (Ch 2)

- ACL (Ch 2)
- Group policies (Ch 2)
- Password policy (Ch 2)
- Domain password policy (Ch 2)
- User names and passwords (Ch 2)
- Time of day restrictions (Ch 2)
- Account expiration (Ch 2)
- Logical tokens (Ch 2)

3.6 Summarize the various authentication models and identify the components of each. (Ch1)
- One, two and three-factor authentication (Ch1)
- Single sign-on (Ch1)

3.7 Deploy various authentication models and identify the components of each. (Ch 1, 4)
- Biometric reader (Ch1)
- RADIUS (Ch1)
- RAS (Ch1)
- LDAP(Ch1)
- Remote access policies (Ch 4)
- Remote authentication (Ch 4)
- VPN (Ch 1)
- Kerberos (Ch 1)
- CHAP (Ch 1)
- PAP (Ch 1)
- Mutual (Ch 1)
- 802.1x (Ch 1, 4)
- TACACS (Ch 1)

3.8 Explain the difference between identification and authentication (identity proofing). (Ch1, 2)

3.9 Explain and apply physical access security methods. (Ch 2)
- Physical access logs/lists (Ch 2)
- Hardware locks (Ch 2)
- Physical access control—ID badges (Ch 2)
- Door access systems (Ch 2)
- Man-trap (Ch 2)
- Physical tokens (Ch 2)
- Video surveillance—camera types and positioning (Ch 2)

4.0 Assessments & Audits

4.1 Conduct risk assessments and implement risk mitigation. (Ch 7)

4.2 Carry out vulnerability assessments using common tools. (Ch 7)

- Port scanners (Ch 7)
- Vulnerability scanners (Ch 7)
- Protocol analyzers (Ch 7)
- OVAL (Ch 7)
- Password crackers (Ch 7)
- Network mappers (Ch 7)

4.3 Within the realm of vulnerability assessments, explain the proper use of penetration testing versus vulnerability scanning. (Ch 7)

4.4 Use monitoring tools on systems and networks and detect security-related anomalies. (Ch 7)

- Performance monitor (Ch 7)
- Systems monitor (Ch 7)
- Performance baseline (Ch 7)
- Protocol analyzers (Ch 7)

4.5 Compare and contrast various types of monitoring methodologies. (Ch 4)

- Behavior-based (Ch 4)
- Signature-based (Ch 4)
- Anomaly-based (Ch 4)

4.6 Execute proper logging procedures and evaluate the results. (Ch 7)

- Security application (Ch 7)
- DNS (Ch 7)
- System (Ch 7)
- Performance (Ch 7)
- Access (Ch 7)
- Firewall (Ch 7)
- Antivirus (Ch 7)

4.7 Conduct periodic audits of system security settings. (Ch 7)
- User access and rights review (Ch 7)
- Storage and retention policies (Ch 10)
- Group policies (Ch 7)

5.0 Cryptography

5.1 Explain general cryptography concepts. (Ch 1, 9)
- Key management (Ch 9)
- Steganography (Ch 9)
- Symmetric key (Ch 9)
- Asymmetric key (Ch 9)
- Confidentiality (Ch 1, 9)
- Integrity and availability (Ch 1, 9)
- Non-repudiation (Ch 1, 9)
- Comparative strength of algorithms (Ch 9)
- Digital signatures (Ch 9)
- Whole disk encryption (Ch 9)
- Trusted Platform Module (TPM) (Ch 9)
- Single vs. Dual sided certificates (Ch 9)
- Use of proven technologies (Ch 9)

5.2 Explain basic hashing concepts and map various algorithms to appropriate applications. (Ch 9)
- SHA (Ch 9)
- MD5 (Ch 9)
- LANMAN (Ch 9)
- NTLM (Ch 9)

5.3 Explain basic encryption concepts and map various algorithms to appropriate applications. (Ch 4, 9)
- DES (Ch 9)
- 3DES (Ch 9)
- RSA (Ch 9)

- PGP (Ch 9)
- Elliptic curve (Ch 4, 9)
- AES (Ch 9)
- AES256 (Ch 9)
- One time pad (Ch 9)
- Transmission encryption (WEP TKIP, etc.) (Ch 4)

5.4 Explain and implement protocols. (Ch 4, 5, 9)
- SSL/TLS (Ch 4, 5, 9)
- S/MIME (Ch 9)
- PPTP (Ch 4)
- HTTP vs. HTTPS vs. SHTTP (Ch 5, 9)
- L2TP (Ch 4)
- IPSEC (Ch 4, 9)
- SSH (Ch 9)

5.5 *Explain core concepts of public key cryptography.* (Ch 9)
- Public Key Infrastructure (PKI) (Ch 9)
- Recovery agent (Ch 9)
- Public key (Ch 9)
- Private keys (Ch 9)
- Certificate Authority (CA) (Ch 9)
- Registration (Ch 9)
- Key escrow (Ch 9)
- Certificate Revocation List (CRL) (Ch 9)
- Trust models (Ch 9)

5.6 Implement PKI and certificate management (Ch 9).
- Public Key Infrastructure (PKI) (Ch 9)
- Recovery agent (Ch 9)
- Public key (Ch 9)
- Private keys (Ch 9)
- Certificate Authority (CA) (Ch 9)
- Registration (Ch 9)

- Key escrow (Ch 9)
- Certificate Revocation List (CRL) (Ch 9)

6.0 Organizational Security

6.1 Explain redundancy planning and its components (Ch 8).

- Hot site (Ch 8)
- Cold site (Ch 8)
- Warm site (Ch 8)
- Backup generator (Ch 8)
- Single point of failure (Ch 8)
- RAID (Ch 8)
- Spare parts (Ch 8)
- Redundant servers (Ch 8)
- Redundant ISP (Ch 8)
- UPS (Ch 8)
- Redundant connections (Ch 8)

6.2 Implement disaster recovery procedures. (Ch 8)

- Planning (Ch 8)
- Disaster recovery exercises (Ch 8)
- Backup techniques and practices—storage (Ch 8)
- Schemes (Ch 8)
- Restoration (Ch 8)

6.3 Differentiate between and execute appropriate incident-response procedures. (Ch 10)

- Forensics (Ch 10)
- Chain of custody (Ch 10)
- First responders (Ch 10)
- Damage and loss control (Ch 10)
- Reporting—disclosure of (Ch 10)

6.4 Identify and explain applicable legislation and organizational policies. (Ch 10)

- Secure disposal of computers (Ch 10)
- Acceptable use policies (Ch 10)
- Password complexity (Ch 10)
- Change management (Ch 10)
- Classification of information (Ch 10)
- Mandatory vacations (Ch 10)
- Personally Identifiable Information (PII) (Ch 10)
- Due care (Ch 10)
- Due diligence (Ch 10)
- Due process (Ch 10)
- SLA (Ch 10)
- Security-related HR policy (Ch 10)
- User education and awareness training (Ch 10)

6.5 Explain the importance of environmental controls. (Ch 8)

- Fire suppression (Ch 8)
- HVAC (Ch 8)
- Shielding (Ch 8)

6.6 Explain the concept of and how to reduce the risks of social engineering. (Ch 6)

- Phishing (Ch 6)
- Hoaxes (Ch 6)
- Shoulder surfing (Ch 6)
- Dumpster diving (Ch 6)
- User education and awareness training (Ch 6)

CompTIA Security+ Assessment Exam

Use this assessment exam to test your knowledge of the topics before you start reading the book, and again before you take the live exam. An answer key with explanation is available at the end of the assessment exam.

1. A biometric system has identified an authorized user as an unauthorized user. What is this?
   A. False acceptance
   B. False rejection
   C. False positron
   D. Biometric strength

2. CHAP is used to authenticate a client using a handshake process. When does this handshake process occur? (Choose two.)
   A. When the connection is first established
   B. When the connection is closed
   C. When the connection needs to be reestablished
   D. During the connection

3. Your network uses both smart cards and strong passwords for authentication. You are asked what could be done to increase authentication. What should you suggest?
   A. Retinal scanner
   B. Pass phrases
   C. PINs
   D. AES

4. Which authentication mechanism creates a token when you log on, destroys it when you log off, and uses it to determine if access to a resource is granted or denied?
   A. KDC
   B. Smart cards
   C. CHAP
   D. Security token

5. Which of the following authentication mechanisms uses a KDC and symmetric-key cryptography?

    A. Smart cards

    B. TACACS

    C. Kerberos

    D. CHAP

6. When an individual is trying to prove who he is, when would proofing occur?

    A. During the purchasing phase

    B. During the authentication phase

    C. During the identification phase

    D. During the validation phase

7. A user logs on once with a single username and password. The user can then access multiple computer applications without logging on again. What is this process called?

    A. DAC

    B. MAC

    C. RBAC

    D. Single sign-on

8. What port does Kerberos use by default?

    A. Port 22

    B. Port 80

    C. Port 88

    D. Port 143

9. Which of the following statements is false concerning the MAC model?

    A. MAC is a static model.

    B. MAC uses security labels.

    C. MAC uses a lattice.

    D. The MAC model does not allow users to share their resources dynamically.

10. Which access control model gives the owner full control of the objects?

    A. MAC

    B. DAC

    C. RBAC

    D. SSL

11. Which of the following is used with the MAC access control model?

    A. AppleTalk

    B. Sensitivity labels

    C. Role membership

    D. Object ownership

12. Which access control model uses roles to establish access?

    A. MAC

    B. DAC

    C. RBAC

    D. RAID

13. Which one of the following statements is true?

    A. Dynamic NAT uses a single public IP address and a many-to-many mapping.

    B. Static NAT uses multiple public IP addresses and a many-to-one mapping.

    C. Dynamic NAT uses multiple public IP addresses and a one-to-one mapping.

    D. Static NAT uses a single public IP address and a one-to-one mapping.

14. Your company wants to host a server that only business partners can use to check the availability and shipping status of parts they have ordered. Where should this server be placed?

    A. Intranet

    B. Extranet

    C. DMZ

    D. SSL

15. You want to allow un-trusted Internet clients access to services hosted by your company, but you don't want these un-trusted clients to be able to access your internal network. What should you use?

    A. DMZ

    B. Extranet

    C. HIDS

    D. NIDS

16. What can cause a switch to function like a hub?

    A. Layer 3 programming

    B. Router tables

    C. MAC flooding

    D. SYN Flood

17. What ports are commonly used for email? (Choose three.)

    A. 21

    B. 22

    C. 25

    D. 80

    E. 88

    F. 110

    G. 143

18. A network administrator suspects that her network has been attacked. Specifically, she suspects that an intruder from the Internet has gotten through security and is accessing internal network resources. What should she check first to investigate the intrusion?

    A. Network firewall logs

    B. Personal firewall logs

    C. ACLs

    D. HIDS

19. Which transmission media is least susceptible to vampire taps?

    A. Twisted pair

    B. Coax

    C. SLA

    D. Fiber optic

20. What type of IDS requires the use of a baseline?

    A. Behavior-based

    B. Signature-based

    C. Heuristic-based

    D. Host-based

21. Of the following, what is considered to be a benefit of TACACS?

    A. It can interact with Kerberos.

    B. It provides more secure encryption of the data than RADIUS.

    C. It provides more secure encryption of the data than IPSec.

    D. It provides protection against network intrusions.

22. What is a VPN?

    A. A virtual private network that provides access to a public network over a private network

    B. A virtual private network that provides access to a private network over a public network

    C. A virtual public network that provides access to a public network over a private network

    D. A virtual public network that provides access to a private network over a public network

23. Which one of the following protocols does not provide encryption?

    A. SSL

    B. L2TP

    C. HTTPS

    D. TLS

24. What encryption protocol is used by WEP?

    A. SSL

    B. RC4

    C. AES

    D. WTLS

25. What is bluejacking?

    A. A Smurf attack launched by zombies

    B. The unauthorized access of an 802.11 wireless network

    C. The unauthorized sending of messages through someone else's Bluetooth device

    D. The unauthorized access to or theft of information from someone else's Bluetooth device

26. Of the following, what is the least effective step to take when hardening a server?

    A. Using a security baseline

    B. Changing administrator defaults

    C. Installing a HIDS

    D. Installing a personal firewall

27. What can be measured to determine network utilization of an individual server?

    A. Switch bandwidth

    B. Router bandwidth

    C. Performance baseline

    D. Security baseline

28. What should be done to reduce the attack surface of a server?

    A. Change defaults

    B. Enable necessary services

    C. Update the system

    D. Disable unneeded protocols

29. Of the following choices, what would be a core method to harden a workstation? (Choose all that apply.)

A. Change defaults

B. Enable a firewall

C. Apply system patches and hotfixes

D. Apply service packs

30. What preventative measure should be taken to reduce vulnerabilities on an Internet-facing server?

A. Disable ports 80 and 443

B. Enable ports 80 and 443

C. Enable auditing

D. Apply the most recent vendor patches and updates

31. An administrator plans to modify a system setting. What process should be followed before implementing the modification?

A. Change management

B. Chain of custody

C. Full/differential backup

D. Privilege escalation

32. What can be used to install malicious code on a server and then overwrite the return address of a program to execute the malicious code?

A. Rootkit

B. Buffer overflow

C. Worm

D. Patch

33. Sally uses her web browser to go to a well-known antivirus web site, but she notices that the URL has changed and she is instead redirected to another site encouraging her to download and install a free version of antivirus software. What is likely occurring?

A. MAC flooding

B. DNS poisoning

C. Kiting

D. DoS attack

34. Where does a Java applet run? (Choose two.)

   A. In a JVM

   B. In a sandbox

   C. In a playpen

   D. In the overflowed buffer

35. Email is being sent through a third-party mail relay. Why would this be considered a risk?

   A. Spammers can send email through a third-party relay.

   B. Email can't be filtered for spam when sent through a third-party relay.

   C. Email can't be filtered for malware when sent through a third-party relay.

   D. Blacklists often restrict the usage of third-party relays.

36. You are designing a backup plan to ensure that accounts accidentally deleted from Active Directory on a Microsoft server can be restored. What should be backed up?

   A. System State data

   B. Active Directory

   C. Data files on the domain controller

   D. Registry

37. Why would a security professional use virtualization?

   A. To test malware in a public environment

   B. To test malware with minimal risk to the virtual environment

   C. To test malware with minimal risk to the host's equipment and software

   D. To deploy malware onto a network

38. What's the difference between a Trojan horse and a worm?

   A. A worm is delivered through email, but Trojan horses travel autonomously over the network.

   B. Trojan horses are considered malware, but worms are not considered malware.

   C. Trojan horses can replicate over the network, but worms must be executed.

   D. Worms can replicate over the network, but Trojan horses must be executed.

39. A string of code spreads from file to file when the host file is executed, but the code cannot spread from system to system through the network. What is this?

    A. Virus

    B. Trojan horse

    C. Worm

    D. Logic bomb

40. What's commonly used to block adware?

    A. Antivirus software

    B. Rootkits

    C. Layer 3 switches

    D. Pop-up blockers

41. What can you use to locate a rootkit?

    A. Protocol analyzer

    B. Sniffer

    C. Port scanner

    D. Malware scanner

42. Of the following, what is commonly used in a DDoS attack? (Choose two.)

    A. Spyware

    B. Zombies

    C. Botnet

    D. Smurf

43. You suspect that multiple computers within your one-hundred-computer network are acting as zombies on an Internet botnet. What could you do to verify your suspicions?

    A. Run anti-spyware software on each computer.

    B. Check the network firewall logs.

    C. Check the System logs on each individual computer.

    D. Check the system firewall logs on each computer.

44. An attacker is attempting to transfer DNS zone data. What is the attacker involved in? (Choose two.)

  A. Reconnaissance attack

  B. A port scan attack

  C. A sniffing attack

  D. Null session attack

45. What is a common method attackers use to spoof email?

  A. Anonymous open relays

  B. Disabled open relays

  C. Replay attack

  D. DLL injection

46. Which one of the following attacks will intercept communication packets and then later resend them while pretending to be one of the clients in the original communication session?

  A. Active replay

  B. Replay

  C. Eavesdropping replay

  D. Man-in-the-middle

47. Which one of the following describes an active interception attack?

  A. Capturing traffic for the purpose of later resending it to impersonate a client

  B. Disconnecting one of two connected clients and taking over the session

  C. Sending ARP packets to mislead computers about the MAC address of a system

  D. Placing a computer between a sender and receiver to capture traffic

48. Which of the following techniques are commonly used by social engineering attackers? (Choose all that apply.)

  A. Conning

  B. Flattery

  C. Assuming a position of authority

  D. Impersonation

49. What can be done to reduce the success of social engineering attacks? (Choose all that apply.)

    A. Security awareness training

    B. Identity verification methods

    C. Logon banners

    D. Posters

50. What is the goal of risk management?

    A. Eliminate risks

    B. Reduce risks to a level acceptable to the organization

    C. Reduce risks to a level lower than the ALE

    D. Reduce risks to a level lower than the SLE

51. What is Nessus?

    A. Protocol analyzer

    B. Port scanner

    C. Vulnerability assessment tool

    D. Password cracker

52. What is external security testing when discussed in the context of a pentest?

    A. A test conducted outside of the LAN but in the DMZ

    B. A test conducted outside the organization's security perimeter

    C. A test conducted inside the firewall

    D. A test conducted outside the physical spaces of the building

53. You suspect an attacker is launching an attack by sending malformed or fragmented packets against a server. What can you use to verify your suspicions?

    A. Wireshark

    B. Nmap

    C. Nessus

    D. John the Ripper

54. Which of the following tools can be used to capture data traveling over a network?

    A. Sniffer

    B. Scanner

    C. Spammer

    D. Scooper

55. During a vulnerability assessment, a port scanner identifies several unexpected open ports on a server. What should be done?

    A. Rerun the port scanner

    B. Investigate the open ports to determine if they are needed

    C. Disable all services on the server and rerun the port scanner

    D. Close the unexpected open ports

56. Which of the following attacks can occur through email? (Choose all that apply.)

    A. Dictionary attack

    B. Brute force attack

    C. Trojan horse

    D. Virus

57. Where can you store security logs to protect them from being modified?

    A. On another server

    B. CD-R

    C. DVD-RW

    D. USB flash drive

58. What is the purpose of OVAL?

    A. Identify a standard for malware

    B. Identify a standard for spyware

    C. Identify a standard for vulnerability assessment tools

    D. Identify a standard for firewalls

59. What backup type will back up files that have changed since the last full or incremental backup?

    A. Full

    B. Differential

    C. Incremental

    D. System stat

60. Of the following choices, which can be effectively used to combat an electrical fire while also preventing damage to equipment and protecting personnel?

    A. Foam

    B. Halon

    C. CO

    D. Heat

61. What is the purpose of a Faraday cage? (Choose all that apply.)

    A. To mitigate data emanation

    B. To prevent interference

    C. To detect network attacks

    D. To detect attacks on host

62. Which of the following is considered the most secure symmetric algorithm?

    A. DES

    B. 3DES

    C. AES

    D. IDEA

63. Which of the following is considered the least secure encryption algorithm?

    A. DES

    B. 3DES

    C. AES

    D. MD5

64. On what layer of the OSI model does SSL encrypt data?

    A. Application

    B. Session

C. Sockets

D. Transport

65. Mathematics includes a principle that large prime numbers cannot be factored. Which algorithm uses this principle to create a strong encryption scheme?

A. AES

B. RSA

C. Diffie-Hellman

D. ECC

66. What can be used to pick the best security associations for multiple clients connecting to a VPN using L2TP/IPSec?

A. PPTP

B. SSL

C. TLS

D. IKE

67. What type of encryption does PGP use to encrypt data?

A. Symmetric

B. Asymmetric

C. SSL

D. TLS

68. Which of the following is considered the strongest hashing algorithm?

A. LANMAN

B. NTLMv1

C. NTLMv2

D. Bluetooth

69. You are preparing to download some new driver files from a manufacturing site. The drivers are listed with an MD5 number. What does this number represent?

A. It's a unique number generated by a hash function and can be used to verify the file after the download.

B. It's a session key and can be used to decrypt the file after the download.

C. It's a unique number generated by a hash function and can be used to decrypt the file after the download.

D. It's a session key and can be used to verify the file after the download.

70. What is it called when the hash of two different files is the same?

A. Variation

B. Deviation

C. Collision

D. Conflict

71. Which of the following can use a PSK?

A. Asymmetric encryption

B. PKI

C. TPM

D. PGP

72. What can be used to enforce non-repudiation? (Choose two.)

A. Audit logs

B. Digital signature

C. Encryption

D. Hashing

73. The chief financial officer of a company wants to send out an email to several executives within the company. She wants to ensure that others have assurances that the email actually came from her, so she decides to use a digital signature. What asymmetric key is used to encrypt the digital signature?

A. Pre-shared key

B. Her public key

C. Her private key

D. Public keys of the recipients

74. Key pairs are generated on individual client computers. What type of PKI architecture is this called?

    A. Decentralized

    B. Centralized

    C. Individual

    D. Client-side

75. What can be implemented to reduce collusion among staff?

    A. Defense in depth

    B. Need-to-know

    C. Implicit deny

    D. Job rotation

76. What are the significant security risks related to removable storage? (Choose all that apply.)

    A. Loss of PII

    B. Confidentiality of data

    C. Malware distribution

    D. Lack of storage space

77. Sally is tasked with transporting a hard drive that was seized as evidence in a possible crime. She will deliver it to a computer forensics professional who will analyze the disk. What form should she use when performing this task?

    A. Chain of custody

    B. Evidence transmittal form

    C. Affidavit of transmittal

    D. Forensics evidence transmittal form

78. What should be done to a hard drive to remove sensitive data from it before reuse?

    A. Sanitize it

    B. Format it

    C. Clean it

    D. Destroy it

Assessment Exam Answers

When checking your answers, take the time to read the explanation given. Understanding the explanations will help ensure you're prepared for the live exam. The explanation also shows the chapter or chapters where you can get more detailed information on the topic.

1. **B.** False rejection occurs when a biometric system incorrectly rejects an authorized user. False acceptance occurs when a biometric system incorrectly identifies someone as an authorized user. Positrons are related to electrons with electronics, but not with biometrics. Biometrics are susceptible to both false acceptance and false rejection if the technology isn't implemented properly, but neither of these is considered a strength.
See Chapter 1.

2. **A, D.** The CHAP handshake authentication process occurs when the connection is first established and occasionally during the connection. There is no need to complete the authentication when the session is closed, and if a connection needs to be reestablished, the process starts over.
See Chapter 1.

3. **A.** The existing authentication is already two of three factors of authentication (something a user knows and something he has), but not the third factor (something he is). Biometrics (such as fingerprint scanners or retinal scanners) could be used to authenticate users with the third factor. Strong passwords are already being used, so adding another requirement for something a user knows (such as pass phrases or PINs) wouldn't increase the authentication.
See Chapter 1.

4. **D.** The security token system is used to identify a user's permissions by matching the contents of a security token with the permissions granted to a resource. In Windows, the token includes SIDs, and it is matched to SIDs contained within DACLs of resources to determine access. The token is created when the user logs on or the session begins, and is destroyed at the end of

the session. The Key Distribution Center (KDC) is used by Kerberos to issue tickets. Smart cards include certificates issued by a PKI. CHAP uses a challenge handshake process including passing a nonce.

See Chapter 1.

5. **C.** Kerberos uses a Key Distribution Center (KDC) and symmetric-key cryptography to prevent unauthorized disclosure. Only Kerberos uses a KDC. Smart cards have embedded certificates from a Public Key Infrastructure (PKI) and use asymmetric encryption, not symmetric encryption. CHAP, TACACS, and TACACS+ are used with remote access servers to provide authentication but do not use a KDC.

See Chapter 1.

6. **C.** Identity proofing performed during the identification phase is the process of verifying that someone is who he says he is prior to issuing credentials. Credentials are later used for authentication. Purchasing and validation are not used to prove someone is who he claims to be.

See Chapter 1.

7. **D.** Single sign-on (SSO) authentication is used to allow users to enter credentials only once to access all resources, instead of entering credentials at each server or application for normal work. Instead, users authenticate once, then the supplied credentials are used throughout the session. DAC, MAC, and RBAC are all access control models, not authentication mechanisms.

See Chapter 1.

8. **C.** Kerberos uses port 88 by default. Port 22 is used by SSH. Port 80 is used by HTTP. Port 143 is used by IMAP with email.

See Chapter 1.

9. **D.** The Mandatory Access Control (MAC) model does not allow the users to share resources dynamically. It is a relatively static model that uses both security labels and a lattice.

See Chapter 2.

10. **B.** The Discretionary Access Control (DAC) model gives the owner full control of the objects, including the ability to assign permissions. Permissions and privileges are predefined in the MAC model and based on role membership in the RBAC model. SSL is an encryption protocol commonly used with HTTPS through port 443, not an access control model.
See Chapter 2.

11. **B.** The Mandatory Access Control (MAC) model uses sensitivity labels (sometimes referred to as security labels) to determine access and a lattice to determine security levels. AppleTalk is a networking protocol previously used with Apple's Macintosh computers, but current Apple Macs use TCP/IP. The RBAC model assigns access based on role membership. The DAC model uses object ownership where every object has an owner that has explicit control over the object.
See Chapter 2.

12. **C.** The Role Based Access Control (RBAC) model uses roles to establish access. The system administrator establishes access in the MAC model. The owner establishes access permissions in the DAC model. RAID is used to provide fault tolerance to disk subsystems.
See Chapter 2.

13. **D.** Static Network Address Translation (NAT) uses a single public IP address and one-to-one mapping to translate private addresses to the single public IP address. Dynamic NAT allows a NAT server to use multiple public IP addresses and decide which public IP address to use based on load.
See Chapter 3.

14. **B.** An extranet is used to provide partners with access to a limited number of resources in your network. The intranet is your internal network. A DMZ would be used to host Internet-facing servers that are accessible to anyone with Internet access, not just partners. SSL is an encryption protocol used with HTTPS (and other protocols); HTTPS uses port 443.
See Chapter 3.

15. **A.** A demilitarized zone (DMZ) is used to host Internet-facing servers accessible from un-trusted clients on the Internet and is an area located between the Internet and the internal network. The extranet is used to host a limited number of servers or services that are accessible from trusted clients or partners. Host-based intrusion detection systems (HIDS) and network-based intrusion detection systems (NIDS) are used to detect and sometimes respond to attacks.
See Chapter 3.

16. **C.** MAC flooding attempts to overload a switch by passing multiple packets with different MAC addresses, overloading its internal memory capabilities. It can then go into "failopen" mode where it functions like a hub. A router (or a layer 3 switch) operates on layer 3, and layer 3 programming does not cause a switch to operate on layer 1 where a hub operates. Router tables are not on switches. A SYN Flood attack withholds the third packet to a three-way TCP handshake.
See Chapter 3.

17. **C, F, G.** Email uses Simple Mail Transfer Protocol (SMTP) on port 25, Post Office Protocol (POP 3) on port 110, and Internet Message Access Protocol (IMAP4) on port 143. FTP uses ports 20 and 21. SSH uses port 22. HTTP uses port 80. Kerberos uses port 88.
See Chapter 3.

18. **A.** If the intruder is coming from the Internet, he would be coming through a network firewall, and the network firewall logs should have a record of the intrusion. This assumes the network has a network firewall because if it didn't, the problems would be much more severe. Personal firewall logs could be checked if a single system was attacked, but the question states the network resources (not just one resource) are being accessed. Access control lists identify what is allowed, not what got through. A host-based IDS would only be able to provide feedback on a single server.
See Chapter 3.

19. **D.** Fiber-optic media is least susceptible to vampire taps. A vampire tap attempts to tap in to the line to capture the signals. Twisted pair (both unshielded and shielded) and coaxial cables are easily tapped into. A service level agreement (SLA) is an agreement between a company and a vendor that stipulates performance expectations, such as minimum uptime and maximum downtime. See Chapter 3.

20. **A.** A behavior-based (or anomaly-based) IDS requires a baseline. The baseline identifies normal behavior, and the IDS can constantly compare current behavior against the baseline. A signature-based IDS uses a database of definitions or signatures. Heuristics are used for antivirus software to detect viruses that don't have definitions or signatures. It doesn't matter whether it's host-based or network-based.
See Chapter 4.

21. **A.** Terminal Access Controller Access-Control System+ (TACACS+) is an authentication mechanism used in remote access systems, such as VPNs, and it can interact with systems using Kerberos. TACACS does not provide encryption of data, but it does encrypt the entire authentication process. It does not act as an intrusion detection system.
See Chapter 4.

22. **B.** A virtual private network (VPN) provides access to a private network over a public network such as the Internet. A VPN does not provide access to a public network via a private network. A VPN is not a virtual public network.
See Chapter 4.

23. **B.** The Layer 2 Tunneling Protocol (L2TP) does not include encryption. L2TP is combined with IPSec for encryption. SSL is an encryption protocol, and HTTPS uses SSL for encryption. TLS is an encryption protocol.
See chapters 4 and 9.

24. **B.** Wired Equivalent Privacy (WEP) uses RC4 stream cipher encryption. SSL is commonly used with HTTPS over port 443 and can also be used to encrypt

other traffic. AES is used by WPA2 and is much more secure than RC4. WTLS is used to encrypt traffic for smaller wireless devices but is not used by WEP. See Chapter 4.

25. **C.** Bluejacking is the unauthorized sending of text messages from a Bluetooth device. A Smurf attack sends a broadcast ping message with the source IP spoofed to cause the pings to attack the victim, but it doesn't use zombies. Bluejacking is done on a Bluetooth network not an 802.11 wireless network. Bluesnarfing is the unauthorized access to or theft of information from a Bluetooth device. See Chapter 4.

26. **D.** A host-based intrusion detection system (HIDS) is the least effective of the given steps to harden a server. In general, the steps to harden a server include starting with a security baseline, changing defaults, eliminating unneeded protocols and services, enabling a software-based firewall, and keeping the system up-to-date. See chapters 4 and 5.

27. **C.** A performance baseline can be measured to determine network utilization (the ratio of current network traffic to the maximum network traffic). It can also be used to measure the utilization of the processor, memory, and disk subsystem. The bandwidth of network devices (such as routers and switches) won't tell you the network utilization of a server. A security baseline is used to standardize security settings but won't measure network utilization. See Chapter 5.

28. **D.** The attack surface of a system can be reduced by disabling unnecessary services, protocols, and applications. Other hardening practices include changing defaults and keeping the system up-to-date, but these aren't referred to as reducing the attack surface. See Chapter 5.

29. **A, B, C, D.** Hardening a workstation is the same as hardening a server. It includes changing defaults (such as default accounts and passwords), enabling a firewall, and keeping the system up-to-date with service packs, patches, and hotfixes. Additionally, unneeded services and protocols should be disabled or removed.
See Chapter 5.

30. **D.** Any server should have the most recent patches and fixes applied to keep it up-to-date and reduce vulnerabilities. This applies to Internet-facing servers (such as web servers, mail servers, or any other server accessible from the Internet) and internal servers. A web server using HTTP and HTTPS would have ports 80 and 443 open, and a non-web server would have these ports closed, but not all Internet-facing servers are web servers. While auditing is a good step to take, it doesn't reduce vulnerabilities as much as it helps to troubleshoot and detect attacks.
See Chapter 5.

31. **A.** A change-management process should be followed to ensure that changes to a system, network, or software application do not have unintended negative consequences. Chain of custody is a process used to ensure that the evidence presented is the same as the evidence that was collected. Depending on what is being modified, a backup may be desirable, but a change-management process should still be the first step. Privilege escalation is when an attacker or malware is able to gain elevated permissions.
See Chapters 5 and 10.

32. **B.** A buffer overflow can pass more code than a program expects, install malicious code, and then overwrite the return address of the program to execute the malicious code. A rootkit is a group of programs designed to hide by modifying the operating system processes. A worm is malware that travels autonomously over the network. A patch is used to update software or an operating system.
See Chapter 5.

33. **B.** A DNS poisoning attack will change the name resolution data for a host to another IP address. This can cause traffic destined for one site to be redirected to another site. MAC flooding can cause a switch to operate as a hub. Domain name kiting is the practice of repeatedly registering a domain name, and then deleting it before five days have passed to avoid paying for it. A denial-of-service (DoS) attack attempts to disrupt a server from providing normal services but wouldn't change a specific URL.
See Chapter 5.

34. **A, B.** A Java applet runs in a Java Virtual Machine (JVM). It's also said to run in a sandbox, where it is isolated and cannot access local data. A playpen is not a valid location for a Java applet. A buffer overflow attack will exploit a vulnerability with a server, but a Java applet would not run here by default.
See Chapter 5.

35. **A.** A third-party relay can be a risk if it isn't protected, and spammers are able to send email through the third-party relay. By disabling anonymous open relays on this third-party server, the company can reduce the risk. Email can still be filtered for spam and malware, even if it goes through a third-party relay. As long as the third-party relay isn't spamming and doesn't have anonymous open relays enabled, it wouldn't be placed on blacklists.
See Chapter 5.

36. **A.** System State data should be backed up on a Microsoft domain controller to back up Active Directory. System State data includes the registry, system data files, and Active Directory on a domain controller, but Active Directory can't be backed up by itself. A domain controller should not include any data files.
See Chapter 5.

37. **C.** Malware can be executed within a virtual machine with minimal risk to the host's equipment and software. A primary benefit of virtual servers from a security perspective is that the virtual servers can be isolated from each other and the host, and malware released on the virtual server won't reach the public

network. While the malware may destroy the virtual server, it can easily be restored.
See Chapter 5.

38. **D.** Worms can self-replicate over the network, but Trojan horses must be executed. Trojan horses can be delivered through email, but only worms can travel autonomously over the network. Both are considered malware.
See Chapter 6.

39. **A.** A virus is a string of code that embeds itself into a host application and executes when the host application executes. It spreads by infecting other host applications when it is executed (spreading from file to file), but only a worm can spread from system to system over a network. A Trojan horse appears to be one thing (such as a screen saver) but includes other malicious code. A logic bomb executes in response to an event such as on a specific date or when a specific program is run.
See Chapter 6.

40. **D.** Pop-up blockers are commonly used to block adware since adware often comes in the form of pop-up windows. While some antivirus software provides limited protection against pop-ups, pop-up blockers are much more effective. Rootkits are malware themselves and don't block pop-ups. A layer 3 switch wouldn't provide any protection against a pop-up window.
See Chapter 6.

41. **D.** A malware scanner, such as some antivirus scanners and some anti-spyware scanners, can detect rootkits. A protocol analyzer can capture packets going across the network, and a protocol analyzer is commonly called a sniffer. A port scanner can detect open ports on a system.
See Chapter 6.

42. **B, C.** Distributed denial-of-service (DDoS) attacks often make use of botnets with zombies remotely controlled by a command and control center. A DDoS attack is one launched from multiple computers against a single organization.

Spyware is software that is installed on a user's system without his awareness or consent. A Smurf attack is where a single computer sends out a broadcast ping with the source address spoofed with a victim's IP.
See Chapter 6.

43. **B.** If the computers were zombies as part of a botnet, the network firewall logs would show each of the zombies checking in with the same computer on the Internet that is not a known resource for the company. Checking each individual computer would be much harder than just checking the logs on the firewall between the computers and the Internet.
See Chapter 6.

44. **A.** A reconnaissance attack attempts to locate as much information as possible about a system or network. This type of attack very often includes using a port scanner to learn about open ports, querying DNS to download DNS zone data, and using protocol analyzers (or sniffers) to capture and analyze data. A null session attack allows an unauthenticated user in older Windows operating systems to access resources intended to be secured.
See Chapter 6.

45. **A.** Anonymous open relays are commonly used by attackers to spoof email if they are left open or enabled. When mail relays are disabled, attackers cannot exploit them. A replay attack is when an attacker captures traffic with the intent to later resend it and impersonate a client. DLL injection is used by attackers to inject code into a process and can be used by security professionals as part of penetration testing.
See Chapters 5 and 6.

46. **B.** A replay attack captures traffic for the purpose of later resending it to impersonate a client. Active replay or eavesdropping replay attacks aren't formally defined. Active interception (or active eavesdropping) attacks are also known as man-in-the middle attacks, where a computer is placed between a sender and receiver to capture information.
See Chapter 6.

47. **D.** Active interception (also known as a man-in-the-middle attack) uses a computer placed between a sender and receiver to capture information. A replay attack captures traffic for the purpose of later resending it to impersonate a client. A TCP/IP hijacking attack disconnects one of two connected clients and takes over the session. An ARP poisoning attack sends ARP packets to mislead computers about the MAC address of a system.
See Chapter 6.

48. **A, B, C, D.** Social engineers use conning, flattery, assuming a position of authority, and impersonation to encourage people to perform an action or reveal information.
See Chapter 6.

49. **A, B, C, D.** The success of social engineering attacks can be reduced through several different methods, including security awareness training, identity verification methods, logon banners, and posters.
See Chapter 6.

50. **B.** The goal of risk management is to reduce risk to a level that the organization will accept. It is not feasible to eliminate risks. Management can look at annualized loss expectancy (ALE) and single loss expectancy (SLE) to make decisions, but the ultimate decision is based on the level of risk a company will accept.
See Chapter 7.

51. **C.** Nessus is a popular vulnerability assessment tool. Wireshark is a popular protocol analyzer that can be used to capture and analyze packets sent over the network. Nmap is a popular port scanner that can be used to detect open ports. John the Ripper and Cain and Abel are password crackers.
See Chapter 7.

52. **B.** External security testing is done outside the organization's security perimeter; this includes the physical security perimeter and the logical security perimeter. The tester has no more access than any outside attacker may have.

An outside attacker wouldn't have access to the DMZ or within a firewall. If only physical access is restricted, the tester may have access to the network using remote technologies, but if remote access is allowed, it isn't a true external test. See Chapter 7.

53. **A.** A protocol analyzer (such as Wireshark) could be used to capture and analyze packets. It could be used to verify if the packets are malformed or fragmented. Nmap is a port scanner. Nessus is a vulnerability assessment tool, and John the Ripper is a password cracker.
See Chapter 7.

54. **A.** A sniffer (also known as a protocol analyzer) such as Wireshark can capture and analyze packets on a network. A port scanner can detect open ports. A spammer sends unsolicited email (spam). A scooper scoops ice cream.
See Chapter 7.

55. **B.** Unexpected open ports should be investigated to determine if they are needed. Rerunning the port scanner will result in the same results if a change isn't made. Disabling all services will close all ports, but any host needs some services running and some ports open. It's possible an administrator enabled a service resulting in the unexpected open port; disabling will cause this service to stop functioning.
See Chapter 7.

56. **C, D.** Malware (including Trojan horses and viruses) is frequently sent through email. Dictionary attacks and brute force attacks are used in password-cracking attempts.
See chapters 6 and 7.

57. **B.** Write once, read many (WORM) media such as CD-R can be used to protect files from being modified. Files stored on another server, on a rewritable DVD-RW, or on a USB flash drive can be modified.
See Chapter 7.

58. **C.** The Open Vulnerability and Assessment Language (OVAL) is an international standard that can be used for security tools and services such as vulnerability assessment tools. It does not include standards for malware, spyware, or firewalls.
See Chapter 7.

59. **C.** Incremental backup types back up all the data that have changed since the last full or incremental backup. Differential backup types back up all the files that have changed since the last full backup. A full backup will back up all the files specified regardless of what files have changed. System State backs up key system files such as boot files and the registry; on a domain controller, System State includes Active Directory.
See Chapter 8.

60. **B.** Halon is the only available choice that would be used on an electrical fire. Foam (and other water-based agents) is conductive and may damage the equipment or pose electrical shock hazards to personnel. Carbon dioxide (CO_2) could be used to fight fires, but not carbon monoxide (CO). Heat is an element of fire, and adding heat won't help put it out.
See Chapter 8.

61. **A, B.** A Faraday cage is designed to mitigate data emanation and also prevents EMI/RFI from entering the enclosures. NIDS would be used to detect network attacks, and HIDS would be used to detect attacks on a host.
See Chapter 8.

62. **C.** Advanced Encryption Standard (AES) is considered the strongest symmetric algorithm of those presented. DES has been compromised. 3DES replaced DES, and AES replaced 3DES. IDEA is sometimes used with PGP but is not considered the most secure of those listed.
See Chapter 9.

63. **A.** Data Encryption Standard (DES) is the least secure encryption algorithm of those listed. It is considered compromised and was replaced with 3DES.

3DES was replaced with AES, which is a fast, secure algorithm. MD5 is a hashing algorithm used for integrity, not encryption.
See Chapter 9.

64. **B.** Secure Sockets Layer (SSL) encrypts data on the Session layer; as a memory technique, remember that SSL starts with an S and Session starts with an S. TLS secures data on the Transport layer.
See Chapter 9.

65. **B.** RSA's success is due to the principle that large prime numbers can't be factored. AES is a strong and fast symmetric algorithm that is the standard today. Diffie-Hellman is an asymmetric algorithm that uses TLS to privately share a session key. ECC is used in smaller wireless devices and uses mathematical equations to create curves and identify points on the curves.
See Chapter 9.

66. **D.** The Internet Key Exchange (IKE) is used to create and manage security associations for IPSec. PPTP is the predecessor of L2TP. SSL and TLS are not a part of L2TP/IPSec.
See Chapter 9.

67. **A.** Pretty Good Privacy (PGP) uses both asymmetric and symmetric encryption, but it uses symmetric encryption to encrypt the data. Asymmetric encryption is used to encrypt the session key. PGP has used the asymmetric algorithm RSA and the symmetric algorithms of IDEA, CAST, and 3DES.
See Chapter 9.

68. **C.** NTLMv2 is considered the strongest hashing algorithm of those listed. LANMAN, NTLMv1, and NTLMv2 use hashing as part of the encryption process. LANMAN is significantly weak; NTLMv1 provided some improvement; and NTLMv2 is strong enough to make it nearly impossible to discover the original value. Bluetooth is a wireless technology used in personal area networks.
See Chapter 9.

69. **A.** MD5 is a hashing algorithm used to verify the integrity of files or messages. The MD5 number would be the hash that can be used to verify that the file hasn't been modified. A session key can be used to encrypt and decrypt files, but posting it would defeat the purpose of confidentiality. A session can't be used to validate a file, and a hash can't be used to decrypt a file.
See Chapter 9.

70. **C.** A hash collision occurs when two completely different files produce the same result using the same hashing algorithm. The other terms listed aren't related to hashes.
See Chapter 9.

71. **C.** A trusted platform module uses a pre-shared key (PSK) to encrypt and decrypt data such as entire disks. Asymmetric encryption uses two keys—public and private. Both PGP and PKI also use asymmetric encryption.
See Chapter 9.

72. **A, B.** Both audit logs and digital signatures can be used to enforce non-repudiation. Non-repudiation is provided through a digital signature by encrypting a hash of the message with the private key of the sender. The encrypted hash can be decrypted by the receiver using the sender's public key (which is matched to the sender's private key); since only the sender has the private key, and the hash can be decrypted by the matching public key, the hash must have been encrypted with the private key, and the sender can't deny sending it. Audit logs will log who, what, when, and where. The "who" provides non-repudiation.
See Chapters 7 and 9.

73. **C.** A digital signature is an encrypted hash of the message and is encrypted with a private key. A pre-shared key is used with a TPM. The matched public key is used to decrypt the digital signature. Public keys of the recipients are not used for a digital signature.
See Chapter 9.

74. **A.** A decentralized PKI architecture allows keys to be generated on individual client computers. All keys would be generated on a central server in a centralized PKI architecture. *Individual* and *client-side* are not valid terms for PKI architecture. See Chapter 9.

75. **D.** Job rotation can help prevent collusion (when two or more employees engage in secret activity for the purpose of fraud). Defense in depth is the principle that employs multiple security layers for protection. Need-to-know is a core principle that specifies that individuals are given only enough information to perform their jobs, no more. Implicit deny is a principle often used with routers and firewalls, where rules are created to allow traffic, but all other traffic is blocked or denied.
See Chapter 10.

76. **A, B, C.** The greatest security risk associated with removable storage (such as USB flash drives or USB external drives) is the confidentiality of data. If data falls into the wrong hands, confidentiality has been lost. This includes the loss of confidentiality of Personally Identifiable Information (PII). Removable media (especially USB flash drives) are often inadvertently used for malware distribution.
See Chapters 6 and 10.

77. **A.** A chain of custody form should be used whenever moving evidence to verify it is kept in control the entire time it is in custody. While companies may create internal documents, such as an evidence transmittal form, an affidavit of transmittal form, or a forensic evidence transmittal form, none of these will take the place of a chain of custody form.
See Chapter 10.

78. **A.** Drives that hold sensitive data should be sanitized before use. Formatting a drive doesn't remove the data. Cleaning it will clean the outside but not the data. If it is destroyed, it won't be able to be reused.
See Chapter 10.

Chapter 1

Mastering the Basics of Security

CompTIA Security+ objectives covered in this chapter

3.1 Identify and apply industry best practices for access control methods.

- Implicit deny

3.6 Summarize the various authentication models and identify the components of each.

- One, two, and three-factor authentication
- Single sign-on

3.7 Deploy various authentication models and identify the components of each.

- Biometric reader
- RADIUS
- RAS
- LDAP
- VPN
- Kerberos
- CHAP
- PAP
- Mutual
- 802.1x
- TACACS

3.8 Explain the difference between identification and authentication (identity proofing).

5.1 Explain general cryptography concepts.

- Confidentiality
- Integrity and availability
- Non-repudiation

* * *

Before you dig into some of the details of security, you should have a solid understanding of core security principles. This chapter will present many of these core principles as an introduction. The second part of the chapter will cover authentication—how systems and users can provide credentials to a system to verify who they are—including authentication used in remote access systems.

Core Security Principles

Security starts with several core principles that are integrated throughout an organization. These principles drive many security-related decisions at multiple levels. Understanding these basic concepts helps to give you a solid foundation in security.

Confidentiality, integrity, and availability together are often referred to as the security triad. Each is important to address in any security program. Additionally, many other core security principles are intertwined in many aspects of a company's security program.

Confidentiality

Confidentiality is implemented to prevent the unauthorized disclosure of data. This is done through multiple methods, such as using authentication, access controls, and cryptography. Authentication is presented later in this chapter, and access controls are covered in Chapter 2.

Cryptography provides confidentiality by encrypting data. There are many different encryption algorithms that can be used. Chapter 9 covers the relevant algorithms (such as AES, SSL, and IPSec) that you'll need to understand for the CompTIA Security+ exam. Two of the key concepts related to confidentiality are these:

- **Confidentiality prevents the unauthorized disclosure of information**. Unauthorized personnel are prevented from having access to the information through authentication and access control mechanisms.
- **Confidentiality is enforced with encryption.** Various encryption algorithms can be used to encrypt or cipher the data to make it unreadable. Encryption algorithms are intended to be secure enough so that if the encrypted data falls into the wrong hands, the unintended recipient will not be able to read it.

> **Remember**
> Confidentiality is used to prevent the unauthorized disclosure of data and is enforced with encryption. If there is a risk of sensitive data falling into the wrong hands, it should be encrypted to make it unreadable.

Other elements of security also help to enforce confidentiality. These include elements such as authentication, access control methods, physical security, and permissions to ensure only authorized personnel can access the data. All of these methods will be presented within this book.

Integrity

Integrity is implemented to verify that data is not modified, tampered with, or corrupted. Hashing is used to enforce integrity. Chapter 9 will also present the relevant hashing algorithms such as MD5 and SHA1. Two key concepts related to integrity are as follows:

- **Integrity is used to verify that data has not been modified**. Hashes are created at the source and destination. If the hashes are the same, integrity is maintained. If the two hashes are different, data integrity has been lost.
- **Integrity is enforced with hashing**. A hash is simply a numeric value created by executing a hashing algorithm against a message or file.

> **Remember**
> Integrity is used to verify that data has not been modified. Integrity is commonly enforced with hashing algorithms such as MD5 or SHA1. A hash is simply a number created by applying the algorithm to a file or message. The hash created at the source is compared to the hash created at the destination to verify that integrity has been maintained.

Acronyms

Don't you just love all of these acronyms? MD5, SHA1, RAID. There are actually three different meanings of MAC within the context of CompTIA Security+:

1. Message authentication code (MAC) used for integrity similar to how a hash is used

2. Mandatory Access Control (MAC) model as one of the three testable access control models

3. Media access control (MAC) addresses that are the physical addresses assigned to NICs

If you're having trouble keeping them all straight, don't feel alone. All of the acronyms used within the book are spelled out with short descriptions in the back of this book.

For example, a simplistic hash of a message could be 123. The hash is created at the source and sent with the message. When the message is received, the received message is hashed. If the hash of the received message is 123 (the same as the hash of the sent message), data integrity is maintained. However, if the hash of the received message is 456, then you know that the message is not the same. Data integrity is lost.

Hashes can be applied to messages such as email, or any other type of data files. Some email programs use a message authentication code (MAC) instead of a hash to verify integrity, but the underlying concept works the same way.

Hashing techniques are commonly used to verify that integrity is maintained when files are downloaded or transferred. If a file loses even a single bit during the download process, the program doing the download will detect it by comparing the source hash with the destination hash.

Similarly, if a file on a file server was infected with a virus, the hash on the infected file would be different than the hash on the original file. Many programs can detect that the hashes are different, know that integrity has been lost, and report the problem to the user.

Availability

Data and services must be available when they are needed. For some companies, this simply means that the data and services must be available between 8 a.m. and 5 p.m., Monday through Friday. For other companies, this means they must be available 24 hours a day, 7 days a week, 365 days a year.

Availability concepts will be covered in more depth in Chapter 7. From a broad perspective, availability includes:

- **Disk redundancies**. Fault-tolerant disks such as RAID-1 (mirroring) and RAID-5 (striping with parity) allow a system to continue to operate even if a disk fails.

- **Server redundancies**. Failover clusters can be implemented that will allow a service to continue to be provided even if a server fails. In a failover cluster, the service switches from the failed server in a cluster to an operational server in the same cluster.

- **Site redundancies**. If a site can no longer function due to a disaster, such as a fire, flood, hurricane, or earthquake, the site can move functionality to another site. The other site can be a hot site (ready and available 24/7), a cold site (a location where equipment, data, and personnel can be moved to when needed), or a warm site (somewhere in the middle of a hot site and cold site).

- **Backups**. Important data is backed up so that when it is lost, it can be restored. Data can be lost due to corruption, deletion, application errors, and even hungry gremlins that can randomly eat your data. If data is not backed up, then when it is lost, it will be lost forever.

Non-repudiation

While non-repudiation isn't one of the core principles in the security triad, it is closely related and specifically mentioned in the objectives, making it an important concept to understand. Non-repudiation provides definitive proof of a sender's identity and can be used to prevent a party from denying he took a specific action.

In commerce, non-repudiation is commonly used with credit cards. If I buy something with a credit card and sign the receipt, I can't later deny making the purchase. My signature can be used to repudiate me if I deny making the purchase. In other words, my signature is used for non-repudiation.

Chapter 9 will cover how digital signatures work in detail, but, as a general concept, digital signatures are commonly used for both authentication and non-repudiation. Additionally, due to how a digital signature is created, it also provides integrity.

Remember
Non-repudiation is used to prevent an entity from denying an action took place. Email that is digitally signed prevents someone from later denying he sent it. An audit log provides non-repudiation since audit log entries include who took an action in addition to what the action was, where the action took place, and when it occurred.

Some common examples of non-repudiation within computer systems are:

- **Using digital signatures to verify someone sent a message**. If I send you an email that is signed with a digital signature, you know definitively that I sent it and I can't later deny doing so. This also allows you to verify the message's origin, or, in other words, the digital signature provides authentication.

- **Logging activity in an audit log.** Audit logs will log details such as who, what, when, and where. The "who" in the audit log provides non-repudiation.

Defense in Depth

Defense in depth refers to the security practice of implementing several layers of protection. You can't simply take a single action such as implementing a firewall or installing antivirus software and consider yourself protected. You must implement security at several different layers.

Remember

Security is never "done." Instead, security is constantly monitored and updated to add to and improve existing methods. A single layer of security is easily beatable. Defense in depth employs multiple layers to make it harder for attacks to exploit a system or network.

As an example, if I drive my car to a local Wal-Mart, put a five-dollar bill on the dash, and leave the keys in the car and the car running, there's a very good chance the car won't be there when I come out of the store. On the other hand, if I ensure nothing of value is visible from the windows, the car is locked, and it has an alarm system and stickers on the windows advertising the alarm system, it's a lot less likely that my car will be stolen. Not impossible, but less likely.

You've probably heard this as "there is no silver bullet." If you want to kill a werewolf, you can load your gun with a single silver bullet and it will find its mark. The truth is that there is no such thing as a silver bullet. (Of course, there's no such thing as a werewolf either.)

Applied to computers, security must be implemented at every step, every phase, and every layer. IT professionals can never rest on their laurels with the thought they have done enough and no longer need to worry about security.

Implicit Deny

Implicit deny indicates that unless something is explicitly allowed, it is denied. Routers and firewalls often have access control lists (ACLs) that explicitly state what traffic is allowed. If traffic doesn't meet any of the explicit rules allowing it through the device, it is denied.

For example, if you had a firewall that was configured to allow HTTP or HTTPS traffic to a web server on ports 80 and 443 respectively, then the firewall would have explicit rules defined to allow this traffic to the server. However, if no other rules were defined, then all other traffic would be implicitly denied. For example, any SMTP traffic sent to this web server on port 25 would be implicitly denied since there isn't an explicit rule allowing the traffic.

Use Devices as Intended

A less quoted principle, but no less important, is the principle that devices should be used as intended. Devices intended for security should be used for only security. Devices intended for serving data should not be mixed with security devices. When usage is mixed, there is more potential for security compromises.

Chapters 3 and 4 cover network concepts in more depth, but in short, some network devices such as firewalls are intended to add to security while other devices such as web servers or mail servers are intended to serve data or services.

Firewalls are security devices intended to keep threatening or non-authorized traffic out of a network. Firewalls are often placed at the boundary between the Internet and an internal network and protect the internal network from attacks on the Internet. Web servers and mail servers are often placed behind a firewall or in a DMZ and serve web pages and email to users on the Internet.

A violation of this principle would be to place the firewall and the web server on the same device. For example, Microsoft's Internet Security Accelerator (ISA) is a firewall, and Microsoft's Exchange Server is a mail server. Both ISA and Exchange should not be placed on the same server.

Authentication

Authentication is used to prove identity through the use of some type of credential that is previously known by the authenticator. Authentication can be used to prove the identity of a user, a service, or a process, or even a workstation, a server, or a network device.

Credentials are known or held by two entities and then presented from one entity to another. For example, a user knows her username and password, and an authenticating server also knows the user's username and password. The user presents the credentials to the server, and if correct, the user is authenticated. Mutual authentication is accomplished when both entities authenticate each other.

The importance of authentication cannot be understated. You can't have any type of access control if you can't identify a user. Note that authentication isn't the same as authorization. Just because you can prove who you are, you won't automatically be granted access to everything. Access control restricts access once authentication has been accomplished.

Chapter 2 will present different access control models. However, the first step is implementing some method of authentication, such as the use of complex passwords, smart cards, or biometrics.

Three Factors of Authentication

Authentication is often simplified down to three factors. Entities can authenticate with any one of these factors, and often, two or more factors are combined to provide multifactor authentication. The three factors are:

- Something you know (such as username and password)
- Something you have (such as a smart card)
- Something you are (such as a fingerprint or other biometric identification)

Something You Know

The *something you know* authentication typically refers to a shared secret such as a password or a username and password or even a personal identification number (PIN). This is the least secure form of authentication.

> ### *Remember*
> The first factor of authentication (something you know, such as a password or PIN) is the weakest. Passwords should be strong, never shared with another person, and stored in a safe if written down. Technical means (such as group policies in a Microsoft domain) should be used to ensure that users regularly change their passwords and don't use the same passwords.

Some general rules about passwords to ensure they are secure include:

- **Passwords should be strong.** This means they are at least eight characters and include multiple character types.
- **Passwords should not be written down.** If the password absolutely must be written down, store it in a safe (not just a safe place).

- **Passwords should not be shared**. Only one person should know the password to any single account.
- **Passwords should be regularly changed**. Users should be forced to change their passwords on a regular basis through the use of password expiration policies.
- **Passwords should not be reused**. Password histories can be maintained to prevent users from using the same passwords over and over.
- **Account lockout policies should be used**. If the wrong password is entered too many times, the account will be locked, preventing password guessing attempts.
- **Default passwords should be changed**. If a system comes with a default password, that default password should be changed before the system is brought in to service.

Strong Passwords

One method used to make passwords more secure is to require them to be strong. A strong password is at least eight characters in length and combines three of the four following character types:

- Uppercase characters
- Lowercase characters
- Numbers
- Special characters

A few examples of strong passwords are: IL0veSec+, IL0veThi$B00k, and IWillP@$$. Note that each includes both uppercase and lowercase letters, one or more numbers, and one or more special characters. These passwords are also known as pass phrases since they are a combination of words that are easier to remember than a nonsensical string of characters such as 4*eiRS@<].

It's widely understood that if you make a password too complex you make it less secure. Read that again. It's not a typo. More complexity equates to less security. The reason is that the more complex a password is, the less likely it is the user will remember it. Instead, he will write it down, significantly reducing the security.

Storing Passwords

Passwords should not be written down unless absolutely necessary. If they are written down, they should be stored in a safe. Note that this is not simply a "safe place."

Many users have simply written down their passwords on a Post-it note and stuck it to the bottom of their keyboard, thinking no one would ever look there. Hackers, crackers, attackers, and even curious fellow employees who have physical access to your system will think to look under a keyboard. At one place I worked, this was so prevalent that when a computer was disposed of, the computer sanitization checklist included checking under the keyboard.

Sharing Passwords

Only one person should know the password, and users should not share their passwords with anyone. This is a difficult message to ingrain in the minds of end users, resulting in many successful social engineering attempts.

Chapter 6 will cover social engineering in more depth, but, for now, just be aware that attackers often gain information just by asking. They can ask over the phone, in person, or via email with increasingly sophisticated phishing attacks.

Social engineers use trickery and conniving to convince users to give out their passwords. If a user is trained by an administrator to believe that sometimes it's OK to share a password, when the social engineer goes into action, the user quickly becomes convinced that this is one of those times. On the other hand, if a user consistently hears the message that passwords should NEVER be shared, alarm bells will ring in the user's head when the social engineer tries to get her password.

Changing Passwords

In addition to being strong, passwords should also be changed regularly. In most networks, users are automatically required to change their passwords regularly. In a Windows domain, group policies are used to force users to change their passwords at regular intervals, such as every thirty, sixty, or ninety days.

I can tell you from experience that if a user is not forced to change his password through technical means, he often simply doesn't. It doesn't matter how many reminders you give him. On the other hand, if Group Policy locks his account until he changes his password, the user will change it.

Password History

Passwords should not be reused. Forcing users to change their passwords is a good first step, but some users will change back and forth between two passwords that they constantly use and reuse.

A password history system can remember past passwords and prevent the user from reusing passwords that have been used before. It's common for Group Policy settings to remember the last twenty-four passwords that a user has used and prevent any of these twenty-four passwords from being used again.

Account Lockout Policies

Accounts will typically have lockout policies preventing users from guessing the password. If the wrong password is entered a specific number of times (such as three times or five times), then the account will be locked. Two key terms are associated with account lockout policies:

- **Account lockout threshold.** This is the maximum number of times a wrong password can be entered. When the threshold is exceeded, the account is locked.
- **Account lockout duration.** This indicates how long an account will be locked. It could be set to 30, indicating that once the account lockout threshold is reached, the account will be locked out for thirty minutes; after thirty minutes, the account will automatically be unlocked. If the duration is set to 0, the account will remain locked until an administrator unlocks it.

Change Defaults

In Chapter 5, you'll learn the basics of hardening systems, including changing defaults, removing unnecessary protocols and services, and keeping the system up-to-date.

Many systems and devices have default passwords. A basic security practice is to change these defaults as soon as the system or device is installed. As an example, many wireless routers have default accounts named "admin" with a default password of "admin." If you don't change these defaults, someone can log in to your network and have full control of the router, even going so far as locking you out of your own network.

Changing defaults also includes changing the default name of the Administrator account, if possible. In many systems, the Administrator account can't be locked out through regular lockout policies, so an attacker can continue to try to guess the password of the Administrator account without risking being locked out. By changing the name of the Administrator account to something else, the attacker can't try to guess the password of the Administrator account since the username is unknown. Some administrators go a step further and add a dummy user account named "administrator." This account has no permissions. If this account is discovered to be locked out, the administrator knows that someone was trying to guess the password.

Previous Logon Notification

A simple technique used to alert a user when her account may have been compromised is to provide notification to users when they last logged on. This is sometimes shortened to "previous logon notification."

As an example, consider Sally, who took Friday off last week. She was at work and logged in on Thursday. When she comes in to work on Monday, the system informs her that the last time she logged in was on Friday. If she's paying attention to this message, she'll realize that someone else logged into her account, meaning that her credentials are compromised.

The primary challenge with this system is that users will tend to ignore the notification. More than 99 percent of the time, the message will tell users what they already know. So, instead of reading the message, users tend to ignore it.

Something You Have

The *something you have* factor refers to something you can physically hold. The two common items in this category are smart cards and key fobs (such as those sold by SecureID).

- **Smart cards.** Smart cards are credit-card-size cards that have embedded certificates used for authentication. The smart card is inserted into a card reader similar to how a credit card is inserted into some credit card readers.
- **Key fobs.** A key fob (sometimes simply called a fob) is an electronic device about the size of a remote key for a car. It has an LED display that displays a number that is synced with a server.

> **Remember**
> The second factor of authentication (something you have, such as a smart card or key fob) is commonly combined with *something you know*. Smart cards have embedded certificates issued by a Public Key Infrastructure (PKI). Both smart cards and key fobs provide a significant level of secure authentication, especially when used with another factor of authentication (multifactor authentication).

Smart Cards

Smart cards require smart card readers. The smart card is inserted into the reader, and the certificate is read. The embedded certificate allows the use of a complex encryption key that provides much more secure authentication than is possible through the use of a simple password. Requirements for a smart card are:

- **Embedded certificate.** A certificate is embedded in the smart card. The certificate holds a user's private key (which is only accessible to the user) and is matched with a public key (that is publicly available to others). The private key is used each time the user logs on to a network.
- **Public Key Infrastructure (PKI).** Chapter 9 will cover PKI in more depth, but in short, the PKI allows the issuance and management of certificates.

Smart cards are often used with another factor of authentication. For example, a user may also enter a PIN or username and password in addition to using the smart card.

Key Fobs

Fobs are sometimes referred to as fob-based authentication or token-based authentication. In its generic use, a fob refers to a small object that can be placed in a pocket, and fobs used for authentication are small enough to carry around in a pocket. Similarly, tokens are small objects that can be carried around in a pocket.

RSA sells SecureID, a popular token used for authentication. You can Google "SecureID picture" to easily see a picture of one of these tokens.

The LED displays a number that will change every sixty seconds. The fob is synced with a server that knows what the number will be at any moment. A user will often authenticate via a web site by entering the number displayed on the fob. As long as the numbers are the same, the user is authenticated.

Fob-based authentication is usually combined with another factor of authentication such as something you know. In other words, the user will also enter a PIN or his username and password. This provides multifactor authentication (something the user has and something the user knows).

One-time Password

One-time passwords are sometimes used to make it more difficult for an attacker. Just as the name implies, a one-time password is used only once.

Fob-based authentication is an example of a one-time password. A user enters the number that is displayed on the LED and known by the server. Even if this number is intercepted, it will quickly become invalid.

Something You Are

The third factor of authentication refers to *something you are*, identified through biometrics. Biometrics is considered the strongest form of authentication, as opposed to passwords, which are considered the weakest. Several different biometric methods are in existence:

- Fingerprint or hand readers
- Retinal scanners (scanning the retina of one or both eyes)
- Signature geometry (handwriting analysis)

Remember

The third factor of authentication (something you are, defined with biometrics) is considered the strongest method of authentication when implemented correctly. Biometrics often uses fingerprints or retinal scans to authenticate individuals.

Just a few years ago, most people only saw examples of biometrics in the movies, but today, examples are frequently seen in day-to-day life. Some examples include:

- **Amusement parks**. Many amusement parks sell annual passes, but they don't want these passes shared with everyone in the neighborhood. Biometric hand scans are frequently used to authenticate someone as the owner of a pass. If someone else tries to use the pass, the hand scan fails.
- **Computers**. Many laptops and some keyboards include fingerprint scanners that can be used to unlock access to a computer.
- **USB flash drive**. Some USB flash drives include a fingerprint scanner. Often four fingerprints can be stored, allowing access to up to four people.
- **Police records**. The use of fingerprinting has been popular for decades, and more recently, programs have been created to automate the search for matching identities.

While the use of DNA is possible in the future for authentication, it's unlikely it'll be used in the near term. Besides the lack of ability to identify DNA in a timely manner, most users will likely balk at having to prick their fingers to provide a blood sample to authenticate to a computer.

Biometrics can be very exact when the technology is implemented accurately. However, it is possible for a biometric sales company to take shortcuts and not implement it correctly, resulting in false readings. Two possible false readings are:

- **False acceptance**. This is when a biometric system incorrectly identifies an unauthorized user as an authorized user.
- **False rejection**. This is when a biometric system incorrectly rejects an authorized user.

True readings occur when the biometric system indicates a match. Two possible readings are:

- **True acceptance**. The biometric system accurately determines a positive match.
- **True rejection**. The biometric system accurately determines a non-match.

A local grocery store had problems with false acceptance. They allowed shoppers to register their debit cards with fingerprints. Once the debit card was registered, a shopper could place her finger in a fingerprint scanner to debit her bank account instead of swiping a debit card and entering a PIN. Then one day, all the fingerprint scanners disappeared. I later learned that the scanners were falsely accepting some users. Users who had not registered their debit cards tried the fingerprint scanners to pay for groceries, and it worked. Someone else's bank account was charged instead.

Amusement parks often have problems with false rejection later in the season. Families are often the biggest customer of these annual passes. Children often grow enough during the season that the handprint recorded for them early in the season no longer matches for them later in the season.

Multifactor Authentication

Multifactor authentication is the use of more than one factor of authentication. As mentioned previously, this is frequently done with smart cards or fobs and PINs or usernames and passwords, where the user must have something and know something.

It's also possible to combine biometrics with one of the other factors of authentication. In very secure environments, you may even see all three factors of authentication used.

Identity Proofing

Identity proofing is the process of verifying that someone is who he says he is prior to issuing credentials to that person, or later when credentials are lost.

Before credentials are issued, individuals are often required to show other forms of identification such as a driver's license. In some environments, individuals are also validated by a trusted employee who states that the individual is who he says he is.

A second use of identity proofing is after credentials have been issued. When the user performs some critical activity (such as transferring money between bank accounts), her identity can be verified before the action is taken. This is often done by having the user verify key information that third parties are highly unlikely to know.

Identity Proofing vs. Authentication

Identity proofing isn't the same as authentication, but both processes are typically employed prior to granting access to a network. Identity proofing validates someone's identity before credentials are issued or is used as a secondary method. Authentication is accomplished simply by providing previously known credentials to the authenticator.

As an example, consider a new employee who needs a new user account to access the network. Before this account information is created and given out, some form of identification is used to verify the identity of the new employee.

Identity proofing may occur out of view of the IT person creating the account, but it still occurs. For example, HR personnel typically are charged with in-processing new hires and ensuring all the paperwork is in order. Later, HR may simply introduce the new employee to an IT professional to create an account. This introduction by the HR person is all the identity proofing needed by the IT worker.

Identity Proofing for Verification

Identity proofing is sometimes used as a verification mechanism to prevent impersonation through the use of stolen credentials. This is common in online banking.

If you've signed up for online banking recently, you've probably seen this. You are presented with a list of questions such as what is the name of your first pet, the name of your closest childhood friend, the middle name of your oldest or youngest sibling, etc. The chances of an attacker knowing these answers is quite slim, and therefore, the list works well as an identity proofing method.

In the past, identity proofing consisted of very few items such as: your birth date, Social Security number, and mother's maiden name. Because so many entities requested this information and didn't always protect it, it became easy for attackers to obtain this information and use it to steal identities. Identities have been stolen just from information visible on a renter's application.

Some banks even record information about the computer you use to access the online site. If you later use a different computer, or a computer with a different IP address, you may be prompted to answer one of the identity proofing questions. If an attacker somehow steals your credentials and uses them to access your bank account, identity proofing will reduce the risk of the attacker's success. Asking the attacker a question that he is less likely to be able to answer, such as what was the name of the street where you grew up, increases security.

Password Reset Systems

An additional use of identity proofing is with password reset or password management systems. These systems are extremely useful in systems with a large number of users and can actually reduce the total cost of ownership of the system.

Instead of an IT professional spending valuable time resetting passwords, the process can be automated with a self-service password reset or password retrieval system that makes use of identity proofing.

Some online systems include a link such as "Forgot Password." By clicking on this link, your password may be emailed to your previously given email address or an identity proofing system may be invoked. The identity proofing system will ask you questions that only you should know, and once your identity is proved, you're given the opportunity to change your password to something different.

Of course, an online password reset system won't help a user if she can't get online. Some organizations utilize password reset systems using the phone system. A user who has forgotten her password can call the password reset system and reset her password by using an identity proofing method such as a PIN.

Kerberos

Kerberos is the authentication mechanism used within Windows domains and some UNIX environments. Kerberos was originally developed at MIT for UNIX systems. Kerberos was later released as an RFC and is now used by other operating systems such as in Microsoft Active Directory domains.

Several requirements must be met for Kerberos to work properly. They are:

- **Time synchronization**. Kerberos version 5 requires all systems to be synchronized and within five minutes of each other. The clock that provides the time synchronization is used to time-stamp tickets, ensuring they expire within five minutes. This helps to prevent replay attacks where a ticket is intercepted and later used to impersonate a client.
- **A database of subjects or users.** In a Microsoft environment, this is Active Directory, but it could be any database of users.
- **A method of issuing tickets used for authentication.** The Key Distribution Center (KDC) uses a complex process of issuing *ticket-granting tickets*, which are later presented to request tickets that can then be used to access objects.

> **Remember**
>
> Kerberos is a commonly used authentication protocol within a Windows Active Directory domain or UNIX realm. It uses a database of objects such as Active Directory and a KDC to issue time-stamped tickets, and requires internal time synchronization. Kerberos uses port 88.

Kerberos uses port 88 by default. As with any Well Known Ports, this can be changed to another port, but it rarely is changed from port 88. Ports and their usage will be explained more fully in Chapter 3.

Additionally, Kerberos uses symmetric-key cryptography to prevent unauthorized disclosure and to ensure confidentiality. Chapter 9 will explain algorithms in more depth, but in short, symmetric-key cryptography uses a single key for both encryption and decryption.

In contrast, asymmetric encryption uses two keys: one key to encrypt and one key to decrypt. Asymmetric encryption requires a PKI to issue certificates. The two keys used in a PKI are a public key and a private key. Depending on what is being accomplished, sometimes the public key encrypts and the private key decrypts; other times, the private key encrypts and the public key decrypts.

As a memory trick, you may like to remember: Symmetric uses one key. Asymmetric adds a syllable ("a"), and it also adds a key, using two keys.

LDAP

The Lightweight Directory Access Protocol (LDAP) specifies formats and methods to query directories. In this context, a directory is a database of objects.

As an example, Active Directory used in Windows environments uses LDAP. Active Directory is a directory of objects (such as users, computers, and groups). Queries to Active Directory use the LDAP format.

LDAP is an extension of the X.500 standard that was used extensively by Novell and early Microsoft Exchange Server versions. LDAP v2 can be encrypted with SSL, and LDAP v3 can be encrypted with TLS.

The Well Known Ports used by LDAP are 389 and 636 when encrypted with either SSL or TLS.

Mutual Authentication

Mutual authentication is accomplished when both entities in a session authenticate with each other prior to exchanging data. Chapter 6 will cover different types of attacks, including attacks where an attacker may try to impersonate a server. Instead of a client sending sensitive data to this server, mutual authentication provides assurances that the server's identity is verified.

Many current authentication processes commonly implement mutual authentication. For example, an improvement of MS-CHAPv2 over MS-CHAP is the implementation of mutual authentication.

Single Sign-on

Single sign-on (SSO) refers to the ability of a user to log on to multiple systems by providing credentials only once. SSO increases security, since the user only needs to remember one set of credentials and is less likely to write them down. It's also much more convenient for users to access network resources if they only have to log on once.

> ### Remember
> Single sign-on enhances security by requiring users to use and remember only one set of credentials for authentication. Once signed on using SSO, this one set of credentials is used throughout a user's entire session. The temptation to write down usernames and passwords increases when users are forced to remember multiple sets of credentials.

As an example, consider a user who needs to access multiple servers within a network to perform normal work. If SSO was not implemented, the user would need to know the credentials to log on to her local system, and each time she accessed a server such as a file server or email server, she would be prompted to provide a different set of credentials. Many users would resort to writing these credentials down to remember them.

Alternatively, if a network has implemented SSO, the user would need to log on to the network once, and these credentials would be used during his entire logon session. Each time the user accesses a network resource, the SSO credentials would be presented.

To fully understand how SSO is implemented, you should understand the use of SIDs, DACLs, and logical tokens.

SIDs and DACLs

Discretionary Access Control Lists (DACLs) are used to identify who can access any object (such as a file or folder) in a system using the Discretionary Access Control (DAC) model. Chapter 2 covers all of the access control models in depth, but for this discussion, you should just know that Microsoft uses the DAC model to protect files and folders with NTFS.

Each user is uniquely identified with a security identifier (SID), although you will rarely see it. A SID is a long string of characters that is meaningless to most of us and may look like this: S-1-5-21-3991871189-223218. Instead of a SID being displayed, the system will look up the name associated with the SID, such as a username or group name, and display the name.

Groups within a system are also identified with SIDs. Groups are used for ease of administration. For example, if you wanted to grant Sally full and complete control to a local system, you could add Sally's user account to the Administrators group. All the appropriate rights and permissions are already granted to the Administrators group, and simply by being a member of this group, Sally has the same rights and permissions of the group.

Without the use of groups, you would have to individually assign all the specific rights and permissions for every individual user. This may work for one or two users but quickly becomes unmanageable with any significant number of users.

Figure 1.1 shows an example of the DACL for a folder named Security+ Study Notes on a Windows Vista system.

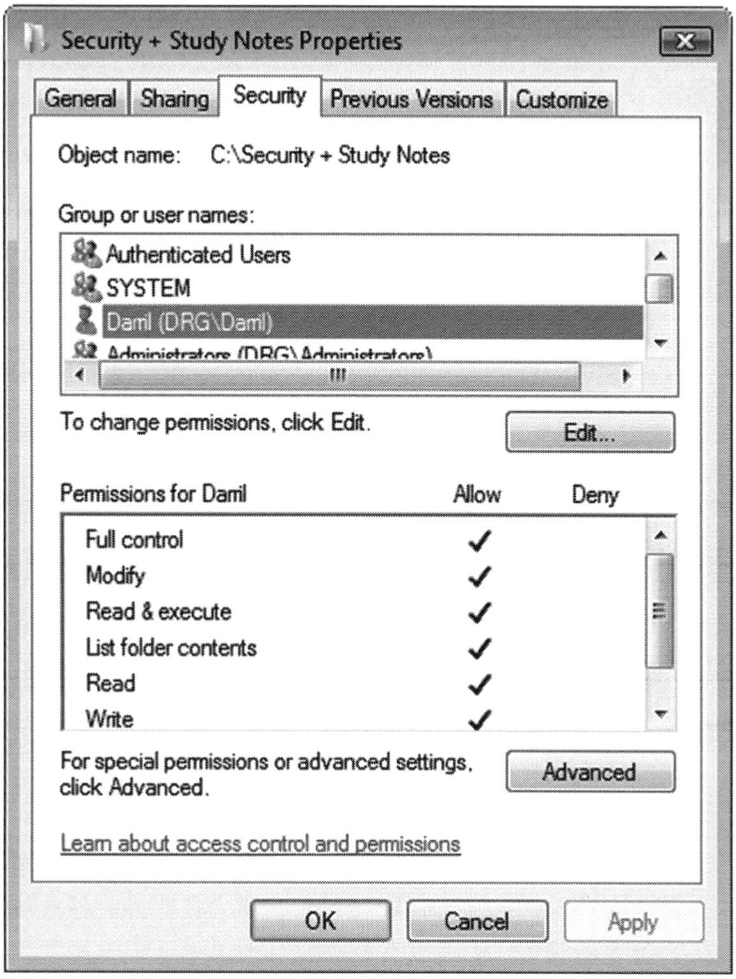

Figure 1.1: DACL in NTFS

The DACL is a list of Access Control Entries (ACEs). Each ACE is composed of a SID and the permission(s) granted to the SID. You can view a DACL on a Microsoft system by following these steps:

1. Press the Open Window+ E keys to launch Windows Explorer. (The Open Window key is just to the left of the left Alt key on most keyboards.)
2. Open up the C: drive to access the folders.
3. Right click any folder and select Properties.
4. Select the Security tab.

a. You will see either user accounts, group accounts, or both. These accounts are actually held in the ACE as SIDs, but the system has looked up and displayed their names.

b. Underneath the Group or User Names box, you will see the Permissions box showing the assigned permissions for the group or user that is selected. If you select a different group or user, you will see the permissions assigned to that group or user.

Logical Tokens Used with SSO

While logical tokens can be used in multiple situations, such as within a Windows environment or on an Internet session, for clarity, I'll stick to explaining one method. The following explanation shows how logical tokens are used within a Microsoft Windows environment. It applies to either a workgroup or a domain.

Logical tokens are used to store the SIDs associated with any individual user. For example, imagine you are a member of the following groups on your system: Administrators, Backup Operators, and a special group called G_PassedSecurityPlus.

When you log on, the system creates a logical token for you. This token includes the SID for each of the groups you are a member of and the SID for your user account.

Now each time you try to access a resource such as a file or folder, the system will examine the DACL on the resource, examine your logical token, and see if there is a match. As long as one or more of the SIDs on your logical token matches one or more of the SIDs on the DACL, you are granted appropriate access to the resource. If more than one SID matches, you are granted the combination of all the permissions matching all the SIDs on your logical token.

This token is created each time a user logs on and is destroyed each time a user logs off.

Some operating systems or applications will actually hide resources if the user's logical token indicates that she doesn't have access. Other operating systems allow the user to see that the resource exists but will indicate that access is denied if a user tries to access it.

IEEE 802.1x

The IEEE 802.1x protocol is a port-based authentication protocol, meaning it is designed to provide authentication when a user connects to a specific access point or, in this context, a logical port. Its primary purpose is to secure the authentication process prior to a client actually gaining access to a network. While 802.1x can be used in both wired and wireless networks, it is often closely associated with wireless networks.

The Institute of Electrical and Electronic Engineers (IEEE, often pronounced as I Triple E) is an international organization that is actively involved in the development of many different protocol standards. Protocols and standards are created by the IEEE or prefaced with IEEE. For example, different wireless standards developed by the IEEE are IEEE 802.11a, 802.11b, 802.11g, and 802.11n.

Chapter 4 will cover wireless networks in more depth, but an important concept to grasp with wireless networks is that there are significant security issues.

The Wired Equivalent Privacy (WEP) protocol was intended to provide security on a wireless network similar to that on a wired network, but it has significant vulnerabilities and is commonly understood to be cracked. WEP was improved with Wi-Fi Protected Access (WPA) as an interim fix to WEP, and later with Wi-Fi Protected Access v2 (WPA2). WPA was cracked in November 2008.

IEEE 802.1x can be implemented with WEP, WPA, or WPA2, providing an added layer of protection. By using 802.1x, the authentication portion of the wireless session is protected from interception.

Remote Access Authentication

Remote Access Service (RAS) is used to provide access to an internal network from an outside source. Chapter 4 will cover RAS in more depth, but this section will cover different authentication mechanisms that can be used with RAS.

RAS is sometimes called Network Access Service (NAS). A RAS server can also be a virtual private network (VPN) server. A VPN is used to access a private network over a public network (such as the Internet).

All of these are useful for personnel who need access to the private network from remote locations. However, no matter what method of remote access you use, you still need to ensure that only authorized clients can access your network remotely. Authorization begins with authentication, and there are multiple methods of authentication that can be employed.

The different authentication mechanisms that may be used with RAS are:

- **PAP**. Password Authentication Protocol. Passwords are sent in clear text, so PAP is rarely used today.
- **CHAP**. Challenge Handshake Authentication Protocol. CHAP uses a handshake process where the server challenges the client with a nonce (a number used once). The nonce is added to a shared secret, encrypted, and returned to the server for verification.
- **MS-CHAP**. Microsoft's implementation of CHAP, which was dedicated to Microsoft clients only.
- **MS-CHAPv2**. An improvement over MS-CHAP. A significant improvement was the ability to perform mutual authentication.
- **RADIUS**. Remote Authentication Dial-In User Service. RADIUS provides a centralized method of authentication for multiple RAS servers.
- **TACACS/TACACS+**. Terminal Access Controller Access-Control System (TACACS) and TACACS+ are used as alternatives to RADIUS. TACACS and TACACS+ are commonly used in UNIX and Cisco remote access systems. A benefit of TACACS+ is that it can interact with Kerberos, allowing it to work with a broader range of environments, including Microsoft. Additionally, TACACS+ encrypts the entire authentication process (RADIUS encrypts only the password).

PAP

Password Authentication Protocol (PAP) is used in Point-to-Point Protocol (PPP) to authenticate clients. It replaced the Serial Line Interface Protocol as a much more efficient method of connecting to remote servers such as Internet Service Providers (ISPs). However, a significant weakness of PAP is that passwords are sent in clear text, presenting a significant security risk.

PPP is primarily used with dial-up connections. Believe it or not, there was a time when the thought of someone wiretapping a phone was rather remote. Because of this, security was an afterthought with PPP. Today, PPP would only be used as a last resort due to passwords being passed in clear text.

Throughout this book, you'll read that sending data across a line in clear text is a security risk. It's not just PPP that has this risk, but also FTP, SNMP, NetBIOS, and many other protocols. It's relatively easy for someone to download and use a free protocol analyzer (such as Wireshark) to capture packets. These packets can easily be analyzed with the protocol analyzer, and the data within the packets can be read. Protocol analyzers are commonly referred to as sniffers.

CHAP

Challenge Handshake Authentication Protocol has often been used to authenticate users in the past. It is often replaced with more secure forms of authentication, but you should be aware of what CHAP is and how it works.

The goal of CHAP is to allow the client to pass credentials over a public network (such as a phone or the Internet) without allowing attackers to intercept the data and later use it in an attack.

Take a look at figure 1.2 for a simplified explanation of the CHAP handshake process.

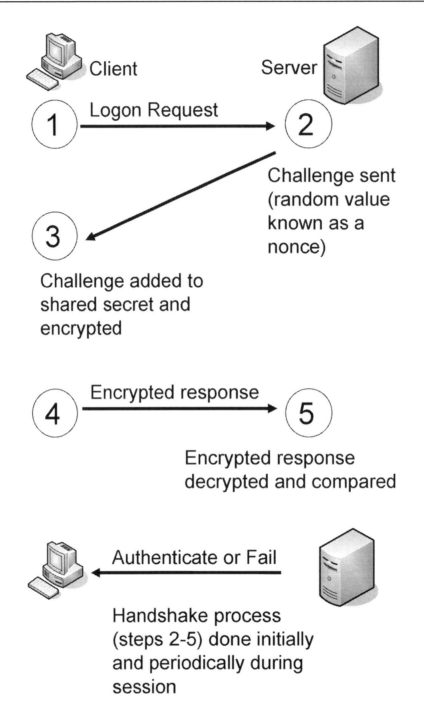

Figure 1.2: CHAP Handshake Process

1. When a client tries to log on, the logon request is sent to the server.
2. The server creates a nonce (a number used once) as a challenge mechanism. The nonce is then sent to the client.
3. The client will add a shared secret (such as a PIN or username and password) to the nonce and encrypt the combined data. Both the server and the client will know the shared secret.
4. The encrypted response is sent to the server. If this information is intercepted by an attacker, the encryption prevents the attacker from easily reading it.
5. The server decrypts the response and compares it to the original nonce and shared secret. As long as the decrypted response includes both the original nonce and the correct shared secret, the client is authenticated and authorized. If the information doesn't match, the authentication fails.

This entire process is done when the client initially tries to connect to the server and at different times during the connection. If the handshake wasn't repeated, an attacker could capture the encrypted response from step 4 and use it in a hijacking attempt.

A hijacking attempt will disconnect the legitimate client, and the attacker will present himself as the legitimate client. However, since the server randomly challenges the client with a different nonce, the attacker will not be able to authenticate to the server.

MS-CHAP and MS-CHAPv2

Microsoft introduced Microsoft Challenge Handshake Authentication Protocol (MS-CHAP) as an improvement over CHAP for Microsoft clients. MS-CHAP supported clients as old as Windows 95. Later, Microsoft improved MS-CHAP with MS-CHAPv2.

A significant improvement of MS-CHAPv2 over MS-CHAP is the ability to perform mutual authentication. Not only does the client authenticate to the server, but the server also authenticates to the client. This provides added protection to ensure that the client doesn't send data to a server that may be impersonating the live remote access server.

RADIUS

Remote Authentication Dial-In User Service (RADIUS) is a centralized authentication service. Instead of each individual RAS server needing a separate database to identify who can authenticate, authentication requests are forwarded to a central RADIUS server.

One of the ways to visualize this is to think of a dial-up ISP such as America Online (AOL). AOL provides dial-in services for just about any city in the United States. While anyone can dial-in to an AOL server, only those with accounts in good standing will be authenticated and allowed access.

Imagine you live in Atlanta, Georgia. You could sign up for AOL, pay the required fee, and access the AOL service via a server in Atlanta. AOL could maintain a database on the server in Atlanta showing your account is in good standing.

However, what if you travel to Virginia Beach, Chicago, Las Vegas, San Francisco, or somewhere else? Since you paid your fees, you would reasonably expect to be able to access AOL no matter where you travel. If the databases were stored on individual servers, then when a user's account changed because he joined or left AOL, every single server in the United States would need to be updated. Clearly, this would take a lot of work.

Instead, a centralized RADIUS server could be implemented as shown in figure 1.3.

This centralized RADIUS server would hold the database. Now if you tried to access AOL from any city, that AOL server would then contact the RADIUS server to check your account.

While this example with AOL works well to illustrate how RADIUS works, you don't need servers all over the country to take advantage of RADIUS. You could have as few as two or three RAS servers. Instead of having authentication databases on each server, you could configure a centralized RADIUS server.

RADIUS is a generic term. Microsoft uses Internet Authentication Service (IAS) as a RADIUS implementation in Microsoft domains. Authentication requests are forwarded from RAS servers to IAS, and IAS, in turn, can pass authentication requests to Active Directory.

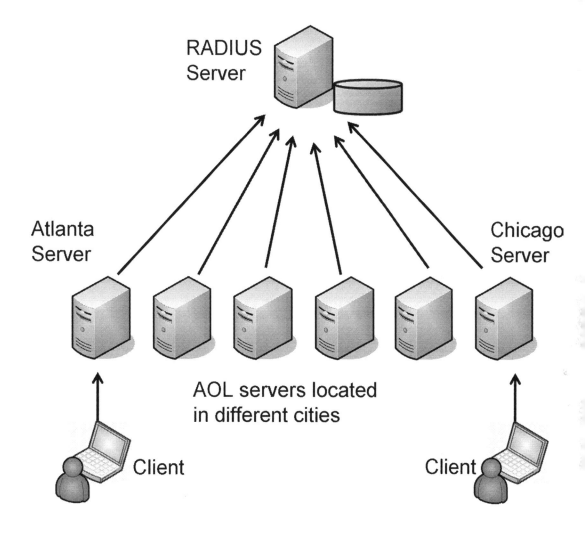

RADIUS
Server

Atlanta
Server

Chicago
Server

AOL servers located
in different cities

Client

Client

Figure 1.3: RADIUS

Remember

MS-CHAPv2 is used to authenticate Microsoft clients and includes mutual authentication. TACACS+ is used by Cisco and UNIX for authentication and can use Kerberos, allowing it to interact with a Microsoft environment. Additionally, TACACS+ encrypts the entire authentication process, while RADIUS encrypts just the password.

TACACS/TACACS+

Terminal Access Controller Access-Control System (TACACS) and TACACS+ are Cisco's alternatives to RADIUS. TACACS has been replaced with TACACS+ in most implementations, but you may still see TACACS.

In addition to using TACACS+ for remote access, it can also be used for authentication with routers and other networked devices.

While TACACS+ is proprietary to Cisco, a significant benefit is that it can interact with Kerberos. This allows a Cisco RAS server or VPN concentrator to interact with a Microsoft Active Directory environment. As a reminder, Microsoft's Active Directory uses Kerberos for authentication.

Both TACACS and TACACS+ use port 49.

Exam Topic Review

When preparing for the exam, make sure you understand these key concepts, which were covered in this chapter.

Core Security Principles

- Confidentiality – Preventing unauthorized disclosure through encryption.
- Integrity – Verifying that data has not been modified with hashing or message authentication codes.
- Availability – Ensuring that data and services are available when needed.
- Non-repudiation – Preventing someone from denying an action through the use of logging or digital signatures.
- Defense in depth – Employing several layers of security.
- Implicit deny – Specifically allowing certain traffic or permissions and blocking everything else. What isn't explicitly allowed is implicitly denied.
- Use devices as intended – Use security devices such as firewalls only for security purposes.

Authentication

Authentication allows entities to prove who they are by using credentials known to another entity. The different methods of authentication covered in this chapter were:

- Three factors of authentication
    - Something you know (such as a username and password)
    - Something you have (such as a smart card or key fob)
    - Something you are (using biometrics)
- Multifactor authentication – employs two or more of the three factors.
- Identity proofing vs. authentication – Identity proofing is verifying that someone is who he says he is before issuing credentials. Identity proofing can also be used to identify someone if she has forgotten her credentials or to validate an identity before a critical activity is approved.
- Kerberos – The authentication mechanism used in domains and UNIX realms. Kerberos requires a KDC to issue time-stamped tickets and uses port 88.
- Mutual authentication – Two hosts authenticate each other before sharing information.
- Single sign-on – Users are issued a single user account, which can access multiple resources on a network.

Remote Access Authentication

Remote access authentication is used when a user accesses a private network from outside the network, such as using a dial-in connection or a VPN connection. The authentication mechanisms used with remote access covered in this chapter were:

- PAP – Password Authentication Protocol is rarely used since passwords are passed in clear text.
- CHAP – Challenge Handshake Authentication Protocol uses a challenge-response authentication process.
- MS-CHAP and MS-CHAPv2 – Microsoft CHAP is Microsoft's improvement over CHAP. CHAPv2 provides mutual authentication.

- RADIUS – Remote Authentication Dial-In User Service provides central authentication for multiple RAS servers. RADIUS encrypts the password during the authentication process.
- TACACS/TACACS+ – Terminal Access Controller Access-Control System is used by some Cisco and UNIX remote access systems as an alternative to RADIUS. TACACS encrypts the entire authentication process. TACACS uses port 49.

Practice Questions

1. You want to ensure that data has not been tampered with or modified. What are you trying to ensure?

   A. Confidentiality

   B. Integrity

   C. Availability

   D. Need-to-know

2. You want to ensure that data is not disclosed to unintended persons. What are you trying to maintain?

   A. Confidentiality

   B. Integrity

   C. Availability

   D. Least privilege

3. You discover that a web server has been added to a firewall in your network. What principle does this violate?

   A. Defense in depth

   B. Implicit deny

   C. Use a device as intended

   D. Least privilege

4. Of the following, what can be used as a first step toward implementing access control?

   A. Requiring complex passwords

   B. Implicit deny

   C. Need-to-know

   D. Job rotation

5. What can be used to validate a message's origin?

   A. Confidentiality

   B. Integrity

    C. Availability

    D. Non-repudiation

6. Which one of the following describes the principle of implicit deny?

    A. Denying all traffic between networks

    B. Denying all traffic unless it is specifically granted access

    C. Granting all traffic to a network that is explicitly granted

    D. Granting all traffic to a network unless it is explicitly denied

7. A biometric system has identified an unauthorized user as an authorized user. What is this?

    A. False acceptance

    B. False rejection

    C. False positron

    D. Biometric frailty

8. Which of the following accurately explains a challenge-response session used for authentication?

    A. A user is challenged to provide a password, and if the password is correct, the user is granted access.

    B. A server produces a random challenge string. The user answers with the challenge string and a PIN.

    C. A server uses specialized hardware to create proximity codes used in a cryptography system.

    D. A user is challenged to provide his PIN, and if the PIN is correct, the user is granted access.

9. What would be set on an account to ensure that it is locked out for fifteen minutes after the maximum number of attempts to log on have failed?

    A. Kerberos ticket expiration

    B. Kerberos time-stamp

    C. Lockout threshold

    D. Lockout duration

10. What types of identification mechanisms are used by many fob-based authentication systems? (Choose three.)

    A. Username and passwords

    B. PINs

    C. Tokens

    D. Fingerprint scanners

    E. Certificates

11. Which authentication mechanism uses the following sequence of events to authorize a user: logon request, challenge, encrypted response, authenticate or fail?

    A. Biometrics

    B. Smart cards

    C. Kerberos

    D. CHAP

12. Why is time synchronization used in Kerberos?

    A. To ensure that tickets expire correctly

    B. To ensure that the challenge-response handshake process is synchronized

    C. To generate random keys used by the KDC

    D. To measure performance

13. Which one of the following protocols will protect wireless authentication requests?

    A. WEP

    B. IEEE 802.11g

    C. IEEE 802.11n

    D. IEEE 802.1x

14. What is a significant benefit of MS-CHAPv2 over MS-CHAP?

    A. MS-CHAPv2 provides multifactor authentication, whereas MS-CHAP does not provide multifactor authentication.

    B. MS-CHAPv2 provides mutual authentication, whereas MS-CHAP does not provide mutual authentication.

C. MS-CHAPv2 can be used instead of IEEE 802.1x authentication for wireless authentication, whereas MS-CHAP cannot replace IEEE 802.1x.

D. MS-CHAPv2 encrypts PAP, whereas MS-CHAP does not provide encryption.

15. What type of authentication requires a user to have something?

  A. Kerberos

  B. PAP

  C. IEEE 802.1X

  D. Smart cards

16. You are using a smart card to log on to your network. What key is being used?

  A. Symmetric

  B. Private

  C. Public

  D. PSK

17. What type of strategy would be implemented to prevent users from entering their credentials at each server or application that requires authentication?

  A. SSO

  B. SSL

  C. Multifactor

  D. Mutual

18. Which authentication mechanism has built-in protections to prevent replay attacks?

  A. PAP

  B. Smart cards

  C. PPTP

  D. Kerberos

19. What authentication process allows a user to access several different resources without the need for multiple credentials?

  A. Implicit deny

  B. Need-to-know

C. Single sign-on

D. Single-factor authentication

20. A user is authenticated by entering a username and password and scanning a finger on a fingerprint scanner. What type of authentication is being used?

A. Biometrics

B. Mutual

C. Multifactor

D. SSO

21. A new employee will start work tomorrow. What security actions should be done prior to granting the new employee access to the network?

A. Confidentiality and availability

B. Availability and integrity

C. Authentication and integrity

D. Authentication and identification

22. Your organization has over one thousand users and is trying to reduce costs while maintaining security. You are asked to recommend a system to manage passwords. What should you recommend?

A. Passwords of at least fifteen characters

B. Removal of account lockout policies

C. Complex passwords created by an administrator and issued to users, and a policy preventing the users from changing their passwords

D. Self-service password reset system

23. Which of the following password rules are often created in a network to ensure password security? (Choose all that apply.)

A. Complex passwords should be created by an administrator and given to the users while ensuring the password can't be modified.

B. Users should be prevented from changing their passwords.

C. Passwords must be at least eight characters and include three different character types.

D. Passwords should expire, requiring users to create new passwords.

24. What could be implemented to help users know when unauthorized access to their account has occurred?

    A. Strong authentication

    B. Identity proofing

    C. Previous logon notification

    D. Account lockout policies

25. Which one of the following would be considered a complex password?

    A. a46bt521

    B. IL0veThi$B00k

    C. password

    D. p@$$word

Practice Question Answers

1. **B.** Integrity is used to verify that data has not been modified and is enforced with hashing or message authentication codes. A hash is created at the source and then again at the destination with identical algorithms. If the hashes are identical, the data hasn't changed and retains integrity, but if the hashes are different, you know the data lost integrity.
Confidentiality is used to prevent the unauthorized disclosure of information. Availability includes several redundant technologies that ensure that data and services are available when needed. Need-to-know is a core principle that specifies that individuals are given only enough information to perform their jobs, but no more.

2. **A.** Confidentiality is used to prevent the unauthorized disclosure of information and is enforced by encrypting the data. Integrity is used to verify that data has not been modified. Availability includes several technologies that ensure that data and services are available when needed. The principle of least privilege specifies that individuals or processes are granted only the rights and permissions needed to perform their assigned tasks or functions.

3. **C.** The principle of using a device as intended specifies that devices intended for security are used only for security. Using a device to serve web pages and a firewall violates this principle. Implicit deny is a principle often used with routers and firewalls where rules are created to allow traffic, but all other traffic is blocked or denied. Defense in depth is the principle that employs multiple security layers for protection. The principle of least privilege specifies that individuals or processes are granted rights and permissions needed to perform their jobs, but no more.

4. **A.** Before access control methods can be implemented, some type of authentication, such as the use of complex passwords, must first be implemented. The only answer that addresses authentication is the first one, requiring complex passwords. Implicit deny is a principle often used with routers and firewalls where rules are created to allow traffic, but all other traffic is blocked or denied.

The need-to-know principle specifies that individuals are given access to the data they need, but no more. Job rotation can provide more oversight of past transactions by rotating new personnel into the job.

5. **D.** Non-repudiation provides definitive proof of a sender's identity, which can validate a message's origin. It is also used to prevent a party from denying he took a specific action. Confidentiality is used to prevent the unauthorized disclosure of information. Integrity is used to verify that data has not been modified and is enforced with hashing or message authentication codes. Availability includes several redundant technologies that ensure that data and services are available when needed.

6. **B.** Implicit deny indicates that unless traffic or permissions are explicitly allowed, they are denied. It isn't used to deny all traffic but instead used to deny all traffic that isn't explicitly granted or allowed.

7. **A.** False acceptance occurs when a biometric system incorrectly identifies someone as an authorized user. False rejection occurs when a biometric system incorrectly rejects an authorized user. Positrons are related to electrons with electronics, but not with biometrics. There is no such thing as biometric frailty.

8. **B.** The Challenge Handshake Authentication Protocol is a classic challenge-response authentication mechanism that uses a random challenge string and a shared secret such as a PIN. The server produces a random challenge string called a nonce and sends it to the client. The client then adds the nonce to the shared secret and encrypts it. The encrypted data is sent back to the server for decryption and comparison for verification. A challenge-response session is much more than just a password or a PIN, and it does not use proximity cards or readers. Proximity codes are embedded in a proximity card.

9. **D.** The lockout duration specifies how long an account is locked out after the maximum number of password attempts have been tried. The lockout threshold specifies how many times an incorrect password can be entered before an account is locked out. Kerberos is used for authentication and will lock out

accounts that aren't synchronized, but Kerberos can't lock out an account for a specified period.

10. **A, B, C.** Fob-based authentication systems are also known as token-based authentication systems and are frequently used for multifactor authentication, where the user must have the fob or token and know something such as a PIN or username and password. Fingerprint scanners are not part of fob-based authentication. Certificates are required in smart cards but are not used with fobs.

11. **D.** The Challenge Handshake Authentication Protocol (CHAP) uses a challenge-response mechanism. After the client requests to logon, the server challenges the client with a nonce. The client combines a shared secret with the nonce, encrypts it, and passes it back to the server. The server then decrypts the response and either authenticates the client or the process fails. Biometrics, smart cards, and Kerberos all use other processes for authentication.

12. **A.** Kerberos uses time synchronization to time-stamp the tickets and ensure the tickets expire correctly. This helps prevent replay attacks. CHAP uses a challenge-response handshake process that does not require time synchronization. Kerberos does not use a challenge-response process. The clock is not used to generate keys or to measure performance.

13. **D.** The IEEE 802.1x is used to protect the authentication portion of a wireless connection. Wired Equivalent Privacy (WEP) can be used to provide limited security for a wireless network but is known to have significant vulnerabilities; 802.1x specifically improves the security within a WEP session. IEEE 802.11g and 802.11n are wireless connection protocols, but they don't specify authentication mechanisms.

14. **B.** A significant improvement of MS-CHAPv2 over MS-CHAP is that MS-CHAP provides mutual authentication between both the client and the server in the authentication process. Both MS-CHAP and MS-CHAPv2 can be used in combination with other authentication mechanisms to provide multifactor

authentication. IEEE 802.1x is commonly used to encrypt the authentication process in wireless networks; it can be used in conjunction with MS-CHAPv2, but MS-CHAPv2 does not replace its functionality. PAP is unencrypted and cannot be encrypted with either MS-CHAP or MS-CHAPv2.

15. **D.** Both smart cards and fob-based authentication mechanisms require a user to have something. Kerberos requires a KDC and time synchronization, but users do not need to physically do anything to use Kerberos. PAP allows users to authenticate with remote access servers by entering passwords, which are sent in clear text, but PAP only requires the user to know something. IEEE 802.1x provides security for an authentication session prior to data being passed, but it doesn't require physically having something.

16. **B.** A smart card has an embedded certificate issued by a PKI, and the certificate holds a private key that is used when a user logs on to a network with a smart card. A private key always stays private and is matched to a public key in asymmetric encryption (not symmetric). Pre-shared keys are symmetric keys used in some encryption protocols such as those used on wireless networks or trusted platform modules.

17. **A.** Single sign-on (SSO) authentication is used to prevent users from entering credentials at each server or application for normal work. Instead, users authenticate once and the supplied credentials are used throughout the session. SSL is an encryption protocol commonly used with HTTPS on port 443. Multifactor authentication makes use of two or more of the three authentication factors. Mutual authentication is when both sides of a session authenticate to each other before data is sent.

18. **D.** Kerberos uses a Key Distribution Center (KDC) to issue time-stamped tickets. These time-stamped tickets expire, helping to prevent replay attacks. PAP is the weakest form of authentication as passwords are passed in clear text. Smart cards use certificates and require a PKI, but they don't have preventions against replay attacks. PPTP is a tunneling protocol used for VPNs, but PPTP doesn't provide protection against replay attacks.

19. **C.** Single sign-on (SSO) authentication is used to prevent users from entering credentials at each server or application for normal work. Instead, users authenticate once and the supplied credentials are used throughout the session. Implicit deny is a principle often used with routers and firewalls where rules are created to allow traffic, but all other traffic is blocked or denied. Need-to-know is a core principle that specifies that individuals are given only enough information to perform their jobs, no more. Single-factor authentication uses one of the three authentication factors.

20. **C.** Multifactor authentication is when more than one of the three authentication factors of authentication (something you know, something you have, or something you are) are being used. The username and password is one factor, and the fingerprint is a second factor. While the fingerprint scan uses biometrics, biometrics as the answer doesn't take into account the second factor of a username and password. Mutual authentication is when two entities both authenticate with each other. SSO authentication is used to prevent users from entering credentials at each server or application for normal work.

21. **D.** The user's identity should be verified with some type of identity proofing method such as showing a driver's license. Once the identification is accomplished, credentials can be issued to the new employee. She can then use these credentials to authenticate herself on the network. Confidentiality is used to prevent the unauthorized disclosure of information. Availability includes several redundant technologies that ensure that data and services are available when needed. Integrity is used to verify that data has not been modified and is enforced with hashing or message authentication codes.

22. **D.** Self-service password reset systems allow users to reset their passwords without requiring intervention from IT professionals and are often recommended in larger networks to reduce costs. Passwords of fifteen characters may result in more users forgetting their passwords unless they write them down, reducing security. Removal of account lockout policies will weaken security. If passwords are created by an administrator, then at least two people know the password,

thus weakening security; additionally, if passwords can't be changed, security is weakened.

23. **C, D.** Passwords should be strong, meaning they have at least eight characters and are using at least three of the four different character types (uppercase, lowercase, numbers, and special characters). Users should be required to change their passwords regularly; this is accomplished by causing the passwords to expire. Passwords should be known by only one person, so if an administrator creates a password and gives it to a user, two people know the password. One problem with this is, if a user causes damage, he could claim he didn't do it; it must have been the administrator who knows his password.

24. **C.** Previous logon notification can be used to inform users of the last time their account was accessed. If the notification indicates a time when the user didn't log on, it provides notification that the account has been compromised. Strong authentication and identity proofing are both important concepts related to authentication, but they wouldn't notify users of unauthorized access. An account lockout policy could cause an account to be locked if someone tried to guess the password, but it would indicate an unsuccessful attempt, not actual unauthorized access.

25. **B.** A complex password would be at least eight characters and include at least three of the four character types: uppercase, lowercase, numbers, and special characters. Only one of the passwords (IL0veThi$B00k) includes all four character types. The other choices include only one or two of the four character types.

Chapter 2

Controlling Access

CompTIA Security+ objectives covered in this chapter

3.2 Explain common access control models and the differences between each.
- MAC
- DAC
- Role & Rule based access control

3.3 Organize users and computers into appropriate security groups and roles while distinguishing between appropriate rights and privileges.

3.5 Compare and implement logical access control methods.
- ACL
- Group policies
- Password policy
- Domain password policy
- User names and passwords
- Time of day restrictions
- Account expiration
- Logical tokens

3.9 Explain and apply physical access security methods.
- Physical access logs/lists
- Hardware locks
- Physical access control – ID badges
- Door access systems
- Man-trap
- Physical tokens
- Video surveillance – camera types and positioning

* * *

Once you've ensured personnel have adequately identified themselves with authentication, you can now move to different methods to restrict or control access. This chapter will cover the following access control topics:

- **Access control models.** The different access control methods covered include MAC, DAC, and RBAC.
- **Physical security methods.** Physical security includes the basics such as locking doors and securing equipment. More advanced methods include using badges, proximity cards, mantraps, and video surveillance.
- **Logical access control methods.** Logical access control methods include using ACLS, Group Policy within a Microsoft environment, and controlling accounts.

Access Control Models

If you've never studied access control models before, these topics might seem a little foreign to you. As models, they are largely theoretical and used in the design stage of defining access control methods. The in-depth knowledge laid out in these models helps the experts create the logical access control methods that IT professionals implement and maintain.

Most IT professionals implement and maintain the security within the networks; they don't design the networks, so the details of the underlying theories aren't as important as knowing how to manage them within a system or network. You don't need to know enough to write a master's thesis on these models.

You're probably familiar with some of these topics, but the terms *MAC, DAC,* and *RBAC* may be unfamiliar. By understanding a little more of the underlying design principles, you'll understand why some of the imposed rules are important, and you'll be better prepared to ensure that security principles are followed. The models you'll learn are:

- Mandatory Access Control (MAC)
- Discretionary Access Control (DAC)
- Role and Rule Based Access Control (RBAC)

Often, when using any of the models, you'll run across the following terms:

- **Subjects**. Subjects are typically users or groups that will access an object. Occasionally, the subject may be a service that is using a service account to access an object.
- **Objects**. Objects are items such as files, folders, shares, and printers that are accessed by subjects.

Some files may be proprietary, private, or classified and need to be protected depending on the classification. The access control model (MAC, DAC, or RBAC) will determine how the protection is implemented.

Mandatory Access Control

The MAC model uses labels (sometimes referred to as sensitivity labels or security labels) to determine access. Both subjects (users) and objects (files or folders) are assigned labels. When the labels match, the appropriate permission is granted.

SELinux (Security Enhanced Linux) is one of the few operating systems that use the MAC model.

> ### *Remember*
> The MAC model uses sensitivity labels for users and data. Levels of security are defined in a lattice model, and associated permissions are set by the administrator. Access privileges are predefined and stay relatively static.

Military units make wide use of this model to protect data. You may have seen movies where a folder is shown with a big red and black cover page with a label of Top Secret. The cover page identifies the sensitivity label for the data contained within.

Only users who have a Top Secret label (a Top Secret clearance) and a need to know are granted access to the folder. If someone doesn't have a Top Secret clearance, he shouldn't be granted access.

Labels and Lattice

The MAC model uses different levels of security to classify both the users and the data. These levels are defined in a lattice. The lattice can be a complex relationship between different ordered sets of multiple labels that define upper-level bounds and lower-level bounds.

You can think of a lattice like a trellis used to guide climbing plants like ivy or roses. The different levels of the trellis allow the plant to reach and climb to different levels. A lattice similarly has different levels, but these are defined as security levels such as Top Secret, Secret, and Confidential in the MAC model. Each level on the lattice identifies the start or end of a different security level, and the tiers between the levels identify security boundaries.

Classification levels could be generically identified as proprietary, private, and public based on the needs of the company. A government entity may identify the levels as Top Secret, Secret, and Confidential.

The names of the labels aren't as important as how they're used. Data is categorized according to these defined labels, and users have clearances defined by these same labels. Users can only access data categorized by sensitivity labels that are assigned to them.

Establishing Access

An administrator is responsible for establishing access, but only after this access has been defined by a higher authority.

Typically, a security professional is assigned the task of identifying who is cleared for specific access and is responsible for upgrading and downgrading an individual's access when needed. This person is also responsible for identifying privileges required to access different data. Note that this is all done via paperwork by the security professional, not on the computers. Additionally, multiple approval levels could be involved in the decision-making process.

For example, in the military this could be done by an officer who coordinates with higher-level entities that actually approve or disapprove clearance requests.

Within the network, an administrator would be responsible for actually establishing access to the different users based on the clearances identified by the security professional. From the IT administrator's point of view, all the permissions and access privileges are predefined.

If someone needed different access, the administrator would forward the request to the security professional, who may approve or disapprove the request. Or the security professional could forward the request to higher entities based on established procedures. This process takes time and results in limited flexibility.

Discretionary Access Control

In the DAC model, every object (such as files and folders) has an owner, and the owner establishes access for the objects. Many operating systems, such as Windows and most UNIX-based systems, use the DAC model.

> ### Remember
> The DAC model specifies that every object has an owner, and the owner has full explicit control of the object. Access is established by the owner, who assigns permissions to users or groups. The owner can easily change permissions, making this a dynamic model. A notable flaw with DAC is its susceptibility to Trojan horse malware.

A common example of the DAC model is the file system in Windows—NTFS. NTFS was discussed briefly in Chapter 1 in the single sign-on section. As a reminder, each object has a Discretionary Access Control List (DACL). The DACL is a list of entries that specify what users are granted access and, specifically, what permissions they have.

In Chapter 3, you'll learn about routers and firewalls. Routers and firewalls also use access control lists (ACLs), but the terminology is a little different. In a router, rules are implemented in the form of ACLs that specifically define what traffic is allowed or what traffic is denied.

The Owner Establishes Access

If a user creates a file or folder, she is designated as the owner. This is sometimes referred to as explicit control. As the owner, she can modify the permissions on the object by explicitly adding user or group accounts to the DACL and assigning the desired permissions.

The DAC model is significantly more flexible than the MAC model. MAC has predefined access privileges, and the administrator is required to make the changes. With DAC, if you want to grant me access to a file you own, you simply make the change, and I have access.

Beware of Trojans

An inherent flaw associated with the DAC model is the susceptibility to Trojan horses. Chapter 6 will present malware in much more depth, but for this discussion, you should understand how Trojan horses work.

Trojan horses are executable files that masquerade as something useful but are actually malicious software. For example, a user might decide to download and install a program that someone raved about. After installation, he decides it's not so great and forgets about it. However, the damage is done.

What really happened? When the program was installed, it also installed malicious software. Moreover, if the program was installed when a user was logged on with administrative privileges, the Trojan is able to run with these administrative privileges.

A common policy for anyone with an administrative account is to also have a regular user account. Most of the time, a user will be logged on with the regular account, and if that account is infected with some type of malware, it won't have the elevated permissions of an administrator.

Role and Rule Based Access Control

Role Based Access Control (RBAC) uses roles to manage rights and permissions for users. The roles are created, and specific rights and permissions are granted to these roles instead of to the users. When a user is added to the role, she has all the rights and permissions of the role.

Rule Based Access Control (with the same acronym of RBAC) uses rules that define specific conditions to determine if access is granted to resources. These rules can be implemented in more complex scenarios where rules can actually be scripted in real time. Rule Based Access Control can be used to complement or enhance a Role Based Access Control model.

For the purpose of this chapter, we'll focus on Role Based Access Control, and for clarity, when the RBAC acronym is being used, it represents Role Based Access Control.

> ### Remember
> The RBAC model uses roles to grant access by placing users into roles based on their assigned jobs, functions, or tasks. It is also referred to as both a hierarchical-based model and a task-based model. Rights and permissions are assigned to the roles. A user is placed into a role, inheriting the rights and permissions of the role.

Using Roles Based on Jobs and Functions

An example of the RBAC model is in Microsoft's Project Server. The Project Server can host multiple projects managed by different project managers. It includes the following roles:

- **Administrators**. Members of the Administrators role have complete access and control over everything on the server, including all of the projects.
- **Executives**. Members of the Executives role can access data from any project held on the server but don't have access to modify system settings on the server.
- **Project Managers**. Members of the Project Managers role have full control over their own projects but do not have any control over projects owned by other project managers.
- **Team Members**. Team Members can typically report on work they are assigned and complete, but they have little access outside the scope of their assignments.

Project Server includes more roles, but you can see the point with these four. Each of the roles has rights and permissions assigned to it, and to give someone the associated privileges, you'd simply add his account to the role.

RBAC is also called hierarchy based, or job based.

- **Hierarchy based**. In the Project Server example, you can see how top-level roles such as the Administrators role have significantly more permissions than lower-level roles such as the Team Members role. Roles may mimic the hierarchy of an organization.

- **Job, task, or function based**. The Project Server example also shows how the roles are centered on jobs or functions that users need to perform.

Establishing Access

Access is established in the RBAC model based on the role membership. Each role has the rights and permissions assigned, and you simply add the user to the role to grant appropriate access.

A looser, more relaxed implementation of the RBAC model is in Microsoft's built-in groups, and specially created groups that are available in both workstations and domains. For example, if you want someone to be able to perform backups and restores, you can simply add her to the Backup Operators group, and she automatically has the appropriate access.

Built-in groups have rights and permissions already assigned. It's also possible to make changes to the built-in groups, giving this model some flexibility. More often, additional groups are created that can be used to meet specific needs. For example, to separate the backup and restore responsibilities, a special group can be created that can only back up data and another special group can be created that can only restore data.

In Windows domains, groups are often created to correspond to departments of an organization, such as sales, marketing, and IT. User accounts for users working in any of the departments are added to the group representing their department. Rights and permissions can be assigned to the groups based on their jobs and functions. When a new employee is hired for a department, the employee's user account is added to the department's group, and he instantly has the appropriate access.

Summary of MAC, DAC, and RBAC Models

Use the following summary as a review of the relevant access control model points for the CompTIA Security+ exam.

MAC

- Uses labels (sometimes called security labels or sensitivity labels) to identify subjects and objects.
- System administrator establishes access.
- Permissions are predefined.
- Uses a lattice model to define security levels.
- Relatively static model – not easy to make changes.

DAC

- Every object has an owner, and the owner has full control of the object.
- The owner establishes access by setting permissions explicitly for users or groups.
- DAC uses access control lists to identify who has access.
- File access can be granted to users or groups.
- Dynamic model – owner can easily make changes to permissions.
- A significant flaw is the susceptibility to Trojan horse attacks.

RBAC

- Roles are used to grant access.
- RBAC is sometimes referred to as a hierarchical-based model or task-based model.
- Access control is based on the role or responsibilities users are expected to have in an organization.
- Access is based on jobs or tasks that role members will perform.
- Roles are granted permissions and rights.
- Users are added to a role, and permissions and rights are granted to all users based on role membership.
- RBAC is more flexible than MAC, which is relatively static.

Physical Security Methods

Physical security includes all the elements employed to restrict physical access to buildings and hardware devices, such as servers, routers, and switches. It includes physical locks; access control mechanisms, such as ID badges; and video monitoring.

Unlike the MAC, DAC, and RBAC models that are theoretical, physical security is physical in the sense that you can physically touch the different elements.

Access Controls

Access controls are used to control entry and exit at different boundary points. The different boundaries that can be controlled are:

- **Perimeter**. Military bases and many companies have a fence around the entire perimeter of the location. Access is often controlled at gates.
- **Building**. A building may have access controls to ensure that only authorized personnel are allowed in. Even when access isn't restricted, many buildings employ video cameras to monitor access.
- **Secure work areas**. Some companies restrict access to specific work areas where some type of classified or restricted access work is accomplished.
- **Server and network devices**. Servers and network devices such as routers and switches are normally stored in areas where only the appropriate IT personnel can access them. These spaces may be designated as server rooms or wiring closets. Providing additional physical security helps ensure they are not tampered with and ensures that illicit monitoring hardware such as a sniffer is not installed to capture traffic.

Physical Access Control – ID Badges

Identification badges (ID badges) are commonly used to provide visual confirmation that someone is authorized in a certain area. ID badges will usually include information on the holder and a picture.

Access points are used to ensure that everyone who enters has an ID badge. Additionally, within secure areas, the ID badges are displayed so that others can see that the person is authorized. ID badges are commonly clipped to pockets or connected to lanyards, which personnel wear around their necks.

ID badges can also be used with other electronic measures. In other words, instead of just identifying the user with a name and a picture, the badge can also function as a proximity card or a smart card, or simply have a magnetic strip similar to a credit card. In addition to providing physical verification that someone is authorized, it can also be used to record entry and exit.

Physical Access Logs and Lists

When access points are controlled with electronic measures such as proximity cards, access logs can be used to verify exactly when someone enters or exits a building. When used for this purpose, the ID badges need to uniquely identify each holder to support accurate logging.

Logging can also be used to identify some security vulnerabilities. If a log shows that a user exited a building but does not show that the user entered the building, it indicates piggybacking or tailgating has occurred.

Piggybacking

Piggybacking is where one user follows closely behind another user. If this often occurs with authorized users, it indicates the environment is susceptible to a social engineering attack where an unauthorized user follows closely behind an authorized user.

As an example, a contractor was hired to perform a vulnerability assessment. She saw that access to the building was controlled with badges. She loaded herself up with a book bag and a laptop, ensuring her hands weren't free. She timed her approach carefully and followed closely behind someone with a badge. Sure enough, the authorized person held the door open.

We're trained to be polite, not rude, and social engineers take advantage of this training.

Access lists can also be used. An access list is a printed list that a guard checks to verify that someone should be granted access.

Door Access Systems

A door access system is one that only opens after some access control mechanism is used. It includes cipher locks and proximity cards.

Cipher locks often have four or five buttons labeled with numbers. By pressing the numbers in a certain order, the lock is unlocked. For example, the cipher code could be 1, 3, 2, 4. By entering the code in the right order, you can gain access.

To add complexity and reduce brute force attacks, many cipher locks include a code that requires two numbers entered at the same time. Instead of just 1, 3, 2, 4, the code could be 1/3 (entered at the same time), then 2, 4, 5.

Physical Tokens

Chapter 1 included information on authentication. Tokens were described as fobs or key fobs such as those sold by SecureID. While these tokens are most often used for authentication, they can also be used for access control.

As a reminder, key fobs have an LED display that shows a number that regularly changes, such as every sixty seconds. This number is synchronized with a server that knows what the number on the key fob is at any time.

The number could then be entered into the door access mechanism to allow someone to gain access to a secure space.

Proximity Cards

Proximity cards are small credit-card-sized cards that can be activated when they are in close proximity to a card reader. These can be used for access points, such as the entry to a building or the entry to a controlled area within a building.

You've probably seen proximity card readers as credit card readers. They are often found at gasoline pumps and many fast-food restaurants. Instead of swiping the credit card, you can simply pass it in front of the reader (in close proximity to the reader), and the information on the card is read.

It's intriguing how this is done. The card doesn't require its own power source. Instead, the electronics in the card include a capacitor and a coil that can accept a charge from the proximity card reader. When the card is placed close to the reader, the reader excites the coil and stores a charge in the capacitor. Once charged, the card will transmit information to the reader using a radio frequency.

Proximity card technology can be used in:

- **Access points**. Mantraps such as turnstiles can use proximity cards to provide access. Additionally, access to rooms can be controlled with proximity cards and readers.
- **Credit cards**. Many credit cards include this technology.
- **Mass transit entry points**. Cards can be sold with a set number of passes for bus or subway rides.

As a side note, one of the worrisome issues related to these cards is that attackers can build or purchase systems that can read your credit cards if they operate as proximity cards. The reader is placed in a purse or bag and then positioned close to your wallet or purse, perhaps by standing behind you in the elevator, a store, or a line. The electronics on the card would charge and then transmit without your knowledge. The collected information can be used later to make unauthorized purchases.

> ### Remember
> Proximity cards are credit-card-sized access cards that only need to be waved or placed in close proximity to a card reader. Data on the card is then read by the card reader. Proximity cards are used as an additional access control in some areas.

About the only way to prevent this is to wrap your credit cards in some type of shielding, like aluminum foil. I've heard of companies selling credit card shield protectors for as much as $29.95. Of course, you can make your own shield with a couple of well-placed pieces of aluminum foil in your wallet or purse.

Mantraps

A mantrap is a physical security mechanism designed to control access to a secure area through a buffer zone. Mantraps get their name due to their ability to lock a person between two areas such as an open access area and a secure access area.

> **Remember**
>
> Mantraps are used to control the access between a secure area and a nonsecure area. They can be highly technical, including rooms made of bulletproof glass, or simplistic, similar to a turnstile used in subways. A mantrap should be able to trap the individual halfway through, preventing him from moving forward or backward if necessary. Mantraps are commonly used to prevent the social engineering tactic known as tailgating or piggybacking.

Mantraps can be sophisticated or simple.

A sophisticated mantrap is a room, or even a building, that creates a large buffer area between the secure area and the unsecured area. Access through the entry door and the exit door is tightly controlled, either through the use of guards or with an access card such as a proximity card.

An example of a simple mantrap is a turnstile that can be locked before the turnstile turns completely through to the other side.

Mantraps can be an effective deterrent against the social engineering tactic of tailgating or piggybacking. A tailgating attack is when a person who isn't authorized to enter an area does so by following closely behind someone who is authorized.

Hardware Locks

Of course, simple physical security can be implemented to prevent access to certain areas. A hardware lock could be just like the locks you have at your home to restrict access.

Hardware locks are frequently used in smaller companies that don't have the resources to employ advanced security systems. Server rooms and/or wiring closets are frequently just smaller rooms used to house servers and network devices such as routers and switches.

Video Surveillance

Security cameras are increasingly being used in the workplace and surrounding areas for video surveillance. In addition to monitoring, most video surveillance systems include a recording element. By recording activity, it can be played back later for investigation and even prosecution.

Video cameras are often used within a work environment to protect employees and enhance security in the workplace. However, they can also be used to monitor the work environment and prevent theft by employees.

When using video surveillance in a work environment, it's important to respect privacy and to be aware of privacy laws.

Some things to consider are:

- **Only record activity in public areas**. People have a reasonable expectation of privacy in certain areas, such as locker rooms or restrooms, and it is often unlawful to record activity in these areas.
- **Notify employees of the surveillance**. If employees aren't notified of the surveillance, legal issues related to the video surveillance can arise. This is especially true if the recordings are used to take actions against the employee.
- **Do not record audio**. Recording audio is often illegal without the express consent of all parties being recorded. Many companies won't even sell surveillance cameras that record audio.

Camera Types

Multiple different camera types can be used depending on your needs. They include:

- **Wireless**. Wireless cameras have built-in transceivers that can be used to transmit the video to a wireless receiver, often up to seven hundred feet away. This is similar to how any wireless device such as a wireless laptop may connect to a wireless network. The benefit is that additional wiring doesn't need to be run. Additionally, while a wired connection can be cut to stop the recording, a wireless connection doesn't have any cable to cut.

- **Wired.** Wired cameras are more common and include the wiring to carry the video back to the recorder or display.
- **Low-light.** Low-light (or low-lux) cameras have the ability to record activity even in low-light conditions. This prevents someone from simply killing the lights to prevent any video recording. Low-light cameras usually use either infrared or thermal technologies.
- **Color.** Most video cameras are color unless they are specifically designed to capture activity in low-light conditions. For regular lighting conditions, a color camera provides a better picture with no appreciable increase in cost.
- **Black-and-white.** Low-light cameras are generally black-and-white since both thermal and infrared technologies can't capture the color in low-light conditions.

Camera Positioning

When considering the use of video cameras, the basic question to ask is, "What do you want to record?" The answer will dictate where you'll place the camera. Cameras can be placed where they can monitor the entrances and exits of buildings or individual rooms. They can also be placed where they can monitor the activity of specific high-risk areas.

Some rooms may require the use of multiple cameras: one could record everyone who enters the room; another camera could record everyone who exits the room; and a third wide-angle camera could record all the activity within the room.

In addition to deciding how and where a camera is positioned, you can also consider whether the camera should be stationary or adjustable. Video surveillance cameras are classified as:

- **Fixed.** A fixed camera can only look at one area and doesn't include any zooming or repositioning ability.
- **PTZ.** Some cameras can pan (move left and right), tilt (move up and down), and zoom to get a closer or a wider view. Panning, tilting, zooming (PTZ) cameras are often used in public establishments that have the security personnel to man the cameras. PTZ cameras are more expensive than fixed cameras.

Logical Access Control Methods

Logical access control methods are implemented through a technology such as access control lists or Group Policy. They control access to the logical network as opposed to controlling access to the physical areas of a building or physical access to devices within the network.

The different methods that can be used to provide logical access control include:

- Access control lists
- Group Policy
- Account control

Access Control Lists

Access control lists (ACLs) are used to specifically identify what is allowed and what is not allowed. An ACL can define what is allowed based on permissions or based on traffic.

ACLs typically operate using an implicit deny policy. For example, NTFS uses a Discretionary Access Control List (DACL) to identify who is allowed access to a file or a folder. Unless permission has been explicitly allowed for a user to access the file (either through an account or through group membership), permission is implicitly denied.

Routers also use ACLs. An ACL in a router is a list of rules that define what traffic is allowed. If the traffic meets the requirements of one of the rules, it is allowed. If it doesn't meet the requirements for any of the rules, the traffic is denied.

Group Policy

Group Policy is used in Windows domains to manage multiple users and computers in a domain. It allows an administrator to configure a setting once in the group policy object (GPO) and apply this setting to many users and computers within the domain.

As an example, you may want to ensure that the firewall is configured a certain way on all the systems in your domain. You can configure a GPO appropriately, link the GPO to the domain, and all the systems will be automatically configured. The magic of Group Policy is that it doesn't matter if you have five systems or five thousand systems. The policy still only needs to be set once to apply to all of them.

Group Policy can also be targeted to groups of users or computers. Active Directory allows you to organize both user accounts and computer accounts into organization units (OUs). You can then create a GPO and link it to the OU to have more specific settings apply to all the users and/or computers in this OU.

Password Policy

One of the core security policies that Group Policy can be used to enforce is a password policy. A password policy includes several elements that can be enforced as a part of a GPO. A password policy would include the following elements:

- **Maximum password age.** The maximum password age defines when a user must change her password. For example, if the maximum password age is set to 45, the user must change her password before the forty-sixth day, or her account is locked out until she changes it.
- **Minimum password age.** The minimum password age defines how long a user must wait before changing his password again. If this is set to two days, the user wouldn't be able to change his password again until two days have passed. This prevents a user from changing his password right back to a familiar password.
- **Enforce password history.** Password history can be set to a number such as 24. If set to 24, the password policy will remember the last twenty-four passwords the user has used and prevent the use of any of those previously used passwords.
- **Minimum password length.** The minimum password length setting ensures that users have a minimum number of characters in a password. Generally, eight characters are considered strong enough for regular user passwords, and fifteen characters are specified for accounts with administrative access.

- **Passwords must meet complexity requirements.** A complex password is defined in a Microsoft policy as being at least eight characters long and including three of the four character types: uppercase, lowercase, numbers, and special characters. In other words, "password" isn't complex enough since it is all lowercase, but "P@ssw0rd" is complex enough since it is eight characters long and uses at least three of the four character types. "P@ssw0rd" actually includes uppercase (P), lowercase (sswrd), a special character (@), and a number (0).
- **Store passwords using reversible encryption.** Reversible encryption significantly weakens security and this setting is rarely enabled in a password policy. A password stored using reversible encryption can easily be read by a knowledgeable attacker.

Domain Password Policy

In Windows Server 2000 and 2003 domains, a single password policy could be created that would apply to all users in the domain. It doesn't matter if the domain has five users or five thousand users, by setting the password policy, it applies to all users.

> ### Remember
>
> Password policies can be implemented using Group Policy to enforce a more secure use of passwords. The password policy only needs to be set once, but all users with domain accounts are required to comply with the password policy.

A drawback in a Windows Server 2000 or Server 2003 domain is that the domain can have only one password policy. Windows Server 2008 added the capability to apply additional password policies to different groups. For example, a standard password policy could be applied to all users in the domain, and then a special password policy could be created requiring anyone in a group defined by the administrator to use a stronger fifteen-character password.

Device Policy

It's also possible to use Group Policy to enforce the restriction of portable devices in a network. Small devices such as flash drives and portable media players can easily become infected with viruses, and once infected, those devices can insert the virus into a system.

When these small devices are inserted into a computer, the operating system detects the installation and can be configured to automatically run software on the device. If a system becomes infected with malware, the malware can spread to the small device. Now, when the device is inserted into another system, the malware spreads to the other system.

If the malware includes a worm component, it can quickly spread through the network after the USB is inserted and the malware is installed on a single system. Many companies employ two protections against this threat, both of which can be enforced with Group Policy:

- **Disable Autorun.** Autorun causes an application to run as soon as a device is inserted into a system. Malware adds a virus to the device and modifies the autorun.inf file to run this virus each time the device is inserted into a system. When Autorun is disabled, the executables identified in the autorun.inf file are not executed by default.

- **Prevent the installation of small devices.** The installation of drivers such as for USB flash drives or MP3 players can be completely prevented or reserved only for administrators.

- **Detect the use of small devices.** A written policy can be enforced through automatic detection. As an example, one company told all employees via email and logon banners that USB drives were expressly forbidden. Further, an executive stated publicly that the company took this rule very seriously and there would be serious consequences if anyone violated the rule. Within a week, an employee plugged in a USB drive and was looking for another job the next day.

USB Flash Drives and Malware

One security professional was hired to perform a vulnerability assessment for a bank. He dropped multiple USB flash drives in the bank's parking lot before the bank opened and then more inside the bank in areas accessible by bank employees.

Eventually, one of the employees found one of the flash drives and inserted it into his system. Bingo! Simply inserting the flash drive into the system exploited a vulnerability. The Start program on the flash drive (launched through Autorun) installed malware including a keylogger that captured the employee's keystrokes and later emailed the captured data to the security professional performing the vulnerability assessment.

Employees finding these USB drives could have good intentions. Perhaps they want to return the USB flash drive to the owner, so they look on the flash drive to see if any data would identify the owner. However, the intentions of the employee don't really matter. The malware that is installed onto USB flash drives and the attackers behind the malware don't have good intentions.

This widely known example is a key reason why many organizations restrict the use of flash drives on company computers. It may be inconvenient, but it's also a sound layer of security.

Accounts

Access control methods can also be implemented on individual user accounts within a Windows domain environment. These can be used to control when and where users can log on.

As a reminder, users have user accounts with passwords that they use to authenticate. The user knows the username, but Active Directory identifies the user account with a security identifier (SID), which is unique to each user.

User accounts can be managed in a centralized or decentralized environment.

- **Centralized.** All user accounts are stored in a central database (such as Active Directory in Windows). A centralized user account database helps provide single sign-on since users only need to sign on once to the domain.

- **Decentralized**. User accounts are stored on each individual workstation or server. A user could have multiple accounts to access multiple systems. On Windows systems, the local database storing local user accounts is the Security Accounts Manager (SAM). The SAM provides a decentralized user account database.

Remember

A centralized user account database (such as in Windows Active Directory) enables single sign-on. Users only need to authenticate one time. The database is held on a central server called a domain controller. Many networks include additional domain controllers for redundancy, and each domain controller includes a full copy of the database. A decentralized database has user accounts on each individual system and does not utilize single sign-on.

Time-of-day Restrictions

Time-of-day restrictions can be used to specify when users can actually log on to a computer. If a user tries to log in to the network outside the restricted time frame, access will be denied.

Figure 2.1 shows the time-of-day restrictions for a user account in a Windows domain.

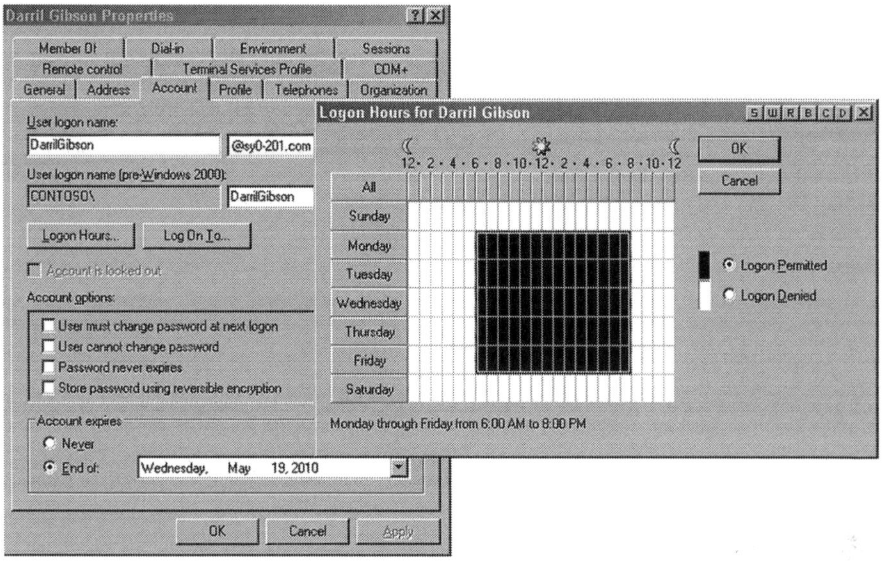

Figure 2.1: User Account Properties

As an example, a company may operate between 8 a.m. and 5 p.m. on a daily basis and decide they don't want regular users logging in to the network except between 6 a.m. and 8 p.m. Time-of-day restrictions could be set, and if someone tried to log in outside the restricted time (such as at 5 a.m. or at 9 p.m.), the logon attempt would be denied.

Account Expiration

Accounts can be set to expire automatically. An expired account will be disabled, and a user will not be able to log in using the account.

The use of account expiration is common with temporary accounts. For example, a contractor may be hired for a ninety-day period to perform a specific job. Leaving the account operational after the ninety days would be a security risk, so an administrator should ensure the account is either disabled or deleted after ninety days.

Some systems allow an administrator to enter an account expiration date that will be used by the system to automatically disable the account after the period has expired. Figure 2.1, shown previously in the time-of-day restrictions section, also shows the account expiration setting.

Logical Tokens

Logical tokens are used within a single sign-on environment to identify a user and a user's group membership. Users and groups are uniquely identified with security identifiers (SIDs), and the logical token includes all of the SIDs associated with a user—the user's SID and the SID of each group that includes the user account.

Chapter 1 explored logical tokens in greater depth. In short, you can control someone's access by controlling his group membership. By adding a user account to a group with greater permissions and privileges, you grant the user greater permissions and privileges.

Exam Topic Review

When preparing for the exam, make sure you understand these key concepts, which were covered in this chapter.

Access Control Models

Expect the three access control models to be heavily tested in the CompTIA Security+ exam. You should be familiar with the key concepts of each:

- **Mandatory Access Control (MAC)**. MAC uses security or sensitivity labels to identify objects (what you'll secure) and subjects (users). The administrator establishes access based on predefined security labels that are typically defined with a lattice to specify the upper and lower security boundaries.
- **Discretionary Access Control (DAC)**. In DAC, every object has an owner. The owner has explicit access and establishes access for any other user. NTFS uses the DAC model with every object having a Discretionary Access Control List (DACL) to identify who has access and what access they are granted. A major flaw of the DAC model is its susceptibility to Trojan horses.
- **Role (or Rule) Based Access Control (RBAC)**. In RBAC, access is granted to users based on their jobs or the tasks they perform. It's also called a hierarchical- or task-based model.

Physical Security Methods

Physical security includes implementing different access control methods with technology you can touch, such as:

- Hardware locks
- ID badges
- Door access systems
- Proximity cards
- Mantraps
- Video cameras

Logical Security Methods

Logical security methods include those elements that are implemented through technological means. Logical security methods include:

- Access control lists
- Group Policy (such as a domain password policy)
- Account controls (such as time-of-day restrictions and account expiration)

Practice Questions

1. The system administrator establishes access permissions to network resources in the _____ access control model.

    A. MAC

    B. DAC

    C. RBAC

    D. SSO

2. Which one of the access control models is sometimes referred to as hierarchical-based on positions held within an organization?

    A. MAC

    B. DAC

    C. RBAC

    D. IPSec

3. What is a known flaw associated with DAC?

    A. It uses predefined access privileges, making it inflexible.

    B. Passwords are sent across the network in clear text.

    C. It is susceptible to Trojan horses.

    D. Every object has an owner, and every user must be a member of the Administrators group to manipulate the objects.

4. Which access control model uses security labels to determine if a user can access specific data?

    A. MAC

    B. DAC

    C. RBAC

    D. SSH

5. How is access control established in the RBAC model?

    A. Access is established by the administrator.

    B. Access is established by the owner of objects.

C.Access is established based on roles.

D.Access is established based on relationships.

6. In which access control model can rights be assigned explicitly to a user?

A. MAC

B. DAC

C. RBAC

D. IMAP

7.Which of the following is true for the MAC model? (Choose all that apply.)

A. It uses labels to determine access.

B. It uses a lattice to determine security levels.

C.All objects have owners.

D. It is susceptible to Trojan horse attacks.

8.Your organization includes several departments, including sales, marketing, HR, and IT.You want to implement an access control model that can be used to grant access based on which department an employee works in.What model could you use?

A. MAC

B. DAC

C. RBAC

D. KDC

9.Who establishes access permissions in the DAC model?

A.Administrator

B. Owner

C. Job role

D. HVAC installer

10.Which access control model restricts access to resources based on the identity of the user or group?

A. MAC

B. DAC

C. RBAC

D. DMZ

11. You want to restrict the use of small devices such as portable media players and USB flash drives. What could you use to automatically restrict or detect the use of these devices by all users within a domain?

    A. Domain password policy

    B. Group Policy

    C. Administrative policy

    D. A DACL

12. A company has a secure area of the building that only personnel with specific clearances are allowed to access. The company wants to create a security buffer zone between the spaces requiring a clearance and the spaces that do not require a clearance. What is this zone called?

    A. DMZ

    B. Mantrap

    C. Proximity cards

    D. ID badges

13. What can be done to ensure that end users employ strong passwords and that they change their passwords regularly?

    A. Implement a password policy.

    B. Strong passwords can be created by administrators and given out to the users.

    C. Configure an administrative policy specifying the use of passwords of at least fifteen characters.

    D. Ensure passwords are stored using reversible encryption.

14. What would be used in a Windows domain to ensure all users change their passwords after forty-five days?

    A. Written password policy

    B. A DRP

    C. RAID

    D. Domain password policy

15. What is a PTZ camera?

    A. A camera used for private surveillance

    B. A camera that is used for privately transmitting Z-axis data

    C. A camera that can pan, tilt, and zoom

    D. A camera that records using PTZ technology for low-light conditions

16. What should be done to prevent an attacker from installing a protocol analyzer on the monitoring port of a switch?

    A. Ensure the switch is operating in promiscuous mode.

    B. Ensure the switch is operating in non-promiscuous mode.

    C. Install anti-spyware software on the switch.

    D. Ensure the switch is protected with physical security.

17. What type of camera can be used to capture video in low-light conditions? (Choose all that apply.)

    A. PTZ

    B. Infrared

    C. Thermal

    D. Color

18. What can be used to prevent a specific user from logging in to a computer after normal business hours?

    A. A group policy object

    B. Account expiration setting

    C. Logical tokens

    D. Time-of-day restriction setting

19. What is used to specifically allow or deny access?

    A. MAC

    B. DAC

    C. RBAC

    D. ACL

20. Where would user accounts be stored in a decentralized environment?

    A. On a domain controller hosting Active Directory

    B. On a decentralized environment (DCE) server

    C. On DNS

    D. On individual workstations or servers

Practice Question Answers

1. **A.** The system administrator establishes access permissions in the Mandatory Access Control (MAC) model. The owner establishes access permissions in the DAC model. Access permissions are set based on role membership in the RBAC model. SSO is used not as an access control model but instead to prevent users from entering credentials at each server or application for normal work.

2. **C.** The Role Based Access Control (RBAC) model is based on jobs, functions, or tasks that users must perform. Functions are often hierarchical within an organization where the top level of the hierarchy has the most responsibilities for different jobs, functions, or tasks, and the lower levels have fewer responsibilities. While MAC can use a lattice to define security levels, the security levels are related to clearances and not related to functions or tasks. In DAC, the owner has full control and can set permissions in any way she decides. IPSec is an encryption protocol commonly used with the VPN tunneling protocol of L2TP.

3. **C.** An inherent flaw with the Discretionary Access Control (DAC) model is its susceptibility to Trojan horses. MAC uses predefined access privileges, not DAC. Passwords are handled through authentication, not access control, so none of the access control models define how passwords are sent. While every object does have an owner in the DAC model, users don't need to be in the Administrators group to manage objects they own.

4. **A.** The Mandatory Access Control (MAC) model uses security or sensitivity labels assigned to subjects, such as users, and security labels are assigned to objects, such as files and folders. Neither DAC nor RBAC uses labels. SSH is an encryption protocol that uses port 22.

5. **C.** The Role Based Access Control (RBAC) model uses roles to establish access. The system administrator establishes access permissions in the MAC model. The owner establishes access permissions in the DAC model. None of the models uses relationships to establish access.

6. **B.** In the DAC model, rights and permissions can be assigned explicitly to another user by the owner of the object. In the MAC model, objects have predefined privileges. Rights are based on the role a user belongs to in the RBAC model. IMAP is used for mail and uses port 143.

7. **A, B.** The Mandatory Access Control (MAC) model uses security labels to determine access and a lattice to determine security levels. All objects have owners in the DAC model, not the MAC model. The DAC model is susceptible to Trojan horse attacks.

8. **C.** The Role Based Access Control (RBAC) model uses roles to establish access, and these roles can easily be associated with the hierarchy of an organization. The system administrator establishes access in the MAC model based on labels, which wouldn't easily work based on jobs associated with departments. The owner establishes access permissions in the DAC model. The KDC issues tickets for Kerberos authentication.

9. **B.** The owner establishes access permissions in the Discretionary Access Control (DAC) model. The system administrator establishes access permissions in the MAC model. Access permissions are set based on role membership in the RBAC model. HVAC is used for environmental control, not access control.

10. **B.** The Discretionary Access Control (DAC) model uses Discretionary Access Control Lists (DACLs) to identify who, such as a user or group, can access an object. Access is granted based on labels in the MAC model and based on role membership in the RBAC model. A DMZ is a protected area between the Internet and an intranet, not an access control model.

11. **B.** Group Policy can be used to configure a setting once and have it apply to multiple users within a Microsoft domain. Group Policy includes settings that can prevent the use of some devices and detect the use of other devices. A domain password policy (a specific group policy object) can enforce password requirements. An administrative policy is a written policy and is often enforced

through technical means such as through Group Policy. A DACL can restrict access to resources, but it would not restrict or detect the use of devices.

12. **B.** A mantrap is used to control the access between a secure area and a nonsecure area by creating a buffer zone. A DMZ is a buffered area of the network between two firewalls used to host Internet-facing servers. Proximity cards can be used to provide access to mantraps, but the proximity card isn't a buffer zone. An ID badge isn't a buffer zone.

13. **A.** A password policy can be implemented as part of Group Policy to ensure users employ strong passwords and passwords are regularly changed. If a password is created by the administrator and given to the user, then the password is no longer known *only* by the user, and the administrator can impersonate the user. Specifying passwords of at least fifteen characters in an administrative policy is a good first step, but it doesn't ensure that users change their passwords regularly. Reversible encryption significantly weakens security.

14. **D.** A domain password policy requiring all users within the domain to change their passwords after a specified time frame can be implemented. A written policy could specify that users change their passwords, but it wouldn't enforce the policy. A DRP is used to help an organization predict and prepare for disasters. RAID is used to provide redundancy to the disk subsystem.

15. **C.** A PTZ camera can pan, tilt, and zoom. Any camera can be used for video surveillance of personnel but should not be used to record areas where people have a reasonable expectation of privacy. Cameras aren't classified as transmitting Z-axis data. Thermal and infrared cameras are used to record in low-light conditions.

16. **D.** Switches (and computers) should be protected with physical security. A protocol analyzer can operate in promiscuous mode to capture all traffic that reaches its NIC, or non-promiscuous mode to capture only traffic that is addressed to or from its NIC, but a switch doesn't operate in promiscuous or

non-promiscuous mode. Anti-spyware isn't installed on network devices such as a switch.

17. **B, C.** Infrared and thermal cameras can capture traffic in low-light conditions. A PTZ camera can manipulate the position of the camera but doesn't specify the lighting. Infrared and thermal cameras are always black-and-white.

18. **D.** Time-of-day restriction settings can be used to restrict when a user can log on to a computer. A GPO can be created to specify settings for multiple users, but it would not be used for a single-user account. Account expiration can specify when an account should be automatically disabled. A logical token is used to help identify a user's permissions after logon, but it wouldn't be able to restrict logon activity.

19. **D.** An access control list (ACL) is used to specifically allow or deny access to objects based on permissions, and an ACL is also used to specifically allow or deny traffic through network devices based on rules. MAC, DAC, and RBAC are all access control models but wouldn't specifically allow or deny access themselves. The DAC model specifies that every object has an owner, and the owner can modify permissions by modifying the access control lists.

20. **D.** A decentralized user management environment stores user accounts on each individual workstation or server. A centralized environment stores the user accounts on a central server such as a domain controller hosting Active Directory in a Windows environment. There's no such thing as a DCE server. DNS is used for name resolution of host names to IP addresses.

Chapter 3

Understanding Basic Network Security

CompTIA Security+ objectives covered in this chapter

1.4 Carry out the appropriate procedures to establish application security.

- P2P

2.1 Differentiate between the different ports and protocols, their respective threats and mitigation techniques.

- Antiquated protocols

2.2 Distinguish between network design elements and components.

- DMZ
- VLAN
- NAT
- Network interconnections
- Subnetting

2.3 Determine the appropriate use of network security tools to facilitate network security.

- Firewalls
- Proxy servers
- Internet content filters

2.4 Apply the appropriate network tools to facilitate network security.

- Firewalls
- Proxy servers
- Internet content filters

2.6 Explain the vulnerabilities and mitigations associated with various transmission media.

- Vampire taps

* * *

CompTIA expects prospective CompTIA Security+ exam takers to have at least two years of networking experience. However, even with that amount of experience, there are often holes in an IT professional's or security professional's knowledge. For example, you may have spent a lot of time troubleshooting connectivity but rarely manipulated ACLs on a router or modified firewall rules.

In this chapter, you'll review some basic network concepts and how they relate to network security. Topics covered in this chapter include:

- A review of basic networking concepts
- Logical ports
- Common network zones
- Network devices
- Peer-to-peer networks
- Transmission media

Reviewing Basic Networking Concepts

Before you can tackle any of the relevant security issues on a network, you'll need a basic understanding of networking. This section isn't intended to teach you all of the relevant network topics, but instead to review some basic networking concepts.

If any of these concepts are completely unfamiliar to you, you may need to pick up a networking book to review them. This section includes a very brief overview of the OSI model and a review of many of the different protocols and networking devices that have a relevance to security.

> **Remember**
> Networking includes many acronyms, and you'll see a lot of them in this chapter. You can refer to the acronym list at the back of the book for a quick reminder of what each acronym represents.

OSI Model

The Open Systems Interconnection (OSI) reference model is used to conceptually divide the different networking requirements into seven separate layers. Most people studying for the CompTIA Security+ exam have been exposed to the OSI model, but since it's mostly theoretical, it's knowledge that simply slips away.

However, when preparing for the CompTIA Security+ exam, you should know some of the details of the OSI model, including:

- Layer names and numbers
- Some protocols matched to specific layers
- Some devices matched to specific layers

If you recently studied for Network+ or CCNA exams, you probably have these mastered. If not, this section is for you.

Know the Layers

The layers are:

- Physical (layer 1)
- Data (layer 2)
- Network (layer 3)
- Transport (layer 4)
- Session (layer 5)
- Presentation (layer 6)
- Application (layer 7)

Mnemonics such as "All People Seem To Need Data Processing" are often used to remember the layers. The first letter of the mnemonic represents the first letter of the layer, so in this example, the A in All stands for Application, People for Presentation, Seem for Session, To for Transport, Need for Network, Data for Data, and Processing for Physical. Another common mnemonic is "Please Do Not Throw Sausage Pizza Away" (for Physical, Data, Network, Transport, Session, Presentation, and Application).

After mastering the mnemonic, you also need to remember which layer is layer 1 and which layer is layer 7. The following memory technique may help. You may have heard about a "layer 8 error." This is another way of saying a user error.

What does a user interact with? Applications. A user on the mythical layer 8 interacts with applications, which are on layer 7.

I don't mean to belittle users or user errors—I make my fair share of errors as a user. However, this memory trick has helped me and a lot of other people remember that the Application layer is layer 7, the layer closest to the user.

Know the Protocols and Devices

You should be familiar with several of the different TCP/IP protocols and network devices and which layers they operate on. The protocols and devices listed here aren't meant to be a complete list, just some of the more common devices and protocols.

> ### Remember
> The Application layer includes application protocols such as HTTP, HTTPS, FTP, DNS, SMTP, and SNMP. SSL operates on the Session layer (notice the S as the first letter of both SSL and Session). TLS operates on the Transport layer. The Network layer includes IP, IPSec, ICMP, and ARP.

- **Layer 7, Application Layer**
  - o Devices: Application-proxy firewall operates on all layers up to the application layer
  - o Protocols: HTTP, HTTPS, FTP, DNS, SMTP, SNMP, and more
- **Layer 6, Presentation Layer**
  - o Protocols: ASCII, EBCDIC, TIFF, JPG
- **Layer 5, Session Layer**
  - o Protocols: SSL, NetBIOS
- **Layer 4, Transport Layer**
  - o Protocols: TLS, TCP, UDP
- **Layer 3, Network Layer**
  - o Devices: Routers, and layer 3 switches operate here
  - o Protocols: IP, IPSec, ICMP, ARP
- **Layer 2, Data Layer**

- o Devices: Switches
- o Protocols: MAC, PPP
- **Layer 1, Physical Layer**
  - o Devices: Hubs, NICs
  - o Protocols: Ethernet, Token Ring

Remember

Hubs have no intelligence and operate on layer 1. Switches operate on layer 2. Routers (and advanced layer 3 switches) operate on layer 3. Application-proxy firewalls operate on layer 7 (Application layer).

Protocols

Networking protocols provide the rules needed for computers to communicate with each other on a network. TCP/IP is a full suite of protocols used on the Internet and many internal networks. Some of the TCP/IP protocols, such as TCP, UDP, and IP, are used for basic connectivity. Other protocols, such as HTTP and SMTP, are used to support specific types of traffic, such as web traffic or email.

Many other protocols have fallen out of use and can be considered antiquated protocols. This section includes information on common networking protocols, application protocols, and antiquated protocols.

Chapter 5 covers the different steps to take to harden or secure a server. One of the primary steps to take is to disable unneeded services and protocols. Before you can identify what is unneeded, you need to understand what is needed.

Common TCP/IP Protocols

TCP/IP isn't a single protocol but, instead, a full suite of protocols. Obviously, there isn't room in this book to teach the details of all the TCP/IP protocols. This section is intended just to remind you of, or possibly expose you to, some of the commonly used protocols.

If any of these protocols are completely new to you, you might like to do some additional research to ensure you understand the basics. I've grouped these protocols into the following sections:

- Basic connectivity protocols
- Application protocols
- Email protocols
- Encryption protocols
- Remote access protocols

Basic Connectivity Protocols

Some basic protocols used within the TCP/IP suite for basic connectivity and testing basic connectivity include:

- **ARP.** Address Resolution Protocol is used to resolve IP addresses to MAC addresses (physical addresses). ARP is required once the packet reaches the destination subnet. ARP poisoning uses ARP packets to give clients an incorrect MAC address for a host, making the host unreachable.
- **TCP.** Transmission Control Protocol is used to provide connection-oriented traffic (guaranteed delivery). TCP uses a three-way handshake. A frequent attack on systems is the SYN Flood attack, which holds back the third packet of the three-way handshake.
- **UDP.** User Datagram Protocol is used to provide connectionless sessions (without a three-way handshake). UDP is used with ICMP traffic and with audio and video streaming. UDP is often used in network-based denial-of-service (DoS) attacks. All TCP/IP traffic is either connection-oriented TCP traffic or connectionless UDP.
- **IP.** The Internet Protocol is used to identify hosts in a TCP/IP network and deliver traffic from one host to another using IP addresses. IPv4 uses 32-bit addresses and is represented in dotted decimal format, such as 192.168.1.100. IPv6 uses 128-bit addresses.
- **IGMP.** Internet Group Management Protocol is used for multicasting.
- **ICMP.** Internet Control Message Protocol is used for diagnostics, such as ping, Pathping, and Tracert. As an example, ping can check for basic connectivity between two systems. Many DoS attacks use ICMP. ICMP uses UDP instead of TCP.

> **Remember**
>
> TCP is connection-oriented, uses a three-way handshake, and provides guaranteed delivery. UDP is connectionless. ICMP uses UDP, and UDP is often used in DoS attacks.

Application Protocols

Many different applications are used on the Internet and within an intranet. The most common you probably use almost every day is HTTP to access web pages on the Internet. Some of the more commonly used application protocols are:

- **HTTP**. Hypertext Transfer Protocol is used for web traffic on the Internet and in intranets. The most common traffic is HTML traffic transmitted between web servers and web browsers. HTTP uses port 80.

- **HTTPS**. Hypertext Transfer Protocol over Secure Socket Layer is used for secure web traffic. Web browsers commonly indicate that a secure session is using HTTPS by displaying a lock icon, and HTTPS can be seen in the URL. HTTPS uses port 443.

- **FTP**. File Transfer Protocol is used to upload and download files to and from an FTP server. FTP uses TCP ports 20 and 21.

- **TFTP**. Trivial File Transfer Protocol uses UDP and is used to transfer smaller amounts of data such as when communicating with network devices. TFTP has been used in attacks and is not an essential protocol.

- **NNTP**. Network News Transfer Protocol is used to host newsgroups. Many newsgroups are now referred to as forums, or simply groups, and can be accessed using HTTP instead of, or in addition to, using NNTP. NNTP uses port 119.

- **SNMP**. Simple Network Management Protocol is often used to manage network devices such as routers or switches. This includes using SNMP to modify the configuration of the devices or have network devices report status back to a central network management system. The first version of SNMP had vulnerabilities such as passing passwords across the network in clear text and is no longer recommended. SNMP v2 and SNMP v3 are much more secure.

- **DNS**. Domain Name System is used to resolve host names to IP addresses. DNS servers host the DNS service and respond to DNS queries. DNS uses port 53.

- **LDAP**. Lightweight Directory Access Protocol is the language used to communicate with directories such as Microsoft's Active Directory or Novell's Netware Directory Services (NDS). LDAP uses port 389. LDAP can be encrypted with either TLS or SSL and uses port 636 when encrypted.

- **Telnet**. Telnet can be used to connect to a remote machine over the network and access the command line. Data is sent in clear text, making telnet vulnerable to sniffing attacks. It is sometimes encrypted with SSH. Telnet uses port 23, and SSH uses port 22.

- **Kerberos**. Kerberos is the authentication protocol used in Windows domains and some UNIX environments. It uses a KDC to issue time-stamped tickets. Kerberos uses port 88.

- **Remote Administration, Terminal Services, or Remote Desktop Services**. Remote administration allows a client to remotely access another system. Microsoft previously called this Terminal Services and then renamed it in Server 2008 R2 to Remote Desktop Services. Microsoft's Remote Assistance allows one user to assist another remotely. Microsoft's Remote Desktop Protocol (RDP) allows an administrator to remotely administer servers from her desktop computer. Terminal Services (and Remote Desktop Services) uses port 3389.

Remember
Application protocols are typically assigned a logical port also known as a Well Known Port. Logical ports must be opened in a firewall to allow the protocol's traffic through. HTTP uses port 80, HTTPS port 443, FTP ports 20 and 21, NNTP port 119, DNS port 53, LDAP port 389, secure LDAP port 636, telnet port 23, Kerberos port 88, and remote administration via Terminal Services uses port 3389.

Email Protocols

Some common protocols used for email include:

- **SMTP**. Simple Mail Transport Protocol is used for transferring email between clients and SMTP servers and between SMTP servers. SMTP uses port 25.

- **POP3**. Post Office Protocol v3 is commonly used to transfer emails from servers down to clients. POP3 uses port 110.

- **IMAP4**. Internet Message Access Protocol is used to store email on an email server. IMAP4 allows a user to organize and manage email in folders on the server. IMAP4 uses port 143.

Encryption Protocols

Any traffic sent across the wire in clear text is subject to sniffing attacks with a protocol analyzer. One way to protect against this vulnerability is to encrypt the data. Some protocols used to encrypt traffic include:

- **SSH**. Secure Shell can be used to encrypt a wide variety of traffic such as telnet and FTP. A popular application is PuTTY, which uses SSH to secure traffic. SSH uses port 22, and telnet uses port 23.

- **SSL**. Secure Sockets Layer protocol is used to encrypt many different types of traffic, but most notably, it is used to secure HTTP traffic as HTTPS. SSL can also be used to encrypt other types of traffic such as LDAP. SSL uses port 443 when encrypting HTTP and operates on the Session layer of the OSI.

- **TLS**. Transport Layer Security protocol has been identified as a replacement for SSL. The RFC for TLS was released in 1999, but SSL is still being used in many applications (most notably with HTTPS). TLS operates on the Transport layer and can be used instead of SSL in just about any application.

- **WTLS**. Wireless Transport Layer Security is used with smaller wireless devices such as personal digital assistants (PDAs). It isn't as resource intensive as TLS, requiring significantly less processing power.

- **IPSec**. Internet Protocol Security is used to encrypt IP traffic at the Network layer. It can be used to encrypt traffic between two systems but is most notably used with L2TP (shown as L2TP/IPSec). IPSec includes two components: Authentication Header (AH) identified by protocol ID number 51 and Encapsulating Security Payload (ESP) identified by protocol ID number 50.

> ### Remember
> When data is sent across the network in clear text, it is susceptible to sniffing attacks from a protocol analyzer. To mitigate the threat, you either don't use the protocol or encrypt the data. Protocols that can be used for encryption include: SSL, which is commonly used for HTTPS on port 443, and IPSec, which is commonly used with L2TP. IPSec includes two components: Authentication Header (AH) identified with protocol ID number 51 and Encapsulating Security Payload (ESP) identified with protocol ID number 50.

Remote Access Protocols

Some common remote access and virtual private network (VPN) tunneling protocols include:

- **PPP**. Point-to-Point Protocol is used to create dial-up connections between a dial-up client and a remote access server, or between a dial-up client and an Internet Service Provider (ISP).
- **L2F**. Layer 2 Forwarding was frequently used by Cisco systems for VPNs. L2F has been largely replaced with L2TP.
- **PPTP**. Point-to-Point Tunneling Protocol is a tunneling protocol used with VPNs that has some known vulnerabilities. Today, L2TP is often used instead. PPTP uses UDP port 1723.
- **L2TP**. Layer 2 Tunneling Protocol was created by combining the strengths of L2F and PPTP. L2TP is commonly used with IPSec for VPNs. Since NAT breaks IPSec, L2TP/IPSec can't go through a device running NAT. L2TP uses TCP port 1701.
- **RADIUS**. Remote Authentication Dial-In User Service is used to provide central authentication to remote access clients. When more than one remote access server is being used, each remote access server can forward authentication requests to the central RADIUS server.

- **TACACS/TACACS+**. Terminal Access Controller Access-Control System and TACACS+ are used as alternatives over RADIUS. TACACS+ is commonly used with Cisco VPN concentrators and is a better alternative than RADIUS since it encrypts the entire authentication process. TACACS uses port 49.

Remember

The most commonly used tunneling protocols for virtual private networks (VPNs) are L2TP and PPTP. L2TP uses port 1701, and PPTP uses port 1723.

Routing Protocols

Routers are used to connect subnets of hosts together. Each router knows the subnets it is connected with, and when it communicates with other routers, it can learn the path to any host on the network. Routers communicate with routing protocols such as:

- **RIP**. Routing Information Protocol and RIPv2 are used in smaller networks of less than fifty routers.
- **OSPF**. Open Shortest Path First is commonly used on internal networks with more than fifty routers. OSPF is more efficient than RIP and RIPv2.
- **BGP**. Border Gateway Protocol is the primary routing protocol used on the Internet. ISPs must use BGP.

Antiquated Protocols

Many protocols have fallen out of use. While you may still run across these in isolated situations, it will be rare. Antiquated protocols include:

- **NetBEUI**. NetBIOS Extended User Interface was frequently used to quickly and easily set up an isolated network. NetBEUI is not routable, meaning traffic cannot pass a router.
- **IPX/SPX**. IPX/SPX was the primary protocol suite used by Novell in previous versions. Novell has moved to TCP/IP, making the IPX/SPX

protocol suite obsolete except in old Novell networks that haven't been upgraded.

- **AppleTalk.** AppleTalk is a proprietary networking protocol used on Apple computers. MAC OS X uses TCP/IP, making AppleTalk obsolete.

Subnetting

Subnetting is used to divide a single range of IP addresses into several smaller ranges of IP addresses. This is often done to isolate traffic and increase efficiency. You don't need to know how to subnet for the CompTIA Security+ exam, but you should be familiar with the concept and how it can be used to isolate users onto different subnets.

As an example, you could have multiple users on a single Class C network. Some of the users may be running applications that stream audio and video across the network; others may upload and download files back and forth to servers on the network; several users may regularly upload and download data via the Internet; and a fourth group could be users with just occasional access to the network. The Class C network could be subnetted into four smaller subnets to isolate each of these user groups.

Imagine that the original Class C network is 192.168.1.0 / 24. It could hold 254 host addresses (192.168.1.1 through 192.168.1.254). This can be subnetted into four smaller subnets as follows:

- **Subnet 1**. 192.168.1.1 / 26 through 192.168.1.62 / 26—use for streaming audio and video
- **Subnet 2**. 192.168.1.65 / 26 through 192.168.1.126 / 26—use for upload and download of files to internal servers
- **Subnet 3**. 192.168.1.129 / 26 through 192.168.1.190 / 26—use for upload and download of files on the Internet
- **Subnet 4**. 192.168.1.193 / 26 through 192.168.1.254 / 26—use for regular users

By dividing the network into the four subnets, you can increase the efficiency by reducing collisions on each individual network. This can effectively improve the performance of each subnet.

Understanding Ports

Ports are logical numbers used by TCP/IP to identify what service or application should handle any data received by a system. Ports are used by both TCP and UDP with a total of 65,535 TCP ports and 65,535 UDP ports.

The ports are organized as follows:

- **Well Known Ports: 0–1023**. Commonly used protocols use these Well Known Ports. Well Known Ports are designated by the Internet Corporation for Assigned Names and Numbers (ICANN). (ICANN was previously known as Internet Assigned Numbers Authority [IANA], so you may occasionally see references to IANA.)

- **Registered ports: 1024–49,151**. These ports are registered with ICANN for use that may be proprietary to a company or to be used with multiple companies for a specific standard. As an example, L2TP (port 1701) and PPTP (1723) are registered in this range.

- **Dynamic and private ports: 49,152–65,535**. These ports are available for use by any application.

While virtually all of the ports are subject to attack, the Well Known Ports are attacked most often. Port scanners will often simply check to see if a Well Known Port is open. For example, SMTP uses the Well Known Port 25, so if port 25 is open, the system is likely running SMTP.

IT personnel who regularly work with routers and firewalls can readily tell you what protocol is associated with which Well Known Port, such as 21, 25, 80, 88, 110, 143, or 443. However, if you don't work with the ports often, you'll need to spend some extra time studying to ensure you're ready for the exam.

Well Known Ports

There are 1024 Well Known Ports, but you don't need to know them all. However, at a minimum, you should know the ports listed in table 3.1.

Protocol	Port	Protocol	Port
FTP	20,21	NNTP	119
SSH	22	IMAP4	143
Telnet	23	LDAP	389
SMTP	25	LDAP/TLS	636
TACACS	49	LDAP/SSL	636
DNS	53	POP3	110
Kerberos	88	L2TP	1701
HTTP	80	PPTP	1723
HTTPS	443	Terminal Services	3389
SSL	443		

Table 3.1: Some commonly used Well Known Ports

When you take the SY0-201 exam, you can write down your own notes as soon as you start. Many successful test takers memorize the ports in this table and write down the table as their very first action when they start the exam. Later, when they come across a question that requires the knowledge of a port number, it's as simple as looking at their notes. If you don't know these ports now, practice writing this table from memory so you're ready when it's time for the live exam.

Combining the IP Address and the Port

At any moment, a computer could be receiving dozens of packets, and these packets are handled by multiple different services, protocols, and applications. Each of these packets includes a destination IP address and destination port.

The system has to identify if the traffic should be handled by the server (based on the destination IP address) and, if so, what the system should do with the packet. It wouldn't do much good to pass an SMTP email packet to the HTTP service or send an HTTP request packet to the SMTP service.

The easiest way to understand the use of a port is to consider traffic between two hosts. For example, say you want to visit the web site sy0-201.com.

You could use a web browser such as Internet Explorer and type the URL into the browser, and the home page will appear.

In the packet sent from your computer to sy0-201.com, the IP address of the server and port 80 are included in the destination section of the packet. Your computer's IP address and a source port are included in the source section of the packet. Two concepts work together to handle this traffic:

- The IP address is used to locate the host and deliver the packet.
- The port is used to identify the correct service, protocol, or application that will process the packet.

IP Address Used to Locate Hosts

Imagine that the IP address of sy0-201 is 64.34.163.18, and the address assigned to your computer from your ISP is 78.161.48.5. TCP/IP uses these IP addresses to get the packets from your computer to the web server and the web server's answer back to your computer.

There's a lot more that occurs under the hood with TCP/IP (such as DNS, NAT, and ARP), but the main point is that the server's IP address is used to get the requesting packet from your computer to the server. The server gets the response packets back to your computer using your IP address (or the IP address of your NAT server).

Server Ports

Different protocols are enabled and running on a server. These protocols have Well Known or registered port numbers, such as port 80 for HTTP, port 443 for HTTPS, and so on. When traffic is received on a system with a destination of port 80, the system knows to send it to the service handling HTTP.

Any web browser knows that the Well Known Port for HTTP is 80. Even though you don't see port 80 in the URL, it is implied as http://www.sy0-201.com:80. If you leave the port blank, port 80 will be used, but you can also include port 80 in the URL.

Popular web servers on the Internet include Apache and Internet Information Services (IIS). Apache is free and is often run on UNIX or Linux systems, which are also free. IIS is included in Microsoft Server products, such as Windows Server 2003 or Windows Server 2008.

Client Ports

TCP/IP works with the client operating system to maintain a table of client side ports. This table associates port numbers with different applications that are expecting return traffic. Client side ports start at port 1024 and increment up to 4096. If the system uses all the ports between 1024 and 4096 cycles through all the ports before being rebooted, it'll start over at 1024.

When you use your web browser to request a page from a site, your system will record an unused client port number such as 1024 in an internal table to handle the return traffic. When the packets containing the web page are received from the web browser, port 1024 is included in the packets, letting your system know that they need to be sent to the web browser application for processing. The browser receives the traffic and displays the page.

The Importance of Ports in Security

Routers, and the routing component of firewalls, filter packets based on:

- IP addresses
- Ports
- Some protocols such as ICMP or IPSec

Access control lists on routers and firewalls include rules that are used to specifically allow or deny traffic. For example, if you wanted to allow SMTP traffic, a rule would be created to grant traffic on port 25.

Usually, routers and firewalls operate based on an implicit deny policy. In other words, all traffic is denied unless it is explicitly allowed with a rule, and traffic would only be allowed if there was a specific reason to do so.

Allowing traffic by creating a rule is commonly referred to as opening the port. These are logical ports, not physical ports. Opening a port is done through software and is often referred to as an exception.

Every open port represents a risk, since it can be used as a path into the protected network. Only ports that are required and actively being used should be open. Attackers often scan systems with port scanners to determine what ports are open and discover what services are running.

Port Scanners

A port scanner is a tool used to query a host to determine which ports are open. It can be used by system administrators as part of an overall vulnerability assessment. It is also used as part of an overall reconnaissance or fingerprinting attack, where an attacker tries to learn as much about a server as possible.

The port scanner sends queries to ports of interest, and, based on the reply, the attacker learns what services and protocols are likely running on the server. For example, if port 25 is open, the SMTP protocol is probably enabled on the server, and the server may be a mail server. If port 80 is open, HTTP is probably running, and the server may be a web server such as Apache or IIS.

Even though it's not recommended for services to use ports other than the Well Known Ports for specific services, it is possible. Because of this, an open port doesn't definitively say the related service or protocol is running.

The attacker will use other methods for verification. For example, a fingerprinting attack will send specific protocol queries to the server and analyze the responses. These responses can verify that the service is running and will often include other details about the operating system since different operating systems often respond differently to specific queries.

A common TCP port scan will send a TCP SYN packet to a specific port of a server as part of the TCP three-way handshake. If the server responds with a SYN/ACK packet, the scanner knows the port is open. However, instead of completing the three-way handshake, the scanner sends an RST to reset the connection and then repeats the process with the next port.

Many port scanners can scan all of the ports or be configured to only scan specific ports of interest. For example, an attacker may only wish to identify web and email servers. He may choose to configure the scanner to scan ports 20 and 21 for FTP; ports 25, 110, and 143 for SMTP, POP3, and IMAP4; and ports 80 and 443 for HTTP and HTTPS.

Two commonly used port scanners are:

- **Nmap**. Nmap can scan a network to determine which hosts are operational (host discovery), perform port scanning to determine the open ports, and determine the operating system and hardware characteristics of some hosts.

- **Superscan**. Superscan can also scan a network to determine which hosts are operational and perform port scanning to determine the open ports. Superscan 4 includes additional features that can provide additional information on Windows targets.

Basic Network Zones

Networking zones are divided into areas of trust. Areas with very little trust require a significant amount of security, while areas of high trust require less security.

Figure 3.1 shows the different basic zones that you'll find in many corporate networks. These areas are defined in the following sections.

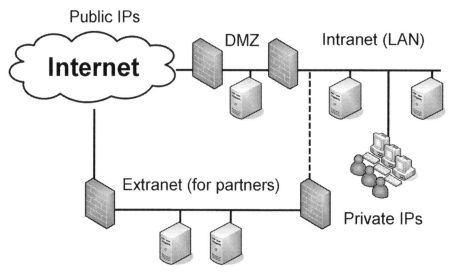

Figure 3.1: Areas of Trust

Intranet

The intranet is the internal network of a company. Since the clients are internal to the company, they are highly trusted, and internal attacks are less likely. An intranet would still have several security precautions implemented, but it does have a higher level of trust than the Internet or a DMZ.

Intranets use private IP addresses, and resources contained in the intranet are not accessible to un-trusted users from the Internet. A few hosts could be connected together in a simple local area network (LAN), or thousands of computers could be connected together using private wide area networks (WANs) to connect multiple LANs.

Very often, users on the intranet have access to the Internet. Firewalls provide a layer of protection between the Internet and the intranet, and Network Address Translation (NAT) is used to translate private addresses used on the intranet to public IP addresses used on the Internet.

Internet

The Internet is the area of least trust. If your system has a public IP address, it is accessible from anywhere in the world by any other system with a public IP address.

Make no mistake. If you have a public IP address, you will be attacked. There are a significant number of people on the Internet constantly looking for vulnerabilities and exploiting them as opportunities arise.

This requires any system with a public IP address to have a significant amount of security to protect it. Instead of putting systems directly on the Internet, most companies (and even many households today) protect Internet-facing systems behind a firewall.

Public IP Addresses

Any IP address that is used on the Internet is referred to as a public IP address. Both IPv4 and IPv6 use public and private IP addresses, but I'll limit this discussion to IPv4. While the details between IPv4 and IPv6 are different, the overall concepts of public IP addresses and private IP addresses are the same.

IPv4 addresses are composed of 32 bits and are often expressed in dotted decimal format such as 12.45.212.34. There are about four billion addresses, but many of the address ranges have been reserved for other uses. Any address that is not reserved for another use can be used as a public IP address.

Public IP addresses are tightly controlled. You can't just use any public IP address; instead, you must either purchase or rent it. ISPs purchase entire ranges of IP addresses and issue them to customers. If you access the Internet from home, you are very likely receiving a public IP address from an ISP.

Private IP Addresses

Several IP address ranges are reserved for private use. Private addresses can be used on any private network. Private address ranges include:

- **10.x.y.z.** (10.0.0.1 through 10.255.255.254)
- **172.16.y.z–172.31.y.z.** (172.16.0.1 through 172.31.255.254)
- **192.168.y.z.** (192.168.0.1 through 192.168.255.254)

Any IP address must be unique within its network. Within a company's network, no two computers can have the same private IP address. However, it's possible for one company to use the same private IP addresses used at another company. For example, one company could be using 192.168.1.1/24 in its network, and another company could be using the same IP address in its network. Since both networks are separate, this doesn't present a conflict.

Private IP addresses will never be used on the Internet. Most routers on the Internet include rules to specifically drop any traffic that is coming from or going to a private IP address.

NAT

Network Address Translation (NAT) is a protocol that translates public IP addresses to private IP addresses and private addresses back to public. NAT is often enabled on the Internet-facing firewall. If you run a network at your home (such as a wireless network), the router that connects to the Internet is very likely running NAT.

> ### Remember
> Private IP addresses are internal to a network, and public IP addresses are accessible on the Internet. NAT translates private IP addresses to public and public back to private, allowing internal clients access to the Internet while still hiding them from attackers on the Internet. Static NAT uses a one-to-one mapping.

Some of the benefits of NAT include:

- **Public IP addresses don't need to be purchased for all clients**. A home or company network can include multiple computers that can access the Internet through one router running NAT. Larger companies requiring more bandwidth may use more than one public IP address.
- **Private computers are hidden from the Internet**. Computers with private IP addresses are isolated and hidden from the Internet. NAT provides a layer of protection to these private computers since they aren't as easy to attack and exploit from the Internet.

One of the drawbacks to NAT is that it is not compatible with IPSec. IPSec is commonly used with L2TP in a VPN and also used to encrypt traffic between computers on an internal network. Any design that includes IPSec going through NAT must be reconsidered.

NAT is generally classified as either static NAT or dynamic NAT.

- **Static NAT**. Static NAT uses a single public IP address. This is often referred to as one-to-one mapping.
- **Dynamic NAT**. Dynamic NAT uses multiple public IP addresses, and NAT can decide which public IP address to use based on load. For example, if several users are using the connection on one public IP address, NAT can map the next request to the less used public IP address.

DMZ

A buffered zone between a private network (intranet) and the Internet is commonly called a demilitarized zone (DMZ). It is used to provide a layer of protection to servers that are accessible from the Internet.

Remember, the Internet is where attackers lurk—the area of least trust. Servers hosted directly on the Internet are certain to be attacked and need to have strong security. The DMZ provides a layer of security for Internet-facing servers.

The DMZ is often designed with two firewalls creating a buffer zone between the Internet and the internal network as shown previously in figure 3.1. One firewall separates the DMZ from the Internet. The second firewall is between the intranet and the DMZ. Each firewall would have detailed rules designed to filter traffic and protect both the internal network and the public servers.

Internet-facing servers such as web servers, mail servers, or FTP servers accessible from the Internet would be placed in the DMZ. The firewall connected to the Internet would be configured to allow specific traffic to and from these servers. The firewall connected to the internal network would prevent traffic allowed to the servers in the DMZ from accessing servers in the internal network.

Extranet

An extranet is used to provide access to a limited number of services or servers on your network to business partners, such as vendors, suppliers, or customers. An extranet is often accessible via the Internet, but it can also be designed so that partners can access it via a dedicated line used in a VPN.

If you look back to figure 3.1, you can see how the extranet looks similar to the DMZ when it's accessible via the Internet. The significant difference between the DMZ and the extranet is that the extranet is intended to provide access to only a limited number of users (such as business partners), while the DMZ hosts servers intended to serve any users on the Internet.

The actual access provided on the extranet can vary widely depending on need. As shown in the figure, an extranet may be configured to provide access to almost all of a company's internal resources to a highly trusted partner such as a subsidiary. Another extranet might be configured to provide access to only a single server to a business partner for the purchase and tracking of products or materials.

Remember

The significant difference between the DMZ and the extranet is that the servers in the DMZ are intended to be accessed by any clients on the Internet, while servers in the extranet are limited only to trusted clients such as business partners. Both can host servers that are accessible from the Internet (Internet-facing servers). An extranet provides only a limited number of services to only a limited group of clients.

Network Devices

Any network will include one or more network devices used to provide connectivity to the devices in the network. Different devices having different capabilities are implemented based on the desired needs.

When discussing the different devices, it's important to remember how TCP/IP traffic is addressed. There are three possibilities:

- **Unicast**. One-to-one traffic. Packets are sent by one host and addressed with a specific destination IP address of another host. Only the host with the destination IP address will process the packet.
- **Broadcast**. One-to-all traffic. Packets are sent by one host and addressed with an IP address of 255.255.255.255. Broadcast traffic is processed by every host that receives the broadcast packet. Hubs and switches pass broadcast traffic, but routers do not pass broadcast traffic.
- **Multicast**. One-to-many traffic. Packets are sent by one host and addressed with a multicast address. Any host that has joined the multicast IP address will process the packet. Multicast traffic is managed with IGMP.

Hub

A hub has multiple physical ports used to provide basic connectivity to multiple computers. Hubs commonly have between four and thirty-two physical ports. In an Ethernet network, the hub would have multiple RJ-45 ports that are used to connect to NICs on the host computers using twisted pair cable.

Most hubs are active, meaning they have power and will amplify the output to a set level. Active hubs are sometimes called multiport repeaters.

Hubs have zero intelligence. Whatever goes in one port goes out to all ports. This presents a security risk because if an attacker installs a protocol analyzer on any computer connected to the hub, it can be configured to capture all the traffic passing through the hub.

Chapter 7 will cover tools in more depth, but to fully understand the risks of hubs and the benefits of switches, you should understand the basics of a protocol analyzer. A protocol analyzer (sometimes referred to as a sniffer) can capture traffic at the packet level. Packets can then be analyzed, and any data sent in clear text can be viewed.

It's not uncommon for some companies to specifically restrict the use of hubs in their networks. In these companies, all hubs are replaced by switches.

Switch

A switch has the ability to learn which computers are attached to which physical ports and can create internal switched connections for two computers communicating with each other.

Consider figure 3.2. When the switch turns on, it starts out without any knowledge other than knowing it has four physical ports. Imagine that the very first session after the switch is turned on is Sally starting a TCP/IP conversation with Joe.

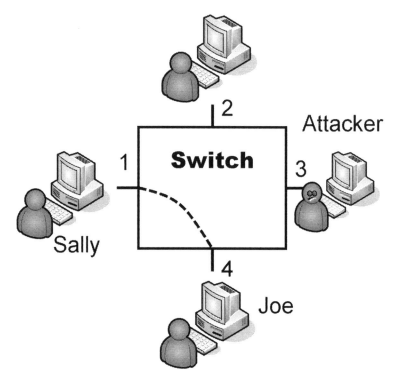

Figure 3.2: Switch

When Sally sends the first packet, it includes the MAC address of the destination computer. However, since the switch doesn't know which port Joe's computer is connected to, it forwards this first packet to all ports.

Included in that first packet is the MAC address of Sally's computer. The switch logs this information into an internal table, knowing that any future traffic addressed to Sally's MAC address should be internally switched to port 1.

When Joe's computer receives the packet, it will respond. Embedded in this return packet is the MAC address of Joe's computer. The switch captures Joe's MAC address and logs it with port 4 into the internal table. From here on, any unicast traffic between Sally's and Joe's computers are internally switched.

Switches do pass broadcast traffic to all ports. Only unicast traffic is internally switched.

While a switch is valuable in a network to reduce traffic on subnets and increase efficiency, it also has an added security benefit.

Security Benefit of a Switch

Most of the previous discussion is basic networking, but what you really need to know is why it's relevant in security.

If an attacker installed a protocol analyzer on a computer attached to another port (such as port 3 in figure 3.2), he would not be successful at capturing all traffic going through the switch. The unicast traffic is internally switched to only ports 1 and 4, so the sniffer on port 3 will not be able to see or capture the traffic.

This is exactly why switches are often used to replace hubs in many corporate networks. The switch reduces the ability of attackers to actively sniff the network.

Remember

Hubs are often replaced with switches in secure networks to mitigate the risk of sniffing attacks using a protocol analyzer from any connection on the switch. The switch must still be protected with physical security to prevent access to the switch's monitoring ports. Successful MAC flood attacks will cause the switch to act like a hub.

MAC Flooding

Normally, each physical port on a switch will have one computer attached to it with only one MAC address. The switch will map the port to the MAC address. However, a MAC flooding attack attempts to overwhelm a switch with multiple packets with different MAC addresses.

The switch has a limited amount of memory to store the internal table, and when the table is filled, a switch can default to "failopen" mode where it acts like a hub.

More advanced switches can protect against MAC flooding attacks by shutting down ports with too many MAC addresses or specifying the MAC addresses for any given port.

Physical Security of a Switch

Most switches have a port that can be used for monitoring traffic. Unlike the normal ports that only see traffic specifically addressed to the port, the monitoring port will see all traffic into or out of the switch, even if the traffic is being internally switched to two regular ports.

The monitoring port is useful for legitimate troubleshooting, but if the switch isn't protected with physical security, it can also be useful to an attacker.

A switch must be protected with physical security by keeping it in a secure area such as a locked wiring closet. Physical security is used to ensure that attackers don't have physical access to the switch and other network devices.

VLAN

A virtual LAN (VLAN) uses a switch to group several different computers into a virtual network.

Normally, a router would group different computers onto different subnets, and the subnets are typically based on physical locations. All the computers in a routed segment are located in the same physical location such as on a specific floor or wing of a building.

The primary benefit of using a switch in a VLAN configuration instead of using a router is that the VLAN allows computers to be grouped together based on logical needs rather than physical location. Additionally, the switch can easily be reprogrammed to add or subtract computers from any subnet if needs change.

For example, a group of users who normally work in separate departments may begin work on a project that requires them to be on the same subnet. The switch can be reprogrammed, even if the computers are physically located on different floors or different wings of the building. When the project is over, the switch can be reprogrammed to return the computers to their original subnets.

Because traffic can be isolated between computers in a VLAN, it does provide a measure of security. However, security isn't the primary goal of a VLAN.

Router

Routers are used to connect multiple network segments together into a single network by routing traffic between the segments. As an example, the Internet is effectively a single network hosting billions of computers. Routers are responsible for routing the traffic from segment to segment, host to host.

Since routers don't pass broadcasts, they effectively reduce traffic on any single segment. Segments separated by routers are sometimes referred to as broadcast domains. If a network has too many computers on a single segment, broadcasts can result in excessive collisions and reduced network performance. Moving computers to a different segment separated by a router can significantly improve overall performance.

Cisco routers are the most popular, but many other brands exist. Most routers are physical devices, and physical routers are the most efficient. However, it's also possible to add a routing software component to multi-homed systems (systems with more than one NIC). For example, Windows Server products (such as Windows Server 2003 and Windows Server 2008) can function as routers by adding the RRAS service.

Routers can be quite sophisticated. They can be programmed with ACLs and are often configured to communicate with other routers to learn paths to any other host in the network. Different routing protocols include Routing Information Protocol (RIP) and RIPv2, Open Shortest Path First (OSPF), and Border Gateway Protocol (BGP).

Routers and ACLs

Access control lists (ACLs) are rules implemented on a router to identify what traffic is allowed and what traffic is denied. When implemented on a router, ACLs can control inbound and outbound traffic. ACLs are normally implemented using an implicit deny philosophy. In other words, all traffic is blocked (implicitly denied) unless a rule in the ACL explicitly allows the traffic.

As an example, your internal network could be using addresses in the private IP range of 10.1.0.1 to 10.10.255.254. An ACL could be created to allow traffic to or from IP addresses in this range. Traffic with source or destination addresses outside this range would be blocked.

> ### Remember
> Routers perform basic filtering by adding an access control list (ACL), which defines what traffic is allowed. Any traffic not included in the ACL is implicitly denied.

Routers and Firewalls

An integral component of any firewall is the routing component. The ACL within a router defines what traffic is allowed and what traffic is blocked.

First-generation firewalls are simply packet-filtering routers that implement ACLs to define traffic that is allowed. A packet-filtering firewall can include rules to allow or block traffic based on the following:

- **IP addresses.** Traffic to or from specific IP addresses can be filtered. For example, a rule could be created on a NIC to allow all traffic in the IP range of 10.1.0.1 to 10.10.255.254 and implicitly deny any traffic not sent to or from this IP range.
- **Ports.** Traffic destined to or from specific ports can be filtered. For example, port 80 is used for HTTP traffic. Traffic with a destination of port 80 can be allowed so that users can access web sites on the Internet, but inbound traffic using port 80 can be blocked to prevent any Internet users from accessing a web server on the intranet.

- **Some protocols such as ICMP and IPSec**. Firewall rules can be created to specifically allow or deny ICMP traffic. Many denial-of-service (DoS) and distributed denial-of-service (DDoS) attacks use ICMP, and firewall rules can be modified on the fly by an automated intrusion detection system in response to such attacks.

Packet-filtering firewalls operate at layer 3 of the OSI reference model.

Firewall

A firewall is designed to filter traffic. Firewalls are primarily used to filter incoming traffic, but they can also be used to filter outgoing traffic.

The purpose of a firewall in a network is similar to a firewall in a car. The firewall in a car is placed between the engine and passenger compartment. If a fire starts in the engine compartment, the firewall will provide a layer of protection for passengers in the passenger compartment. Similarly, a firewall in a network will try to keep the bad traffic (often in the form of attackers) out of the network.

Of course, an engine has a lot of moving parts that can do damage to us if we accidentally reach into it while it's running. The firewall in a car also protects passengers from accidentally reaching into the engine and causing bodily harm. A network can also block users from going to places that an administrator deems dangerous. For example, since damaging files could inadvertently be downloaded, the firewall could prevent FTP downloads.

A firewall can be hardware-based or software-based.

- **Hardware-based**. A hardware-based firewall is a dedicated system with additional software installed to monitor, filter, and log traffic. For example, a popular hardware-based firewall used in many larger environments is Sidewinder. This is a dedicated server with proprietary firewall software installed. A hardware-based firewall would have two or more network interface cards (NICs).

- **Software-based**. A software-based firewall is simply software that will monitor traffic passing through the NIC. Many operating systems include software-based firewalls that can be implemented on individual workstations and servers. Microsoft has included a software-based firewall on operating systems since Windows XP. Third-party software-based firewalls were available before then.

In addition to filtering traffic, most firewalls have logs that can be enabled. Firewalls typically allow you to log all traffic that has been allowed, all traffic that has been blocked, or both.

Firewalls start with a basic routing capability for packet filtering. More advanced firewalls go beyond simple packet filtering and include stateful firewalls and application layer firewalls.

Stateful Firewall

A stateful firewall has the ability to examine multiple packets involved in a network connection. Only packets that are determined to be legitimate packets for any given TCP/IP connection, or network conversation, are allowed.

You may remember from your studies of basic networking the three-way handshake used by the TCP protocol. Figure 3.3 shows the handshake process. Packets set flags such as synchronize (SYN), synchronize/acknowledge (SYN/ACK), and acknowledge (ACK).

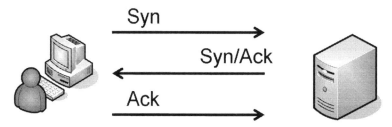

Figure 3.3: TCP Handshake Process

To start a TCP session, the client sends a packet with the SYN flag set. The server responds with a SYN/ACK packet, and the client completes the third part of the handshake with an ACK packet. Once the ACK is sent and received, the connection is referred to as established. TCP is often referred to as connection-oriented providing guaranteed delivery since all sessions begin by first establishing connectivity with this three-way handshake.

SYN Flood Attack

The SYN Flood attack is a common denial-of-service (DoS) attack. In the SYN Flood attack, the attacker sends multiple SYN packets but never completes the third part of the handshake. The last ACK packet is held back, leaving the server with several open sessions waiting to complete the handshake.

Each uncompleted session consumes resources on the server, and if the SYN Flood attack is not detected and stopped, it can actually cause the server to crash. Some servers reserve a certain amount of resources for connections, and once these resources are consumed by the attack, additional connections are not allowed. Instead of crashing the server, legitimate users are prevented from connecting to the server.

An intrusion detection system (IDS) can detect a SYN Flood attack. An active IDS may respond by modifying the ACL of the firewall to block all traffic from the attacking IP address, and closing all the open sessions from the attacking IP address.

The stateful firewall uses the three-way handshake to identify valid TCP connections between two clients. TCP packets that aren't part of an established connection are blocked.

Many stateful firewalls can also track connections using UDP. UDP is connectionless, meaning there is no three-way handshake; instead, a client just sends the data hoping it reaches the other end.

UDP is commonly used with ICMP, such as for a simple ping, and also for streaming audio and video. The stateful firewall uses the first UDP packet to indicate a session is started and tracks it afterwards.

Application Firewall

An application firewall (sometimes called an application-proxy firewall) operates on the application layer of the OSI model. It examines packets based on the application layer protocol being used.

For example, an application layer protocol could include an HTTP proxy component that has the capability to examine all HTTP traffic. It could specifically allow and deny traffic based on application commands such as Get and Put. Similarly, an FTP proxy could be added to examine FTP traffic and allow or deny specific FTP application commands.

While the application-proxy firewall is transparent to the client and the server, all traffic must go through the firewall, and each packet is examined. Undesirable traffic can be blocked.

Content Filtering

Many advanced firewalls have the capability to perform content filtering. Content filtering actually means different things depending on the context. Content filters can filter based on:

- **Content – Spam**. Unwanted email can frequently clog a user's in-box. A content filter can identify and filter out some known spam. Spam can be filtered at a firewall (if it includes spam filtering capabilities) or more commonly at an email server.
- **Content – Attachments**. Some files are known to be malicious, and a content filter can screen incoming data for known malicious files and block them. Files can be filtered at a firewall (if it includes content filtering capabilities), or more commonly at an email server.
- **URLs**. A proxy server can filter a user's request to specific web sites and block sites that a company considers inappropriate for the work environment. Some companies subscribe to lists to block traffic to specific categories of web sites.
- **Certificates**. Certificates can be checked to see if they were issued by a trusted Certificate Authority (CA) and to ensure they have not been revoked. Sources that present invalid or untrusted certificates can be blocked.

> ### Remember
> Content filters have the capability to filter data, such as attachments or unwanted email, URLs that a user tries to access, or certificates. Content filtering is additional software that can be installed or enabled on some firewalls, email servers, and proxy servers. Some companies market an all-in-one solution as an appliance that is easy to configure and implement.

A firewall that includes content filtering is frequently referred to as an appliance. Similar to a washer or dryer appliance you may have at your home, these appliances have dedicated jobs and are often easy to use—simply plug them in and follow some basic steps for usage.

Content filtering would typically be done on a network-based firewall, and many firewall appliances can be purchased with content filtering built in.

Firewall Logs

Firewalls include logs to record any activity of interest. The logs can include all traffic that reaches the firewall, only the traffic that is blocked, or only the traffic that is allowed. A firewall log is often the first place that an administrator might check to investigate a possible intrusion.

The review of the logs can also be automated through scripting and applications. As an example, intrusion detection systems frequently use firewall logs as a raw data source to help identify intrusions.

No matter how the logs are reviewed, they will include valuable information that might signal an attack. As a simple example, a port scan attack will query different logical ports of an IP address to see what ports are open. Based on what ports are open, the attacker can determine what services or protocols may be running on the server. A portion of the firewall log may look like this:

Time	Source IP	Destination IP	Port
10:01	12.34.67.89	89.67.34.12	22
10:02	12.34.67.89	89.67.34.12	23
10:03	12.34.67.89	89.67.34.12	24
10:04	12.34.67.89	89.67.34.12	25

You can see that the source and destination IP addresses are the same, and the port is incrementing. This is typical behavior of a port scan. If the scan on port 25 provides a response back to the scanner, it indicates this port is open. Since SMTP uses port 25, this system is very likely running SMTP and may be an email server.

Network-based Firewalls

A network-based firewall is used to protect multiple systems within a network. It does this by filtering traffic based on firewall rules to ensure that only authorized traffic is allowed into or out of a network.

One example of a network-based firewall is placing the firewall between the Internet and an internal network. Taking this a step further, a second network-based firewall can be added to create a DMZ to host Internet-facing servers.

Network-based firewalls are typically dedicated servers or appliances, or hardware-based firewalls as described earlier. These firewalls would be dedicated to security and would not host any services that aren't security related.

> ### Remember
> Network-based firewalls are often dedicated servers and should only be used for security purposes. Host-based firewalls are software-based and are installed on end users' systems to provide a layer of protection. Users should enable host-based firewalls especially when in public places such as in a hotel, airport, coffee shop, or eatery.

Host-based Firewalls

A host-based firewall is a firewall used to protect a single system such as a workstation or server. The firewall is just another software element running on the system and is often referred to as a personal firewall.

Microsoft has included a host-based firewall on current operating systems such as Windows XP, Vista, Windows 7, and server operating systems such as Windows Server 2003 and Windows Server 2008. Additionally, there are many third-party firewall products that can be installed on systems as an added layer of protection similar to installing antivirus or anti-spyware programs. Figure 3.4 shows the host-based Windows Firewall on Windows Vista. This is a good example of a software firewall.

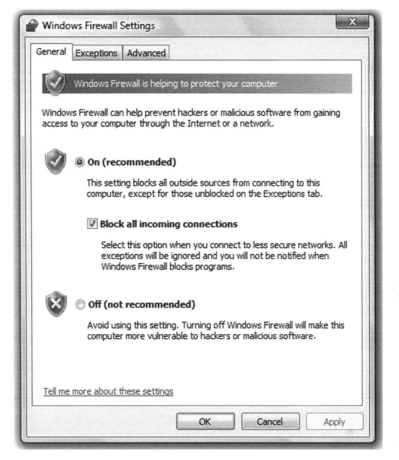

Figure 3.4: Personal Firewall on Windows Vista

Personal firewalls should be implemented on systems especially when accessing the Internet in a public place. Free Wi-Fi Internet access is often available in public places such as airports, hotels, and many fast-food establishments such as Starbucks and even McDonald's. However, connecting to a public Wi-Fi hotspot without the personal firewall enabled is risky.

Proxy Server

Proxy servers are often used in networks. They can improve performance by caching content and can restrict users' access to inappropriate web sites by filtering content. A proxy server would be placed on the edge of the network bordering the Internet and the intranet as shown in figure 3.5.

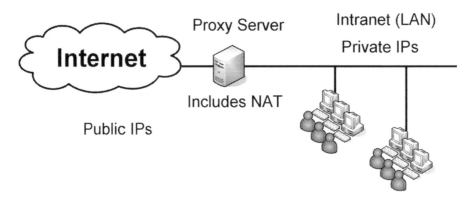

Figure 3.5: Proxy Server

One NIC is connected to the Internet with a public IP address. The other NIC is connected to the internal network with a private IP address. The proxy server would include the Network Address Translation (NAT) protocol to translate the private IP addresses to public and the public IP addresses back to private.

Static NAT uses only one public IP address and uses a one-to-one mapping for the client's private IP address to the public IP address.

In larger environments, it's possible to use multiple public IP addresses. Dynamic NAT can use multiple IP addresses and can pick which public IP address a client will use based on the load. For example, a proxy server with two public IP addresses could use dynamic NAT to map half the requests from private IP addresses to one NIC and half of the requests to the other NIC.

All internal clients would be configured to send requests through the proxy server. The proxy accepts the request, retrieves the content from the Internet, and then returns the data to the client.

A proxy server is typically only used to act as a proxy for HTTP and HTTPS. However, proxy servers can also proxy other Internet protocols such as FTP and NNTP.

Caching Content for Performance

The proxy server can be used to increase the performance of Internet requests by caching each result received from the Internet. Any data that is in the proxy server's cache wouldn't need to be retrieved from the Internet to fulfill another client's request.

In this context, *cache* simply means "temporary storage." Cache could be a dedicated area of RAM, or in some examples, it could also be an area on a high-performance disk subsystem.

As an example, if one user in the network retrieved a web page from sy0-201.com, the proxy server would store the result in cache. If another user requested the same page, instead of going back through the Internet to retrieve the page, the proxy server would just retrieve it from cache and send it to the client.

Using Content Filters to Restrict Access

Proxy servers can also restrict what users can access with the use of content filters. A proxy server content filter will examine the requested URL and choose to allow the request or deny the request.

Many third-party companies sell subscription lists for content filtering. These sites scour the Internet for web sites and categorize the sites based on what companies typically want to block. Categories may include: pornography sites, gambling sites, anonymizers, and warez sites. Anonymizers are sites that give the illusion of privacy on the Internet and are sometimes used to bypass proxy servers. Warez sites often host pirated software, movies, MP3 files, and hacking tools.

The subscription list can be loaded into the proxy server, and whenever a user attempts to access a site on the content filter block list, the request is blocked. Often, the user is shown a web page indicating that the site he is trying to access is restricted.

Content filters are not restricted to only proxy servers. Windows Vista and Windows 7 include parental controls that perform basic content filtering. Additionally, mail servers perform content filtering to block certain attachments that may be malware.

P2P

P2P is short for peer-to-peer and is often restricted in corporate networks. P2P networks are commonly used to share files such as music, video, and data over the Internet. P2P is commonly referred to simply as *file sharing*.

Instead of a server providing the data to end users, all computers in the P2P network are peers, and any computer in the network can provide resources such as parts of a file or bandwidth. Additionally, any computer in the P2P network can share a file, which often leads to data leakage, or the sharing of files that users didn't intend to share.

A P2P network could include computers from anywhere in the world as long as they all have connectivity to the Internet. Users join the network to have access to files on the network, and also typically agree to participate in file sharing.

A Little History

The first widely used P2P network was Napster, an online music-sharing service that operated between 1999 and 2001. Users were able to easily copy and distribute MP3 files amongst one another. The files were stored on each user's system, and as long as the system was accessible on the Internet, other users could access and download the files.

Napster was ultimately shut down by court order due to copyright issues. However, P2P software and P2P networks continue to appear and evolve.

Some current P2P software includes BitTorrent, LimeWire, and Kazaa.

Data Leakage

A significant risk of P2P networks is data leakage. Users are often unaware of what data they are sharing. Another risk is that users are often unaware of what is being downloaded onto their systems, causing them to host inappropriate data.

Remember

Data leakage occurs when users install P2P software and unintentionally share files. This results in data stored on a system being available to other users in the P2P network. Some attackers specifically target P2P networks to gather data that has been unintentionally shared.

Two examples help illustrate these data leakage risks.

Information concentrators specifically search P2P networks for information of interest. In March 2009, an information concentrator in Iran was discovered with over two hundred documents containing classified and secret U.S. government data. This included classified information about *Marine One*, the helicopter used by the president. While the information about *Marine One* made the headlines, the information gained by attackers was much more important. This specific system included Iraq status reports and lists of soldiers with privacy data.

A user with access to this information installed P2P software on a computer and inadvertently shared a significant amount of other data. If this user had any Personally Identifiable Information (PII) such as banking information, tax data, or even files that included passwords, all of it could also be available to someone who knows how to search P2P networks.

The media latched onto the news about *Marine One*, so this story was widely published. However, it's widely believed that much more data is being mined via P2P networks. When data on a user's system is captured resulting in a bank account being emptied of $5,000 or so, it may be a catastrophe to the user, but it isn't news.

A second example affected a school-age child. It's popular to use these P2P sharing programs to share music files, but they are often used to share other data. One school-age girl was browsing data she found on her computer and discovered a significant number of pornographic pictures. She did not seek these or deliberately download them. Instead, as a member of the P2P network, her system was used to store files shared by others.

While some people consider P2P networks as grayware that are a nuisance and not a problem, IT security professionals understand they pose significant risks. It's not uncommon to have P2P programs and access blocked in corporate networks.

Transmission Media

Transmission is simply the type of cable used to transmit signals across the network. Any wired network requires some type of transmission media to connect the devices. Wireless networks will be covered in Chapter 4.

When designing, or redesigning, a network, the transmission media deserves a lot of consideration. From the security perspective, the most important element involves the different risks associated with each media type. The risks include vampire taps, EMI, RFI, and signal emissions.

The primary transmission media you'll see in a network are:

- Coaxial – very rare today
- Twisted pair – most common today
- Fiber optic – growing in popularity

Vampire Taps

A vampire tap is any tap that attempts to gain access to the signal on the wire. Virtually any transmission media type is susceptible to vampire taps though some are more susceptible than others.

In older networks, the transmission media was Thicknet coaxial cable, and a vampire tap was used to pierce the cable and allow a device to connect onto the network. The tap actually forced a spike through the cable to connect to the inner conductor.

However, the term *vampire tap* has morphed into any attempt to tap in to the wire to allow an unauthorized device access to the network. As an example, if the wiring isn't protected, it's possible to snip any type of cable, recreate two connectors, and attach a device between the two connections to capture the data.

It's relatively easy to tap in to both coaxial and twisted pair cable. It's more difficult, but not impossible, to tap in to fiber-optic cable.

Interference

Electronic signals can be disrupted by interference. When interference isn't prevented or mitigated, it can actually prevent hosts from communicating with each other. The two primary types of interference are EMI and RFI.

EMI

Electromagnetic interference (EMI) is caused by different types of motors, power lines, and even fluorescent lights. Electronic devices are normally separated from motorized devices to prevent EMI problems.

As an example, a modem placed near a microwave oven or a laser printer could have signals disrupted by these devices. A simple solution is to move the modem.

RFI

Radio frequency interference (RFI) is interference from RF sources such as AM or FM transmitters. RFI can typically be filtered out since it is transmitted on a specific frequency.

As an example, a farmer who owns the land behind my house rented some space for an AM repeater station. The AM signal was strong enough that it could be regularly heard on our phone line and prevented me from sending or receiving faxes. By installing filters on the phone lines, I was able to eliminate this RFI.

Signal Emanations

Signal transmissions that can be captured outside the cable are referred to as signal emanations or emissions. Coaxial cable has a relatively thick core that transmits signals, and emanations from the core are considered a risk. Additionally, two cables lying side by side are susceptible to cross talk, where data from one cable crosses over to the other cable.

If the data is classified or proprietary, you should protect it by either ensuring the cable is adequately shielded or the transmission media is not susceptible to signal emanations. STP cable provides good shielding against emanations. Fiber-optic cable is not susceptible to signal emanations since the signals travel as light pulses.

> **Remember**
>
> All lines can be tapped into using vampire taps. Fiber-optic lines are the most difficult to tap in to. UTP is the most susceptible to EMI, RFI, and signal emanations. STP and coaxial provide a level of protection from EMI and RFI. A primary risk of coaxial cable is data emanation from its core. Fiber optic cable is completely immune to EMI, RFI, and signal emanations.

Coaxial

Coaxial (often called coax) cable has an inner core conductor made of copper and outer shielding. The shielding provides protection against EMI and RFI. However, due to its electrical characteristics, a primary risk of coaxial cable is data emanation from the core.

Most people handle coax cable when connecting their TV to a cable system. Although this type of coax is similar to coax cable used in networks, the cables do have some different electrical characteristics.

Years ago, both Thinnet and Thicknet coax were commonly used in networks, but their usage today is rare. Thinnet is known as 10Base2, and Thicknet is known as 10Base5. In both 10Base2 and 10Base5 networks, both ends of the cable on each cable segment must be terminated with a special connector. If both ends aren't terminated, signal bounce prevents any hosts on the network from communicating.

If any computer connections are disconnected from each other, or any terminator is disconnected, all of the computers on the network go down. While this is quite frustrating to the technicians responsible for maintaining the network, it's also a significant vulnerability. An attacker with physical access to any computer in a 10Base2 or 10Base5 network could take down the entire network by removing one cable.

Due to the high cost of maintenance and the security risk, it's rare to see coaxial cable in a network today.

Twisted Pair

Twisted pair cable is the most common transmission media being used today. It includes multiple pairs of copper wire twisted together. Twisted pair cable used within a network use RJ-45 jacks to connect to NICs and physical network device ports. Common categories are:

- **Cat 5**. Includes four twisted pairs. It carries signals up to 100 Mbit/s.
- **Cat 5e**. Enhanced and superseded Cat 5 cable by defining stricter performance specifications.
- **Cat 6**. Cat 6 is also called Gigabit Ethernet since it can carry signals up to 1 Gbit/s. It is backward compatible with Cat 5 and Cat 5e cable. Twisted pair comes as either shielded or unshielded.
- **UTP**. Unshielded twisted pair has no shielding and is most susceptible to EMI, RFI, and emanations.
- **STP**. Shielded twisted pair includes shielding to prevent signal contamination from EMI or RFI, and signal emanations outside the cable.

Fiber Optic

Fiber-optic cable uses glass or plastic as the medium instead of copper. Light pulses are sent down the cable instead of electrical pulses. Fiber-optic cables can carry a significantly higher or larger amount of data than traditional copper cables.

While fiber is more expensive than copper, it is quickly increasing in popularity. Most new ships, planes, and jets are being built with fiber optics instead of copper, and many new construction homes are being wired with fiber optics. TV cable and telecommunications companies are beginning to run fiber-optic cables to homes instead of traditional copper wire.

Fiber optics is not susceptible to EMI and RFI, and since the signals are light pulses, fiber optics doesn't have any problems with signal emanations outside the fiber-optic cable.

Exam Topic Review

When preparing for the exam, make sure you understand these key concepts covered in this chapter.

Basic Networking Concepts

The OSI model maps different functionalities to different layers. It includes seven layers, and you should be able to name each layer by name and number. In this chapter, you reviewed some key aspects of the OSI model, including the layer names and numbers and some common devices and protocols that are associated with particular layers.

- **Layer 7, Application Layer**. Devices include application-proxy firewalls, which can operate on all layers up to the application layer. Protocols include HTTP, HTTPS, FTP, DNS, SMTP, and SNMP.
- **Layer 6, Presentation Layer**. Protocols include ASCII, EBCDIC, TIFF, and JPG.
- **Layer 5, Session Layer**. SSL is a key protocol on this layer.
- **Layer 4, Transport Layer**. Protocols include TLS, TCP, and UDP.
- **Layer 3, Network Layer**. Devices include routers and layer 3 switches. Protocols include IP, IPSec, ICMP, and ARP.
- **Layer 2, Data Layer**. Devices include switches. Protocols include MAC and PPP.
- **Layer 1, Physical Layer**. Devices include hubs and NICs.

Ports

Logical ports 0 to 1023 are identified as Well Known Ports by ICANN. Ports in this range are commonly used with specific protocols, such as port 25 for SMTP and port 80 for HTTP. While you don't need to know all 1024 ports by rote, you should at least know the ports identified in table 3.1 in this chapter.

Network Zones

Networks are separated into different zones based on the trustworthiness of clients who can access them. The Internet has the least amount of trust since any computer with a public IP can be accessed from any other client on the Internet anywhere in the world. A company's intranet has the most amount of trust since it is protected and can only be accessed by internal clients.

A DMZ provides a buffer zone for Internet-facing servers such as web servers or mail servers. Servers in the DMZ are intended to be accessed from anyone on the Internet, but the DMZ provides a layer of protection not available if the servers are placed directly on the Internet.

An extranet is an area where servers are made available to allow trusted clients or partners to access them. While servers may be accessible via the Internet, they are only accessible to a limited number of users such as trusted clients or partners.

Network Devices

Any network is connected with network devices. For security purposes, hubs are often replaced with switches to mitigate sniffing attacks from attackers using protocol analyzers. All network devices still need to be protected with physical security. Additionally, a MAC flooding attack on a switch can cause it to function as a hub.

Routers are used to subnet a network. Routers can perform basic packet filtering.

Firewalls can be hardware-based or software-based, host-based or network-based. Most host-based firewalls are software-based. Many network-based firewalls are hardware-based and are a dedicated appliance installed in a network for security. Firewalls can be simple packet-filtering firewalls or more advanced stateful or application-proxy firewalls.

A proxy server can be used to improve performance by caching requests, and can restrict users' access to web sites by providing content filtering.

P2P

Peer-to-peer networks are networks where multiple computers connect together as peers and are commonly used for sharing files. P2P is often called file sharing. A significant risk with P2P is data leakage, where users share data they didn't intend to share or host files they would normally consider inappropriate.

Transmission Media

Wired networks transmit data on transmission media. Virtually any transmission media can be tapped into by an attacker, and once tapped, data can be monitored. While fiber-optic cables are more difficult to tap than copper-based media, it still can be done. When a cable is tapped, it is referred to as a vampire tap.

Copper-based cables (such as coaxial and twisted pair) are also susceptible to EMI, RFI, and data emanation problems. Unshielded twisted pair provides the least protection. Fiber-optic cable is immune to EMI, RFI, and data emanation problems.

Practice Questions

1. A packet-filtering firewall operates on layer 3 of the OSI model. What layer does an application-proxy firewall primarily operate on?

    A. Layer 1

    B. Layer 3

    C. Layer 4

    D. Layer 7

2. What layer does SSL operate on?

    A. Layer 3

    B. Layer 4

    C. Layer 5

    D. Layer 7

3. What protocol is commonly used for attacks and is referred to as connectionless?

    A. TCP

    B. SYN Flood

    C. SNMP

    D. UDP

4. Which one of the following protocols is not recommended for use due to being susceptible to a sniffing attack?

    A. UDP

    B. TCP

    C. SNMP

    D. ICMP

5. What protocol is commonly used to manage network devices?

    A. SNMP

    B. SMTP

    C. L2TP

    D. HTTP

6. A web server will create web pages that can be requested by a web browser. What protocol is used to send the web pages over the Internet?

    A. HTML

    B. HTTP

    C. SMTP

    D. SNMP

7. How many TCP ports are subject to attack?

    A. 1024

    B. 4096

    C. 65,535

    D. 131,070

8. What port does HTTPS use?

    A. 80

    B. 88

    C. 22

    D. 443

9. You are checking a firewall that is operating at the boundary between the Internet and your network. You notice that port 49 is open. Why would port 49 be open?

    A. To allow TACACS traffic

    B. To allow SMTP traffic

    C. To allow Terminal Services traffic

    D. To allow secure LDAP traffic

10. What port would need to be opened to allow secure LDAP traffic through?

    A. 88

    B. 53

    C. 389

    D. 636

11. You want to allow VPN traffic through your firewall using L2TP. What port needs to be open on the firewall?

    A. 80

    B. 443

    C. 1701

    D. 1723

12. An email server is being hosted in the DMZ to accept and forward SMTP traffic. What port should be opened to support this?

    A. 20

    B. 22

    C. 23

    D. 25

13. A user has installed a company-purchased program that needs to regularly contact a server on the Internet to validate data. This program uses port 5678 for outbound traffic. After installation, you discover the outbound traffic is being blocked. What should be done?

    A. Reinstall it as an administrator.

    B. Move the user's system to the same subnet as the firewall.

    C. Open the port on the company's firewall.

    D. Replace the firewall with a switch.

14. What type of IP address mapping does static NAT use?

    A. One-to-one

    B. One-to-many

    C. Many-to-one

    D. Many-to-many

15. Of the following choices, what would be the best choice to allow a partner to access your network resources from the Internet?

    A. Intranet

    B. LAN

C. DMZ

D. Extranet

16. An employee was caught capturing and analyzing traffic of other users on the same subnet. Your company wants to upgrade the network to reduce the success of similar attacks in the future. What network device should be used?

A. Hub

B. Switch

C. Router

D. VLAN

17. Where should you place Internet-facing servers to provide added protection?

A. DAC

B. DHCP

C. DMZ

D. NAT

18. What would be used to ensure that only authorized traffic is allowed into or out of a network?

A. Switch

B. Firewall

C. NAT

D. Honeynet

19. You want to perform filtering of traffic in such a way that traffic that is not a part of an established TCP session is blocked. What device would you use?

A. Switch

B. Router

C. Packet-filtering firewall

D. Stateful firewall

20. Your company is considering purchasing an Internet content filtering appliance. What can this appliance analyze? (Choose all that apply.)

    A. Email

    B. Web site addresses

    C. Certificate validity

    D. CRLs

21. What is a security risk of P2P if users within your company use it?

    A. Violation of copyright laws

    B. Increased bandwidth availability

    C. Lower disk usage

    D. Data leakage

22. Why is fiber-optic cable considered safer than UTP cable?

    A. Fiber-optic cable can be tapped into and is not susceptible to interference.

    B. Fiber-optic cable is made of copper, so it is not susceptible to vampire taps.

    C. Fiber-optic cable is not susceptible to vampire taps.

    D. Fiber-optic cable is harder to tap in to and is not susceptible to interference.

Practice Question Answers

1. **D.** An application-proxy firewall operates on the Application layer (layer 7) of the OSI model. Many application-proxy firewalls have the ability to operate on multiple layers, but the primary function of the application-proxy firewall is to inspect packets related to specific application protocols.

2. **C.** SSL operates on the Session layer (Layer 5). As a memory trick, you can think of the S in SSL matching the S in Session. Layer 3 is the Network layer; layer 4 is the Transport layer; and layer 7 is the Application layer.

3. **D.** User Datagram Protocol (UDP) is referred to as connectionless and is commonly used in UDP attacks. TCP is connection-oriented. A SYN Flood attack is a common TCP attack where the third packet of the TCP three-way handshake is held back. SNMP is used to manage and query network devices.

4. **C.** Simple Network Management Protocol (SNMP) sent passwords across the network in clear text and was susceptible to sniffing attacks. SNMP has been upgraded to SNMP v2 and SNMP v3, which are more secure. SNMP is the only listed protocol that uses passwords. All TCP/IP traffic must use either TCP or UDP. ICMP is used for diagnostics such as ping.

5. **A.** Simple Network Management Protocol (SNMP) is commonly used to manage network devices. SNMP is also used to determine equipment status of network devices. SMTP is used for email. L2TP is a tunneling protocol used with VPNs. HTTP is used for common web traffic on the Internet.

6. **B.** Hypertext Transfer Protocol (HTTP) is used to transmit web pages from a web server to a web browser. HTML is the language used to create web pages. SMTP is used for email. SNMP is used to manage network devices.

7. **C.** A total of 65,535 TCP ports are subject to attack by being scanned or exploited. Similarly, 65,535 UDP ports are also subject to attack. The first 1024 ports (ports 0–1023) are designated as Well Known Ports with commonly used

protocols associated with them. While Well Known Ports are attacked more frequently, all ports are subject to attack.

8. **D.** HTTPS uses port 443; HTTPS uses SSL to encrypt HTTP traffic. HTTP uses port 80. Kerberos uses port 88. SSH uses port 22.

9. **A.** Port 49 is used for Terminal Access Controller Access-Control System (TACACS), an implementation of RADIUS. SMTP uses port 25. Terminal Services (such as Microsoft's Remote Desktop Protocol) use port 3389. Secure LDAP traffic uses port 636.

10. **D.** Port 636 is used to allow secure LDAP traffic (such as LDAP/TLS or LDAP/SSL). Kerberos uses port 88. DNS uses port 53, and nonsecure LDAP uses port 389.

11. **C.** L2TP uses port 1701, so port 1701 should be opened on the firewall. Port 80 is for HTTP. Port 443 is for HTTPS. PPTP uses port 1723.

12. **D.** SMTP uses port 25. FTP uses ports 20 and 21. SSH uses port 22. Telnet uses port 23.

13. **C.** Ports on the company's firewall would need to be opened to allow legitimate traffic; additionally, if the host system had a personal firewall, the port should be opened on the personal firewall too. There is no indication this is due to an unsuccessful installation requiring administrative privileges. Routing within a network allows systems to operate on different subnets. Replacing the firewall with a switch would weaken security and may even disable Internet connectivity unless the switch was a layer 3 switch.

14. **A.** Static NAT uses a one-to-one mapping. A single public IP address is used by the NAT server, and internal clients can all use private IP addresses. Dynamic NAT allows a NAT server to use multiple public IP addresses and decide which public IP address to use based on load.

15. **D.** An extranet is used to provide partners with access to a limited number of resources in your network. *LAN* and *intranet* are terms used to describe an internal network. A DMZ would be used to host Internet-facing servers that are accessible to anyone with Internet access, not just partners.

16. **B.** Switches can be used to provide added security when connecting users on the same subnet; a switch will internally connect two communicating hosts, preventing other hosts from capturing the conversation with a protocol analyzer. The scenario implies a hub is currently being used, which provides little security. A router can separate different subnets, but it wouldn't connect multiple users on the same subnet. A VLAN isn't a device.

17. **C.** Internet-facing servers, or public-facing servers, should be placed in a demilitarized zone (DMZ) for added security. DAC is an access control model. DHCP is used to issue TCP/IP configuration information. NAT is used to translate public and private IP addresses.

18. **B.** A firewall can be used to filter traffic to ensure that only authorized traffic is allowed in or out of the network. A switch is used instead of a hub to reduce the vulnerability to protocol analyzers. NAT is used to translate private and public IP addresses. A honeynet is a simulated network used to attract an attacker for the purpose of either distracting the attacker or providing an opportunity to watch the attacker's methods.

19. **D.** A stateful firewall can examine traffic and make decisions based on established sessions. A switch doesn't filter traffic but can only internally direct or switch traffic to specific ports. A router can perform packet filtering, but packet filtering can only make decisions concerning individual packets, not the entire session.

20. **A, B, C.** An Internet content filter appliance can analyze content, such as email and attachments, web site addresses in the form of URLs, certificate validity, and certificate trust paths. A CRL is a list published by a CA to identify

certificates that have been revoked, but a content filter appliance wouldn't analyze the CRL.

21. **D.** Peer-to-peer (P2P) networks allow multiple users to share files via the Internet, and a significant risk is data leakage where users are sharing more data than they realize. While copyrights are concerns to copyright holders, P2P networks can be used to share data that is not copyright protected, and copyright protection isn't the security risk posed to a company. P2P networks result in increased bandwidth usage (and reduced bandwidth availability) and increased disk usage (not lower disk usage).

22. **D.** Fiber-optic cable is harder to tap in to, making it less susceptible to vampire taps, and since signals travel as light pulses, fiber-optic cable is not susceptible to EMI, RFI, or data emanations. While it's harder to tap in to fiber-optic cable than it is to tap in to a copper line, it isn't impossible.

Chapter 4

Securing Your Network

CompTIA Security+ objectives covered in this chapter

1.5 Implement security applications.

- HIDS
- Personal software firewalls

2.2 Distinguish between network design elements and components.

- NAC
- Telephony

2.3 Determine the appropriate use of network security tools to facilitate network security.

- NIDS
- NIPS
- Honeypot

2.4 Apply the appropriate network tools to facilitate network security.

- NIDS

2.7 Explain the vulnerabilities and implement mitigations associated with wireless networking.

- Data emanation
- War driving
- SSID broadcast
- Bluejacking
- Bluesnarfing
- Rogue access points
- Weak encryption

3.7 Deploy various authentication models and identify the components of each.

- Remote access policies
- Remote authentication
- 802.1x

4.5 Compare and contrast various types of monitoring methodologies.

- Behavior-based
- Signature-based
- Anomaly-based

5.3 Explain basic encryption concepts and map various algorithms to appropriate applications.

- Elliptic curve
- Transmission encryption (WEP TKIP, etc.)

5.4 Explain and implement protocols.

- SSL/TLS
- PPTP
- L2TP
- IPSEC

$* * *$

In this chapter, you'll learn about some more advanced network security concepts. Topics in this chapter include:

- **Intrusion detection systems**. IDSs are another method used to protect networks and systems. IDS topics include host-based intrusion detection systems (HIDS) and network-based intrusion detection systems (NIDS), signature-based and anomaly-based detection methods, and passive and active responses.

- **Remote access**. Remote access technologies allow personnel to access private networks from remote locations such as on the road or from home. Topics in this section include dial-up and VPNs, LT2P and PPTP tunneling protocols, IPSec, and network access control (NAC) methods.

- **Wireless networking**. Wireless networks are growing in popularity in homes and businesses. This section includes IEEE 802.11 basics; security protocols such as WEP, WPA, and WPA2; and Bluetooth information.

Intrusion Detection System

Intrusion detection systems (IDSs) are designed to detect attacks on a network. IDSs take a different approach than firewalls. Firewalls will try to block network attacks using ACLs while IDSs instead try to detect the attacks.

The primary types of IDSs you'll see are host-based IDSs (HIDSs) and network-based IDSs (NIDSs). Each of these IDSs detect attacks either through predefined attack signatures or by detecting anomalies. Once an attack occurs, an IDS can respond either passively or actively.

The following items summarize the important concepts related to intrusion detection systems.

- A HIDS is installed on individual servers and workstations.
- A NIDS is installed on network devices such as routers and firewalls.
- Signature-based monitoring detects attacks based on known attack patterns. This is also referred to as definition-based monitoring.
- Anomaly-based (also called behavior-based) monitoring detects attacks by first identifying normal operation through a baseline and then comparing current operation against the baseline to detect abnormal behavior.
- A passive IDS will log an alert. It may also inform personnel of the alert.
- An active IDS will log and possibly inform personnel of the alert, and also take action to change the environment.

IDS vs. Antivirus vs. Firewall

Intrusion detection systems are similar to antivirus software and firewalls in some respects. While these similarities exist, there are distinct differences.

The primary focus of an IDS is to inspect network traffic and detect attacks.

- A HIDS inspects traffic at the NIC and can also monitor system and application activity similar to antivirus software.
- A firewall can inspect traffic passing through a network or an individual system and block or allow traffic based on rules and access control lists.
- A NIDS will inspect the network traffic and can block or allow network traffic.

IDS vs. Antivirus

Antivirus software is used to detect different types of malware such as viruses, Trojans, and worms. Most of the viruses attack files on an individual system, and this is the central protection that antivirus software provides.

A host-based IDS focuses on examining traffic passing through the NIC, but it also observes application activity and can detect abnormal application behavior. While this is similar to antivirus behavior, it doesn't replace antivirus software.

Many viruses and worms can also wreak havoc on a network by sending massive amounts of traffic. As an example, the "I Love You" virus released in 2000 took entire networks to their knees due to the massive amounts of email transmitted.

An installed IDS can provide an extra layer of detection against this type of internal attack. An anomaly-based IDS could detect the abnormal behavior, and administrators would be notified of the problem more quickly and may have a better chance at controlling the outbreak. In this way, the antivirus software and IDS software can work together as part of a multilayered approach to security.

IDS vs. Firewall

Firewalls are designed to examine traffic and either allow or block the traffic. Simple packet-filtering firewalls (first-generation) make decisions based on each individual packet. Second- and third-generation firewalls make decisions based on the entire session.

Similarly, IDSs can examine the traffic and detect attacks based on signatures or behavior. Detected attacks can then be reported and even blocked in active response IDSs.

Firewalls and NIDSs both have similar goals in that they want to control the traffic on a network. These goals are merging in some advanced products, and some companies have released Next-Generation Firewalls. A Next-Generation Firewall includes NIDS capabilities, in addition to the early generation capabilities.

Until Next-Generation Firewalls are more widespread, NIDSs will likely still be deployed in many networks.

HIDS

A host-based intrusion detection system (HIDS) is additional software installed on a system such as a workstation or a server. The primary goal of any IDS is to monitor traffic. For a HIDS, this traffic passes through the network interface card (NIC).

> **Remember**
>
> A host-based IDS (HIDS) is installed on workstations or servers as an additional piece of software. It is used primarily to monitor network traffic passing through the NIC and can't monitor network traffic that doesn't reach the NIC. HIDS software should be checked to ensure it does not impact the performance of the host.

Many host-based IDSs have expanded to also monitor application activity on the system. As one example, a HIDS could be installed on different Internet-facing servers such as web servers, mail servers, and database servers. In addition to monitoring the network traffic, the HIDS could monitor server applications.

Some organizations install a HIDS on every workstation as an extra layer of protection similar to how antivirus protection is installed on every workstation. Just as the HIDS on a server is used primarily to monitor network traffic, a workstation HIDS is primarily used to monitor network traffic. However, a HIDS may also monitor some applications.

HIDS Strengths

The primary strength of a HIDS over a NIDS is its ability to monitor all traffic in or out of the host system. This includes:

- **Encrypted traffic**. Since the host is part of the encrypted session, encrypted traffic can be interpreted by the host.
- **Dial-up traffic directly to the host**. Since a modem isn't connected to a network, dial-up traffic to a host can only be monitored via a HIDS.

HIDS Weaknesses

Some of the more notable weaknesses of a HIDS over a NIDS include:

- **Consumes resources.** A HIDS is another piece of software installed on the system. Systems should be tested to ensure the HIDS doesn't substantially impact the system's performance.
- **Can't monitor network traffic.** A HIDS can only monitor traffic to and from the host.
- **Can be expensive.** A HIDS must be installed on every workstation, which may be cost prohibitive in some environments.
- **Data stored locally.** If the HIDS is corrupted, all local logs and files may be lost.

NIDS

A network-based intrusion detection system (NIDS) monitors activity on the network. NIDSs are installed on network devices, such as routers and firewalls, as sensors or taps. Information gathered by these sensors is reported back to a central server hosting a console to monitor the activity.

A NIDS is not able to detect anomalies on individual systems or workstations unless the anomaly causes a significant difference in network traffic.

Remember

A network-based IDS (NIDS) is installed on network devices, such as routers or firewalls, to monitor network traffic. A NIDS uses sensors or taps installed on network devices that report back to a central NIDS server. A NIDS cannot monitor traffic on individual hosts.

Figure 4.1 shows an example of how a NIDS could be configured. It shows sensors before and after the firewall and on routers. These sensors can monitor network traffic on subnets within the network and report back to the NIDS console.

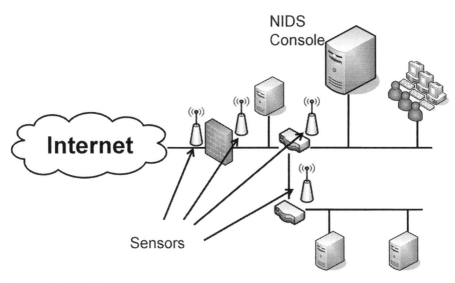

Figure 4.1: NIDS Sensors

The decision on where you want to place the sensors depends on what you want to measure. For example, the sensor on the Internet side of the firewall will see all the traffic. However, the sensor on the internal side of the firewall will only see traffic that has passed by the firewall. In other words, the firewall will filter some attacks, and these attacks won't be seen by the internal sensor.

If you want to see all attacks on your network, put a sensor on the Internet side. If you only want to see what gets through, put a sensor internally only. If you want to see both, put sensors in both places.

Detection Methods

An IDS can only detect an attack. It can't prevent attacks. An attack is generally any attempt by an outside source to compromise security. The two primary methods of detection are signature-based and anomaly-based.

Both a HIDS and a NIDS can detect attacks based on signatures or anomalies, or both. The HIDS will monitor the network traffic reaching its NIC, and the NIDS will monitor the traffic on the network.

Signature-based

Signature-based IDSs use a database of predefined attack patterns. For example, tools are available for an attacker to launch a SYN Flood attack on a server by simply entering the IP address of the system to attack. The tool will then flood the attacked system with SYN packets but never complete the TCP handshake with the ACK packets.

Since this is a known attack, it has a known pattern, such as successive SYN packets from one IP to another IP. The traffic doesn't include matching ACK packets, resulting in the server's open sessions steadily increasing.

Remember

Signature-based IDSs (also called definition-based) use a database of predefined traffic patterns. A signature-based IDS is the most basic form of detection and the easiest to implement.

The IDS can detect these patterns if they are defined in the signature database. This method is also often called definition-based. The process is very similar to what antivirus software uses to detect malware. Both IDS signatures and antivirus definitions must be updated on a regular basis to protect against current threats.

Anomaly-based

Anomaly-based detection first determines what is normal operation or normal behavior and can then later determine if network activity is abnormal. Anomaly-based detection is also referred to as behavior-based IDS.

Normal operation is determined by creating a performance baseline. The baseline identifies normal behavior, and the IDS can constantly compare current behavior against the baseline. When abnormal activity, as compared to the baseline, is detected, the IDS will give an alert indicating a potential attack.

Anomaly-based detection is similar to how heuristic-based antivirus software works. While the internal methods are different, both examine activity and make decisions that are outside the scope of a signature or definition database.

> ### *Remember*
> Anomaly-based IDSs (also called behavior-based) start with a performance baseline of normal behavior. Network traffic is compared against this baseline, and when the traffic differs significantly, the IDS will give an alert. The baseline must be updated any time the environment is changed significantly.

Any time significant changes are made to a system or network that cause normal behavior to change, the baseline should be recreated. Otherwise, the IDS will constantly alert on what is now normal behavior.

Data Sources

Any type of IDS will use various raw data sources to collect information on activity. This includes a wide variety of logs such as firewall logs, System logs, and Application logs.

Some IDSs have the capability to monitor the logs, and each time any log entry is recorded, the IDS can examine the log to determine if it's an item of interest or not. Other IDSs will periodically poll relevant logs and scan new entries to determine if anything of interest has recently been recorded.

Alert

An alert indicates that an IDS has detected an event of interest. An alert is not necessarily an attack. Alerts occur when certain activity reaches a threshold. The goal is to set the threshold of an alert to a level low enough so that you are always informed when an attack occurs and high enough so that you don't get too many false positives or false intrusions.

Consider the classic SYN Flood attack, where the third part of the TCP handshake is held back. A host will send a SYN packet. A server will respond with a SYN/ACK packet. However, instead of completing the handshake with an ACK packet, the attacking host never sends the ACK but instead continues to send more SYN packets, leaving the server with open connections that can ultimately disrupt services.

It's possible for the third packet of a single TCP handshake to never reach a server during normal operation. A host system could start the handshake process but not complete it due to network issues or some other minor problem. This isn't an attack and shouldn't cause an alert.

However, if the same IP address initiated over one hundred TCP sessions in less than sixty seconds and never completed any of the sessions, it is clear this is an attack.

Some number between one and one hundred would be set as the threshold to signal an alert.

IDS Threshold

When setting the threshold, the IDS administrator will try to balance the risks of an attack against the risks of false positives.

Most administrators want to know if their system is under attack. That's the primary purpose of the IDS. However, if an IDS is constantly giving false positives, it will soon be ignored. An IDS that constantly cries "Wolf!" will be ignored when the real wolf attacks.

There is no perfect number that will always indicate an active attack. Thresholds can be adjusted in different networks based on the network's activity level and personal preferences of security administrators.

IDS Responses

When an attack is detected, an IDS will respond. The response can be either passive or active. A passive response primarily consists of logging and notifying, while an active response will also change the environment.

Passive IDS

A passive IDS will simply log the attack and may also raise an alert to notify someone. The notification can come in many forms, including:

- **A pop-up window.** A dialog box can appear notifying the user of the event.
- **A central monitor.** Some large organizations use central monitors to display events of interest.

- **An email.** The IDS can be programmed to send an email to a user or group. Email systems can be configured to forward these to portable devices such as BlackBerry devices.
- **A page.** Email servers can be programmed to accept email and forward it to a phone system to page someone.

Remember

An IDS can respond passively or actively. A passive response will simply log the event and provide a level of notification. An active response will change the environment in some way, such as changing ACLs or closing processes or sessions.

Active IDS

An active IDS will log and notify just as a passive IDS will, but it can also change the environment to thwart or block the attack. The environment can be changed by:

- Modifying ACLs on firewalls to block offending traffic
- Closing processes on a system that were caused by the attack
- Diverting the attack to a safe environment

Consider the common SYN Flood attack, where an attack floods a system with SYN packets but never completes the handshake with the ACK packet.

The attacker is coming from a specific IP address. Access control lists on a router or firewall could be modified to specifically block all traffic from this IP address. The attacker initiated sessions that will never be completed. The IDS could close all of these sessions initiated by the offending IP address.

It's also possible to divert the attack to a honeypot or honeynet.

Diverting to a Honeypot

A honeypot is a sweet-looking server—at least it's intended to look sweet to the attacker. It's actually a server that is left open or appears to have been sloppily locked down, allowing an attacker relatively easy access. The intent is for the server to look like an easy target so that the attacker spends his time in the honeypot instead of in a live network.

As an example, a honeypot could be an FTP server that has some protection but can be thwarted by an attacker. If the server is left completely open, it may look too suspicious to experienced attackers, and they may simply avoid it.

Honeypots would never hold any valuable data. The data may appear to be valuable at first, but its disclosure does no harm. Honeypots have two primary goals:

- **Divert attackers from the live network.** As long as an attacker is spending time in the honeypot, he is not attacking live resources.
- **Allow observation of an attacker.** While an attacker is in the honeypot, security professionals are able to observe the attack and learn from the attacker's methodologies.

Remember

A honeypot is used to divert an attacker from a live network and/or allow IT administrators an opportunity to observe methodologies used in an attack. A honeynet is a group of honeypots staged in a virtual environment.

Sun Tzu famously wrote in *The Art of War*, "All warfare is based on deception," and "Know your enemies." Security professionals on the front lines of network and system attacks recognize that these attacks mimic warfare in many ways, and it's sometimes referred to as cyber warfare. Honeypots and honeynets are extra tools that security professionals can use in the war.

Honeynets

A honeynet is a group of virtual servers contained within a single physical server. The honeynet is intended to mimic the functionality of a live network.

As an example, a single powerful server could be installed with a significant amount of RAM and processing power. This server could host multiple virtual servers where each virtual server is running an operating system and applications.

A physical server hosting six virtual servers will appear as seven systems on a subnet. An attacker looking in will not be able to tell that six of the servers are virtual.

The purpose of this virtual network is to attract the attention of an attacker similar to how a single honeypot tries to attract the attention of an attacker. While the attacker is in the honeynet, he isn't in the live network and his actions can be observed.

Counterattacks

An active response IDS would rarely perform a counterattack. A counterattack would be an attack back on the attacker. Some network security professionals specialize in attacks or counterattacks, but regular administrators should avoid them.

Consider basic human nature. If one person bumps into another in a crowd, the second person could simply ignore it or give a smile and a nod indicating "no problem," and the event is over. On the other hand, if the response is an aggressive push of the first person, the event is escalated. It can turn ugly quickly.

Consider some basic facts about attackers today.

- **Attackers are professionals.** Attackers aren't just bored teenagers passing their time away like Matthew Broderick in the movie *War Games*. Most attackers today are professional attackers similar to how you might consider a seasoned car thief a professional car thief. They are often very good at what they do. Attackers' skills steadily increase, and their tools are increasingly more sophisticated.

- **Attackers have unlimited time.** Attackers usually have the luxury of spending 100 percent of their time on attack strategies and methodologies. Compare this to network administrators who have a host of other duties and rarely can spend 100 percent of their time on security.

If an administrator has some extra time and decides to have some fun, trace back an IP address, and launch a counterattack, he will likely be discovered. The original attacker will very likely escalate the attack. Instead of moving on from your network, he may make the attack personal. He now has a mission, and this administrator's network is the target.

NIPS

A network intrusion prevention system (NIPS) is an extension of NIDS and is designed to react in real time to catch an attack in action.

Prevention is somewhat of a misnomer. You can't actually stop the attacker from attacking. However, NIPS will act in real time to block offending traffic while still allowing safe traffic.

A significant difference between NIDS and NIPS is that NIPS would be placed in line. In other words, NIPS could be placed on the firewall that accepts all incoming and outgoing traffic. In contrast, NIDS would have sensors that monitor and report the traffic on the firewall back to a console located elsewhere. This in-line configuration allows NIPS to perform much quicker than NIDS.

Remote Access

Remote access is the group of technologies that allow users to access an internal network from remote locations. Remote Access Service (RAS) is provided through dial-up or virtual private networks (VPNs). RAS is also referred to as Network Access Service (NAS).

Several components come together to form a successful Remote Access Service. They include:

- **Access method**. Users can access a RAS server through dial-up or VPN.
- **Authentication**. A secure authentication mechanism must be used since users may connect over unsecure lines.
- **Access control**. Once a user is authenticated, remote access policies can be implemented to verify that the user is authorized to connect and to control the connection.

Dial-up RAS

Dial-up RAS uses phones and modems. Both the client and server need access to phone lines, and each must have a modem. The dial-up RAS allows the client to have access to a remote network over POTS (plain old telephone system).

As a simple example, I was a traveling trainer for many years. While I was on the road, I was able to dial in to the RAS server using a laptop with a modem anytime I needed access to the company network. Once I connected, I could access resources on the network similar to how I could access the resources if I was at my desk at work—just not as quickly since I was using a 56K modem.

Figure 4.2 shows the dial-up configuration. The client has a modem and access to a phone line and can dial directly into the RAS server. The RAS server also has a modem and access to a phone line. Once connected, the RAS server provides access to the internal network.

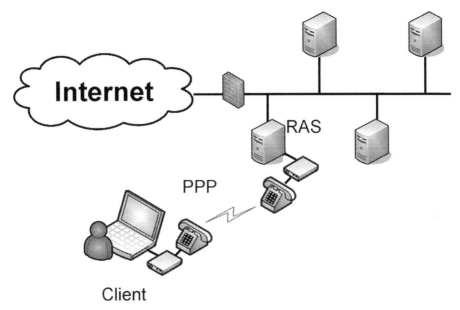

Figure 4.2: Dial-up Remote Access

The primary protocol used for dial-up access is the Point-to-Point Protocol (PPP). When it was developed, tapping phone lines was considered rare, so PPP didn't include any security. Additionally, long-distance phone costs can make this solution cost prohibitive. VPNs provide security and can reduce phone costs.

Dial-up remote access includes telephony technologies—the use of telephone technologies to connect computers. Telephony also includes combining the use of computers and telephone technologies to provide voice-over IP.

VPN

A virtual private network (VPN) allows a connection to a private network over a public network. The public network is most commonly the Internet, but it can also be a semiprivate leased line from a telecommunications company. Since the telecommunications company will often lease access to one physical line to several companies, the leased line is not truly private.

Since access is over a public network, security has been a core concern with VPNs. Different tunneling protocols have been developed to encapsulate and encrypt the traffic to protect the data from unauthorized disclosure.

Tunneling

Figure 4.3 shows an example of how a tunneling protocol would work within a VPN. The figure is focused on showing the VPN server, so it doesn't show firewalls, but in a normal configuration, you would have at least one firewall protecting the internal network. The VPN server has a public IP address, making it accessible from any other host on the Internet.

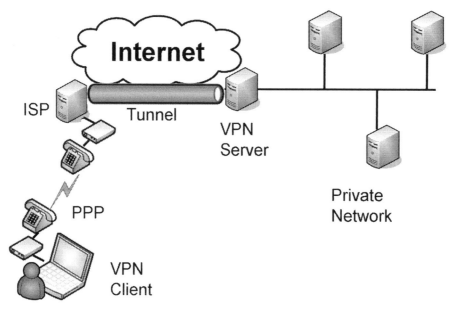

Figure 4.3: Tunneling to a VPN Server

Clients can use PPP to dial up a local Internet Service Provider (ISP) to get a public IP address. If clients already had a public IP address, such as through a broadband always-on connection, they wouldn't need to use PPP to dial up a local ISP and get a public IP address.

Once connected to the Internet with a public IP address, a tunneling protocol is used to create a protected tunnel through the Internet to the VPN server. Some common tunneling protocols used by VPN connections are:

- **L2F**. Layer 2 Forwarding protocol was developed by Cisco and used as a tunneling protocol for VPNs. This is not used much anymore.
- **PPTP**. Point-to-Point Tunneling Protocol was commonly used by Microsoft and was encrypted using Microsoft's Point-to-Point Encryption. PPTP has known vulnerabilities. PPTP uses TCP port 1723.
- **L2TP**. Layer 2 Tunneling Protocol was developed by Cisco and Microsoft and combines features of L2F and PPTP. L2TP is the most common tunneling protocol used today. It does not encrypt the tunnel itself but is commonly encrypted with IPSec (L2TP/IPSec). L2TP uses UDP port 1701.
- **SSTP**. Secure Socket Tunneling Protocol is used to encrypt L2TP or PPP traffic using SSL over port 443. SSTP was developed to overcome the limitation of IPSec. IPSec is not compatible with NAT. In the past, if VPN traffic had to pass through a NAT server, the less secure PPTP was often selected. Today, SSTP can be used instead though it is still relatively new.

> ### Remember
> The two most common tunneling protocols are PPTP and L2TP. PPTP has known vulnerabilities, so it is falling into disuse in favor of L2TP. PPTP uses port 1701, and L2TP uses port 1723. As a memory aid, remember that 1701 is before 1723, and L is before P in the alphabet (L2TP is before PPTP). L2TP commonly uses IPSec (L2TP/IPSec) to encrypt the tunnel.

L2TP and IPSec

While it is possible to use L2TP to create a tunnel between devices, L2TP doesn't include any encryption, so it does not provide confidentiality of the data. IPSec is used to provide security for the VPN tunnel. IPSec provides security in two ways:

- **Authentication**. IPSec includes an Authentication Header (AH) to allow each of the hosts in the IPSec conversation to authenticate with each other before data is exchanged. AH is identified with protocol ID number 51.
- **Encryption**. IPSec includes Encapsulating Security Payload (ESP) to encrypt the data and provide confidentiality. ESP is identified with protocol ID number 50.

The term *protocol ID number* may look like a typo, but it isn't. AH and ESP are identified with protocol ID numbers, not port numbers.

Remember

IPSec is used to encrypt traffic. IPSec includes an Authentication Header (AH), which can be used by itself for authentication, or Encapsulating Security Payload (ESP), which includes authentication and encryption. AH is identified with protocol ID 51, and ESP is identified with protocol ID 50.

While the focus of IPSec in this chapter is its use with L2TP, IPSec can also be used by itself to encrypt traffic. This may be desirable if sensitive data is being transferred between two hosts on a network.

Routers and firewalls were discussed in Chapter 3. You may remember that a basic packet-filtering firewall can route packets based on IP addresses, ports, and some protocols, such as ICMP and IPSec. Packet filters use the protocol ID numbers to identify AH and ESP traffic.

NAT and IPSec

IPSec and Network Address Translation (NAT) are not compatible with each other. NAT manipulates the IP header of the packets when it translates the addresses. This change causes the receiving end of the VPN tunnel to discard the packet as invalid.

If the path to the VPN server is through a NAT server, then a method other than L2TP/IPSec must be selected.

Gateway-to-gateway VPNs

A gateway-to-gateway VPN includes two VPN servers that act as gateways for multiple clients to access a remote network over a public connection. Each of the VPN servers acts as a gateway for multiple users in the different networks.

Figure 4.4 shows an example of a gateway-to-gateway model. The two VPN servers are used as gateways to connect a remote office network with a larger headquarters LAN.

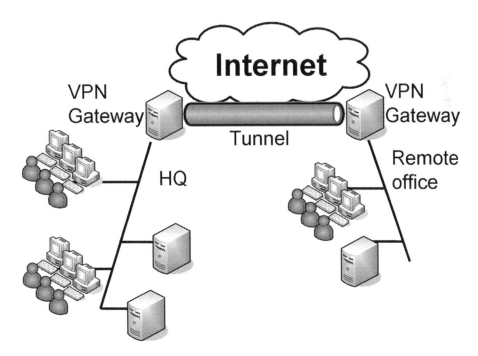

Figure 4.4: Gateway-to-gateway VPN Server

A big benefit of the gateway-to-gateway model is that it connects both networks without requiring additional steps on the part of the user. If users want to connect to a server in headquarters, they're able to connect to the remote server just as they would connect to a server in their local office. Connecting to the remote server may be slower than connecting to a local server, but otherwise, it's transparent to the users.

In contrast, a host-to-gateway model is where the end user makes the direct connection to the VPN server and is very much aware of the process.

Network Access Control

Allowing unrestricted access to your private network can expose your network to a significant number of problems. Network access control methodologies are used to provide a measure of control.

Network access control includes three primary components:

- **Authentication**. Before you can determine if a client is allowed access, you need to know who he is. Clients provide credentials for authentication.

- **Remote access policies**. Once clients are authenticated, remote access policies can be used to control many different elements of the connection, such as who can access the network and when.

- **Inspection and control**. Clients can be inspected to ensure they meet specific predefined health conditions, such being up-to-date and running anti-malware software. Healthy clients are allowed full access. Clients that don't meet the predefined conditions are only allowed limited, quarantined access.

RAS Authentication

Chapter 1 presented authentication, including the different mechanisms that can be used with authentication. To connect the two topics, it's worth a short review of the authentication mechanisms used with RAS.

- **CHAP**. Challenge Handshake Authentication Protocol introduced a challenge-response mechanism for authentication. It has largely been replaced with other methods.

- **MS-CHAPv2**. Microsoft improved CHAP with MS-CHAP and MS-CHAPv2. The significant improvement MS-CHAPv2 provided was mutual authentication, requiring both the client and the server to authenticate before data was shared.

- **RADIUS**. Remote Authentication Dial-In User Service uses a central server for authentication when multiple RAS or VPN servers are used. A weakness with RADIUS is that only the password is encrypted in the authentication process.

- **TACACS/TACACS+**. Terminal Access Controller Access-Control System (TACACS) and TACACS+ are commonly used with Cisco VPN concentrators as a replacement for RADIUS. A strength of TACACS+ over RADIUS is that TACACS+ encrypts the entire client-server negotiation process, not just the password.

Remote Access Policies

Remote access policies are used after authentication to control access to a network. A remote access policy can be used to simply allow or deny access to the remote access connection or specify several different conditions that must also be met.

As an example, Microsoft's RRAS service can be used for remote access. Remote access policies are used to control access. A remote access policy in RRAS includes three elements:

- **Condition**. One or more conditions must be met for access to be granted. Conditions can include specific user groups that are allowed access, specific days or times when users can use the connection, or even specific phone numbers users should dial into.
- **Permission**. The two permissions are allow and deny.
- **Profile**. A profile can be used to further control the connection such as disconnecting inactive connections or limiting the overall time allowed for connections.

Remote access policies can be used to control how and when users connect to the remote access server. This includes users who are authorized to work from home or users who access the network while traveling.

Inspection and Control

More advanced network access control includes the inspection of clients that attempt to access a network and only allowing access to clients that meet predefined conditions.

Within a network, clients can be well controlled. An administrator can make sure all the clients are kept up-to-date, have antivirus software installed with up-to-date definitions, and take other proactive management steps. However, the administrator doesn't have much control over systems kept at employees' homes or used while employees are traveling.

Network access control techniques allow an administrator to create policies that inspect the computer. Within a Microsoft environment, Windows Management

Instrumentation scripts can inspect just about every nook and cranny of a system to determine exactly what it is, what is installed, and how it is maintained.

After inspection, network access control can determine if the system meets the administrator's predefined conditions, such as having antivirus software installed with up-to-date definitions. If the conditions are met, the client will be identified as healthy. If the system doesn't meet the conditions, it is identified as unhealthy. Healthy clients can be granted full network access. Unhealthy clients can be granted access to an isolated, quarantined network that can be used to update the client to a healthy status.

Wireless Networking

Wireless local area networks (WLANs) have become quite popular in recent years, especially in home networks. A wireless network is easy to set up and can quickly connect several computers without the need to run cables.

The significant challenge with wireless networks is security, and wireless networks are well known to have significant vulnerabilities. You can lock down a wireless network, but interestingly, many more wireless networks are left wide open than are secured.

Figure 4.5 shows a typical home wireless network. A single connection is used to connect to the Internet through an ISP. This connection can be a regular modem or broadband cable modem.

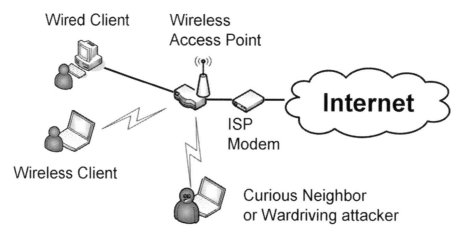

Figure 4.5: Typical Home Wireless Network

A wireless access point (WAP) connects to the modem to share Internet access and connects all the computers in the network. When used this way, the WAP also includes routing capabilities and network address translation. Most WAPs include wired ports and transceivers that can be used to connect wireless clients.

Since wireless networks broadcast on known frequency bands, other wireless users can often see a wireless network. This can be a curious neighbor who occasionally looks around or a dedicated attacker war driving your neighborhood looking for open wireless networks to attack.

IEEE 802.11

IEEE 802.11 is a group of several protocols that define the standards for wireless networks. Some of the common wireless standards, their maximum throughput, and operating frequencies are:

- **802.11a**. 54 Mbit/s. 5 GHz.
- **802.11b**. 11 Mbit/s. 2.4 GHz.
- **802.11g**. 54 Mbit/s. 2.4 GHz.
- **802.11n**. 600 Mbit/s. 2.4 GHz and 5 GHz. 802.11n is expected to be finalized in December 2009.

The 802.11-2007 standard was approved in 2007 and includes all of the accumulated changes for 802.11a, b, d, e, g, h, i, and j protocols.

Every connection to a WAP won't achieve the maximum throughput. Instead, the client and WAP negotiate the highest throughput that can be achieved without errors. A wireless device in the same room as the WAP will be quicker than a wireless device separated by space, walls, and floors.

Additionally, wireless devices don't operate on exactly 2.5 GHz or 5 GHz. Instead, there are multiple channels within these bands where the devices will transmit and receive data.

Data Emanation

A significant vulnerability of wireless networks is that they broadcast all the traffic over the air. The data emanates and can be received by anyone with a receiver tuned to the correct frequency. Since these frequency bands and channels are formally defined in IEEE standards, they are easy to learn by dedicated attackers.

One method employed within some wireless networks is to limit the footprint of a wireless network. The footprint is the area where the wireless traffic can be received. By decreasing the power output of a WAP, the footprint can be reduced.

Decreasing the footprint isn't always successful. Most common wireless devices use omnidirectional antennas to receive a wireless signal from any direction, but an attacker can create a unidirectional antenna that can receive wireless traffic from a specific direction.

While an omnidirectional antenna requires a strong signal, a unidirectional antenna can be pointed in the specific direction of the wireless transmitter and capture a very weak signal. In other words, the wireless footprint can be reduced for omnidirectional antennas, but the dedicated hacker with a unidirectional antenna can still capture the traffic from the wireless network.

IEEE 802.1x

Chapter 1 presented different authentication protocols. As a reminder, the IEEE 802.1x protocol is used to protect the authentication process during connection sessions. IEEE 802.1x can be used in both wired and wireless networks, but it is most closely associated with wireless networks. IEEE 802.1x protects the authentication process from interception prior to allowing access to a network.

Security Protocols

Since wireless networks broadcast over the air, anyone who has a wireless transceiver can intercept the transmissions. Wireless networks can be secured with several different steps, but the most important step is to implement a security protocol. The available security protocols are:

- **WEP**. Considered compromised.
- **WPA**. Considered compromised.
- **WPA2**. Current standard.

WEP

Wired Equivalent Privacy (WEP) was the original security protocol used to secure wireless networks. As the name implies, it was intended to provide the same level of privacy and security within a wireless network as could be achieved in a wired network.

Unfortunately, WEP has significant vulnerabilities, and tools are available to break into WEP-protected networks. The biggest problem with WEP was related to poor encryption key management. Due to the widely published vulnerabilities of WEP, it was deprecated in 2004 with WPA, identified as an interim replacement, and WPA2 as a permanent replacement.

Even though WEP has vulnerabilities, using WEP is better than using nothing at all. If your NICs and/or WAP aren't compatible with WPA, WEP should still be used.

Leaving your network without any security is like leaving your car running when you run into a store. Yes, it's possible no one will steal your car, but it is quite a temptation. Adding WEP is like turning your car off and locking it. Can a dedicated thief still steal your car? Yes, but it's unlikely it'll be stolen by a casual passerby.

WEP uses RC4 stream cipher encryption. Chapter 9 will cover encryption in greater depth, but in general, stream cipher encryptions are susceptible to vulnerabilities and aren't considered as secure as block ciphers.

Additionally, most encryption methods (such as RC4 stream cipher) use both an algorithm and a key. The encryption method is widely known, but the keys should be kept secret and regularly changed. WEP had significant problems with key management allowing an attacker to discover the keys.

WPA

Wi-Fi Protected Access (WPA) was created as an intermediate replacement for WEP after WEP's vulnerabilities became widely known and exploited. Even when WEP was replaced, it was recognized that WPA wasn't solid enough to last for any extended period of time. Instead, it was intended only to provide better security until WPA2 could be ratified.

WPA uses RC4 stream encryption with Temporal Key Integrity Protocol (TKIP) to better manage the encryption keys. TKIP addresses several of the specific flaws that were discovered and exploited in WEP.

TKIP was designed as a replacement for WEP without the need to replace the hardware. As newer hardware was developed, WPA and TKIP's usage diminished and is now considered deprecated, but you may still see some legacy hardware supporting both WEP and WPA.

A successful attack method against WPA was published in November 2008. However, WPA2 had already been ratified by then.

WPA2

Wi-Fi Protected Access v2 (WPA2) is the permanent replacement for WEP and WPA. WPA2 was ratified in 2004 and published as the IEEE 802.11i standard. Any devices sold today that bear the Wi-Fi logo must support WPA2.

WPA2 uses the Advanced Encryption Standard (AES) instead of RC4. AES is much more secure and is used in many different scenarios where a secure encryption protocol is needed to ensure confidentiality. WPA2 also uses much more secure methods of managing the encryption keys.

> ### Remember
> The most important security precaution is to enable WPA2 on your wireless components. If your wireless components do not support WPA2, and they can't be upgraded, you should at least enable WPA or WEP. While both WEP and WPA are considered compromised, they are better than nothing.

The single biggest step you can take to secure a wireless network is to ensure WPA2 is enabled. Other steps are possible and certainly can be used to provide a defense in depth solution, or layered security, but clearly WPA2 is the most important.

Of course, you also need to make sure that the default administrator password has been changed so that an attacker can't simply log in to your WAP and turn off WPA2.

What Wireless Security Are You Using?

What wireless security are you using? WEP, WPA, WPA2, or nothing at all?

I frequently ask this question when teaching CompTIA Security+ classes. Many students simply don't know, and this question often starts a lot of whispering among students as some realize they may not even be using WEP.

The next day, many of the students report back, and it's common to hear that they've upgraded security on their wireless networks. Many WAPs and wireless NICs can be upgraded to support WPA and WPA2 if they don't already. Some of the older ones can only be upgraded to WPA.

How about you? What wireless security are you using? If you don't know, check. The single most important step you can take to secure your wireless network is to upgrade to WPA2. Go ahead. Dig out the manual for your wireless access point or wireless router and check it out now.

WTLS and ECC

Two other security protocols you may run across are Wireless Transport Layer Security (WTLS) and elliptic curve cryptography (ECC). WTLS and ECC are sometimes used in smaller wireless devices.

Smaller wireless devices such as PDAs and cell phones don't have the same processing power as servers and desktop computers and can't easily handle the processing requirements of advanced security protocols such as WPA2.

Instead, WTLS or ECC is used.

- **WTLS**. WTLS is a wireless implementation of TLS. TLS will be explored further in Chapter 9.
- **ECC**. ECC elegantly exploits a field of mathematics that can use a formula to create a curve and another formula to identify one or more points on the curve. The point(s) on the curve are used to create the encryption key.

Other Security Steps

While the use of WPA2 is clearly the single most important step you can take to secure a wireless network, there are other steps to take. These additional steps are:

- Change default administrator password
- Implement authentication
- Disable SSID broadcasting
- Change default SSID
- Enable MAC filtering

These settings are normally accessible via a group of web pages hosted by your router. You can often access the web pages by using your web browser and entering either http://192.168.0.1 or http://192.168.1.1 to access the home page.

Change Default Administrator Password

Many WAPs come with a default Administrator account of "admin," and default passwords of "admin." Some even ship with blank passwords. The defaults are documented in the instruction manual, and most manuals stress changing the password, but quite simply, it's not always done.

> ### *Remember*
> Wireless access points and wireless routers have default Administrator accounts and default passwords. The default password of any device should be changed as soon as it is placed into service.

If the default password isn't changed, anyone who can access your WAP can log in and modify the configuration. Even the most secure wireless network can be circumvented if the administrator password is not changed. The attacker can log in and simply turn off the security. Unless you go back into the WAP configuration, you may never know that the security has been turned off.

Implement Authentication

A wireless network provides another layer of security by combining authentication with a security protocol. As a reminder, authentication is used to prove who someone is by providing credentials. Authentication was covered in depth in Chapter 1.

Some hotels and resorts use pay-as-you-go Wi-Fi access. For example, some Las Vegas hotels and Walt Disney resorts have wireless access for $15 per day. If you choose to pay for this service, you create an account with a username and password. To access the wireless network, you authenticate with the credentials.

Authentication systems are more advanced than most home networks need, but they can be implemented. A combination of both a security protocol and an authentication system would significantly mitigate the chances of a successful access attack against a wireless system.

Disable SSID Broadcasting

One of the goals of 802.11 wireless networks is ease of use. The designers wanted wireless computers to be able to easily find each other and work together. They certainly achieved this goal. Unfortunately, attackers can also easily find your networks.

One method used to make a wireless network harder to find is to disable security set identifier (SSID) broadcasting. The SSID is a network name used to identify a wireless network. When it is broadcasting, other devices can automatically discover the WAP. While this is a great feature when initially configuring devices, it's a good practice to disable it after the devices have been configured.

As an example, my next-door neighbor's name is Linda, and she's a lawyer. The name of her wireless network is "LindasLegal." Occasionally, when I use my wireless network, I can see her network as one of the many wireless networks discovered by my wireless NIC. I can see her wireless network because the SSID is broadcasting.

Most WAPs allow you to disable SSID broadcasting by just checking a box in the WAP's configuration. Details for specific WAPs are described in the WAP's manual.

> **Remember**
>
> The service set identifier (SSID) identifies the name of the wireless network and should be secured by taking two steps. The name should be changed from the default SSID, and SSID broadcasting should be turned off.

Change Default SSID

In addition to disabling the SSID broadcast, the default SSID should be changed. Wireless access points and wireless routers come with a default SSID, and the default SSID is set to broadcast by default.

As an example, a Linksys WAP often comes with the default SSID of "Linksys" or "linksys-g." If SSID broadcasting is disabled, but the default SSID is still being used, attackers may be able to guess the SSID and connect to the wireless network.

Enable MAC Filtering

An additional step you can take to protect a wireless network is to enable MAC filtering. MAC filtering is used to allow traffic sent by computers that hold specific MAC addresses and block all other traffic.

The media access control (MAC) address is a 48-bit address used to identify network interface cards (NICs). It is commonly displayed as six pairs of hexadecimal characters such as: 00-16-EA-DD-A6-60. The MAC is also known as the physical address.

By entering the MAC address of the specific computers in your home, you can use MAC filtering to allow these systems to connect but block traffic by computers with different MAC addresses.

This may sound very secure, but if a dedicated attacker is able to learn what MAC addresses are allowed into a wireless network, the MAC addresses can be spoofed. Using a spoofed MAC, the attacker is able to bypass MAC filtering. Some war driving software will detect and display MAC addresses.

War Driving

War driving is the practice of looking for a wireless network. While war driving is more common in cars, it can just as easily be done by walking around in a large city. If the SSIDs are broadcasting, the wireless networks are easy to locate.

Software such as NetStumbler can be used to locate a wireless network even if the SSID isn't broadcasting. War driving software can identify details of the wireless network such as the network name, MAC addresses, signal strength, and the security protocol (if any) that is being used. Other tools such as Aircrack-ng and AirSnort can be used to break the encryption.

Many current operating systems often include software to identify wireless networks that are broadcasting the SSID. For example, Microsoft's Windows Vista and Windows 7 include tools that allow you to view details about wireless networks that are in range (if the SSID is broadcasting). The software also shows which security protocol is being used, such as WPA2, WPA, or WEP, or if the network is left unsecured.

Rogue Access Points

Generically, a rogue is thought of as a crook or a villain. A rogue access point is a wireless access point (WAP) placed within a network by someone with some type of attack in mind. Clearly, if a rogue is a crook or villain, then rogue access points should be avoided.

Attackers have been known to connect rogue access points to network devices in wireless closets that don't have adequate physical security. This access point acts as a sniffer to capture traffic passing through the wired network device and then broadcasts the traffic using the wireless capability of the WAP. The attacker can then capture the traffic from the parking lot.

Remember
If a rogue wireless access point is discovered, it should be disconnected. The first response to a security incident is to contain or isolate the threat.

If an unauthorized WAP is discovered, it should be disconnected. A basic first step to take when an attack is discovered is to contain or isolate the threat. By simply unplugging an Ethernet cable, the sniffing attack from an unauthorized WAP can be stopped.

Often, administrators will use war driving tools such as NetStumbler to periodically scan their networks for rogue access points.

Bluetooth Wireless

Bluetooth is a short-range wireless system that was created for personal area networks (PANs) or a network of devices close to a single person. Bluetooth devices include phones, personal digital assistants (PDAs), and computer devices.

The range of Bluetooth was originally designed for about three meters (about ten feet), but the range is often farther, which, ultimately, extends beyond a person's personal space. Attackers have found that personal area networks aren't necessarily restricted to the person and attacks are possible. Two common attacks are bluesnarfing and bluejacking. Both attacks are made much easier by Bluetooth devices that are left in discovery mode.

Discovery Mode

When Bluetooth devices are first configured, they are configured in discovery mode. One of the risks occurs when a Bluetooth device is left in discovery mode. Attackers are able to easily discover and connect to the Bluetooth device and access or steal information on the device.

While in discovery mode, a Bluetooth device is easily discoverable and visible to other devices. Bluetooth devices are identified with a MAC address just as a NIC has a MAC address. In discovery mode, the Bluetooth device broadcasts its MAC address, allowing other devices to see it and connect to it.

Once a device connects with another device, it is paired to open the communication channel. The pairing process often includes configuring a PIN or a password. Pairing with a PIN or a password provides a layer of security.

If the device is left in discovery mode, it is relatively easy for an attacker to use either bluesnarfing against your device to access the data on the device or bluejacking to send email or text messages through the device.

Non-Discovery Mode

After the pairing process, the Bluetooth device should be changed from discovery mode to non-discovery mode. Non-discovery mode is also referred to as invisible mode. While in non-discovery mode, the device doesn't broadcast information about itself. Additionally, many devices add encryption to the communication process when in non-discovery mode.

Bluesnarfing

Bluesnarfing is any unauthorized access to or theft of information from a Bluetooth connection. Information that can be accessed through bluesnarfing includes:

- Email
- Contact list
- Calendar
- Text messages

Any Bluetooth device that is turned on and in discovery mode is easily exploited through a bluesnarfing attack. Users with a Linux system and Bluetooth capabilities can exploit the vulnerability with just a few command line entries using hcitool and obexftp.

Remember

Bluesnarfing and bluejacking are two threats against Bluetooth devices that are left in discovery mode. Bluesnarfing is the unauthorized access to or theft of information from a Bluetooth device. Bluejacking is the unauthorized sending of text messages from a Bluetooth device.

Bluejacking

Bluejacking is the practice of sending text messages over someone else's Bluetooth device without her permission or knowledge. A bluejack message may only be text, but it can also include sound and text on some Bluetooth devices.

Hijacking (such as hijacking a car or plane) is more serious than snarfing (which relates to pilfering). Similarly, bluejacking is considered more serious than bluesnarfing.

Often the user won't have any idea that the message has been sent. Bluejacking has been used to send advertising via someone's Bluetooth device but can also be much more malicious in nature.

Imagine your device is bluejacked. If someone sends a threatening text message to a political figure, guess who that gets traced back to? You! And, if sound and text can be sent, it's only a short leap for someone to figure out how to send malware. If someone releases the next I Love You virus via your Bluetooth device, guess who they'll track the release of this virus back to? You again!

Clearly, the best defense for Bluetooth devices is to ensure the device stays in non-discovery mode.

Exam Topic Review

When preparing for the exam, make sure you understand these key concepts, which were covered in this chapter.

Intrusion Detection Systems

- A host-based IDS (HIDS) is installed on servers and workstations and can detect attacks on the hosts but not on the network. A HIDS will impact the host's performance and primarily monitors activity on the NIC.
- A network-based IDS (NIDS) is installed on network devices such as routers and firewalls and can detect attacks on the network. A NIDS uses sensors or taps that report back to a central console.
- Signature-based detection methods use a database of predefined signatures and detect attacks that match patterns in the signatures. A signature-based IDS is a basic IDS, while anomaly-based is more advanced.
- Anomaly-based (also called behavior-based) detection methods start with a performance baseline. Ongoing performance is measured against the baseline to determine abnormal behavior or anomalies.
- A honeypot is a server designed to look valuable to an attacker but doesn't actually contain anything valuable. It is created to divert an attacker from valuable resources and can also be used to observe an attacker's methodologies.
- A honeynet is a network of honeypot servers.
- A passive response IDS will log activity and often notify administrators of events through methods such as email or paging.
- An active response IDS will also change the environment by taking actions such as modifying ACLs on routers or firewalls and closing sessions or processes.

Remote Access

- Remote access can be achieved via dial-up or virtual private networks (VPNs).
- A VPN allows access to a private network over a public network such as the Internet.
- VPNs use tunneling protocols such as PPTP and L2TP. PPTP uses port 1723, and L2TP uses port 1701. Neither PPTP nor L2TP by itself will encrypt data within a tunnel.
- IPSec is used to encrypt L2TP. IPSec includes an Authentication Header (AH) and Encapsulating Security Payload (ESP) for authentication and encryption, respectively. AH is identified with protocol ID 51, and ESP is identified with protocol ID 50.
- IPSec is not compatible with NAT.
- RADIUS and TACACS/TACACS+ are often used for authentication of network access clients. RADIUS only encrypts the password, while TACACS+ will encrypt the entire authentication process.
- Network access control includes authentication, remote access policies, and inspection and control elements.
- Gateway-to-gateway VPNs allow multiple clients in remote locations to access resources in a main location, such as remote offices accessing resources at headquarters. Gateway-to-gateway VPNs are transparent to the users.
- Network access policies (sometimes called remote access policies) are used to control who can and who cannot connect to remote access servers.

Wireless Networking

- IEEE 802.11 protocols identify different wireless standards.
- Security protocols include WEP, WPA, and WPA2. WEP was cracked, and WPA was released as an interim measure. WPA was cracked in November 2008. WPA2 is a final standard.
- WEP and WPA used the less secure RC4 stream cipher encryption. WPA2 uses the more secure AES.

- Security protocols can be combined with authentication methods to mitigate the success of attacks on wireless networks.
- The SSID is the network name of a wireless network. SSIDs should be changed from the default, and SSID broadcasting should be disabled.
- Bluetooth is used for personal area networks (PANs).
- Bluesnarfing is the unauthorized access to or theft of information from a Bluetooth device.
- Bluejacking is the unauthorized sending of text messages from a Bluetooth device.
- Discovery mode allows attackers to find and exploit Bluetooth. After devices are connected and paired on a Bluetooth network, they should be placed into non-discovery mode.

Practice Questions

1. What are some weaknesses of a HIDS over a NIDS?

    A. A HIDS is not able to detect network attacks but improves overall performance.

    B. A HIDS is not able to detect network attacks and has a negative impact on the host's performance.

    C. A HIDS can't easily detect attacks on web servers and has a negative impact on the host's performance.

    D. A HIDS can easily detect attacks on web servers and improves overall performance.

2. You are preparing to implement an anomaly-based IDS. What should be created first?

    A. A behavior-based database

    B. Heuristics

    C. A baseline

    D. A database of signatures or definitions

3. You have installed a new suite of software applications on a system. When does this require the creation of a new baseline?

    A. When the HIDS is behavior-based

    B. When the HIDS is signature-based

    C. When the NIDS is signature-based

    D. When the NIPS are signature-based

4. You want to monitor the activity of an application on a server. What should you use?

    A. NIDS

    B. NIPS

    C. HIDS

    D. NAT

5. Any system has four primary resources: the CPU, memory, disk(s), and NIC(s). What does a HIDS primarily monitor?

    A. CPU

    B. Memory

    C. Disk(s)

    D. NIC(s)

6. You are considering adding an IDS that will detect attacks based on specific network traffic. What type of IDS is this?

    A. NIDS

    B. HIDS

    C. Signature-based

    D. Anomaly-based

7. Which type of IDS provides the most basic detection of attacks?

    A. Signature

    B. NIPS

    C. Heuristic

    D. Anomaly

8. What looks like a collection of servers on a network and is specifically designed to attract attackers?

    A. NIDS

    B. Honeypot

    C. Honeynet

    D. Virtual honey

9. What's the purpose of a honeypot? (Choose two.)

    A. Allow security professionals an opportunity to observe attacks

    B. Divert attackers from the live environment

    C. Divert attackers to the live environment

    D. Allow attackers an opportunity to practice attacks

10. What is a primary difference between TACACS+ and RADIUS?

   A. TACACS+ encrypts the entire authentication process, but RADIUS only encrypts the password.

   B. RADIUS encrypts the entire authentication process, but TACACS+ only encrypts the password.

   C. RADIUS can interact with Kerberos, but TACACS+ cannot.

   D. TACACS+ is generic, while RADIUS is proprietary.

11. What is RADIUS?

   A. A VPN service used for tunneling

   B. An authentication mechanism used for dial-up and other connections

   C. An encryption protocol used with remote access servers

   D. A remote access server that is proprietary to Cisco

12. Which of the following are tunneling protocols used for VPN connections? (Choose all that apply.)

   A. PPP

   B. NNTP

   C. SMTP

   D. PPTP

   E. L2TP

   F. FTP

13. What prevents IPSec from working in some VPN tunnels?

   A. L2TP

   B. PPTP

   C. NAT

   D. DNS

14. Employees are accessing the internal network from remote locations, such as their homes or hotel rooms while on business trips. What can be used to secure these connections?

   A. PPP

   B. L2TP

C. IPSec

D. ECC

15. A VPN provides access to a private network over what?

A. An intranet

B. The Internet

C. An extranet

D. A DMZ

16. Users in a remote office are able to access server resources at the headquarters LAN without taking any additional steps using a VPN model that is transparent to the users. What VPN model is being used?

A. PPTP VPN

B. L2TP VPN

C. Host-to-gateway VPN

D. Gateway-to-gateway VPN

17. What would be used to control which users can connect to an internal network while traveling?

A. Remote access policy

B. L2TP

C. PPTP

D. RAS authentication

18. What can be done to reduce the risk that an 802.11 network will be automatically discovered?

A. Enabling the SSID broadcast

B. Disabling the SSID broadcast

C. Changing the default administrator password for the WAP

D. Renaming the default SSID

19. What is an SSID?

A. A security identifier for a user or group

B. The security protocol used with wireless

C. A tool used to exploit NetStumbler

D. The network name used to identify a wireless network

20. Of the following, what could be used to secure a wireless network? (Choose all that apply.)

A. WEP

B. WPA

C. WPA2

D. WLAN

21. Which of the following choices would provide the highest level of protection for a wireless network?

A. WPA and authentication

B. WPA2 and identification

C. WEP and authentication

D. WPA and disabling SSID broadcast

22. Which of the following are known threats or vulnerabilities related to Bluetooth technologies? (Choose all that apply.)

A. Bluejacking

B. Bluesnarfing

C. Discovery mode

D. Broadcasting SSID

Practice Question Answers

1. **B.** A host-based IDS (HIDS) is not able to detect network attacks, and the HIDS can have a negative impact on the host's performance. Since the HIDS is software running on the host, it consumes resources and will not improve overall performance. A HIDS would be good for detecting attacks on individual servers such as web or database servers.

2. **C.** An anomaly-based IDS (also known as a behavior-based IDS) requires a baseline to be created. The baseline identifies normal behavior, and the IDS can constantly compare current behavior against the baseline to determine if any significant anomalies are occurring. Antivirus software can use heuristics to detect malware that doesn't have a signature. A signature-based IDS uses a database of signatures or definitions.

3. **A.** Behavior-based (or anomaly-based) IDSs require the baseline to be recreated when the environment changes significantly, such as when installing new software. Signature-based IDSs use a database of signatures or definitions and don't require the use of a baseline.

4. **C.** A host-based intrusion detection system (HIDS) could be used to monitor activity on a server. NIDS and NIPS would be used to monitor activity on the network. NAT is used to translate IP addresses from public to private, not monitor activity.

5. **D.** A host-based IDS (HIDS) is used to monitor network intrusions on a host and would primarily monitor the network interface card (NIC). While other resources can be monitored by the HIDS, network traffic is the primary focus.

6. **C.** A signature-based IDS will detect attacks based on specific network traffic; the specific traffic is interpreted as patterns and defined in a signature database. Both HIDS and NIDS can be either signature-based or anomaly-based.

An anomaly-based IDS starts with a baseline and identifies traffic patterns that significantly deviate from the baseline.

7. **A.** A signature-based (or definition-based) IDS is the most basic form of detecting attacks. NIPS is an advanced implementation of NIDS. Heuristic is an advanced method used to detect malware and used by antivirus software. An anomaly-based IDS is more advanced than signature-based and more complex.

8. **C.** A honeynet is a group of virtual servers designed to attract an attacker to divert him from a live network and allow the attack to be observed. A honeypot is a single server for the same purpose. A NIDS is used to monitor the network and detect attacks. There is no such thing as virtual honey in IT security.

9. **A, B.** The two purposes of a honeypot are to allow security professionals an opportunity to observe attacks and divert attackers away from the live environment. You don't want to divert attackers to your live environment or allow them to practice their attacks.

10. **A.** A benefit of Terminal Access Controller Access-Control System+ (TACACS+) over Remote Authentication Dial-In User Service (RADIUS) is that TACACS+ encrypts the entire authentication process, but RADIUS only encrypts the password. TACACS+ can interact with Kerberos, but RADIUS cannot. RADIUS is generic, and TACACS+ is proprietary to Cisco.

11. **B.** Remote Authentication Dial-In User Service (RADIUS) is an authentication mechanism used for dial-up and VPNs. It is not dedicated to only VPNs and is much more common with dial-up. It encrypts the password but doesn't encrypt any data or even the entire authentication process. RADIUS is generic, while TACACS+ is proprietary to Cisco.

12. **D, E.** Point-to-Point Tunneling Protocol (PPTP) and Layer 2 Tunneling Protocol (L2TP) are tunneling protocols used for VPN connections. Point-to-Point Protocol (PPP) is used for dial-up connections and doesn't create a tunnel.

Network News Transfer Protocol (NNTP), Simple Mail Transport Protocol (SMTP), and File Transfer Protocol (FTP) all are not tunneling protocols.

13. **C.** Network Address Translation (NAT) and IPSec are not compatible due to the changes made to the IP header by NAT. L2TP is commonly used with IPSec (and shown as L2TP/IPSec). PPTP uses MPPE, not IPSec. DNS is used to resolve host names to IP addresses and goes through port 53.

14. **C.** IPSec is an encryption protocol that can be used to secure these connections. The connections are remote access connections and can be either dial-up or VPN connections. Dial-up would use PPP, but PPP isn't encrypted by itself. L2TP is a tunneling protocol but isn't encrypted by itself. IPSec is commonly used with L2TP and provides encryption for the L2TP/IPSec connection. ECC is an encryption protocol used with wireless devices but isn't used in remote access scenarios.

15. **B.** A VPN provides access to a private network over a public network such as the Internet. The private network is the intranet. An extranet provides access to a limited number of resources to trusted business partners. A DMZ provides protection to Internet-facing servers that are accessible to any clients on the Internet.

16. **D.** A gateway-to-gateway VPN model is transparent to the end users and allows them to access resources in the distant end network without taking any additional steps. A host-to-gateway VPN model is where an end user directly connects to the VPN server to access the back-end network and isn't transparent to the user. PPTP and L2TP are tunneling protocols used in both host-to-gateway and gateway-to-gateway VPN models and aren't considered VPN models themselves.

17. **A.** A remote access policy can be used to control which users can connect to a remote access server, such as those who may try to connect while traveling or from home. L2TP and PPTP are two common tunneling protocols used with VPNs. RAS authentication is implemented to allow users to prove who they

are; after authentication, a remote access policy can be used to control who can connect.

18. **B.** Disabling SSID broadcasting on a WAP will prevent the WAP from being automatically discovered. SSID broadcasting is typically enabled by default but should be disabled after clients are connected and configured. Changing the default administrator password for the WAP is a good security practice but doesn't affect the WAP's discoverability.

19. **D.** A Service Set Identifier (SSID) is used to identify an 802.11 wireless network. Security identifiers are used to identify users or groups. WEP, WPA, and WPA2 are security protocols used with wireless networks. NetStumbler is a war driving tool used to discover wireless networks.

20. **A, B, C.** WEP, WPA, and WPA2 are security protocols that can be used to secure wireless networks. WEP was used first but had significant vulnerabilities. WPA was released as an interim fix, and WPA2 was released as a permanent fix. WLAN is a wireless local area network.

21. **A.** Combining a strong security protocol with an authentication system will mitigate the chances of a successful attack against a wireless network. WPA combined with authentication is the best answer given. While WPA2 is a stronger security protocol, it isn't paired with authentication. Identification is not the same as authentication. WEP is the weakest security protocol. Disabling SSID broadcasting is a good security precaution, but the SSID is discoverable with war driving tools such as NetStumbler.

22. **A, B, C.** Bluejacking, bluesnarfing, and discovery mode are known threats. Bluesnarfing is the unauthorized access to or theft of information from a Bluetooth device. Bluejacking is the unauthorized sending of text messages from a Bluetooth device. Discovery mode allows attackers to find and exploit Bluetooth; devices should instead be placed into non-discovery mode after pairing. A broadcasting SSID is a vulnerability for an 802.11 wireless network, but not Bluetooth.

Chapter 5

Securing Your Servers and Network Devices

CompTIA Security+ objectives covered in this chapter

1.1 Differentiate among various systems security threats.

- Privilege escalation

1.2 Explain the security risks pertaining to system hardware and peripherals.

- BIOS

1.3 Implement OS hardening practices and procedures to achieve workstation and server security.

- Hotfixes
- Service packs
- Patches
- Patch management
- Group policies
- Security templates
- Configuration baselines

1.4 Carry out the appropriate procedures to establish application security.

- ActiveX
- Java
- Scripting
- Browser
- Buffer overflows
- Cookies
- SMTP open relays
- Instant messaging
- Input validation
- Cross-site scripting (XSS)

1.5 Implement security applications.

- Antivirus
- Anti-spam
- Popup blockers

1.6 Explain the purpose and application of virtualization technology.

2.1 Differentiate between the different ports & protocols, their respective threats and mitigation techniques.

- DNS poisoning

2.5 Explain the vulnerabilities and mitigations associated with network devices.

- Privilege escalation
- Weak passwords
- Back doors
- Default accounts
- DOS

3.4 Apply appropriate security controls to file and print resources.

4.4 Use monitoring tools on systems and networks and detect security-related anomalies.

- Performance monitor
- Systems monitor
- Performance baseline

5.4 Explain and implement protocols.

- SSL/TLS
- HTTP vs. HTTPS vs. SHTTP

* * *

This chapter focuses on hardening servers and network devices. There are several core steps you can follow to secure any server, and these steps can be streamlined by using baselines. Once the core system is hardened, you can also take additional steps to harden or secure specific servers such as web servers and mail servers. Last, virtualization is presented with some tips on how it can be used to help security professionals perform testing within an isolated environment.

Hardening a System

Hardening a system is the practice of making it more secure from the default installation. Hardening a server or workstation includes the following primary steps:

- Change defaults
- Eliminate unneeded protocols, services, and software
- Enable a software firewall
- Keep the system up-to-date

The first three steps are often implemented through the use of a security baseline. Multiple security baselines can be implemented, such as one for end-user systems, another for generic servers, and another for specialized servers.

Security is maintained on systems by using different methodologies to ensure that the operating system and software are kept up-to-date.

Additionally, each group of servers requires extra steps to keep them secure. For example, FTP servers, email servers, and DNS servers all require additional steps to secure them after the initial operating system has been installed and secured.

> ### Remember
> The key steps to harden a workstation or a server are to change defaults; eliminate unneeded protocols, services, and software; and enable the software firewall. Additionally, the system must be kept up-to-date by installing patches and hotfixes after they have been released and tested.

Changing Defaults

Many systems come with default passwords for key accounts, default accounts, and even enabled back doors. A basic principle in hardening a system is to change these defaults as soon as the system is installed.

Default Accounts and Passwords

As an example, Windows systems have two default accounts: Administrator and Guest. Best practices with these accounts include:

- **Rename the Administrator account**. Most accounts are subject to lockout policies; if the wrong password is entered a certain number of times (such as three or five), then the account will be locked. However, the Administrator account cannot be locked out. By renaming the Administrator account, attackers are prevented from guessing this account's password.

- **Disable the Guest account**. The Guest account provides only limited access, and anyone using this account won't be authenticated. This account is rarely enabled. It is disabled by default in current implementations of Windows.

Wireless devices come with predefined accounts and passwords. For example, some Linksys wireless routers come with an Administrator account named "admin" and a password of "admin." Unless this password is changed, an attacker can easily break into the network and cause considerable damage.

So Easy, a Ten-Year-Old Can Do It

A video was circulating on the Internet a while ago showing a ten-year-old hacking into his neighbors' wireless network. He was successful only because the default administrator password wasn't changed.

The neighbors had the same wireless router that was being used in the boy's home. He turned off his wireless access point (WAP) and connected to the neighbors' using the defaults shown in the manual. He then made a few changes to their WAP, effectively locking them out but allowing him access.

Locking the neighbors out of their own network was humorous to this ten-year-old. However, a war driving attacker could do much more damage. If the defaults aren't changed in a network, just about anyone with a manual or some basic knowledge of defaults can break in.

Eliminate Back Doors

A back door is an access to an application or service that bypasses normal security mechanisms. Back doors are often used by developers for legitimate means to view the internal workings of an application or for ease of administration. Some malware will purposely open up back doors with the express purpose of later exploiting the system.

Back doors have been widely used in the past. For example, Microsoft's NT 4.0 server products included several server applications, such as Microsoft Exchange and Microsoft SQL Server, that were collectively known as Back Office.

Back Office included several back doors that were exploited. Attackers created a program specifically designed to exploit these back doors in Back Office and named it Back Orifice.

NetBus is another program developed to exploit back doors in Microsoft systems. NetBus exploited back doors in Windows 95, 98, and NT.

While the use of back doors is largely discouraged in most released software today, some developers still do use back doors. If you learn of them, they should be closed whenever possible.

BIOS Settings

It's also possible to lock the Basic Input/Output System (BIOS) for a system. The BIOS are the system's firmware and are used to configure basic settings such as which device the system will try to boot from.

Most BIOS can be password protected. Password-protected BIOS will prevent personnel from accessing the BIOS and changing different control settings.

However, this password provides only limited protection. A knowledgeable technician with unrestricted physical access to the system can open the box and reset this password by manipulating a jumper on the motherboard.

Remove Unnecessary Services, Protocols, and Software

A core principle associated with hardening a workstation or server includes removing all unnecessary services, protocols, and software. This is often referred to as reducing the attack surface of the system.

If a service is not running, it can't be attacked. If a protocol is not installed, it can't be attacked. On the other hand, if unneeded services, protocols, and software are running on a system, it's highly unlikely they are being actively managed, and they may even be left with the default configuration. Attacks on unmanaged services and protocols may not even be noticed.

> **Remember**
> Removing unnecessary services, protocols, and software reduces the overall attack surface of a system. If a protocol has been removed or a service disabled, it is no longer susceptible to an attack. Nonessential services and protocols that are running often aren't managed or correctly configured, and attacks may go unnoticed.

Microsoft took the concept of reducing the attack surface a step further in a version of Windows Server 2008 called Server Core. Server Core includes only the most basic operating system components to reduce the attack surface. It doesn't even include a GUI but instead only presents a command-line interface.

Eliminate Unnecessary Services and Protocols

Chapter 3 included information on many of the protocols with a focus on TCP/IP protocols. Some protocols, like TCP, UDP, IP, and ARP, are absolutely necessary for connectivity within a TCP/IP network.

Other protocols, like HTTP, SMTP, NNTP, FTP, and more, are application protocols and only need to be running to support the underlying service. If the server is a web server, it needs HTTP. If the server is an email server, it needs SMTP. However, an email server doesn't necessarily need HTTP, and a web server doesn't necessarily need SMTP.

The point is that all of the services and protocols should be examined to determine if there is a need for them to be running on each server or workstation. If the protocol is needed to support the system, leave it running. If it is not needed, ensure the service is disabled and/or the protocol is removed.

Similarly, antiquated protocols such as IPX/SPX and NetBEUI are rarely needed and should only be enabled to support a specific need.

Eliminate Unneeded Software

Just as unnecessary services and protocols should not be running, unneeded software should be uninstalled from systems. Software frequently has bugs and vulnerabilities that appear. While patching software will frequently close these vulnerabilities, if the software is not running at all, the vulnerability simply doesn't exist.

Years ago, I was working at a small training company. One of the servers had a default installation of Windows 2000. We were using the server as a file server, but since it wasn't hardened from the default installation of Windows 2000, it was also running Internet Information Services (IIS), Microsoft's web server.

Then, the Nimda virus was released into the wild—active and spreading on the Internet. Microsoft released a patch for IIS, but since IIS was installed by default and we weren't using it, we also weren't managing it. Ultimately, the Nimda virus found our server, and the worm component of Nimda quickly infected our network.

If the IIS software hadn't been installed, the server wouldn't have been vulnerable to the attack. The same goes for unneeded services and protocols. By only running what is needed, the attack surface is significantly reduced.

Enable a Software Firewall

Most operating systems include software firewalls that operate as software on the system. Software firewalls are also called personal firewalls when running on workstations. For a more detailed explanation of the different types of firewalls, see Chapter 3.

A software firewall operates as an additional application on a system to provide an added layer of protection. It can be especially effective at mitigating the effectiveness of malware that is released within a network. The only drawback is that it takes additional processing power from the operating system.

Use Baselines

A baseline is a known starting point. In the context of the CompTIA Security+ exam, two baselines are important:

- **Security baseline.** A security baseline is a secure starting point for any system or group of systems that can be deployed through imaging or Group Policy. It can be used to perform the basic hardening steps of changing the defaults, removing unnecessary protocols and services, and enabling firewalls.
- **Performance baseline.** A performance baseline is a measurement of performance for a system including the core resources of processor, memory, disk, and network. Performance Monitor is used on Microsoft systems to create performance baselines.

Security Baselines

A security baseline is a secure starting point for an operating system. The first step in creating the security baseline is creating the written security policy. Once the policy is created, different methods can be used to deploy the baseline.

> ### Remember
> The first step in creating a security baseline is creating the security policy. The security policy identifies what should be locked down in a system.

Creating the security policy is no trivial matter. It can take months to identify all the elements that should be locked in a system.

A security baseline can be used to enforce the basics of hardening a system, such as:

- **Changing defaults.** Administrator or Guest accounts can be renamed or disabled. Users can be forced to change default passwords.

- **Eliminating unneeded services, protocols, and software**. Unnecessary services such as telnet can be disabled. Antiquated protocols can be removed. Unneeded applications such as games or other software found to be risky can be removed.
- **Enabling a software firewall**. Software firewalls can be enabled and configured for proper operation. Configuration could include ensuring the firewall will accept updates from a patch-management server or is configured for remote administration.

By including these basic steps in the baseline, all deployed systems start in a secure configuration. Common methods of deploying security baseline settings are imaging and Group Policy.

- **Imaging**. Imaging tools such as Symantec's Ghost can be used to capture an image of a reference computer, and this image can then be deployed to other computers.
- **Group Policy**. Group policy objects (GPOs) can be created and linked with a Microsoft domain environment so that any computer that joins the domain automatically receives these settings. Multiple GPOs can be deployed within a domain to meet differing needs.

These methods can be used individually to create a baseline or together to provide a more comprehensive baseline solution. The image would be used to create the system with a starting baseline, and Group Policy can be used to provide ongoing maintenance and implement changes to the baseline.

Several security baselines could exist within an IT environment. End-user operating systems could be created with a single baseline; generic servers could be created with another baseline; and specialty servers could be locked down with more defined baselines.

Imaging

The process of creating an image includes installing the operating system, installing and configuring any desired applications, and modifying security settings. Once the system is configured exactly the way you want the deployed system to be configured, the system is prepared and the image is captured.

Once the image is captured, it can be deployed to multiple computers with only minimal tweaking required afterwards.

Imaging provides two important benefits:

- **Secure starting point**. Personnel who deploy the system don't need to remember or follow detailed checklists to ensure that new systems are set up with all the detailed configuration and security settings. The deployed image retains all the settings of the original image. Additional settings, such as the computer name, can be configured after the image is deployed.

- **Reduce TCO**. Total cost of ownership (TCO) is reduced when the systems are deployed identically. Support personnel don't need to learn multiple different end-user system environments; instead, they learn just one. Each system they troubleshoot is created and maintained in the same way, allowing support personnel to focus on the problem at hand.

Once systems are deployed with an image, they are often joined to a domain, and Group Policy is used to provide additional security or configuration settings.

Group Policy

Group Policy is used within Windows 2000 and later domains to manage computers and users within a domain environment. The magic of Group Policy is that a setting can be configured one time and easily deployed to many users or computers within the domain.

Settings are created within group policy objects (GPOs), and a GPO is linked to a site, domain, or Organizational Unit (OU). Once the GPO is linked, it applies to all the users and computers located in the site, domain, or OU.

There are literally hundreds of security settings in a GPO and thousands of overall configuration settings. Just a few of the possibilities with GPOs include:

- Enforce password policies
- Enforce lockout policies
- Restrict installation of device drivers
- Restrict use of portable devices
- Configure different applications such as Internet Explorer
- Deploy applications
- Restrict the use of applications

As an example, if you wanted to ensure that all users in a domain followed a specific password policy (minimum length, complex, changed regularly, and so on), a GPO could be created and linked to the domain. The policy would enforce the settings for all users in the domain.

Similarly, a GPO can ensure that basic hardening rules are enforced after deployment. While imaging will ensure that the system is deployed with a certain standard, the GPO can ensure that deployed systems continue with the same settings. If changes are attempted on any systems, the GPO will bring them back into compliance.

Default Policies

Two group policy objects exist within Microsoft domains by default. These GPOs can be modified, and additional GPOs can be created as needed. The two default GPOs are:

- **Default Domain Policy.** This policy is linked to the domain and applies to all users and computers in the domain. It includes many default security and configuration settings, but any of these can be modified, and changes will automatically be deployed to users and computers in the domain.
- **Default Domain Controller Policy.** This GPO is linked to the Domain Controllers OU. When a server is promoted to a domain controller, the associated Active Directory computer object is placed in the Domain Controllers OU, so the Default Domain Controller Policy will control the settings on all domain controllers in the domain.

Security Templates

Security templates are used as starting points for security settings. They can be used as part of Group Policy to ensure that systems start with a common security configuration. When modified, they can be used to ensure that all servers comply with a company's security policy.

GPOs include hundreds of security settings. It's difficult for any single administrator to learn and know all the possible security settings. Microsoft has provided many different security templates that can be used to address different needs. Any of the available templates can easily be copied and modified to create additional templates.

These templates are preconfigured with different levels of security by enabling different security settings. By importing a security template into a GPO and applying the GPO to a site, domain, or OU, all of the users and computers are quickly brought up to a common security level.

Security templates include the following sections:

- **Account Policies**. Includes password and lockout policy settings.
- **Local Policies**. Includes many detailed user rights settings.
- **Restricted Groups**. Used to automate the control of group membership such as the administrators and Domain Admins groups.
- **System Services**. Used to enable and disable specific services. Any service can be set to start manually, start automatically, or be disabled.
- **Software Restrictions**. Only specific software can be allowed to run on a system, or specific software can be prevented from running. For example, specific games can be prevented from running on computers.

Configuration Baseline

A configuration baseline is a starting point for the configuration of a system. It is used to specify a set of consistent requirements or a standard load for a system. Configuration baselines are often combined with security baselines.

The differences between a configuration baseline and a security baseline can be a little fuzzy. The purpose of the security baseline settings is strictly security related. The purpose of the configuration baseline settings is for consistent operation. However, since the configuration baseline contributes to improved availability of a system (part of the security triad), it also contributes to overall security.

Some examples of configuration baseline settings include:

- Desktop background and screen saver
- Configuration of printers and shares
- Configuration of applications such as Internet Explorer

Remember

Configuration baselines can be used to ensure that all systems have a standard load. In other words, all systems would have similar settings and applications installed in a standard manner. Standardization makes it easy for help-desk professionals to troubleshoot and reduces overall maintenance costs, since they don't need to relearn each system they troubleshoot.

Performance Baseline

A performance baseline is used to identify the overall performance of a system at a point in time. Later, if performance deteriorates, current measurements can be captured and compared against the baseline. The differences between the current measurements and the baseline help an administrator to quickly identify a problem.

Any system has four primary resources: processor, memory, disk, and NIC. The overall performance of a system can often be tracked by measuring these four resources. Specialized systems, such as a server configured as a database server, will have additional resources that can be measured beyond the four core resources.

- **Processor.** The processor metric shows how busy the processor is over time. Normally, a processor's performance is relatively stable. However, during an attack, the processor may become much busier and even peak at 100 percent.
- **Memory.** Systems love memory as much as a child loves candy. It's often possible to increase the performance of a system significantly by adding more memory that a system can use. Since 32-bit operating systems are limited to 4 GB, adding more than 4 GB won't provide better performance for most 32-bit systems.
- **Disk.** Disk subsystems can load down a system by generating heavy I/O on the disks. Adding different types of RAIDs can improve the performance of the disk subsystem while also providing fault tolerance.
- **NIC.** The NIC handles all the network traffic. Monitoring the NIC can give you insight into the network utilization metric: the ratio of current network traffic to the maximum traffic allowed on the NIC. For example, if there is 10 MB of traffic regularly on a 100 MB NIC, the network utilization is 10 percent.

In Chapter 4, different types of intrusion detection systems (IDSs) were covered. As a reminder, an anomaly-based IDS will first use a baseline to determine normal operation and can compare current operation with the baseline. This comparison of the performance metrics will allow the IDS to detect an attack.

Two tools within Windows systems often used to view system performance are Performance Monitor and Task Manager.

> ### Remember
> Performance baselines can be used to detect performance degradation or abnormalities that may be associated with an attack. Tools such as Performance Monitor and Task Manager can be used to measure basic system resources such as processor, memory, disk, and the NIC.

Performance Monitor

Performance Monitor in Windows systems is used to create performance baselines. A performance baseline will often capture snapshots of the key metrics every thirty minutes throughout a seven-day period. These snapshots will give a good picture of a system's performance during peak performance times and slack times.

It's also possible to keep the Performance Monitor running regularly to keep a running tally of current performance.

Task Manager

Task Manager is a tool that can often detect anomalies on a system. It can be launched by pressing the CTRL + SHIFT + ESC keys. Task Manager includes key metrics that can be used to easily view details of the performance of a system.

Figure 5.1 shows Task Manager with the Performance tab selected. Other tabs allow you to view various metrics on the system.

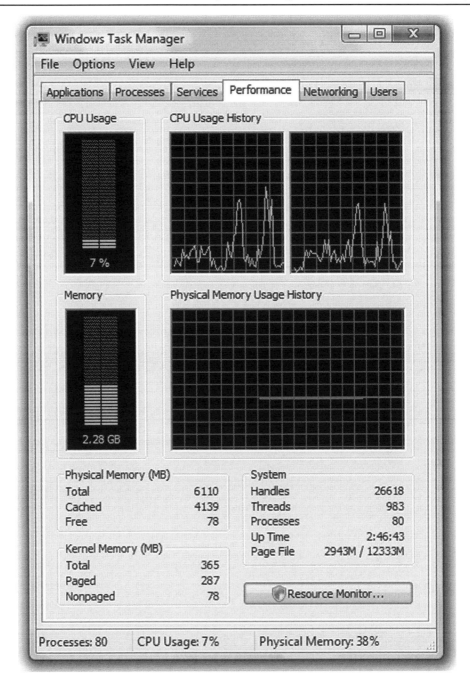

Figure 5.1: Task Manager

When a system is infected with malware, the performance of the system often slows down significantly. Task Manager will show the CPU usage spiking and perhaps even approaching 100 percent. The Processes tab can be used to identify processes that may be consuming most of the resources and can even be used to end the processes.

Identifying high-usage processes and researching their names on the Internet is one method that can be used to identify malware that has infected a system. For example, the Processes tab may show the kernel32.exe process consuming a significant amount of system resources. A Google search on kernel32.exe shows this is a known virus.

Note that the kernel32.**dll** file is a valid system file and shouldn't be deleted. The malware author named the virus similarly (with the extension of **.exe** instead of **.dll**) to add an element of confusion and discourage users from deleting it.

Keeping the System Up-to-date

Software is not secure. There. I said it. As someone who's written a few programs over the years, it's not easy to say. In a perfect world, all bugs, exploits, and vulnerabilities would be discovered through extensive testing before any operating system or application is released. However, since an operating system is composed of millions of lines of code, testing simply doesn't find all the problems.

Instead, most companies make a best effort to test software, and then as problems are discovered, updates are released. Updates can be deployed as patches, hotfixes, or service packs.

Patches

A patch is a small piece of code used to correct a single bug or vulnerability discovered in an operating system or application. Patches are released as software problems are discovered. Since bugs and vulnerabilities can be discovered at any time, it's important to regularly check for patches to ensure a system is kept up-to-date.

Think of a bicycle tire. When the tire gets a puncture and goes flat, you don't replace the entire tire, but instead apply a small patch to fix it. This is very similar to a patch applied to operating systems or applications. A patch is a small piece of code used to correct a problem.

Microsoft releases patches on the second Tuesday of the month, and this is sometimes referred to as Patch Tuesday. Patches can be applied directly to end-user computers or via other patch-management software.

Occasionally, an emerging threat results in an out-of-cycle patch release, where Microsoft doesn't wait until the next Patch Tuesday, but instead releases a patch earlier.

Hotfixes

A hotfix is also a small update similar to a patch. The actual difference between a hotfix and a patch isn't clearly defined, and each means different things to different vendors. The terms *hotfix* and *hotfixes* have been used to describe:

- Patches that can be applied without a reboot
- Patches that are intended to address an immediate threat
- Patches intended to address a specific issue for a narrow market (specific customers)

It's not uncommon to see the terms *hotfixes* and *patches* used interchangeably. The important thing to remember is that if a hotfix or a patch is released that applies to your system, it should be tested and applied.

Zero-Day Attack

A zero-day attack is an attack on an undisclosed vulnerability. The vulnerability has been discovered and some people know of it, but the vulnerability isn't widely known or understood yet.

Zero-day attacks come in two forms:

- **The time between when a patch is released and when it is applied**. Some attackers wait until a patch is released, reverse-engineer it to determine the vulnerability, and then exploit the vulnerability on systems that aren't patched. Some users don't automatically patch their systems, and many companies employ testing before deploying the patches, leaving the systems vulnerable until the patch is applied.
- **A vulnerability without a patch**. When a vulnerability is first discovered, there is no patch. As long as the vulnerability remains undisclosed, systems are susceptible to zero-day attacks.

Service Packs

A service pack is a collection of patches and fixes and can also include additional features. The primary purpose of the service pack is to make it easier to apply a large number of patches and fixes to a system to quickly bring it up-to-date.

Service packs are not released on a schedule, but instead, are released when the vendor chooses. This is often related to the number of patches and fixes that have been released or the desire to release a new feature.

Patch Management

Patch management is a group of methodologies used to ensure that all systems within an enterprise are appropriately patched. It can include separate servers used to download and deploy patches or simply to ensure that systems receive patches automatically. Patch management can include:

- **Testing**. Before patches are deployed to multiple computers, the patch should be tested. The worst that can happen when a patch is deployed is that the system no longer works. It's inconvenient if a single system doesn't work after deploying a patch, but it can be catastrophic if a patch takes down hundreds of computers within an enterprise.
- **Applying changes**. Updates can be applied by allowing the clients to connect to a server (either external or internal) or by pushing the updates to the clients through an enterprise-management system.
- **Auditing for changes**. Enterprise-management system software can audit the clients to ensure that the patches have been successfully applied. Unsuccessful updates can be reapplied, and systems that don't accept updates can even be quarantined.

> ### Remember
> A key component of patch-management software is the ability to audit systems to determine if they have the patch applied. It can deploy the patch if needed and then repeat the auditing process to ensure that the patch was successfully applied. Software firewall settings can prevent the successful deployment of patches and should be checked if patches aren't being successfully deployed.

If the same systems are not receiving patches, they should be checked to identify the source of the problem. As a simple example, a software firewall could be enabled on a system, preventing the patches from being successfully deployed. Obviously, if this is the case, the firewall should be configured to allow the patches to be deployed.

Patch-management Tools

Patch-management tools allow the automation of patch deployment. These tools have the ability to query clients in an enterprise, determine what patches are needed, and deploy the patches. Some of the common patch-management tools are:

- **MBSA**. Microsoft Baseline Security Analyzer is used to query one or multiple computers in an enterprise. It can check for current updates and basic vulnerabilities.
- **WSUS**. Windows Server Update Services is a free product that can be used by an administrator to download and approve updates. Approved updates are deployed to administrator-defined groups of computers. The previous version was called Software Update Services.
- **SMS**. Systems Management Server is a server product that can be used to inventory systems and schedule the deployment of patches. The newer version of SMS is known as System Center Configuration Manager.

Other third-party, enterprise-management system tools exist. The basic goals of any of these tools are to be able to determine what systems need the updates, apply the updates, and then audit the systems to ensure that the updates have been successfully applied.

Change Management

Change management includes the different tools and methodologies used to implement changes to a system or network. While changes can include a lot of different changes, they are frequently applied through patching. Changes applied to reconfigure a system or network are more specifically called change configuration management.

The worst enemies of networks have been unrestrained administrators. Changes made by well-meaning administrators often have unexpected devastating results.

A misconfiguration can take down a server, a network, all email communication, and even an entire enterprise. Before IT organizations embraced effective change-management strategies, these self-inflicted disasters were relatively common. Today, most IT organizations employ some type of change management.

> **Remember**
>
> A change-management process should be followed before implementing any new changes to a server, network, or software application. Change management ensures that changes don't have unintended negative effects.

A change-management process ensures that changes aren't completed until the change has been submitted, reviewed, and approved. While change management is important for all IT servers and network devices, it also applies to software applications.

Many companies have adopted change-management practices that have been popularized by the Information Technology Infrastructure Library framework.

Hardening Network Devices

Hardening a network device is making it more secure than the default configuration. Hardening a network device such as router, switch, or firewall follows the same principles of hardening a server.

- Change defaults.
- Remove unneeded services and protocols.
- Keep it up-to-date.

It may not be apparent if you haven't worked with network devices, but they also run software. For example, Cisco devices run the Cisco IOS software as the operating system on its routers and many of its switches. Just as an operating system on any server can have bugs and vulnerabilities, so can the Cisco IOS.

When bugs and vulnerabilities are discovered, Cisco releases patches and updates. So, just as servers and workstations should be kept up-to-date with patches and fixes, so should network devices. As long as the IOS is kept up-to-date, the routers and switches are less susceptible to the vulnerabilities.

Two topics that weren't mentioned in the server section but are in the objectives for network devices are:

- Privilege escalation
- Denial-of-service (DoS)

Privilege Escalation

Privilege escalation occurs when a vulnerability allows a user or process access to elevated permissions.

As an example, the Cisco Call Manager application used in telephony solutions had a privilege escalation issue. Under certain conditions, users granted read-only access were able to gain administrative access. This allowed an attacker to pose as a regular user but perform administrative tasks.

Cisco quickly released a patch, and as long as systems were kept up-to-date, the vulnerability could not be exploited.

Malware frequently tries to exploit privilege escalation vulnerabilities if they exist and are not patched. Chapter 6 will cover malware in much more depth.

Denial-of-service

A denial-of-service (DoS) is an attack on a system designed to prevent it from performing a service. DoS attacks can be launched against servers, hosts, and network devices.

Many DoS attacks against routers and switches attempt to overwhelm the device by flooding it with packets. Some attacks will send specific commands to the device in an attempt to cause it to reset.

When specific DoS attacks occur, or vulnerabilities to DoS attacks are discovered, vendors of network devices will release updates to the network device software. Keeping network devices up-to-date is a core requirement to protect against DoS attacks.

Chapter 4 covered different intrusion detection systems that can detect and mitigate DoS attacks. Chapter 6 will cover both DoS and distributed DoS (DDoS) attacks in more depth.

Hardening Server Applications

Any server should be hardened following the basics of changing defaults; eliminating unneeded protocols, services, and software; enabling software firewalls; and keeping the system up-to-date. Some servers also require some extra steps. In this section, you'll learn about some specific issues to consider with:

- Web servers
- Mail servers
- File and print servers
- DNS servers
- Domain controllers
- Instant messaging
- Virtualization

Web Servers

Web servers are used to host and serve web pages and web sites. The two primary server applications used for web servers are:

- **Apache.** Apache is the most popular web server used on the Internet. It's free and can run on UNIX and Linux platforms, which are also free; Apache has also been ported to Windows. Free is good, but Apache is a solid product too.
- **Internet Information Services (IIS)**. IIS is Microsoft's web server, and it's included with any server product.

Web servers most commonly host web sites accessible on the Internet. A web server serving Internet content would usually be placed within a DMZ to provide a layer of protection.

It's also possible for a web server to host content used only internally by employees. When used internally, it would be placed on the intranet and not be accessible from the Internet.

Since web servers are easily accessible on the Internet and highly susceptible to attacks, there are multiple issues to consider when securing a web server. These issues include protocols, buffer overflow attacks, ActiveX controls and Java applets, scripting, and the use of web browsers.

Web Server Protocols

Web servers are primarily used to serve web pages in the HyperText Markup Language (HTML) format. The protocols used to deliver the HTML pages over the Internet are:

- **HTTP**. Hypertext Transfer Protocol is an Application layer protocol used to deliver content over the Internet. HTTP uses port 80.
- **HTTPS**. Hypertext Transfer Protocol over Secure Socket Layer is the most common secure implementation of HTTP. Data is encrypted using SSL. SSL operates on the Session layer of the OSI model and uses port 443 to encrypt HTTP traffic. SSL will be explored in more depth in Chapter 9.
- **SHTTP**. Secure Hypertext Transfer Protocol is an alternate method of encrypting HTTP traffic. However, just as Blu-Ray DVDs won the war over HD DVDs, HTTPS won the war over SHTTP. You won't see many HD DVD players or HD DVDs around anymore, and you also won't see many sites using SHTTP.

A web server listens on ports 80 and 443 for HTTP and HTTPS respectively. It's not uncommon to provide protection for the web servers by implementing filters to allow traffic on these two ports only and dropping all other traffic.

Buffer Overflow

A buffer overflow occurs when an attacker sends more input, or different input, to an application that is unexpected. The data causes erratic behavior and allows the attacker to access the internal buffer and insert malware. The unexpected input could be as simple as sending a negative number when a positive number is expected.

An application will normally be programmed to reject the unexpected data, but occasionally, a bug is discovered where a specific string of data can be sent to the application, resulting in erratic behavior. The application gets overloaded, and the attack allows access to areas of memory called a buffer.

The buffer is normally accessed by manipulating the memory's internal heaps and stacks. After the attack, the memory is infected with the malware, which can now infect any user that accesses the application.

Buffer overflow attacks are one of the most common exploits against Internet-facing servers, and web servers are commonly attacked. When a bug is discovered, the best thing to do is patch the server as quickly as possible.

Buffer overflows have a better chance at being prevented if application developers take the following steps:

- **Perform significant testing and code review**. Specifically, checking for data input outside the bounds of expected data often discovers this vulnerability. A simple example of bounds testing is checking to see what happens if five numbers are input but only four numbers are expected.
- **Perform input validation**. Input validation checks that data is within the scope of what is expected. For example, a number less than 1000 may be expected, but a user may enter a number greater than 1000. Input validation will determine if the value is outside what is expected and not use it.

When buffer overflows are detected, vendors are usually quick to release a patch or hotfix. From an administrator's perspective, the solution is easy—keep the servers up-to-date.

Remember

Buffer overflow attacks are caused by an application receiving unexpected data. Keeping servers up-to-date is the single best protection against buffer overflow attacks after the software has been deployed. Code testing, code review, and input validation are some techniques performed by developers to prevent buffer overflow vulnerabilities from occurring.

ActiveX Controls and Java Applets

Web sites earn money through advertising. When you or I click on an ad, the web site hosting the ad earns money. Ads have different rates, but it's possible for a click-through ad to earn a web site ten cents. If a web site can get 1 percent of the traffic to click on an advertisement, then for every one hundred visitors, the site earns ten cents.

Clearly, a web site needs more than one hundred visitors a day to earn money through advertising. If a web site using these ads attracted ten thousand visitors a day, it could earn $1000 a day. Clearly, that's enough to live on for most of us.

The only way to attract that many visitors is to have a well-developed site with lots of pizzazz. It used to be that content was king. All a web site needed was content, but today, successful web sites have both—pizzazz and content.

ActiveX controls and Java applets give a web site pizzazz. Both are mini-programs designed to provide additional features that add to the visitor's experience, keep her there, and encourage her to come back. Talented developers can use these mini-programs to add significant capabilities to a web site.

Signed Code

The problem with both of these is that attackers can also develop these mini-programs. Instead of adding significant capabilities, attackers can use them to launch significant attacks.

Legitimate software developers can differentiate their mini-programs from malicious code by having them signed. Developers can submit a program to a Certificate Authority (CA) to have it signed. The CA validates the identity of the company submitting the program and creates a digital certificate.

When the mini-program is presented to a web browser, the digital signature is presented. Web browsers can be configured to allow signed programs to run, since their identities can be traced. Unsigned programs can be blocked or prompt the user to determine if they should be downloaded and installed.

Think of this from the attacker's point of view. If an attacker creates malicious code packaged as an ActiveX control or Java applet, it's highly unlikely he will submit it to a CA so that it can be traced back to the attacker. With this in mind, it's common to trust signed code and view unsigned code as suspicious.

> **Remember**
> Systems can be protected from malicious Internet code by only allowing
> signed code to be downloaded and run. Java applets run in Java Virtual
> Machines (JVMs), and JavaScript can be run in a sandbox—both the JVM
> and the sandbox provide some isolation and prevent the program from
> accessing local data.

Java Virtual Machines

Java applets provide an added layer of protection. Java applets will run within a
Java Virtual Machine (JVM). The JVM isolates the applet by only allowing it to run
within a confined environment frequently called a sandbox. The sandbox allows
the applet to run but prevents it from accessing local data. Scripts can also be
configured to run in a controlled environment called a sandbox.

JVMs allow applets to run on multiple platforms (Linux, Windows, and Macs).
While the JVM is different on the different platforms, the Java applet only needs
to be written once.

JavaScript Scripting

Scripting is also both beneficial for legitimate web sites and damaging when
misused by attackers. JavaScript is the most popular script language used on the
Internet.

JavaScript is distinctly different from Java. Java (and Java applets) are compiled
programs. JavaScript is an interpreted language; JavaScript is simple text that will
be read and interpreted when executed.

However, they both share the term *sandbox*. Just as a sandbox is used by JVMs
to isolate the applet and prevent it from accessing local data, a JavaScript script
can also be forced to use a sandbox, providing a layer of protection. Scripts that
run in a sandbox have very limited access to system resources.

Cross-site Scripting (XSS)

Cross-site scripting (XSS) is a web application vulnerability where attackers
are able to gather data from a user, without the user's knowledge. The data is

obtained by passing a hyperlink that contains malicious content. Often, all the user has to do is click the hyperlink to execute the malicious XSS code.

XSS can be used to steal cookies off an end user's system, learn a user's identity, and execute JavaScript on a user's local computer, which will run in the less restrictive local zone.

These attacks are much more common than most people realize. Symantec reported in 2007 that 80 percent of web site vulnerabilities were related to cross-site scripting.

The best protection against cross-site scripting is for web developers to use input validation. In short, web developers should never trust user input but should always check it to ensure it is valid and doesn't include extra data.

Users can protect themselves in two ways:

- **Only follow links within a site**. If a link in one site is taking you to another site, enter the URL directly instead of clicking the URL.
- **Turn off JavaScript except when absolutely needed**. This will prevent the malicious code from being executed and can be done by setting security settings to high in Internet Explorer.

Web Browsers

Users access web sites using web browsers. Many versions of web browsers exist, including Microsoft's Internet Explorer, Firefox, and Google's Chrome. The purpose of any browser is to accept the HTML code from the web server and display it.

Several items worth mentioning related to accessing the Internet with web browsers are cookies, pop-up blockers, antivirus software, and anti-spyware software.

Cookies

A cookie is a text file stored on a user's computer that can be used for multiple purposes, but it is often used to track activity. A tracking cookie is often used by spyware to track a user's activities.

Cookies are intended to only be read by the web site that wrote them. However, as just mentioned, cross-site scripting code can be used to read cookies that shouldn't be read.

Cookies are often used legitimately by web sites. As an example, Amazon makes frequent use of cookies. When I visit the site and look at different products, it tracks my activity and places ads on the web site based on my previous searches.

If I purchase something, it records my name and the purchase data in a back-end database. It may record a customer number in the cookie that can pull my customer data. The next time I visit, it can personalize pages with my name and ads targeted at previous purchases.

Pop-up Blockers

It's possible to open up additional windows to present information to users. As a legitimate example, my online bank has rate information that I can view. When I click on this link, it pops up another window showing current rate information, without taking me away from the current page I'm viewing.

Sometimes pop-ups can be helpful.

However, in the hands of attackers or aggressive advertisers, pop-ups can be quite annoying and downright harassing. At their height, pop-ups were sometimes responding to Windows close events by launching five more pop-ups.

Today, web browsers have built-in pop-up blockers that can be used to block these extra windows from popping up. As a user, you're also able to allow the use of some pop-ups. For example, when I visit my bank, I can set the browser to allow pop-ups for the current session or even for the site whenever I visit.

Antivirus and Anti-spyware Software

Both antivirus and anti-spyware software should be installed and maintained on systems where users regularly use the Internet. Chapter 6 will cover the different types of malware in more depth, but it's important to realize that a core protection against malware is the use of antivirus and anti-spyware software.

Antivirus software is intended to protect against viruses, and anti-spyware software is intended to protect against spyware. With this in mind, it's worth defining viruses and spyware.

- **Viruses.** Viruses are software designed to replicate without the permission of the user. Viruses often have another malicious intent, such as the destruction or theft of data. Viruses will often include other types of malware and install them on infected systems. Viruses are different than worms, Trojan horses, and other types of malware.

- **Spyware.** Spyware is software that has been installed on a user's computer without informed consent. It is designed to gather information on the user with the intent of sending that information to an attacker. Information could include Personally Identifiable Information (PII) such as name, Social Security number, birth date, and mother's maiden name. It could also include less harmful information such as surfing habits that can be used for targeted advertising. Spyware has been called adware, but as the malicious intent has increasingly grown, the term *spyware* has become much more popular.

In the past, viruses were considered highly malicious while spyware was considered less so. However, with so many attackers using the Internet for illicit monetary gain, the lines have blurred. Today, both are considered malicious, and systems should be vigorously protected against all types of malware.

Antivirus software targets viruses and other types of malware including worms and Trojan horses. Anti-spyware software targets spyware, but it also includes searches for other types of malware.

The only way to completely avoid getting infected with malware is to never use a computer. If that's not an option, both antivirus software and anti-spyware software should be installed on systems. Additionally, the virus definitions should be kept up-to-date.

Mail Servers

Mail servers are used to send and receive email on the Internet and internal networks. The three primary protocols used by mail servers are:

- **SMTP.** Simple Mail Transport Protocol is used to send email between email servers and from clients to email servers. SMTP uses port 25.
- **POP3.** Post Office Protocol v3 is used to send messages from a POP3 server down to a client. POP3 uses port 110.
- **IMAP4.** Internet Message Access Protocol v4 is used to allow email clients to access email on a server. The email can then be organized

in folders. Note that the email stays on an IMAP server, while it is downloaded from a POP3 server to the client.

As an example, I use Cox Communications as my ISP. They host a POP3 server, which receives messages destined for me. When I connect, the messages "pop" down to my system and are available in my email program but are taken off the server. When I send emails, my email program uses SMTP to send email to an SMTP server.

Two serious problems associated with email are spam and viruses.

Spam

Spam is unwanted email. Spam presents two primary problems:

- **Used to deliver malware**. Much of the malware is delivered en masse to unsuspecting clients. If a client receives malware through spam and executes it, it will be installed on her system. Sometimes the malware arrives as a Trojan horse—it looks like one thing but is actually something else. It's a good rule of thumb to not open up any attachments received from unknown sources.

- **Consumes resources**. Spam consumes bandwidth on the network and network resources on any server that receives the spam. Additionally, spam consumes processor, memory, and disk resources on any server or client that receives it. As much as 85 to 95 percent of all email is reported as spam. Thankfully, many content filters are able to filter out much of it.

Viruses

Viruses are often delivered via email so it's very common to include content filters to check for viruses. In many organizations, a three-pronged approach to scanning for viruses is done:

- **At the firewall**. Traffic is filtered using different content filters to detect malware and block it here.

- **At the mail server**. Mail traffic is filtered using content filters, which strip unwanted attachmens off of email. The email is still delivered, but with a message indicating the attachment was removed.

- **At all workstations and servers**. Antivirus software is run on all workstations and servers to ensure that malware cannot infect the systems through other means.

This may seem like overkill, but the damage that a virus can cause for an enterprise is significant and can be costly. Utilizing defense-in-depth strategies is worth the added cost for most companies.

> ### *Remember*
> Mail servers will often use content filters to scan for viruses and spam. Risky attachments are stripped off before delivery, and the intended recipient is notified of the action. Additionally, traffic from specific email addresses can be filtered so that known spammers' email isn't delivered.

Open Relays

Anonymous open relays can be a significant problem for companies, but before understanding the problem, you need to understand the basic operation. Consider figure 5.2, which represents one possible way email servers can be configured.

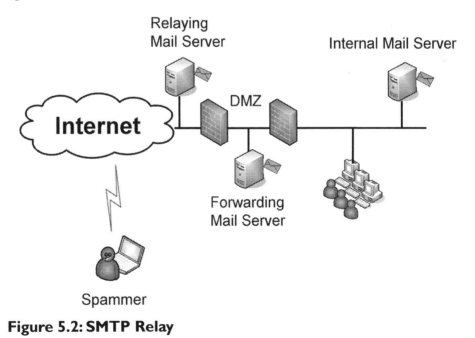

Figure 5.2: SMTP Relay

Internal clients will interact with the internal mail server by sending and receiving email to and from it. When email needs to be sent outside the company, the internal mail server will forward the email to the forwarding mail server, which is typically located in the DMZ.

It's not uncommon to configure this forwarding mail server to forward Internet-destined email to a relaying mail server. This is called mail relay or SMTP relay.

Many ISPs host mail servers that will accept email from paying clients and forward or relay this email to others. When an ISP forwards the mail, it's referred to as third-party mail relay.

It's also possible for the mail server in the DMZ to simply act as the relaying mail server and relay all email to the Internet without using a third-party email server.

Anonymous Open Relays

Both the forwarding mail server and the relaying mail server should not accept email from anonymous clients. This is done by disabling a setting known as anonymous open relays. A mail server can be configured to relay email, but it should only relay email from known clients.

Now, consider the spammer. The spammer performs basic reconnaissance or footprinting attacks. Using a port scanning tool such as Nmap, he can determine which servers have port 25 open and are likely SMTP servers. Reverse lookups will allow him to discover the names of these servers.

The spammer could have a simple script that occasionally sends an email to these known mail servers that is addressed back to him. Most of the time, his email is rejected by the relaying mail server since he's not paying to have his email relayed and anonymous open relays are disabled.

> **Remember**
>
> Anonymous open relays are considered a significant risk. Anonymous open relays are also called anonymous relays, SMTP relays, or mail relays. Email servers should have anonymous relays disabled so that the only clients who can send email through the email server are known clients. If open, a spammer may be able to spoof an email so that it looks like it's coming from the email servers with open relays, rather than from the spammer.

However, if anonymous open relay is ever enabled, the spammer gets a reply to his email. Jackpot! Now he can send a single email to this server with a thousand recipients, and this server with anonymous open relay enabled will be the spammer. Of course, he doesn't stop with a single email. He keeps sending until the hole is plugged.

Spammer Blacklists and Whitelists

Some companies maintain lists of known spammers and sell subscriptions to these lists. These lists are referred to as blacklists, and known spammers are placed on spam blacklists when they are discovered. Subscribers then know to block email from these spammers.

A whitelist is a list of companies known to be valid, legitimate companies that don't engage in spamming. Traffic on a whitelist is intended to be allowed.

Consider the mail server that is misconfigured with anonymous open relay enabled. Since this mail server is acting as a spammer, it will be placed on the blacklist. Now, even legitimate email from this company will be rejected by blacklist subscribers.

More than a few companies have learned the hard way that a simple mistake can land you on one of these lists. While it may be simple to get on the list, it's anything but simple to get off.

Database Servers

Database servers are often used as back-end servers for web servers. In other words, the data provided to a web server is not hosted on the web server, but instead hosted on a database server. Two primary methods are often used to protect database servers in this configuration:

- Protect with firewalls
- Perform input validation

Protect with Firewalls

A database server would rarely be configured to be accessed from the Internet directly. Instead, the database server would be configured behind a firewall that does not allow direct access from the Internet to the database server.

That doesn't mean that data isn't accessible on the Internet. Instead, data is often made available via a web server. Figure 5.3 shows how a database server may be configured to provide data to a web server.

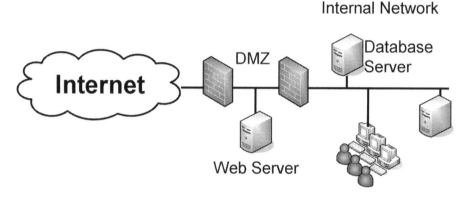

Figure 5.3: Protected Database Server

Notice that the web server is placed in the DMZ so that it is accessible to the Internet, while the DMZ provides a layer of protection. Ports 80 and 443 are opened on the Internet-facing firewall of the DMZ to allow access to the web server from Internet clients.

The web server accepts queries, and when needed, it forwards data requests to the database server internal to the network. The internal firewall allows traffic from the web server to the database server, but traffic directly from the Internet-facing firewall is not allowed to the database server.

While placing the database server behind a second firewall provides a lot of protection, it doesn't protect against SQL injection attacks.

Perform Input Validation

If data isn't examined and validated before being executed against a database server, an attacker can enter other data, performing an SQL injection attack. An SQL injection attack can allow an attacker to execute commands directly against the database through the web server.

Depending on how well the database server is locked down (or not), SQL injection attacks may allow the attacker to get the entire structure of the database and all the data, and even modify data in the database.

However, if the web application developer uses input validation techniques, an SQL injection attack can easily be thwarted.

As an example, a web form may have a text box for a first name. You can logically expect only characters in a first name and no more than twenty-five characters. Input validation is code that is used to check the data input by the user and verify that it includes only characters and is not more than twenty-five characters. If the data is outside the scope of the input validation rules, it is considered invalid and not used.

If you'd like to learn more about SQL injection, check out the book *All-In-One MCITP SQL Server 2005 Database Developer* by Darril Gibson (ISBN 978-0071546690).

File and Print Servers

File and print servers are used internal to a network to allow users to share data and manage print jobs. While some environments don't use a print server at all and instead print directly to the printer, other environments will often use the same server to perform both tasks.

Files are shared by creating shares on a server. Users connect to the share using the Universal Naming Convention path of \\ServerName\ShareName.

The following primary steps can be used to protect data on file and print servers.

- **Create shares on non-system partitions**. Normally the C: drive is both the system and boot partition. Data shared on a file server or print jobs spooled to a print server should be stored on another partition such as D: or E:.

- **Restrict access through the use of permissions**. On Windows servers, both share permissions and NTFS permissions can be combined to restrict access. For example, some users may need full control access, while others may only need read access.

- **Enable quotas.** The NTFS file system allows quotas to be set on partitions. Quotas can be used to restrict how much data users can store on a partition and allow administrators to track usage on a per-user basis.
- **Keep file and print servers internal.** A file or print server shouldn't be accessible from the Internet, so it shouldn't be placed in the DMZ. If it is desirable to share files on the Internet, an FTP server should be used instead.

FTP Servers

A File Transfer Protocol (FTP) server is used to host files on the Internet. FTP servers allow users to upload and download files. FTP servers can have access restricted through the use of credentials. For example, users may be required to log in before uploading or downloading data.

FTP servers have some significant risks. They include:

- **Credentials sent in clear text.** Protocol analyzers (sniffers) can be used to capture credentials. For this reason, some logins simply use "anonymous" as the username and an email address as the password.
- **Data sent in clear text.** Sniffers can capture any data that is transferred from or to an FTP server.
- **Anonymous logins allow unrestricted uploads.** If "anonymous" is used for logins, the FTP server may become a host for warez—pirated software, movies, music, and network attack tools. Or it may simply have malicious software uploaded to it.

Notice that there is a conflict here. Since credentials are sent in clear text, you can choose to allow anonymous access. However, if an FTP server allows anonymous uploads, it may become a warez server.

Often, FTP servers allow anonymous downloads but restrict uploads. FTP can be secured using SSH, and this is one way that credentials can be passed for uploads.

More than a few FTP servers have become unwitting warez hosts. Here are some things you'll likely see if an FTP server is being used by attackers to host files:

- **Increased disk consumption.** You may have a 1 TB hard drive with 900 GB free, but come in after a weekend and find the 1 TB drive is full.
- **Increased NIC activity.** As users are uploading and downloading data, the NIC will be at or near capacity.
- **CPU usage will be higher.** This depends on you knowing what the performance baseline is, but you will also probably see a spike in the CPU usage.

FTP servers use ports 20 and 21.

DNS Servers

Domain Name System (DNS) servers are used for name resolution. Specifically, DNS resolves names to IP addresses. This eliminates the need for you and me to have to remember the IP address of Google. Instead, we simply type "google.com" in the browser, and it connects. Part of the process is a query to DNS for the IP address.

DNS resolves much more than just names to IP addresses. As a few examples, DNS can also:

- Resolve IP addresses to names in a process known as reverse lookup using pointer (PTR) records
- Locate mail servers through the use of Mail Exchange (MX) records
- Locate domain controllers in a network using Service (SRV) records
- Locate domain controllers holding specific roles or running specific services using SRV records

Most environments will include more than one DNS server. Data is shared between DNS servers through a process called zone transfers. The data on a DNS server is contained within a zone. You can think of a zone as a database of records held by the DNS server.

As changes are made to one DNS server, they are transferred to another. It's also possible for the entire zone to be transferred from one server to another. This should be restricted to only known DNS servers.

> **Remember**
>
> DNS zone data should be protected. Zone transfers should only be authorized to specific clients, and auditing should be enabled to monitor any unauthorized zone transfer attempts. Zone transfer attempts are often a part of a reconnaissance attack. DNS cache poisoning can cause web traffic to be redirected to bogus web sites.

Some of the risks to protect against with DNS are:

- **Unauthorized zone transfers**. Data held in DNS zones includes server names, IP addresses, and SRV records identifying key servers. Zone transfers should be strictly restricted, and auditing should be enabled to identify any attempts to access zone data through zone transfers. Reconnaissance attacks frequently try to gain information from DNS servers through unauthorized zone transfers. DNS logging can detect any zone transfer attempts.

- **DNS cache poisoning**. Name resolution results are cached on the server and on the client. DNS cache poisoning can change what should be in cache and redirect clients to bogus web sites. As DNS vulnerabilities are discovered, they should be patched.

- **Internal data should stay internal**. DNS servers can be used internally to resolve internal servers like domain controllers and other servers, and externally to resolve Internet resources. Internal data should not be located on a DNS server that is accessible from the Internet.

- **Altered Hosts File**. The Hosts file (located in the Windows/System32/Drivers/Etc/ folder on end users' systems) is used first to resolve host names to IP addresses. Malware sometimes changes the contents of the Hosts file to bypass DNS.

Domain Controllers

Domain controllers contain Active Directory, which is a database of all the objects (such as user and computer objects) in the domain. Domain controllers require DNS servers in the network. DNS includes SRV records used to find domain controllers.

One of the primary protections for a domain controller is to implement strong physical security. If someone gains unrestricted physical access to a domain controller, it's possible for him to gain a considerable amount of information on your internal enterprise.

Due to how much data is contained in Active Directory, it's important to regularly back it up. On Windows Server 2003 systems and earlier, Active Directory is backed up by backing up System State data.

> **Remember**
>
> Active Directory should be backed up regularly by backing up System State data.

System State data includes system files such as boot files and the registry. On domain controllers, it also includes Active Directory. You can't pick and choose what parts of the System State data you back up, but instead back up all of System State data or none of it.

Instant Messaging

Instant messaging (IM) is used for real-time communications between two or more people. It's similar to a phone conversation in that communication is instantaneous, but the difference is that everything is typed. Some IM systems also include the use of web cams where you can see the other party.

> **Remember**
>
> One of the biggest risks associated with instant messaging systems is the fact that communications are sent over the network in clear text without any encryption. IM communications are highly susceptible to sniffing attacks.

Many public IM systems are available such as AOL Instant Messenger (AIM), Yahoo Messenger, and Google Talk. Some public IM systems have certain risks including:

- **Data transferred in clear text**. Communications are open and unprotected. Everything that a user types is vulnerable to sniffing attacks from protocol analyzers.

- **Lack of security**. IM was created as an easy method to allow people to chat in real time, and it succeeded in that goal, but security was not a goal.

- **Malware can be delivered with messages**. Just as malware can be delivered through email, malware can be delivered through IM systems.

- **Administrative oversight is difficult**. Data and conversations are difficult to monitor and control. If charged with capturing and saving all internal communications (such as from a court order), it is just not possible with a public IM system.

Many enterprises deploy their own private IM systems to overcome many of these weaknesses. As an example, Microsoft's Office Communications Server (OCS) is a server product that can be used within a network, allowing administrators much more administrative oversight and control, while also allowing users to easily communicate using real-time chat capabilities.

Virtualization

Virtualization is a technology that has been gaining a lot of popularity in recent years. Virtualization allows you to host one or more virtual servers on a single physical server.

The different servers can be running different operating systems. It's possible to have a single physical server running multiple virtual systems. The virtual servers could be running Microsoft operating systems, Linux, UNIX, or other operating systems.

The single physical server needs to have beefed-up resources (processor, memory, disk, and NIC), but it's still only one set of hardware. This one physical server requires less electricity, less cooling, and less space.

Several virtualization technologies currently exist, including VMWare, Microsoft's Hyper-V, and Microsoft's Virtual PC (VPC). VMWare has been around the longest as a server product specifically designed to host multiple servers in a production environment. Microsoft's Hyper-V was released with Server 2008 and is a direct competitor with VMWare.

Microsoft's Virtual PC can run on desktop systems and is frequently used for simple test environments. I remember seeing a MAC running OS-X with Virtual PC images of Windows XP, Windows Vista, and Server 2003. It was quick and slick!

> ### Remember
> Virtualization is commonly used by security professionals to perform testing within an isolated environment. Patches can be tested on a virtual server. Malware can be released and patches can be tested in a virtual environment without any negative impact on the host hardware or software.

From a security perspective, the primary benefit of virtual servers is isolation. A secondary benefit is the easy restoration of a crashed virtual server.

Isolation

Online virtual servers are normally configured so that they can communicate easily with other virtual and physical servers. However, it's also possible to configure the virtual systems so that they are completely isolated. They can be isolated from the host operating system and isolated from other virtual servers if desired.

This isolation allows the following benefits:

- **Testing malware**. Malicious software can be released and tested on this isolated server. Malware released on an isolated virtual server presents minimal risk to the hardware and host operating system.
- **Testing applications**. Virtualized applications are applications running in a virtual environment. This can protect the host operating system from malware released within the virtual environment.
- **Isolation of network services and roles**. Since network services (such as DNS, WINS, and DHCP) run on server operating systems, these network services can also be isolated.

Easy Restores

A significant benefit of virtual servers is that the original image can easily be restored. If testing on an isolated server destroys the server, no problem. The image can easily be returned to a previous state, often by simply restoring a snapshot of the image taken previously.

Restoring a virtual server to a previous state is counted in minutes. Compare this to a physical server. If it crashes, the amount of rebuilding may be counted in hours.

Virtualization Weakness

The primary weakness presented by virtualization is that the host operating system becomes a single point of failure. If a host operating system is used to host five virtual servers and the host fails, the five virtual servers also fail.

One way to overcome this weakness for critical servers is to use clustering technologies to provide fault tolerance for the host server.

Exam Topic Review

When preparing for the exam, make sure you understand these key concepts, which were covered in this chapter.

Hardening a System

- Hardening a system increases security from the defaults.
- Hardening includes:
    - Changing defaults such as default accounts, passwords, back doors, and BIOS settings
    - Removing unneeded services, protocols, and software
    - Enabling software firewalls
    - Keeping systems up-to-date with patches, hotfixes, and service packs
- Baselines can be used to harden all systems in a standard format. Baselines can be deployed through imaging or Group Policy.

- Patch-management software can be used to deploy patches and audit systems to determine if the patches were successfully applied.
- Change-management processes can be used to ensure that changes to software and configuration are not changed without being reviewed for unintended consequences.

Hardening Server Applications

- Web servers should be secured with the following actions:
    - Protect against buffer overflow errors by keeping the web server up-to-date. Buffer overflows exist when an application receives more input than it expects and allows attackers to install malware. Buffer overflow vulnerabilities exist due to lack of code review, adequate testing, or enough input validation.
    - Use signed code such as signed ActiveX controls.
    - Allow HTTP and HTTPS over ports 80 and 443.
- Mail servers should be secured with the following actions:
    - Include content filters to filter out spam and viruses.
    - Ensure that anonymous open relays are not enabled.
- File and print servers should be protected by placing data on non-operating system partitions and restricting access with permissions.
- FTP servers should be protected by not allowing anonymous uploads. All data and credentials are passed in clear text unless they are encrypted, such as with SSH.
- DNS servers should restrict zone transfers and have auditing enabled to track zone transfers to unintended clients.
- Domain controllers can be backed up by backing up System State data.
- Instant messaging systems are risky since all data goes across the network in clear text.

Virtualization

- Virtualization technologies allow a single physical server to host multiple virtual servers. Virtual servers can communicate with each other on a network or remain completely isolated.

- Security professionals can use the virtual servers to execute malware in an isolated environment that will not harm the host hardware or operating system.
- The only weakness is that if the physical server fails, all virtual servers hosted on the server also fail.

Practice Questions

1. What should be done to harden workstations and servers? (Choose all that apply.)

    A. Change defaults

    B. Disable or remove unnecessary services and protocols

    C. Install only necessary software

    D. Enable the software firewall

2. What is the primary security reason why unnecessary services should be disabled on a system?

    A. To preserve resources such as processor and memory

    B. To reduce the attack surface

    C. To reduce administrative overhead

    D. To improve the performance of the system

3. What should be done before creating a security baseline?

    A. Create a performance baseline

    B. Create a security policy

    C. Disable unneeded services and protocols

    D. Change defaults

4. What can be used to standardize a set of requirements for a system?

    A. Configuration baseline

    B. Performance baseline

    C. Default services

    D. Patch baseline

5. What can be used to prevent users from running specific graphical user interface (GUI) applications?

    A. SSO

    B. Proximity cards

    C. Router access control lists

    D. Group policy objects

6. You want to ensure that all the systems in your network have a standard load for consistent operation across the enterprise. What can be used to enforce this? (Choose two.)

    A. Imaging

    B. Configuration baseline

    C. Security baseline

    D. Smart cards

7. When should default passwords be changed?

    A. Once a threat has been identified

    B. When the device or software is first enabled

    C. When notified by the vendor

    D. At least every sixty days

8. What is considered a security threat for a newly installed network device?

    A. DoS attack

    B. Spoofed MAC addresses

    C. Spoofed IP addresses

    D. Default passwords

9. A Windows system is responding quite slowly when doing normal tasks, but indicators on the system show that the disk and the NIC are busy. You suspect the system is infected with malware. What can you use to check the CPU usage? (Choose two.)

    A. Performance Monitor

    B. Task Manager

    C. Task Monitor

    D. Windows Firewall

10. A vendor has released an executable file that includes several patches and hotfixes. What is this called?

    A. Service pack

    B. Update

    C. Upgrade

    D. Support patch

11. A security vulnerability has been discovered on an operating system. What would the vendor release to address this issue?

    A. Upgrade

    B. Service pack

    C. Patch

    D. WSUS

12. What would patch-management software perform? Choose the best answer.

    A. Identifying needed patches and applying the patches

    B. Identifying needed patches and auditing for the successful application of patches

    C. Downloading all patches and applying the patches

    D. Identifying needed patches, applying the patches, and auditing for the successful application of patches

13. Of the following choices, which one represents the most common vulnerability of Internet-facing servers?

    A. Buffer overflows

    B. Rogue DHCP servers

    C. Disabled anonymous relay

    D. Installation of Trojan horses

14. A web server is receiving more data than it is programmed to accept. What type of vulnerability is this?

    A. Input validation

    B. Code testing and review

    C. Patch management

    D. Buffer overflow

15. A public web site accesses a database server for data. What should be done to prevent an SQL injection attack launched from the web server?

    A. Keep the servers up-to-date.

    B. Block buffer overflow vulnerabilities.

    C. Validate input.

    D. Open ports 80 and 443.

16. You want to prevent users from unknowingly installing malicious code from Internet web sites. What should you do?

    A. Block ports 80 and 443 at the firewall.

    B. Enable JVMs.

    C. Disable anti-spyware software.

    D. Disable unsigned ActiveX controls.

17. What is used to allow a web script to run in its own environment without accessing other processes or data?

    A. JVM

    B. ActiveX control

    C. Sandbox

    D. Antivirus software

18. What ports need to be open for a web site hosting both encrypted and unencrypted Internet traffic? (Choose all that apply.)

    A. Port 80 inbound

    B. Port 80 outbound

    C. Port 443 inbound

    D. Port 443 outbound

19. What should be done to prevent malware from being sent to email clients?

    A. Keep the mail server up-to-date.

    B. Employ anti-spam and antivirus software.

    C. Enable anonymous relays.

    D. Remove the SMTP protocol.

20. What should an email server be able to do? (Choose all that apply.)

    A. Send email messages using the NNTP protocol on port 25

    B. Create email messages to send to clients

    C. Detect viruses received as attachments in email

    D. Warn clients of detected viruses

21. Why should logging be enabled on a DNS server?

    A. To prevent buffer overflow attacks

    B. To ensure SRV records are maintained

    C. To record any anonymous relay attempts

    D. To identify any unauthorized zone transfer attempts

22. What should be backed up on a domain controller?

    A. System State

    B. System files

    C. Registry

    D. Boot files

23. What type of server can host warez if anonymous logins are enabled?

    A. Web server

    B. FTP

    C. Email

    D. Domain controller

24. Of the following choices, what is considered a security issue related to instant messaging?

    A. Communications are open and unprotected.

    B. Anonymous open relays are allowed.

    C. Buffer overflow attacks are common.

    D. The encryption is easy to break.

25. What are some security reasons why a virtual system is used? (Choose all that apply.)

    A. Malicious software can be executed with minimal impact to the host.

    B. It will isolate the host OS from security threats on the virtual servers.

    C. It can isolate network services and roles.

    D. Threats can be analyzed in a controlled environment.

Practice Question Answers

1. **A, B, C, D.** Basic steps to harden a workstation or server include changing defaults (such as default passwords); disabling or removing unnecessary services, protocols, and software; and enabling the software firewall. Other steps include using a security baseline and keeping the system up-to-date.

2. **B.** Unnecessary services should be disabled to reduce the attack surface of a system and make it less susceptible to attacks. While disabling unnecessary resources will consume less resources, will reduce administrative overhead, and may improve the overall performance of the system, these aren't the primary security reasons to disable unnecessary services.

3. **B.** The first step in creating a security baseline is creating a security policy. A security baseline could enforce security policy settings like disabling unneeded services and protocols, and changing defaults.

4. **A.** A configuration baseline is used to specify a set of consistent settings and requirements for a workstation or server. A performance baseline is taken to capture the performance for a specific time period. Default services should be examined to see if they're needed, but they can't specify or enforce consistent requirements. Patch-management software can be used to ensure that patches are applied consistently, but this is not commonly called a patch baseline.

5. **D.** Software restriction policy within group policy objects can be used to prevent users from running specific applications. Single sign-on allows a user to access multiple resources after logging on once with one set of credentials. Proximity cards are used for access control and activity when placed in close proximity to a card reader. Access control lists can be used to allow or deny traffic on a router.

6. **A, B.** Imaging and configuration baselines can be used to ensure that systems have a standard load across the enterprise. Imaging can be used to deploy an identical configuration to all systems, and configuration baselines can be

configured and deployed through Group Policy to ensure that all systems are configured the same. Security baselines can be used to ensure that security settings are configured the same, but security settings are only a part of the overall load or configuration of a system. Smart cards are used for authentication.

7. **B.** Default passwords should be changed as soon as the device or software is used. If the default password continues to be used, it becomes a vulnerability as soon as the device or software is used, and a notification by the vendor isn't needed. While it's a good practice to change passwords regularly such as every sixty days, once the default is changed, it is no longer the default.

8. **D.** Default passwords are a security threat for any newly installed device. Default passwords should be changed prior to deployment of a device for the first time. While denial-of-service (DoS) attacks are a risk, they aren't the primary risk when a device is first installed. Similarly, spoofed MAC and IP addresses don't represent a primary risk of a newly installed network device.

9. **A, B.** Both the Task Manager and the Performance Monitor can be used to monitor basic resources, such as the processor, memory, disk, and NIC. There is no such thing as a Task Monitor. The Windows Firewall is a software firewall used to protect a system, but it doesn't have the ability to measure a CPU's usage.

10. **A.** A service pack is an executable file or installable package that includes several patches and hotfixes in one comprehensive package. An update would be a single patch or hotfix. An upgrade is the complete change of an operating system (such as from Windows Vista to Windows 7). *Support patch* isn't a common term, but a service pack would not include only one patch.

11. **C.** A patch or a hotfix would be released to address a single security vulnerability. An upgrade is used to upgrade the operating system from one version to another. A service pack is a group of multiple patches and hotfixes. WSUS is an example of patch-management software used to deploy patches and hotfixes.

12. **D.** Patch-management software will be able to identify needed patches for systems, apply the patches, and then follow up by auditing systems to ensure that the patches have been successfully applied. An integral component of this process is being able to audit the systems for the successful application of the patches and to determine what is needed in addition to deploying the updates.

13. **A.** Buffer overflow attacks are the most common exploits for Internet-facing servers from those listed. Buffer overflow attacks are common on web servers. DHCP servers would not be accessible on the Internet. Enabled anonymous relay is a significant threat to SMTP servers, not disabled anonymous relay. A Trojan horse is a program that looks like one thing but actually includes something else in the form of malware and would be executed by a user; a Trojan horse is a threat on workstations since users can execute programs on the workstation but wouldn't be a significant threat on a server, because administrators would rarely install untested additional software on a server.

14. **D.** A buffer overflow attack occurs when an Internet-facing server receives more input than it is programmed to accept. Buffer overflows can often be prevented by the developer if adequate testing and code review is done and/or input validation is done to prevent the unexpected data from being applied.

15. **C.** An effective method of protecting against SQL injection attacks is to use input validation on the web server; data determined to be invalid is not used to query the database server. Servers should be kept up-to-date to protect against vulnerabilities such as buffer overflows, but this won't protect against SQL injection attacks. Ports 80 and 443 would be open to allow HTTP and HTTPS traffic to a web server.

16. **D.** Malicious ActiveX controls will not be signed, so disabling unsigned ActiveX controls will prevent them from being downloaded and installed. Ports 80 and 443 are used for HTTP and HTTPS traffic, so blocking these ports will essentially block all Internet access. Java Virtual Machines (JVMs) are required to run Java applets, so enabling JVMs will allow Java applets to run. Disabling anti-spyware software would reduce the protection, not increase it.

17. **C.** Web scripts can be forced to run within a controlled environment, frequently referred to as a sandbox. Java applets run within a JVM. A script can't run within an ActiveX control; an ActiveX control is a mini-application. Antivirus software can detect viruses but won't be able to ensure that a script only runs in a controlled environment.

18. **A, C.** Unencrypted traffic will come in as inbound HTTP requests on inbound port 80. Encrypted traffic will come in as inbound HTTPS requests on inbound port 443.

19. **B.** Anti-spam and antivirus software are used to prevent malware from being sent to email clients and can be installed on all clients, email servers, and firewalls. Keeping a server up-to-date is a positive step toward keeping it hardened but won't prevent malware. Open anonymous relays are a known vulnerability, and anonymous relays should be disabled. The SMTP protocol is required for the delivery of email.

20. **C.** An email server should have antivirus software installed that can detect viruses sent as attachments, remove risky attachments, and warn clients that the attachment was removed due to the risk. The Network News Transfer Protocol is not used to send or receive email, and it uses port 119. SMTP uses port 25. Email servers send and receive email, but they wouldn't be used to create email.

21. **D.** Logging should be enabled on a DNS server to monitor any unauthorized zone transfer attempts. DNS data is held in DNS zones, and data is transferred in a zone transfer process. Zone transfers are unrelated to buffer overflow attacks (which usually occur on web servers) or anonymous relay problems (which are related to email servers). SRV records are required in an Active Directory domain, but logging is not required to maintain SRV records.

22. **A.** System State data should be backed up on a domain controller to back up Active Directory. System State data includes Active Directory system files, the registry, and boot files.

23. **B.** An FTP server may become a warez server (hosting pirated movies, software, music, and network tools) if anonymous logins are enabled. Web servers may have pages defaced if anonymous logins are enabled. Email servers need to have anonymous relay disabled but don't have logins. Domain controllers don't have anonymous logins.

24. **A.** Communications are open and unprotected on IM servers; data is sent in clear text, making IM communications highly susceptible to sniffing attacks. Anonymous open relays are a risk on email servers. Buffer overflow attacks are common on web servers. IM doesn't use any type of encryption.

25. **A, B, C, D.** Virtualization technologies provide all the benefits listed. Malware can be executed with minimal impact (if any impact) on the host's hardware and software. Security threats can be completely isolated on the virtual server. Virtual environments can host network services and roles to provide isolation. Threats can be released and analyzed in a controlled environment.

Chapter 6

Predicting and Mitigating Threats

CompTIA Security+ objectives covered in this chapter

1.1 Differentiate among various systems security threats.
- Virus
- Worm
- Trojan
- Spyware
- Spam
- Adware
- Rootkits
- Botnets
- Logic bomb

1.5 Implement security applications.
- Antivirus
- Anti-spam

2.1 Differentiate between the different ports & protocols, their respective threats and mitigation techniques.
- TCP/IP hijacking
- Null sessions
- Spoofing
- Man-in-the-middle
- Replay
- DOS
- DDOS
- Domain Name Kiting
- ARP poisoning

6.6 Explain the concept of and how to reduce the risks of social engineering.

- Phishing
- Hoaxes
- Shoulder surfing
- Dumpster diving
- User education and awareness training

* * *

Threats are abundant in information technology. Attackers lurk almost everywhere, and constant vigilance is required by IT professionals and security professionals to predict and mitigate these threats. The first step is to ensure that you know what the threats are.

Malware includes a variety of different software specifically designed to wreak havoc on your network, harvest information, or take control of systems and use them as zombies within controlled botnets. Multiple other attacks are possible even without the use of malware. Any system with a public IP address will be attacked—it's just a matter of time.

Even if the best technology is employed to protect systems and networks, it can be circumvented through social engineering tactics. Attackers use simple conniving and flattery to encourage users to give up critical information.

In this chapter, you'll learn about malware, different attacks, and social engineering.

Malware

Malicious software (malware) is a wide range of different software that has malicious intent. Malware is not software that you would knowingly purchase or download and install; instead, it is installed onto your system through devious means.

The term *virus* is sometimes erroneously used to imply all types of malware. Actually, a virus is a specific type of malware, and malware includes many other types of malicious software including:

- Virus
- Worm
- Trojan horse
- Logic bomb
- Rootkit
- Spyware

Viruses

A virus is a set of malicious code that attaches itself to a host application. The host application must be executed to run, and when the host application is executed, the malicious code will execute. The virus will try to find other host applications to infect with the malicious code. At some point, the virus will activate and deliver its payload, such as causing damage or delivering a message.

Typically, the payload of a virus is damaging. It may delete files, cause random reboots, or enable back doors that attackers can use to access a system over the Internet. Some older viruses merely displayed a message at some point, such as "Legalize Marijuana!"

Most viruses won't cause damage immediately. Instead, they give the virus time to replicate or distribute other malware. Note that not all malware needs a host application to be executed. As an example, worms are not executed, while viruses and Trojan horses are.

A user will often unknowingly execute the virus, but other times, an operating system may execute the virus through an Autorun feature (see the sidebar for one way this is done).

Characteristics

Viruses have specific characteristics. These include:

- **Replication mechanism**. For a virus to survive, it must replicate. When the program hosting the virus is executed, the virus will look for other host applications to infect.

- **Activation mechanism**. This is the point in time when the objective is executed. There is usually a time lag between replication and activation. If a virus performed the objective as soon as it was installed, it wouldn't have much time to replicate.

- **Objective mechanism**. The objective is the damage or the payload the virus seeks to inflict or deliver. Objectives could be to make the hard drive unbootable, to pop up a dialog box with a message, to connect to a botnet control mechanism to download and run other malware, and more.

Remember

Viruses have three different characteristics: replication, activation, and objective. The replication mechanism is used to replicate the virus to different hosts. The activation mechanism is the trigger that tells the virus to deliver the objective. The objective of the payload of the virus is to cause damage or simply to send a message.

Delivery of Viruses

Viruses can be delivered from system to system through a variety of methods, but they are most often spread through email. Spammers often include viruses as attachments and use different techniques to encourage users to execute the virus on their systems.

Many companies include antivirus and anti-spam software on their mail servers. The intent is to filter out malicious content. Instead of forwarding the suspect content, the software strips the attachment, and the user receives the email text with an explanation of what was removed and why. If the sender is known and the attachment is legitimate, then the user at least knows that it was removed.

Other methods used to deliver viruses include:

- **USB flash drives**. USB flash drives are increasingly used to deliver viruses. Many systems have Autorun enabled, so as soon as a USB drive is inserted into the system, the virus can be read and executed.
- **Floppy drives**. Floppy drives have been very popular for delivering viruses. However, since floppies have been removed on many systems and USB flash drives are so common, the use of floppy drives to deliver viruses is less common today.
- **Downloads**. Users can also unwittingly download and install a virus. A Trojan horse is a prime example of this.

Virus Hoaxes

A virus hoax is a message, often circulated through email, that tells of impending doom from a virus that simply doesn't exist. The user may be encouraged to delete files or change her system configuration.

> ### Remember
> A virus hoax can be as damaging as an actual virus. It can trick users into damaging their own systems and increase the help-desk workload.

An example is the teddy bear virus (jdbgmgr.exe), which is not a virus at all. The "victim" may receive an email that says this virus lies in a sleeping state for fourteen days and then it will destroy the whole system. However, if you can find and delete this file now, you will be protected. It then gives instructions on how to find the file (which has an icon of a little bear).

Creating an Autorun File

Attackers often modify the autorun.inf file on systems to have viruses executed as soon as a USB drive is inserted into a system. The following steps show how this can be done on a Windows system.

1. Insert a USB flash drive into your system.
2. Use Windows Explorer to browse to your drive.
3. If an autorun.inf file exists, rename it to oldautorun.inf so that you can restore it at the end of these steps.
4. Right click at the root of the USB drive and select New, Text Document. Double-click the document to open it in Notepad.
5. Add the following two lines to the text document:
   [AutoRun]
   open=calc.exe
6. Save the file at the root (not in a folder) of your USB flash drive with the name **autorun.inf**. Notice that the extension .txt will be replaced with .inf in the saved file.
7. Remove the flash drive and reinsert it. If Autorun is enabled, the Calculator program will automatically start. If Autorun is configured to prompt you, you will be prompted to Run Calc.exe.
8. Clearly the Calculator program is not malicious (unless you're afflicted with math phobia). However, this does show how easy it is for an attacker to configure malware to execute from a flash drive. The virus could be a program hidden within a folder on the USB, and when the USB is inserted, the virus would execute.
9. Delete the autorun.inf file you created.
10. If you had an autorun.inf file on your system, rename it back to autorun.inf.

The program is a Java Debug Manager, important to some users. However, if they followed the steps in the message, they would lose some system capability.

More serious virus hoaxes have the potential to be as damaging as a real virus. If a user is convinced to delete a significantly important file, he may make his system unusable. Virus hoaxes cause the following problems:

- May trick the user into changing the system configuration or deleting key files.
- Can waste help-desk personnel's time due to needless calls about the hoax or support calls if users damaged their systems as a result of the hoax.

There are several resources you can check to determine if a virus threat is valid or a hoax. They include:

- **Antivirus vendor sites**. Sites such as Symantec and McAfee regularly post information on emerging threats and virus hoaxes. They have their own search engines, and other Internet search engines will often take you to the right page.
- **Urban legend sites**. Sites like Snopes.com separate the truth from fiction and have pages dedicated to viruses and virus hoaxes.
- **ProgramChecker.com**. This site is great to determine if a program is valid or not. As an example, a known virus is kernel32.**exe**. This looks similar to a valid file named kernel32.**dll**. A hoax may direct a user to delete kernel32.**dll**, while a valid warning from an antivirus scan would say to delete kernel32.**exe**.

Worms

A worm is malicious software that travels throughout a network without the assistance of a host application or user interaction. A worm resides in memory and is able to use different transport protocols to travel over the network.

One of the significant problems caused by worms is that they consume network bandwidth. Worms can replicate themselves hundreds of times and spread to all the systems in the network, causing each of these systems to also spread the worm. Network performance can slow to a crawl.

> **Remember**
>
> Worms do not need to be executed but can travel autonomously through a network. A virus must be executed (either by a user or through automation). A Trojan horse looks like one thing (such as a screen saver or other legitimate program), but it's something else (malicious software). A logic bomb executes in response to an event, such as when a specific application is executed or a specific time occurs.

Trojan Horses

A Trojan horse looks like one thing that isn't malicious, but it's actually something else that is malicious. Trojan horses are named after the infamous horse from the Trojan War.

In Greek mythology, the Achaeans tried to sack the city of Troy for several years, but they simply could not succeed. At some point, someone got the idea of building a huge wooden horse and convincing the people of Troy that it was a gift from the gods. Warriors hid inside, and the horse was rolled up to the gates.

The people of Troy partied all day and all night, but when the city slept, the warriors climbed down from the horse and opened the gates, and the rest of the warriors flooded in. What the Greek warriors couldn't do for years, the Trojan horse helped them do in a single day.

In computers, a Trojan horse appears as a cool screen saver, a useful utility, a game, or something else that you may be enticed to download and try. Some even masquerade as free antivirus programs. When you allow the program to run on your computer, the hidden malicious code is also allowed in.

Logic Bombs

A logic bomb is a string of code embedded into an application that will execute in response to an event. The event may be when a specific date is reached, a user launches a specific program, or any condition the programmer decides on.

There's an often repeated story about a company that decided they had to lay off an engineer due to an economic downturn. They didn't see him doing much, so they thought they could do without him. Within a couple of weeks after he left, they started having all sorts of computer problems they just couldn't resolve.

They called him back, and within a couple of weeks, everything was fine. A few months later, they determined they had to lay him off again. You guessed it. Within a couple of weeks, things went haywire again.

The engineer had programmed a logic bomb that executed when the payroll program ran. It checked for his name on the payroll, and when it was there, things were fine, but when his name wasn't there, ka-boom!—the logic bomb exploded.

Logic bombs may also be called time bombs.

Rootkits

A rootkit is a group of programs (or in rare instances, a single program) that hides the fact that the system has been infected or compromised by malicious code. A user may suspect something is wrong, but antivirus scans and other checks indicate everything is fine since the rootkit manipulates what is viewed by the user and other applications.

Rootkits intercept calls to the operating system. Antivirus software often makes calls to the operating system that could detect malware, but the rootkit prevents the antivirus software from making these calls. This is why antivirus software will sometimes report everything is OK. In addition to modifying the internal operating system process, a rootkit will often alter the registry.

Some malware scanners (such as antivirus and anti-spyware scanners) can detect rootkits. However, it's important to remember that rootkits are very difficult to detect, since they can hide so much of their activity. A clean bill of health by a malware scanner may not be valid. One method used to detect rootkits is to boot into safe mode, or have the system scanned before boot.

> **Remember**
>
> Rootkits hide themselves by altering the internal process of operating systems so that antivirus and anti-spyware software cannot easily detect them. A rootkit may also alter the registry. Still, some anti-malware software can detect some rootkits.

Spyware/Adware

Spyware is software that is installed on a user's system without her awareness or consent. Its purpose is often to take some level of control over the user's computer to learn information and send this information to a third party.

Some examples of spyware activity are:

- Changing a user's home page
- Redirecting web browsers
- Installing additional software, such as search engines

These examples are rather harmless compared to what more malicious spyware (called privacy-invasive software) may do.

Spyware

Since some spyware has become more malicious, a new term has emerged. Privacy-invasive software is more malicious and is often intended to separate users from their money. This type of spyware is sometimes referred to as data-harvesting software. It attempts to gather information that can be used to empty bank accounts or steal identities.

For example, some spyware will install keyloggers onto a system without the end user's knowledge. A keylogger can be used to capture keystrokes and can be combined with other malware. A logic bomb could lie in wait for a user to visit a specific banking site, and when the site's URL is accessed, it could then launch the keylogger. The keylogger could capture the credentials entered in the keystrokes and then email the data to an attacker.

Adware

When adware first emerged, its intent was usually to learn a user's habits for the purpose of placing targeted advertising. However, as it became more malicious in its intent, the name morphed into spyware.

Adware often launched pop-up windows to show advertisements. Newer web browsers and some web browser add-ins known as pop-up blockers are commonly used to block pop-up ads.

> ### Remember
> The most effective protection against unwanted adware is the use of pop-up blockers in web browsers.

The term *adware* is sometimes still used to identify software that is free but includes advertisements. The user is well aware that the advertisements appear, and often a version of the software can be purchased that does not include the ads. All of this is aboveboard without any intentions of misleading the user.

However, even though adware can be used for legitimate software, its usage is mixed in with spyware, and both have serious negative connotations.

Protection Against Malware

Malware is a significant threat that administrators must address in a network. It's common to have a multi-pronged defense to protect against malware. This includes:

- **Mail server.** The most common method of delivering viruses today is through email as attachments. By scanning all email for malicious attachments, the delivery of many viruses can be prevented.
- **All systems.** All systems (workstations and servers) would also have antivirus software installed. Servers may have specialized antivirus software installed, and workstations may also have anti-spyware software installed.

- **Boundary or firewall.** Many networks include antivirus tools that monitor network traffic through the firewall. Inspecting this traffic reduces the risk of users downloading and installing malicious software.

Of course, the obvious protection against viruses and spyware is the use of antivirus and anti-spyware software.

Antivirus Software

Antivirus software is software specifically designed to detect different types of malware. Notice that the lines have blurred a little. While the term *virus* refers to some malware, antivirus software will often detect more types of malware than just viruses.

Malware that can often be detected by antivirus software includes:

- Viruses
- Trojans
- Worms
- Rootkits
- Spyware
- Adware
- Other potentially unwanted programs (PUPs)

Antivirus software detects viruses using either signature-based detection or heuristic-based detection.

Signature-based Detection

Viruses and other malware have known patterns that can be detected. These patterns are defined in signature files (also called data definition files). Files are scanned to determine if they match a pattern or signature of any known threats. If so, the antivirus software detects the match and deletes or quarantines the viruses, depending on the configuration.

A quarantined virus is not harmful to the system while it is in quarantine, but it can still be analyzed. As an example, a quarantined virus could be released in an unprotected but isolated virtual environment to allow a security professional to observe the actions of the virus.

Since new viruses are constantly being released, an important step is to regularly update signature definition files. Most antivirus software includes the ability to automate the process of checking and downloading updated signature definition files.

Heuristic-based Detection

Some antivirus software includes heuristic-based detection. Heuristic-based detection is used to detect viruses that were previously unknown, so signatures don't exist.

Heuristic-based detection is similar to anomaly-based detection used with intrusion detection systems as discussed in Chapter 4. Both methods detect suspect behavior that can't be detected by signature-based detection alone. However, heuristic-based analysis performs the analysis quite differently than anomaly-based detection.

You may remember that anomaly-based detection starts by creating a baseline of normal behavior and then compares it to current behavior. Heuristic-based analysis instead runs questionable code in a virtualized environment specifically designed to protect the live environment but observe the behavior of the questionable code. Most viruses engage in "viral activities"—actions that can be harmful but are rarely performed by legitimate programs. These viral activities can often be detected.

Additionally, some heuristic analysis programs will attempt to reverse-engineer the suspect program to read the actual source code. This is also known as decompiling the program.

Anti-spyware Software

Anti-spyware software has emerged as a separate application that targets spyware. It is common today for a system to have both antivirus software and anti-spyware software installed.

Some of the lines between spyware and malware have become blurry from the perspective of antivirus software and anti-spyware software. Specifically, antivirus software may catch some spyware, and anti-spyware software may catch some malware. Companies are simply adding additional features to make their programs worth more to end users.

Several anti-spyware programs are available free of charge including:

- Lavasoft's Ad-Aware
- Microsoft's Windows Defender
- Spybot—Search and Destroy

Attacks

While malware is a significant threat to protect against, several other attacks also present risks to systems and networks. In this section, you'll learn about many of these other attacks.

It's important to realize that effective countermeasures exist for all of the attacks listed in this book. But some attackers are actively working on beating the countermeasures. As they do, additional countermeasures will be devised and implemented. Security is a never-ending process.

The goal in this section is to become aware of many of the well-known attacks, and you'll be better prepared to comprehend the improved attacks and the improved countermeasures.

Denial-of-service

A denial-of-service (DoS) attack is an attack intended to make a computer's resources or services unavailable to users. In other words, it prevents a server from operating or responding to normal requests.

There are many different types of DoS attacks, including the SYN Flood attack and the Smurf attack.

SYN Flood Attack

The SYN Flood attack is a common DoS attack used against servers on the Internet. It's also called simply a SYN attack. Any server using TCP/IP is susceptible. SYN Flood was introduced in Chapters 3 and 4 since it is so common.

> **Remember**
> The SYN Flood attack disrupts the TCP initiation process by withholding the third packet of the TCP three-way handshake.

As a reminder, two systems would normally start a TCP session by exchanging three packets in a TCP handshake.

- A client sends a packet with the SYN flag to start the synchronization.
- A server replies with a packet that has the SYN and ACK flags set to acknowledge the connection attempt. The server establishes a session and waits for the client's reply.
- The client replies with the ACK flag set to confirm the connection. The connection is then used for regular communication.

The SYN Flood attack modifies this handshake by withholding the third packet. The client never sends the packet with the ACK flag set, so the server is left with an open session waiting for the connection to complete.

A single session that remains open is no big deal, but a SYN Flood attack floods the server with these half-open connections, consuming the server's resources. Too many of the sessions can cause servers to crash or simply reduce their response times against legitimate requests.

Intrusion detection systems are commonly configured to detect and respond to these types of attacks.

Smurf Attack

A Smurf attack spoofs the source address of a broadcast ping packet. It's worthwhile to break this down.

- **A ping is normally unicast—one computer to one computer**. ICMP echo requests are sent to one computer, and ICMP echo responses are sent back to the requesting computer.
- **The Smurf attack sends the ping out as a broadcast**. In a broadcast, one computer sends the packet to all other computers in the subnet.

- **The Smurf attack spoofs the source IP**. If the source IP address isn't changed, the computer sending out the broadcast ping will get flooded with the ICMP replies. Instead, the Smurf attack substitutes the source IP with the IP address of the victim, and the victim gets flooded with these ICMP replies.

The rumor that a Smurf attack is one where attackers send out little blue packets that report back to a Papa Smurf is simply not true.

Distributed Denial-of-service

A distributed denial-of-service (DDoS) attack is similar to a denial-of-service attack except that it includes multiple attacking computers. These attacking computers are often part of a botnet and are often known as zombies.

> **Remember**
> A distributed denial-of-service (DDoS) attack includes multiple computers attacking a single target. The multiple computers are often zombies as part of a botnet. A botnet includes a command and control center that acts as a master to control the zombies, which act as slaves.

Botnet

A botnet combines the words *robot* and *network*. It includes multiple computers that act as software robots and function together in a network (such as the Internet), often for malicious purposes.

Malware frequently attempts to build botnets by taking control of thousands or even millions of computers. Infected computers will periodically check a computer on the Internet for instructions. These instructions could be:

- Launch a distributed denial-of-service attack at a given time.
- Send spam email. (Botnet operators often sell this service to spammers.)
- Download additional malware, adware, or spyware.

Botnets are controlled by central command and control computers and include many zombie computers.

Zombies

A zombie computer is one that has been infected with some type of malware and is now part of a botnet. The computer may otherwise work fine, but when told to do something by the botnet, it mindlessly does so.

Zombies are remotely controlled by a central command and control center, and the zombie will periodically check with this command and control center. The server hosting the command and control center can be any computer with Internet access. Often public web servers are hijacked to unwittingly perform as command and control centers to issue instructions to zombie computers.

The command and control computer and the zombie computers have a master/slave type relationship.

- **Master.** The command and control center runs an application that can instruct the zombies on what to do.
- **Slave.** The zombies run software that acts as a slave and will periodically check in with the command and control center and do its bidding.

The traffic from these master and slave applications can often be detected on boundary firewalls. Network administrators sometimes discover these master/slave relationships by reviewing the network firewall logs and discovering multiple computers periodically communicating to the same remote server.

Zombies have sometimes been called clones, though the term *clone* is not used as often.

Spoofing

Spoofing is where one person or entity impersonates or masquerades as something else. Spoofing is often used to modify the source IP address or the source email address.

IP Spoofing

In IP spoofing, the source IP address is modified. IP spoofing is used for multiple types of attacks. The Smurf attack uses IP spoofing to target another system as a victim. IP spoofing can also be used to mask the sender's identity or make the packet look more trustworthy.

For example, an attacker on the Internet can attempt to penetrate an internal network by sending traffic through the firewall. Systems on the internal network (with private IP addresses) are more trusted than systems on the Internet (with public IP addresses). Armed with this knowledge, the attacker may try to spoof his Internet IP with a trusted private IP.

Similarly, IP addresses are sometimes used for authentication. When this occurs, the IP address can be spoofed to gain entry.

Email Spoofing

Email spoofing occurs when someone changes the From address to make email appear as though it's coming from someone else. This is actually easy to do with most email software, but it is not done for legitimate purposes. Similarly, the Reply To address is easy to change.

It is possible to block any email from known spammers using the From address, but since the address is easily spoofed, this method is no longer effective. Email spoofing is very effective when anonymous relays are enabled on mail servers. The email looks like it is coming from the email server.

Additionally, many spammers now use software to automate the process of spoofing the source address. They often change the From address to a legitimate email address of someone who is not involved in the spam at all.

While the From and Reply To fields of emails can be spoofed, the SMTP header can often be examined to identify the IP address of the email server that sent the email.

Advanced Attacks

These attacks require more advanced knowledge and often additional hardware. They are possible, and you should know about them, but they are used less often. These advanced attacks include:

- Man-in-the-middle
- Replay attacks
- TCP/IP hijacking

> **Remember**
>
> A man-in-the-middle attack is a form of active interception or eavesdropping where a third party can listen in on a conversation. Advanced man-in-the-middle attacks can even listen in on SSL sessions. A replay attack is used by a third party to capture transmissions (including credentials) that are later used to impersonate a client. A TCP/IP hijack attack is where a third party disconnects one of two connected clients and takes over the session as the original client.

Man-in-the-middle

A man-in-the-middle (MITM) attack is a form of active interception or active eavesdropping. It uses a separate computer that accepts traffic from each party in a conversation and forwards the traffic without modifying it at all.

For example, Sally and Joe could be connected with two computers passing information back and forth. A third computer controlled by hacker Harry could be used to intercept all traffic. Sally and Joe still receive all the information, so they are unaware of the attack. However, hacker Harry also receives all the information.

A more sophisticated form of this attack can attack encrypted SSL sessions. Normally, the two clients would create an SSL session between them, and the SSL session could not be decrypted by a third party. However, the MITM creates two separate SSL sessions.

Take a look at figure 6.1 while considering this scenario.

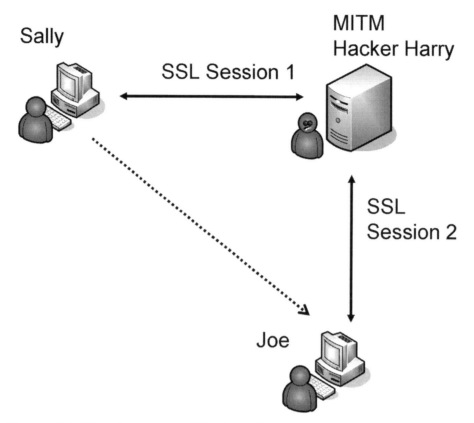

Figure 6.1: Man-in-the-middle Attack

Think about Sally and Joe again. They think that they are creating a single SSL session between each other, but instead, they are creating SSL sessions with hacker Harry. Sally has one SSL session with hacker Harry, and hacker Harry forwards the traffic on to Joe with another SSL session. Since hacker Harry is part of each SSL session, he can read all the data.

Notice that eavesdropping means the same thing with computers as it does in real life—listening in on conversations. Someone can hover close to others to listen in on or overhear a conversation, and clandestine electronic devices can be used to eavesdrop.

Replay

A replay attack is one where an attacker replays data that was already part of a communication session. Replay attacks are often done by third parties to impersonate a client that is involved in the original session.

As an example, Sally and Joe may initiate a session with each other. During the communication, each client authenticates with the other by passing authentication credentials. Hacker Harry intercepts all the data including the credentials and later initiates a conversation with Sally pretending to be Joe. When Sally challenges hacker Harry, he sends Joe's credentials.

In Chapter 1, Kerberos was covered. Kerberos prevents replay attacks with time-stamped tickets that require the internal clocks of all computers to be synchronized within five minutes of each other. The window for a replay attack is restricted to only five minutes.

TCP/IP Hijacking

TCP/IP hijacking is where a third party takes over a session and logically disconnects a client that was originally involved in the session. Many TCP sessions only require authentication at the beginning of a session, allowing this attack to succeed.

CHAP was covered in Chapter 1. CHAP prevents hijacked sessions by periodically requiring the clients to authenticate again using a different nonce each time. If the session is hijacked, it is disconnected when the hijacker is unable to answer the challenge with a new nonce.

ARP Poisoning

ARP poisoning can be used in a denial-of-service attack to mislead computers about the actual MAC address of a system. When used against a single computer, it can stop the computer from communicating with other hosts. When the default gateway is attacked, it can cause entire subnets to become isolated.

As a reminder, the Address Resolution Protocol (ARP) is used to resolve IP addresses to MAC addresses on a subnet. ARP broadcasts a request with an IP address asking anyone with the IP address to respond. The computer with that IP address responds with its MAC address. All computers that hear the ARP reply will cache the data for several minutes.

The vulnerability is that all computers will believe any ARP reply packet. In an ARP poisoning attack used for denial-of-service, an ARP packet is sent out associating a valid IP address with an invalid MAC address. Now, any traffic destined for the victimized client will fail.

If ARP poisoning is used to mislead clients about the MAC of the default gateway, then it will prevent clients from reaching the default gateway and getting any traffic out of the subnet.

Reconnaissance Attack

Reconnaissance is the process of evaluating targets for strengths and weaknesses by learning as much as possible about them. Once the vulnerabilities are learned, the attack is often done quickly and easily.

Of course, reconnaissance shows what targets are easy and what targets are well protected. The easier targets are more likely to get attacked since an attacker has a better chance of getting in and out quickly.

Remember

A reconnaissance attack is used to learn as much as possible about a target. Ping scanners ping IP addresses to identify what systems are operational. Port scanners determine what ports are open. The fingerprinting process analyzes replies to specific queries to learn details about the operating system.

Reconnaissance includes:
- **IP address identification**. IP addresses are assigned geographically, so if an attacker is interested in servers in a specific area, these IP addresses can often be discovered.
- **Ping scanner**. A ping scanner uses ICMP to ping IP addresses and determine what systems are operational. A ping sweeper can simultaneously ping multiple computers to determine which computers are operational.
- **Port scanning**. Using port scanning tools like Nmap, open ports can be discovered to learn what services and protocols are running on a server.

For example, if port 53 is open, the server is likely a DNS server. If port 25 is open, SMTP is likely running. Port scanning can also be used to learn details about the operating system based on how it replies to port scan attempts.

- **Operating system fingerprinting**. Queries sent to the IP address can be used to learn details of the operating system. The response to many protocol queries (such as telnet, HTTP, FTP, SNMP, SMTP, and more) includes details about the operating system. Sometimes server banners are left enabled, which provides details about the operating system, service packs, hotfixes, and even installed applications.
- **DNS probes**. Simple DNS queries can be used to map IP addresses to names or names to IP addresses. Attempts to transfer zone data are used to get entire databases of valuable DNS data.

Individually, the information gained through this reconnaissance may not be valuable. However, combined, it provides a detailed picture.

This is the same way spies operate. Espionage is the process of gathering multiple innocuous details that form the individual pieces of a much larger picture, just as the pieces of a jigsaw puzzle eventually come together to complete a picture. Security professionals need to be aggressive at closing all the holes to significantly limit the amount of information that is available to any attacker.

Null Sessions

A null session is a logon session that represents anonymous users in Windows environments. It takes advantage of a NetBIOS vulnerability allowing unauthenticated clients to access resources such as files, folders, and printers on Windows file and print servers.

In past versions of Windows, the Everyone group was widely used, granting literally everyone, including anonymous users, access to resources. To mitigate this risk, administrators have commonly replaced the Everyone group with the Authenticated Users. This ensured null sessions couldn't be used to access resources intended only for authenticated users.

Microsoft modified the Everyone group in Windows XP and Windows Server 2003 so that it no longer includes the Anonymous group. This effectively plugs the hole for null sessions as long as this security isn't weakened. However, the best practice of replacing the Everyone group with the Authenticated Users group is still recommended.

Domain Name Kiting

Domain name kiting is the practice of repeatedly registering a domain name, and then deleting it before five days have passed. The domain name is free for the first five days, so by canceling it, the name is free, but then it can be registered for another five days. Domain name kitin is sometimes referred to as *domain kiting*, or just *kiting*.

> **Remember**
>
> Domain name kiting is used to avoid paying for domain names. By registering a domain name and then deleting the registration before five days have passed, a user can avoid paying for the domain name.

The purpose of the free period is to allow domain tasting. Domain tasting allows potential purchasers to perform some basic testing to check for traffic to the domain name. If the domain name generates a lot of traffic, it will likely be able to generate revenue from advertising.

Domain tasting was never intended to be used repeatedly for the same domain name. Due to the abuse of domain name kiting, some registrars have begun charging minimal fees to cancel a domain name, which discourages domain name kiting.

Social Engineering

Social engineering is the practice of using social tactics to gain information or access. It's often low-tech or no-tech and encourages a person to do something or reveal some piece of information such as his credentials.

Some of the individual methods and techniques include:

- Flattery
- Conning
- Assuming a position of authority
- Encouraging someone to perform an action
- Encouraging someone to reveal information
- Impersonating someone, such as an authorized technician
- Closely following authorized personnel without providing credentials

In the movie *Catch Me If You Can*, Leonardo DiCaprio played Frank Abagnale Jr., an effective con artist. He learned some deep secrets about different fields by conning and flattering people into telling him. He then combined all he learned to impersonate pilots and doctors, and perform some sophisticated forgery.

Remember

Social engineering bypasses technology protections and encourages uneducated users to perform actions or reveal information. It includes flattery, conning, and impersonation, such as an attacker assuming a position of authority or impersonating a repair technician.

Social engineering can be done in-person as Frank Abagnale Jr. did, over the phone, or via email using phishing tactics.

As an example of a social engineer using the phone, consider this scenario. Sally is busy working and receives a call from hacker Harry, who identifies himself as a member of the IT department.

Hacker Harry: "Hi, Sally. I just wanted to remind you, we'll be taking your computer down for the upgrade today, and it'll only be down for a few hours."

Sally:"Wait. I didn't hear anything about this. I need my computer to finish a project today."

Hacker Harry:"You should have gotten the email. I'm sorry, but I have to get the last few computers updated today."

Sally:"Isn't there any other way? I really need my computer."

Hacker Harry:"Well…it is possible to upgrade it over the network while you're still working. We don't normally do it that way because we need the user's password to do it."

Sally:"If I can still work on my computer, please do it that way."

Hacker Harry:"OK, Sally. Don't tell anyone I'm doing this for you, but if you give me your username and password, I'll do this over the network."

This is certainly a realistic scenario, and many end users will give out their passwords unless training and security awareness education repeatedly repeat the mantra "NEVER give out your password."

Social Engineering Tactics

Many specific social engineering tactics are regularly practiced. These include:

* Phishing
* Piggybacking or tailgating
* Impersonation
* Dumpster diving
* Shoulder surfing

Phishing

Phishing is the practice of sending unwanted email to users with the purpose of tricking them into revealing personal information or clicking on a link.

The classic example is where a user receives an email that looks like it came from eBay, PayPal, a bank, or some other well-known company. The "phisher" doesn't know if the recipient has an account at the company, just as a fisherman doesn't know if any fish are in the water where he casts his line. But, if enough emails are sent out, the odds are good that someone who receives the email has an account and may respond.

The email may look like:

"We have noticed suspicious activity on your
account. To protect your privacy, we will suspend your
account unless you are able to log in and validate your
credentials. Click here to validate your account and
prevent it from being locked out."

The email often includes the same graphics that you would find on the
vendor's web site or an actual email from the vendor. While it may look good, it
simply isn't.

Remember
Phishing is the practice of sending unwanted email to users with the
purpose of tricking them into revealing personal information (such as
bank account information) or clicking on a link. Links within email can
also lead unsuspecting users to install malware.

Legitimate companies simply do not ask you to revalidate your credentials
via email. If you go directly to the site, you may be asked to provide additional
information to prove your identity beyond your credentials, but legitimate
companies don't send emails asking you to follow a link requesting you to input
your credentials to validate them.

Phishing is morphing into other types of methods intending to fool users into
following a link or installing malware.

Phishing to Install Malware

One phishing email looked like it was from a news organization with
headlines of several recent news events. However, if the user clicked it, a dialog
box popped up indicating that the user's version of Flash was older than was
needed to view the story, and gave the question "Would you like to upgrade
your version of Flash?" If the user clicked Yes, Flash wasn't upgraded but instead
malware was installed.

Another email had the subject line as "We have hijacked your baby" and the
following content:

"You must pay once to us $50,000. The details
we will send later. We have attached photo of your
family."

The English seems off, and the receiver may not even have a baby, making this look bogus to most people right away. However, curiosity of the photo is all the attackers seek. If the user tries to open the photo, it instead installs malware.

Remember, the most common method of malware delivery is through email. Phishing is one more technique attackers have added to their arsenal.

Phishing to Validate Email Addresses

A simple method used to validate email addresses is the use of beacons. A beacon is a link included in the email that links to an image on the Internet. The link includes unique code that identifies the receiver's email address.

If the image is displayed in the email, it must be retrieved from a web site on the Internet. When the image is requested, the receiver's email address is validated. This is one of the reasons that most email programs won't display images by default.

Piggybacking or Tailgating

Piggybacking or tailgating is the practice of one person following closely behind another without showing credentials. For example, if Joe uses a badge to gain access to a secure building and Sally follows closely behind Joe without using a badge, Sally is piggybacking.

Remember

Piggybacking or tailgating occurs when one user follows closely behind another user without using valid credentials. Piggybacking can be thwarted with the use of mantraps or security guards.

A solution is the installation of a turnstile to act as a simple mantrap. This could be the same type of turnstile used in subways or bus stations. Imagine two men trying to go through a turnstile like this together. It's just not likely.

Another solution is the use of security guards who can check the credentials of each person. Obviously, employing security guards can be much more expensive than a simple turnstile, but it is warranted in some situations.

Impersonation

Impersonation is where an attacker pretends to be someone else. This is often done to gain access to an area that the attacker would otherwise not be able to easily access.

> ### *Remember*
> Impersonation is a social engineering tactic where an attacker impersonates someone, such as a repair technician, to gain access to a secured area. Identity verification methods can be used to thwart impersonation attempts.

As an example, an attacker can impersonate a repair technician to gain access to a server room or telecommunications closet. After gaining access, he can attempt to access a system to gather information or install hardware such as a rogue access point to capture data and send it wirelessly to an outside collection point.

Identity verification methods are useful to prevent the success of impersonation attacks. Personnel don't simply believe someone is who he says he is or allow him access because he has a uniform. His identity is also verified through a third-party method.

Dumpster Diving

Dumpster diving is searching through trash to gain information from discarded documents. Often a single piece of paper won't have much valuable information on it, but when multiple pieces of paper each contain different snippets of information, the information can be put together to gather meaningful data.

Of course, single documents thrown away can be quite valuable. On a personal basis, preapproved credit applications or blank checks given by credit card companies can be quite valuable to someone attempting to gain money or steal identities. Within a company, if a document is thrown away that contains detailed employee or customer information, it could be easily exploited by attackers.

Documentation with any type of Personally Identifiable Information (PII) should be shredded or burned.

Shoulder Surfing

Shoulder surfing is simply looking over the shoulder of someone to gain information. This can be to learn credentials such as a username and password or a PIN used for a smart card or debit card.

Education and Awareness Training

The single best protection against social engineering attacks is education and awareness training. Most users simply aren't aware of the multiple types of methods that attackers regularly employ. The best technology can easily be rendered ineffective by an internal employee who is unaware of the risks.

> ### *Remember*
> Social engineering attempts succeed due to a lack of security awareness by users and employees. Attackers prey upon this lack of awareness. Education and training can be used to raise awareness and prevent attacks.

In organizations, training and awareness can be accomplished through multiple methods, including:

- Formal classes
- Short informal training sessions
- Posters
- Newsletters
- Logon banners
- Emails

Exam Topic Review

When preparing for the exam, make sure you understand these key concepts, which were covered in this chapter.

Malware

- **Viruses.** A virus is a set of malicious code that infects a host application. The malicious code is executed when the host application is executed. A virus will replicate, and when an activation trigger occurs, it will deliver the objective, which is usually malicious. Email is the most popular method used to spread viruses.

- **Hoaxes.** Hoaxes can be as damaging as real viruses since they can trick users into harming their own equipment and can add workload to help desks.

- **Worms.** Worms can travel autonomously over the network. A worm does not need a host application and doesn't require a user to execute it.

- **Trojan horses.** A Trojan horse is a program that looks like something desirable, such as a screen saver, but includes other malicious code.

- **Logic bombs.** A logic bomb executes in response to an event, such as when a certain date occurs or when another program is launched.

- **Rootkits.** A rootkit is a group of programs that can alter the operating system and the registry to hide its presence. Rootkits can be found by malware scanners.

- **Spyware/adware.** Spyware and adware are software installed without the user's awareness and often attempt to gain Personally Identifiable Information (PII).

- **Antivirus software.** Antivirus software can be placed on all workstations and servers, on the mail server (since most malware is delivered via email), and on boundary firewalls. Antivirus software uses predefined definitions to identify known viruses and heuristic analysis to identify unknown viruses.

Attacks

- **DoS and DDoS**. Denial-of-service attacks attempt to prevent a server or network from performing a normal service. A distributed denial-of-service attack launches a DoS attack from multiple computers.

- **Zombies and botnets**. Computers taken over by malware can join a botnet. A botnet is controlled through a command and control center that acts as a master, with the zombies acting as slaves. Zombies and botnets are frequently used in DDoS attacks. Internal zombies can sometimes be discovered by analyzing network firewall logs.

- **SYN Flood**. A SYN Flood attack disrupts the TCP session initiation process by withholding the third packet of the TCP three-way handshake.

- **Man-in-the-middle**. A man-in-the-middle attack uses a computer placed between a sender and receiver to capture information. It's also known as active interception. A simple MITM attack simply listens in or eavesdrops on a conversation. Sophisticated man-in-the-middle attacks can mimic a single encrypted SSL session by creating two SSL sessions and view all the content involved in the session.

- **Replay**. A replay attack captures traffic (including login credentials) for the purpose of later resending the packets to impersonate a client.

- **TCP/IP hijacking**. In a TCP/IP hijacking attack, the attacker will take over a session and logically disconnect one of the users originally in the session.

- **Reconnaissance attack**. A reconnaissance attack is where an attacker attempts to learn as much about a system or network as possible. It can include ping scans, port scans, DNS transfer attempts, and operating system fingerprinting.

- **Fingerprinting**. Fingerprinting is part of a reconnaissance attack where an attacker attempts to learn details about the operating system by analyzing replies from different queries.

- **Kiting.** Domain name kiting is the practice of repeatedly registering a domain name, and then deleting it before five days have passed to avoid having to pay for it.

Social Engineering

Social engineering bypasses technology protections by using a variety of different tactics and methods to encourage another person to perform a specific action or give up a piece of critical information. Social engineering includes:

- **Conning and flattery**. Social engineering attacks often start as simple con jobs.
- **Phishing**. Phishing is the practice of sending unwanted email to users with the purpose of tricking them into revealing personal information (such as bank account information) or clicking on a link.
- **Piggybacking or tailgating**. Piggybacking or tailgating occurs when one user follows closely behind another user without using valid credentials. It can often be prevented with a mantrap.
- **Impersonation**. Impersonation is a specific social engineering tactic where an attacker masquerades as someone else, such as a repair technician.
- **Dumpster diving**. Dumpster diving is the practice of searching through trash to gain information from discarded documents.

The primary reason social engineering attacks succeed is due to a lack of security awareness by personnel. The primary protection against social engineering tactics is an educated workforce. Personnel can be educated through security awareness training, identity verification methods, logon banners, posters, and more.

Practice Questions

1. What's the most popular method used to spread viruses?

   A. Floppy

   B. Email

   C. DVDs

   D. External USB hard drives

2. What characteristics define a virus?

   A. Replication, activation, and objective

   B. Replication, worm, network control

   C. Execution, payload delivery, replication

   D. Activation, replication, recurrence

3. What can be said about a virus hoax? (Choose all that apply.)

   A. A virus hoax can cause as much damage as a real virus.

   B. A virus hoax is harmless.

   C. A virus hoax is only damaging if the attachment is executed.

   D. A virus hoax is only damaging if it includes a worm.

4. What type of malware doesn't need to be executed but instead travels across the network?

   A. Virus

   B. Trojan horse

   C. Worm

   D. P2P

5. A user downloads and installs a screen saver. Later, he learns that he has been infected with malware that was included with the screen saver. What is this called?

   A. Virus

   B. Trojan horse

   C. Worm

   D. Logic Bomb

6. A piece of code in a legitimate application is scheduled to be executed every year on July 4th and perform a malicious action. What is this?

    A. Virus

    B. Trojan horse

    C. Worm

    D. Logic Bomb

7. A system has been infected with malicious code that has altered the operating system processes and modified some registry entries to hide its presence. What is this?

    A. A port scanner

    B. A rootkit

    C. A worm

    D. Service pack

8. What is a DDoS attack?

    A. An attack launched from the command line, previously known as the DoS prompt

    B. Using multiple computers to attack a single target

    C. Exploiting the TCP session initiation process

    D. An attack launched from a single computer designed to make the resource unavailable to intended users

9. A firewall log shows multiple internal computers routinely communicating with a single computer on the Internet. Research has been unsuccessful at determining the actual function of the server. What is likely occurring? (Choose two.)

    A. The remote server is running command and control master software for a botnet.

    B. The remote server is running slave software for a botnet.

    C. The internal computers are running command and control master software for a botnet.

    D. The internal computers are running slave software for a botnet.

10. What type of attack attempts to overload servers by manipulating the TCP three-way handshake process?

    A. SYN attack

    B. MAC flood attack

    C. Zombie attack

    D. Port scan attack

11. Which one of the following describes a man-in-the-middle attack?

    A. Capturing traffic for the purpose of later resending it to impersonate a client

    B. Disconnecting one of two connected clients and taking over the session

    C. Sending ARP packets to mislead computers about the MAC address of a system

    D. Placing a computer between a sender and receiver to capture traffic

12. Which one of the following describes a replay attack?

    A. Capturing traffic for the purpose of later resending it to impersonate a client

    B. Disconnecting one of two connected clients and taking over the session

    C. Sending ARP packets to mislead computers about the MAC address of a system

    D. Placing a computer between a sender and receiver to capture traffic

13. An attacker monitors a session, then takes over the session, disconnecting one of the parties from the session. What is this?

    A. Replay attack

    B. Man-in-the-middle attack

    C. Active interception

    D. TCP/IP hijacking attack

14. An attacker is trying to determine details about an operating system by querying it with specific protocol traffic. What is this called?

    A. Ping scanning

    B. Port scanning

C. ARP poisoning

D. Fingerprinting

15. An individual is floating domain registrations for five days, canceling them, and then registering them again. What is this called?

A. Kiting

B. Hijacking

C. Fingerprinting

D. ARP poisoning

16. What type of an attack encourages another person to do something or give up some piece of information?

A. Social engineering

B. Impersonation

C. Brute force

D. Shoulder surfing

17. Sally has received an email from her mortgage company requesting her to validate information on her account such as the account number and the bank account number she commonly uses to pay her mortgage. What is this?

A. A virus hoax

B. Social technology

C. Phishing

D. Impersonation

18. A company has a secure room within its building. They are controlling access to the room with a badge and video surveillance but have found that unauthorized personnel occasionally enter. What else could be added?

A. Mantrap

B. Piggybacking log

C. Tailgating lock

D. Access control lists

19. An attacker pretends to be a repair technician coming in after hours to repair a server. He convinces the security guard to allow him access, and while in the server room, he connects a rogue access point to one of the routers. Which one of the following best explains what occurred?

    A. Port scanning attack

    B. Vulnerability assessment

    C. Social engineering

    D. Phishing

20. An attacker wants to retrieve documents discarded by a company. What would this be called?

    A. Phishing

    B. Dumpster diving

    C. Kiting

    D. Shoulder surfing

21. Why do many social engineering attacks succeed?

    A. Use of weak passwords

    B. Use of strong passwords

    C. Use of SSO

    D. Lack of security awareness

Practice Question Answers

1. **B.** Email is the most common method of spreading viruses today. They are included as attachments, and users are encouraged to execute the attachment that installs the virus. Floppies are falling into disuse. DVDs and CDs are typically write-once, so they are only useful if the virus was written on the original media. External USB drives typically don't travel from computer to computer, so they wouldn't be able to spread viruses easily; however, USB flash drives are frequently used to spread viruses.

2. **A.** A virus includes a replication mechanism (where it tries to replicate), an activation mechanism (a trigger that identifies when to achieve the objective), and an objective (such as inflicting damage or delivering a message).

3. **A.** A virus hoax can create as much damage as a real virus. Users can be tricked into changing their system configuration, and help-desk staff can be overwhelmed with user calls.

4. **C.** A worm doesn't need to be executed, doesn't have a host application, and can autonomously travel over the network. Viruses and Trojan horses have host applications that must be executed. P2P software isn't recognized as malware even though it is susceptible to data leakage.

5. **B.** A Trojan horse appears to be one thing but is another. The user thought he was installing a screen saver, but it included malware hidden as a Trojan horse. A virus attaches itself to a host application and runs when the host application runs. A worm travels over the network without needing a host application. A logic bomb executes in response to an event, such as on a specific date or when a specific program is run.

6. **D.** A logic bomb executes in response to an event, such as a specified date or when a specific program is executed. A virus executes when the host application executes. A Trojan horse is malicious code embedded in what appears to be a

legitimate application. A worm uses network resources to replicate throughout the network.

7. **B.** A rootkit is malicious code that may alter the operating system and possibly registry entries to hide its presence. A port scanner is used to detect open ports. A worm is malicious code that travels autonomously over the network without a host application. A service pack may alter the operating system and registry entries, but it is to update the system, not for malicious purposes.

8. **B.** A distributed denial-of-service (DDoS) attack is one launched from multiple computers against a single organization. DDoS attacks often make use of botnets with zombies remotely controlled by a command and control center. There is no formal name for attacks launched from the command line. SYN Flood attacks withhold the third packet of the TCP three-way handshake process. An attack launched from a single computer with the intention of making resources unavailable is known as a DoS attack, not a DDoS attack.

9. **A, D.** Multiple internal computers regularly checking in to a single remote unknown computer is suspicious. More than likely, the remote computer is running command and control master software and controlling the internal computers, which are acting as zombies by running slave software.

10. **A.** A SYN attack (or SYN Flood attack) withholds the third packet in a TCP three-way handshake. A MAC flood attack attempts to overload a switch so that it functions as a hub. A zombie attack can be any type of attack where a command and control center issues commands to zombies in a botnet to perform some type of attack. A port scan attack attempts to identify open ports to learn what services or protocols may be running.

11. **D.** A man-in-the-middle attack (also known as active interception) uses a computer placed between a sender and receiver to capture information. A replay attack captures traffic for the purpose of later resending it to impersonate a client. A TCP/IP hijacking attack disconnects one of two connected clients and

takes over the session. An ARP poisoning attack sends ARP packets to mislead computers about the MAC address of a system.

12. **A.** A replay attack captures traffic (including users' login information) for the purpose of later resending it to impersonate a client. A TCP/IP hijacking attack disconnects one of two connected clients and takes over the session. An ARP poisoning attack sends ARP packets to mislead computers about the MAC address of a system. A man-in-the-middle attack uses a computer placed between a sender and receiver to capture information.

13. **D.** A TCP/IP hijacking attack is where a third party takes over a session and logically disconnects a client that was originally involved in the session. A replay attack captures traffic for the purpose of later resending it to impersonate a client. A man-in-the-middle attack uses a computer placed between a sender and receiver to capture information.

14. **D.** Fingerprinting is part of a reconnaissance attack where an attacker queries an IP address with different protocols to determine details about the operating system or queries ports to determine running services or protocols. A ping scanner uses ICMP to ping IP addresses and determine what systems are operational. A port scanner queries ports on an IP address to determine what ports are open and what ports are likely running. ARP poisoning is used in a denial-of-service attack to mislead computers about the actual MAC address of a system.

15. **A.** Domain name kiting is the practice of repeatedly registering a domain name, and then deleting it before five days have passed; the name comes from the practice of floating checks, which is also called kiting checks. A TCP/IP hijacking attack is where a third party takes over a session and logically disconnects a client that was originally involved in the session. Fingerprinting is part of a reconnaissance attack where an attacker queries an IP address with different protocols to determine details about the operating system or queries ports to determine running services or protocols. ARP poisoning is used in a denial-of-service attack to mislead computers about the actual MAC address of a system.

16. **A.** A social engineering attack encourages another person to perform some specific action or reveal a critical piece of information, such as a user's credentials. Impersonation is a specific type of social engineering, but it doesn't require another person to perform an action or give up a piece of information, only to be fooled by the impersonation. Brute force is a password guessing method. Shoulder surfing is looking over someone's shoulder to gain information.

17. **C.** Phishing is the practice of sending unwanted email to users with the purpose of tricking them into revealing personal information or clicking on a malicious link. A virus hoax warns of a nonexistent virus and may trick users into disabling their systems. Social engineering is the low-tech practice of using social tactics to gain information or access; it is not called social technology. Impersonation is another social engineering tactic where an attacker may pretend to be someone, such as a repair technician, to gain access.

18. **A.** A mantrap can be installed to prevent a piggybacking or tailgating attempt, which is a likely method that unauthorized people are using to access the secure area. Piggybacking or tailgating occurs when one user follows closely behind another user without using valid credentials, but there's no such thing as a piggybacking log or tailgating lock. Access control logs (not lists) can also be used to control entry.

19. **C.** Social engineering is the practice of using social tactics to gain information or access; impersonation is a specific social engineering tactic where an attacker masquerades as someone else, such as a repair technician. A port scanning attack scans an IP address for open ports to determine what services or protocols may be running. A vulnerability assessment is performed by a security professional to determine vulnerabilities. Phishing is the practice of sending unwanted email to users with the purpose of tricking them into revealing personal information.

20. **B.** Dumpster diving is the practice of searching through trash to gain information from discarded documents. Phishing is the practice of sending unwanted email to users with the purpose of tricking them into revealing personal information. Domain name kiting is the practice of repeatedly

registering a domain name and then deleting it before five days have passed. Shoulder surfing is looking over someone's shoulder to gain information.

21. **D.** Many social engineering attacks succeed due to a lack of security awareness; the single best protection against social engineering attacks is education and awareness training. Social engineering can bypass the best technical security measures, such as strong passwords, or the use of single sign-on.

Chapter 7

Managing Vulnerabilities and Risks

CompTIA Security+ objectives covered in this chapter

1.2 Explain the security risks pertaining to system hardware and peripherals.

- BIOS
- USB devices
- Cell phones
- Removable storage
- Network attached storage

2.3 Determine the appropriate use of network security tools to facilitate network security.

- Protocol analyzers

2.4 Apply the appropriate network tools to facilitate network security.

- Protocol analyzers

4.1 Conduct risk assessments and implement risk mitigation.

4.2 Carry out vulnerability assessments using common tools.

- Port scanners
- Vulnerability scanners
- Protocol analyzers
- OVAL
- Password crackers
- Network mappers

4.3 Within the realm of vulnerability assessments, explain the proper use of penetration testing versus vulnerability scanning.

4.4 Use monitoring tools on systems and networks and detect security-related anomalies.

- Protocol analyzers

4.6 Execute proper logging procedures and evaluate the results.

- Security application

- DNS
- System
- Performance
- Access
- Firewall
- Antivirus

4.7 Conduct periodic audits of system security settings.

- User access and rights review
- Group policies

* * *

As a security professional, you need to be aware of the different security issues associated with threats, vulnerabilities, and risks and the tools available to combat them. In this chapter, you'll learn about:

- Threats, vulnerabilities, and risks
- Security tools
- Hardware risks
- Logging and auditing

Threats, Vulnerabilities, and Risks

Threats, vulnerabilities, and risks are all intertwined. You can't fully understand one without understanding the others. In this section, I've used a variety of sources to provide accurate definitions of these terms, including The U.S. National Institute of Standards and Technology (NIST).

The Information Technology Laboratory (ITL) at NIST has published a significant number of well-researched documents on computer security, including the Special Publication 800 series (SP800 series). The SP800 series includes research, guidelines, and guides resulting from collaboration from industry, government, and academic organizations.

If you want to dig deeper into any of these topics, the SP800 series is a great place to continue your research: http://csrc.nist.gov/publications/PubsSPs.html.

Threats

A threat is a potential danger. Within the realm of CompTIA Security+, a threat is the possibility that confidentiality, integrity, or availability of data may be compromised due to an exploited or exposed vulnerability.

Threats come in different forms.

- **Natural threats.** This could include hurricanes, floods, tornados, earthquakes, landsides, electrical storms, and other similar events. On a less drastic scale, a natural threat could also mean hardware failure. Protection against these types of threats is discussed in Chapter 8.
- **Malicious human threats.** This includes the different types of attacks launched by malicious users such as malware, network attacks, and system attacks. These threats have been mentioned throughout this book and were covered in depth in Chapter 6.
- **Accidental human threats.** This includes the unintentional deletion or corruption of data or systems or unauthorized access to confidential information.
- **Environmental threats.** This includes long-term power failure, which could lead to chemical spills, pollution, or other possible threats to the environment.

Different locations have different threats. I live in Virginia Beach, Virginia, and while we're concerned about the natural threat of hurricanes during the hurricane season, we aren't very concerned about earthquakes. However, my sister, who lives in San Francisco, helps companies prepare for risks associated with earthquakes there, but she spends very little time or energy considering the risks of a hurricane in San Francisco.

Vulnerabilities

A vulnerability is a flaw or weakness in software or hardware, or a process that could be exploited, resulting in a security breach. Just because a vulnerability exists doesn't mean it will be exploited, only that it *can* be exploited.

Examples of vulnerabilities include:

- **Updates.** If systems aren't kept up-to-date with patches, hotfixes, and service packs, they are vulnerable to bugs and flaws in the software.

- **Default configurations**. If defaults aren't changed in hardware and software configurations, they are susceptible to attacks.
- **Lack of malware protection or updated definitions**. If antivirus and anti-spyware protection isn't used and kept up-to-date, systems are highly vulnerable to malware attacks.
- **No firewall**. If personal and network firewalls aren't enabled or configured properly, they are much more vulnerable to network and Internet-based attacks.
- **Lack of organizational policies**. If job separation, mandatory vacations, and job rotation policies aren't implemented, an organization may be more susceptible to fraud and collusion from employees.

All vulnerabilities aren't exploited. For example, a user may install his wireless router using all the defaults. It is highly vulnerable to an attack, but it may never be attacked. Even if it's never been attacked, it doesn't mean it isn't vulnerable. A war driving attacker can drive by at any time and exploit the vulnerability.

Risks

A risk is the likelihood that a threat will exploit or expose a vulnerability. The vulnerability is a weakness, and the threat is a potential danger.

For example, if a system is not protected with antivirus software, it is vulnerable to malware. A malicious user who wants to install malware on a system is a threat. The likelihood that the malicious user will be able to install malware on a given system represents the risk.

Just because it can happen on any system doesn't mean it will. The likelihood will significantly increase for a system that is connected to the Internet, however, and will increase even more for a system that is used to visit many risky web sites and download and install unverified files.

It's important to realize that a computer cannot be made completely safe while also being usable. While you can make the computer safe by unplugging it, it's not very useful without power. Instead, risk management is practiced.

You probably practice risk management every day. Driving or walking down roads and streets can be a very dangerous activity. Car-sized bullets are speeding back and forth, representing significant risks to anyone else on the road. However, these risks are mitigated by caution and vigilance.

The same occurs with computers and networks. The risks are recognized and mitigated through risk management. The amount of risk that remains after the risk has been mitigated is referred to as residual risk.

Risk Management

Risk management is the practice of identifying, monitoring, and limiting risks to a manageable level. Risk management usually doesn't eliminate the risk; instead, it only limits or mitigates the risk.

The primary goal of risk management is to reduce risk to a level that the organization will accept. Senior management is ultimately responsible for residual risk—the amount of risk that remains after it has been mitigated. Management must choose a level of acceptable risk. They decide what resources (such as money, hardware, and time) to dedicate to mitigate the risk.

> ### Remember
> The goal of risk management is to reduce risk to a level that the organization will accept. Senior management is responsible for managing risk and for any losses suffered from residual risk.

Clearly, senior management has a significant responsibility here. One of the tools available to help them manage risks is a risk assessment.

Risk Assessment

A risk assessment is the first step in risk management. It is used to quantify or qualify different risks based on different values. A risk assessment is also known as risk identification and starts by first identifying the assets that will be evaluated.

Risk analysis is performed to quantify the impact of potential threats with a goal of identifying the potential harm from a risk. Assessments can be based on quantitative measurements or qualitative measurements.

Quantitative measurements use a monetary figure, and qualitative measurements use a value that is defined internally, such as a value between one and ten. Both methods have the same core goal of helping decision makers make educated decisions based on priorities.

> ### Remember
> Risk assessments are used to prioritize risks using variables such as impact and asset values. Quantitative risk assessments use monetary values as the primary metric, and qualitative risk assessments use internally defined values.

These metrics help management make educated decisions on the amount of resources to dedicate to any specific risk.

Quantitative Risk Assessment

A quantitative risk assessment measures the risk using a specific monetary amount. This monetary amount makes it easier to prioritize risks. For example, a risk with a potential loss of $30,000 is much more important than a risk with a potential loss of $1,000.

The measurements used in a quantitative risk assessment would include the impact and asset value expressed in monetary terms.

- **Impact**. The negative result of the event occurring. For example, a successful DoS attack on an Internet-facing web server may stop it from providing the service to customers. A successful virus attack on the library workstation may inconvenience library visitors.
- **Asset value**. The revenue value or replacement value of an asset. A web server may generate $10,000 in revenue per hour. If it goes down, the company will lose $10,000 each hour it's down, possibly the loss of goodwill if customers take their business elsewhere, and the cost to repair it. The library workstation may cost a total of $1000 to completely replace the system.

One quantitative model uses the following values to determine risks:

- **Single loss expectancy (SLE)**. The SLE is the cost of any single loss.
- **Annualized rate of occurrence (ARO)**. How many times this loss will occur annually.
- **Annualized loss expectancy (ALE)**. The ALE is the SLE * ARO.

Imagine that employees at your company lose, on average, one laptop a month. The laptops are stolen when left in conference rooms during lunch, forgotten in cabs, stolen from their homes, or somehow just lost.

Now, imagine that you're able to identify the average cost of these laptops including the hardware, software, and data as $2,000 each. This assumes employees do not store any PII on the systems that can easily result in much higher costs.

A manager can use the following model to determine the annual cost.

- **SLE** – $2,000 for each laptop.
- **ARO** – Employees lose about one laptop a month, so the ARO is 12.
- **ALE** – $2,000 * 12 = $24,000.

Managers are able to look at the ALE and make educated decisions on the cost of mitigating the risks.

For example, it could be determined that simple hardware locks could be purchased to reduce the number of lost or stolen laptops from twelve a year to only two a year. This changes the ALE from $24,000 to only $4,000 (saving $20,000 a year). If the cost to purchase these locks for all laptops is $1,000 a year, this is a sound fiscal decision. The manager is spending $1,000 to save $20,000.

However, if the cost to mitigate the threat exceeds the ALE, it doesn't make fiscal sense. For example, the company could choose to implement several different controls such as locks, biometrics, access controls, Computrace LoJack for Laptops, and more at a cost of $30,000 per year.

Even if a laptop was never stolen again, the company is spending $30,000 to save $24,000, resulting in a higher net loss—they're losing $6,000 more a year. Admittedly, a company could choose to factor in other values, but if using a quantitative risk assessment, these values would need to be expressed in monetary terms.

Qualitative Risk Assessment

A qualitative risk assessment uses numbers or values to categorize risks based on probability and impact. For example, terms such as *low*, *medium*, and *high* could be used or the numbers one through ten.

The two categories often included in a qualitative risk assessment are probability and impact.

- **Probability.** The likelihood an event will occur. For example, the probability that an Internet-facing web server will be attacked is close to 100 percent and could be given a numerical value of 10. However, the likelihood that an internal workstation in the library with no Internet access will be attacked through the Internet is very low, so it could be given a numerical value of 1.
- **Impact.** The negative result of the event occurring. If the web server is down, the impact may be considered significant and given a value of 10. If the library workstation is down, a library patron may be inconvenienced, and it may be given a value of 1.

Now the risk can be calculated by multiplying the probability and the impact.

- **Web server.** 10 * 10 = 100
- **Library computer.** 1 * 1 = 1

A manager can look at these numbers and easily determine how to allocate resources to protect against the risks. More resources would be allocated to protect the web server than the library computer.

One of the challenges with a qualitative risk assessment is gaining consensus on the probability and impact. Unlike monetary values that can be validated with facts, probability and impact are often subject to debate.

Vulnerability Assessments

Vulnerability assessments are performed on a network or system to identify vulnerabilities. More specifically, they are done to identify and correct the vulnerabilities before attackers can identify and exploit the vulnerabilities. A vulnerability assessment is the most effective way for security professionals to identify security holes.

> **Remember**
> The most effective way for security professionals to identify security holes in systems or networks is through a vulnerability assessment. A vulnerability assessment tool will scan for weak passwords, open ports, and more. Nessus is one of the more popular vulnerability assessment tools.

Many tools are available to help with vulnerability assessments. Some of the tools used by administrators are the same tools used by attackers. If an attacker can find security holes with any available tool, an administrator should also be aware of these holes.

Some of the key points associated with vulnerability assessments are:

- **Identified deficiencies should be corrected.** Any holes that aren't plugged remain vulnerabilities.
- **Vulnerability scans should be repeated any time the environment changes.** This includes after holes are plugged, updates are applied, or any other change.

Some of the vulnerabilities that can be discovered by a vulnerability assessment include:

- **Weak passwords.** Most vulnerability assessment tools include a password cracker that can discover weak passwords. Separate password-cracking tools can also be run as part of the assessment.
- **Open ports.** Open ports can signal a vulnerability if the services associated with these ports aren't actively managed. Separate port scanners can be used, or the capability can be built into a combined package.
- **Discover sensitive data.** Data can be scanned to determine if it matches patterns, such as the pattern for Social Security numbers.
- **Audit configuration.** This includes checks, such as security policy settings for password complexity and checking for the deployment of updates.

One of the popular vulnerability assessment tools is Nessus. Instead of administrators or attackers using multiple individual tools, Nessus combines the features of many different tools into a single package.

Nessus is free for personal use and can be used by an external attacker as easily as it can be used by an internal security professional or administrator. Professional licenses can be purchased for corporate use.

Tenable Network Security owns and licenses Nessus. The different versions of Nessus include:

- **Nessus and Nessusd.** Nessusd is the daemon, or service, that does the scanning, and Nessus is the client that controls the scans and displays the results. These versions will run on UNIX and UNIX derivatives such as Linux and even Apple's Mac OS X.
- **Nessus 3.** Nessus 3 was written to run on Windows systems.
- **Nessus 4.** The current version at this writing.

Penetration Testing

Penetration testing (sometimes called pentest) is done to simulate an attack on a computer system or network. The goal is to determine if vulnerabilities exist that can be exploited by an attacker.

> **Remember**
> Penetration testing starts with a vulnerability test and then tries to exploit vulnerabilities by actually attacking or simulating an attack. Penetration testing is much more intrusive than vulnerability testing; penetration testing can actually disrupt services.

A pentest will start with a vulnerability test but take it a step further and actually try to exploit the vulnerability by simulating or performing an attack. Since a pentest can exploit vulnerabilities, it has the potential to disrupt actual operations and is approached cautiously.

Vulnerability testing is less intrusive since it passively tries to discover the vulnerabilities.

DLL Injection

DLL injection is used to inject dynamic link libraries (DLLs) into a process, causing the process to run the code in the DLL. DLL injection is sometimes used with penetration testing, where a security professional simulates an attack.

A DLL is a compiled set of code that can be called from other programs. DLLs are commonly used for reusability of common code. Instead of rewriting subroutines all the time, common subroutines can be written once and compiled in a DLL. This DLL can then be used as a resource for a larger application.

In DLL injection, code is written in a DLL, and a process is forced to load the DLL. The code could be malicious and cause programs to behave in unintended ways. Or, when used in penetration tools, the code could be used to emulate an attacker.

External Security Testing

External security testing is sometimes used in penetration testing. An external security test would be initiated outside the organization's security perimeter. This includes outside the physical perimeter (meaning off the property) and outside the logical perimeter (from outside of the company's firewall).

However, it's not uncommon for testers to utilize social engineering tactics to gain physical access or bypass network access to improve their odds of a successful attack. If the tester can succeed, an actual attacker can succeed.

Security Tools

Several tools are available for use by security professionals and attackers alike. This is a key point to remember—the same tools security professionals use to monitor and protect networks are often used by attackers.

Some of the tools are:

- Protocol analyzers
- Ping scanners
- Port scanners
- Password crackers
- Vulnerability assessment tools
- Penetration assessment tools

Protocol Analyzer

A protocol analyzer can capture and analyze packets on a network. Any data sent across a network in clear text can be captured by the protocol analyzer and easily displayed. Sensitive data is often encrypted to thwart sniffing attacks.

The process of using a protocol analyzer is sometimes referred to as sniffing or using a sniffer. The term *sniffer* comes from the Sniffer Network Analyzer tool, which is trademarked, so it is more correct to refer to a tool that captures packets as a protocol analyzer or a network analyzer.

> ### *Remember*
> Protocol analyzers (such as Wireshark) can be used to capture and display packets. This can be used to discover passwords sent in clear text, analyze TCP/IP traffic to gain more information on SYN Flood attacks or malformed packets, and analyze traffic related to a specific protocol. A protocol analyzer must run in promiscuous mode to capture all traffic.

Some of the common purposes of a protocol analyzer include:

- Analyze traffic over the network for troubleshooting. This can include analyzing traffic as a whole or filtering the captured traffic to analyze only a specific protocol such as SMTP traffic.
- Capturing and displaying clear text sent across the network. Passwords sent across the network in clear text are often sought by attackers.
- Analyzing TCP/IP sessions and traffic.
    - A SYN Flood attack would have only two packets of the three-way handshake, which can easily be displayed.
    - Malformed or fragmented packets are also easy to identify in a protocol analyzer.
- Monitor specific traffic or network traffic for specific users or computers.
- Detect internal computers being used as zombies within a botnet.

Wireshark is a popular protocol analyzer. It was originally written as Ethereal and was available on UNIX and UNIX derivatives, and later ported over to Windows. Wireshark is available as a free download.

Microsoft includes Network Monitor as a free protocol analyzer with any server product. However, this version can't be used in promiscuous mode, while Wireshark can. A full version of Network Monitor is available with Microsoft's Systems Management Server (SMS) or its replacement System Center Configuration Manager 2007 (SCCM).

Promiscuous and Non-promiscuous Modes

Protocol analyzers can work in either promiscuous mode or non-promiscuous mode. This affects what traffic the protocol analyzer can capture.

- **Non-promiscuous mode.** The protocol analyzer will only capture traffic addressed to the NIC (including broadcasts and multicast traffic) or coming from the NIC.
- **Promiscuous mode.** The protocol analyzer can capture all traffic that reaches the NIC regardless of the source and destination IP addresses. Individual NICs can be configured to operate in promiscuous mode.

Careful though. If a protocol analyzer is working in promiscuous mode, it will give telltale signs on the network. I remember teaching a protocol analyzer topic in a college class once. We even downloaded a sniffer, installed it, and captured some traffic. The next day, one of the students decided to do the same thing in his live network. Within about ten minutes, administrators showed up at his desk, peered over his shoulder, and asked, "Hmmm. What are you doing?"

Switches and Promiscuous Mode

It's worth mentioning how a switch functions in relation to promiscuous mode. Using a protocol analyzer in promiscuous mode allows it to capture all the traffic that reaches the protocol analyzer. However, a switch will restrict the data that can reach it.

Remember, a switch will internally switch traffic so that unicast traffic from one host to another host will only appear on two physical ports. If a protocol analyzer is connected to a third physical port, the traffic between the two hosts won't appear on the third port. The protocol analyzer can't capture traffic that doesn't appear on its port any more than you can capture gold coming out of your faucet.

The exception is if the protocol analyzer is connected to the monitoring port of the switch. The monitoring port can capture traffic from all ports of the switch but requires unrestricted physical access to the switch. This is why switches need to be protected with physical security.

Ping Scanner

A ping scanner sends ICMP requests (pings) to IP addresses to determine if an IP address is being used by a host and if the host will respond to ICMP requests. A ping scanner is often used as part of a larger attack. Once the ping scanner discovers that a system is operational, other tools, such as port scanners, may be used to learn more about the system.

Nmap is a popular network mapping tool that combines the features of a ping scanner and a port scanner to learn what systems are operational and what services are running on these systems.

Port Scanner

A port scanner is used to determine what ports are open on a system. Since ports 0 to 1023 are Well Known Ports, users can determine what services or protocols are running on a system based on the open ports.

> ### Remember
> A ping scanner uses ICMP to discover systems on the network. This is often followed with a port scanner to identify open ports and learn what services are running. Administrators should investigate unexpected open ports to determine if an unneeded service is running.

For example, if a host responds to a query on port 25, it is very likely that the host is running the SMTP protocol, since port 25 is the Well Known Port for SMTP. Port scans will often scan successive ports, leaving a telltale sign in firewall logs.

Most port scanners can scan more than just a single host. Network port scanners (sometimes just called network scanners) have the capability to test for open ports on multiple hosts within a network.

Once an attacker discovers open ports, he can use additional fingerprinting tools to learn more about the system.

If an administrator finds unexpected open ports, she should investigate to determine if these ports should be open.

Password-cracking Tools

Password cracking is used to discover passwords that are used for authentication on systems and networks. Password cracking is used by system administrators trying to discover vulnerabilities in their networks, by administrators trying to discover forgotten or changed passwords, and by attackers trying to break into systems or networks.

Password cracking involves different types of comparative analysis or brute force methods including:

- **Dictionary.** A database of common words is used to try to guess a password. Complex passwords that mix uppercase, lowercase, numbers, and special characters can normally beat this type of attack. NTLMv1 passwords are very susceptible to this type of attack.

- **Brute force.** All possible combinations are attempted. Complex passwords of at least eight characters result in a brute force attack taking simply too long to succeed.

Hash attacks will attack the hash of a password instead of the password. Rainbow table attacks are used to speed up the process of a hash attack by using pre-calculated lookup tables. Chapter 9 will cover hashes, hash attacks, and rainbow tables in more detail.

Many password-cracking tools are available. Password crackers use different forms of comparative analysis to discover or crack a password.

Some of the popular password crackers are:

- **John the Ripper**—Can crack passwords on multiple platforms. It's often used to detect weak passwords.
- **Cain and Abel**—Commonly used to discover passwords on Windows systems; can sniff the network, and use dictionary, brute force, and cryptanalysis attacks.
- **Ophcrack**—Used to crack passwords on Windows systems through the use of rainbow tables.
- **Airsnort**—Can discover WEP keys used on 802.11 wireless networks.
- **Aircrack**—Used for both WEP and WPA cracking on 802.11 wireless networks.
- **L0phtCrack**—Can crack passwords on older Windows systems.

Vulnerability Assessment Tools

Vulnerability assessment tools are used to perform vulnerability assessments. They can be used within a company by administrators checking their own systems for vulnerabilities, or they can be used externally. External assessments can be from attackers or authorized personnel specifically contracted to perform assessments.

The most popular vulnerability assessment tool is Nessus, mentioned earlier in this chapter. It can be used to scan for a wide variety of vulnerabilities including weak passwords, open ports, sensitive data stored on the network or sent over the network, and different audit configuration checks.

OVAL

The Open Vulnerability and Assessment Language (OVAL) is an international standard. The goal is "to promote open and publicly available security content, and to standardize the transfer of this information across the entire spectrum of security tools and services."

OVAL standardizes three steps in the assessment process:

1. Collecting system characteristics and configuration information of a system
2. Analyzing the system to determine the current state
3. Reporting the results

It's important to realize that OVAL isn't a vulnerability assessment scanner. Instead, it's a standard that vulnerability assessment scanners can follow. The idea is that if vendors follow this standard, the customer will receive an overall better product.

Hardware Risks

Some hardware has specific risks associated with it and deserves special attention. Hardware that often causes problems for security professionals are removable and network-attached storage and cell phones.

Storage Risks

The risks associated with storage primarily refer to the loss of data. A massive amount of data is easily accessible via network-attached storage and is easily removed using removable storage.

Network-attached storage refers to hard drives or hard drive systems that are attached directly to the network with an IP address. Any system that has access to the network can access data held on a network-attached storage system.

Removable storage refers to any storage system that can be attached to a computer and can easily remove data. It primarily refers to USB hard drives and USB flash drives.

- A USB hard drive has all the same hardware and moving parts (such as platters and heads) as an internal drive.
- A USB flash drive isn't actually a hard drive but is instead non-volatile memory. It uses solid-state memory to store data without the need to keep it powered on.

USB Flash Drives

USB flash drives are as popular today as floppy drives were years ago and present the same types of risks: loss of data and malware distribution.

Due to the high risk these devices pose, it's not uncommon to have their usage restricted. Some of the ways that USB flash drive usage can be restricted are:

- Disabling the USB root hub within the operating system
- Disabling the USB in the BIOS
- Disabling the USB driver via Group Policy in Windows systems
- Using third-party tools

> ### Remember
> USB flash drives present many security risks including the loss of data and inadvertently spreading malware. USB flash drive usage can be restricted by disabling the USB root hub in the operating system, disabling the USB in the BIOS, or disabling the driver supporting USB devices.

Loss of Data

Inexpensive USB flash drives that can fit into your pocket can hold 16 GB or more of data. If an attacker has physical access to a system, he can easily copy that data onto the flash drive.

Employees can also easily copy massive amounts of data onto their systems. While copying data may seem like a necessity, one of the things that commonly occurs is that users become lackadaisical with security when things are easier to do.

As an example, many USB flash drives have been purchased at flea-market-type sales that have data installed. At some foreign bazaars near U.S. military bases, USB flash drives have been purchased that included a significant amount of personal information on personnel stationed at the base.

I doubt that people intentionally gave the USB away with the data on it. Instead, the data was copied onto the drive, not protected, and stolen. In Chapter 9, many different encryption methods will be covered. AES can be used to quickly encrypt data on USB drives, providing confidentiality for the data.

Malware

Malware can easily be installed on USB flash drives and spread from system to system. Two methods are commonly used to install the malware:

- **From the USB.** When an attacker has unrestricted physical access to a USB flash drive, he can install malware on the drive. When the flash drive is installed on the system, the virus can be transferred to the system.
- **To the USB**. Malware can sense when a USB drive is inserted and copy the malware onto the USB. This malware now waits until it's installed in another system and installs itself there.

Cell Phones

Cell phones (and related PDAs) present many different risks. It's not uncommon for cell phones to be restricted from being brought into some secure areas due to their risks.

> ### Remember
> Cell phones present many risks, such as built-in cameras and the ability to have their audio turned on remotely. Their usage is often restricted in secure areas. It's also recommended that cell phones are password protected, preventing their use if stolen.

Some of these risks are:

- **Built-in cameras.** The cell phone can be brought into a work area and easily be used to take photos.
- **Remote capabilities.** While the technology isn't common, it is possible to remotely turn on the audio for a cell phone, making it a transmitter.
- **Eavesdropping.** Cell phones transmit on known frequencies, and if an attacker wants to listen to a phone call, the technology exists to do so.
- **Stolen phone.** If a phone or PDA is stolen, the attacker can use it to make long-distance calls or access any data stored on the device. It's recommended that cell phones be password protected.

Logging and Auditing

Logging and auditing go hand-in-hand. Logs have the capability to record what happened, when it happened, and where it happened. Auditing adds an important detail that isn't always in regular logs—who did it.

One of the primary purposes of logging is to allow someone, such as an administrator or security professional, to review what happened. A log records events as they occur so that someone can come back later and discover exactly what happened and when.

With this in mind, it's tempting to set up logging to record every event and provide as much detail as possible—most logs support a verbose mode that will log additional details. However, a limiting factor is the amount of disk space available.

Additionally, when logging is enabled, there is an implied responsibility to review the logs. The more you choose to log, the more you may have to review.

Auditing has another meaning in the context of security. Auditing is also known as the independent and objective examination of processes and procedures to determine if standards and guidelines are being followed. Audits in this context will be covered in Chapter 10.

Reviewing Logs

The primary purpose of creating logs is so that they can be reviewed. Ironically, this is often the most overlooked step in the auditing process. Often logs are created but only reviewed when a symptom appears. Sometimes, symptoms don't appear until a problem has snowballed out of control.

> ### Remember
> The most often overlooked step in the auditing process is the review of logs. Reviews can be manual or automated, but logs should be reviewed.

Many third-party programs are available that can automate the review of logs for large organizations. For example, NetIQ has a full suite of applications that can be used to monitor multiple computers and servers in a network. When an event occurs, the event is examined to determine if it is an event of interest. If so, it triggers a programmed response, such as sending an email to a group of administrators.

Smaller organizations require administrators to manually review the logs. Windows Vista and later operating systems include many improvements to Event Viewer, making this process easier. For example, subscriptions can be configured to forward events to a central server for easier monitoring.

The process of reviewing the logs and what should be looked for depend on many variables.

- **Operating system logs**. Operating system logs include information on the system's performance and security. For example, the System log would record system events, such as startup and shutdown, and the Security log would include auditable events such as when a user logs on or accesses a file.

- **Application logs**. Applications like SQL Server, Microsoft Exchange, DNS or DHCP have logs specific to the application, and each application will have unique log entries. For example, DNS logs may be monitored to discover unauthorized zone transfers or unsuccessful update attempts.

- **Performance logs**. Performance logs can be configured to monitor system performance and give an alert when preset performance thresholds are exceeded.

- **Firewall logs**. Firewall logs can be configured to log all traffic that is blocked or allowed. Firewall logs will often be checked to detect intrusions or attacks, such as port sniffing attacks, or simply to record traffic through the firewall.

- **Antivirus logs**. Antivirus logs will log all antivirus activity including when scans were run, any malware detected, and whether the malware was removed or quarantined.

Windows Logs

Windows systems have several common logs that are used to record what happened on a computer system. All of these logs are viewable in the Event Viewer. The common logs are:

- **Application**. The Application log records events recorded by applications or programs running on the system. Any application has the capability of recording errors in the Application log.

- **System**. The operating system uses the System log to record events related to the functioning of the operating system. This can include when it starts, when it shuts down, information on services starting and stopping, drivers loading or failing, or any other system component event deemed important by the system developers.

- **Security**. The Security log records auditable events. Some auditing is enabled by default in some systems, but additional auditing can be added by administrators. The Security log will record details such as who did something, when he did it, what he did, and where.

If a system is attacked, you may be able to learn details of the attack by reviewing the operating system logs. Depending on the type of the attack, any of the operating system logs may be useful.

> **Remember**
>
> Windows logs continuously record information that can be useful in troubleshooting and gaining information on attacks. The System log records events related to the operating system (such as when it boots or is shut down), and the Security log records auditable events that can be used for non-repudiation.

Events in most of the logs are classified as information, warning, or error.

- **Information.** Describes the successful operation of a program, driver, or service.
- **Warning.** An event that might indicate a possible future problem.
- **Error.** A significant problem. Errors are often preceded by warnings that may give a fuller indication of the problem.

The Security log includes entries for audited events, such as when someone accessed a file. Audited events are recorded as success or failure.

- **Success.** Success indicates an audited event completed successfully, such as a user successfully logging on or successfully deleting a file.
- **Failure.** Failure indicates that a user tried to perform an action but failed, such as failing to log on or trying to delete a file but receiving a permission error instead.

Audit Logs

Audit logs are used to specifically identify *who* did something, along with other details of the event, such as what the event was, when it occurred, and where it occurred. Auditing is often used to protect resources such as files, folders, and printers. Within Microsoft systems, the Security log stores the audited events.

When auditing is enabled on a resource, it can record all the actions associated with a resource. For example, auditing could show if anyone accessed, modified, or deleted any files in a folder.

Audit logs are one method of enforcing non-repudiation—preventing a party from denying an event. If it is recorded that Joe deleted a file while logged on with his user account, he can't later deny it (at least not with any credibility). Another method of non-repudiation is the use of digital signatures, which is covered in Chapter 9.

Log Maintenance

Most logs will need to be archived on a regular basis. This is simply saving a copy of the log and storing it. Logs can also have several different properties set on them. This includes:

- **File location**. Can be stored on a different partition than the operating system.
- **Maximum size**. Ensures that the log file can't continuously grow and take over the disk space.
- **Action to take if events can't be recorded**. As a best practice, it's recommended to provide notification to an administrator if the log becomes full.

Some files are circular, meaning that they will overwrite old data. Imagine drawing a circle with a pencil. When your pencil reaches the point where it started, you can continue drawing on top of the original circle. The first line will be overwritten. Circular log files just overwrite the oldest events.

Other log files are configured so that old data can't be overwritten. When the maximum file size is reached, no more log entries are allowed. If a log is full and events can't be recorded, an attack can occur without a record.

Remember

Personnel should be notified if a log becomes full. The notification can come in the form of an alert, an email, a page, or some other means.

If a log becomes full, personnel managing the log should be notified. Different people will be notified based on where the log is located—DNS log, workstation log, firewall log, and so on. Additionally, the notification can come in different forms, such as an email or a page.

It is possible to configure a system to shut down if the log becomes full. The idea is that if events can't be logged, you don't want an attacker's actions to go unrecorded. However, this can result in an easy denial-of-service event. All the attacker has to do is perform many auditable events to fill up the log, and the server shuts itself down.

Securing Log Files

Log files have valuable data. Just as you should protect any valuable data, you should also protect log files. Log files should be protected to ensure that they aren't modified or accessed by unauthorized personnel.

> ### Remember
> Log files can be protected by copying or storing them on another server; restricting access to only certain security groups with the use of permissions; storing them on write-once, read-many media; or using hashes for file integrity auditing.

There are several different methods that can be used to secure log files.

- **Secure them with permissions**. Use permissions to ensure that only trusted administrators or security professionals can access the files. You can also do this by only granting access to users in specific security groups.
- **Store them on another server**. Copy or store log files onto a remote server and ensure that the server has adequate security.
- **Store them on WORM media.** You can ensure that files are not modified by storing them on write-once, read-many (WORM) media such as CD-R or DVD-R media.
- **Hash the log files**. Hashing can be used for file integrity auditing. Chapter 9 covers hashing in greater depth, but in short, a hash is a number that can be created by executing a hash algorithm (such as MD5 or SHA1) on the files. Later, the hash algorithm is executed again, and if the hashes aren't the same, you know the files are no longer the same—they have lost integrity.

- **Apply retention policies.** Retention policies define a specific time frame that files should be maintained. After this time frame, the files should be deleted.

Exam Topic Review

When preparing for the exam, make sure you understand these key concepts, which were covered in this chapter.

Threats, Vulnerabilities, and Risks

- **Threat.** A threat is a potential danger that can compromise confidentiality, integrity, or availability of data.
- **Vulnerability.** A vulnerability is a weakness. It could be a weakness in the hardware, software, or configuration of the system or network.
- **Risk.** A risk is the likelihood that a threat will exploit or expose a vulnerability.
- **Risk management.** Risk management attempts to reduce risk to a level that an organization is able to accept. Senior management is responsible for managing risk and the losses associated from residual risk.
- **Risk assessment.** Risk assessments prioritize risks by evaluating variables, such as risk impact and asset values. Both quantitative (monetary values) and qualitative (internally defined) measurements can be used.
- **Vulnerability assessments.** A vulnerability assessment is performed to identify security holes in a network, such as weak passwords and open ports.
- **Penetration test.** A penetration test (pentest) starts with a vulnerability assessment and follows with an attack to determine if the vulnerability can be exploited. A pentest is much more intrusive than a vulnerability test.

Security Tools

- Vulnerability assessment tools are used to test for weaknesses in a system or network. Nessus is a popular vulnerability assessment tool.

- Protocol analyzers (also called sniffers) are used to capture and analyze packets on a network. They can be effective at discovering passwords going across the network in clear text, analyzing TCP/IP traffic, and more.
- Wireshark is a popular protocol analyzer. It can operate in promiscuous mode, allowing it to capture all traffic that reaches the NIC. Or it can operate in non-promiscuous mode, only allowing packets addressed to or from the NIC to be captured.
- A ping scanner uses ICMP requests (pings) to determine if systems are operational. Many network mappers such as Nmap combine a ping scanner with a port scanner.
- Port scanners scan ports of systems to learn what ports are open and what services and protocols may be running.
- Password crackers attempt to discover passwords using comparative analysis techniques. Dictionary attacks use a database of words; brute force attacks attempt every possible combination.
- Password-cracking tools include John the Ripper, Cain and Abel, LophtCrack, and more.

Hardware Risks

- USB flash drives represent a significant risk through loss of data or malware distribution.
- USB devices can often be disabled by disabling the USB root hub in the operating system or the BIOS, or by disabling the driver.
- Cell phones include many additional features, such as cameras, and can hold additional data, such as email and contacts.
- Password protecting cell phones can reduce the risks associated with a lost or stolen phone.

Logging and Auditing

- Logs can be created to record what event occurred, when it occurred, and where it occurred. Auditing adds the additional element of who performed the event and can provide non-repudiation.
- The most overlooked step in auditing is reviewing the logs.

- Windows core logs include the System log, Security log, and Application log. The System log records system events, such as when a server starts or shuts down. The Security log records any auditable events, such as when a user accesses a file. The Application log records events related to specific applications.
- Logs should be monitored to ensure that they are archived before they fill up. If a log does become full, someone should be notified through an automated email or other means.
- Log files should be secured to protect them from inadvertent disclosure or tampering. Files can be secured with permissions, copied to a more secure server, stored on CD-R or DVD-R media, or hashed.

Practice Questions

1. Who is responsible for the residual risk of an attack on a network?

    A. Network administrators

    B. Firewall administrators

    C. Security officers

    D. Senior management

2. What should a quantitative risk assessment be based upon?

    A. Impact and asset value of a given risk

    B. Impact of a given risk

    C. Probability of mitigating a risk to a level that the organization will accept

    D. The person ultimately responsible for the damage from the risk

3. Which one of the following is a vulnerability assessment tool?

    A. Nessus

    B. Wireshark

    C. Honeypot

    D. RADIUS

4. You want to check for the deployment of an update to determine if systems are susceptible to known software bugs. What would be the least intrusive check that could be done to achieve the goal?

    A. Penetration test

    B. Vulnerability test

    C. Ping scan

    D. Use of Wireshark

5. Vulnerability scanners can perform multiple checks. Which of the following vulnerabilities can most vulnerability scanners detect? (Choose all that apply.)

    A. Open ports

    B. Weak passwords

    C. Revoked certificates

    D. Unneeded services

6. A company policy only allows nonintrusive scans on production servers. An administrator ran a vulnerability test and detected that a system was missing a security patch. After applying the patch, what should be done?

    A. Nothing since only nonintrusive scans are allowed

    B. Perform a vulnerability test

    C. Perform a penetration test

    D. Upgrade the server missing the patch

7. What will a penetration test do?

    A. Check for vulnerabilities and provide a report

    B. Simulate an actual attack on a network

    C. Create a baseline used for behavior-based NIDS

    D. Detect and remove malware

8. What tool could an attacker use to discover a password that is sent across the network in clear text?

    A. John the Ripper

    B. Cain and Abel

    C. Port scanner

    D. Protocol analyzer

9. You need to analyze email traffic on your network including the IMAP4, SMTP, and POP3 protocols. What tool could you use?

    A. An email filter

    B. A protocol analyzer

    C. Antivirus software

    D. Nmap

10. You want to determine what ports are open on several different systems in your network. What could be used?

    A. Ping scanner

    B. Network scanner

    C. Malware scanner

    D. Pentest

11. Which tool uses ICMP to detect if hosts will respond?

    A. Port scanner

    B. Ping scanner

    C. Protocol analyzer

    D. TCP scanner

12. What does a password cracker do?

    A. Reads password files

    B. Performs comparative analysis

    C. Prevents passwords from working anymore

    D. Uses the known passwords of a system

13. Which of the following is used to crack passwords? (Choose all that apply.)

    A. John the Ripper

    B. Rainbow table

    C. Cain and Abel

    D. Wireshark

14. What can be done to prevent users from using USB flash drives on company computers? (Choose all that apply.)

    A. Disable the USB root hub driver in the operating system

    B. Disable the USB hub within the operating system

    C. Disable the USB hub in the BIOS

    D. Disable the PS2 ports in the BIOS

15. You are planning a logging strategy for a new server that you will be implementing. What should you consider within your strategy?

    A. The information that is needed to reconstruct events and the amount of memory available

    B. The information that is needed to reconstruct events and the amount of disk space available

    C. The TCP/IP configuration of the system and the amount of memory available

    D. The TCP/IP configuration of the system and the amount of disk space available

16. You suspect that someone rebooted a server to gain access to the root drive using a boot CD. Which Windows log can be checked to see when the server was last booted?

    A. Application

    B. System

    C. Security

    D. Setup

17. What can you do to secure log files? (Choose all that apply.)

    A. Copy the logs to a remote log server

    B. Store the logs on a CD-R

    C. Hash the logs

    D. Secure them with permissions

18. You want to ensure that, if any log files are modified, there is evidence that they have been modified. You choose to use the MD5 hash function to protect the files. What is this called?

    A. Encryption

    B. File integrity auditing

    C. Non-repudiation

    D. Digital signature

19. What step is often overlooked after enabling auditing?

    A. Archiving the logs

    B. Reviewing the logs

    C. Storing the logs on DVD-RW media

    D. Encrypting the logs

20. A computer system was attacked from within the network, and you'd like to identify where the attack originated. What log could you use?

    A. Attacked computer's logs

    B. Attacking computer's logs

    C. Network firewall

    D. DNS logs

21. It's suspected that an employee is using his computer during off-hours and copying proprietary data to a remote location. Audit logging is not enabled on his workstation. What log can be checked to verify this?

    A. Workstation Security log

    B. Workstation System log

    C. Anti-spyware log

    D. Firewall log

22. What should be done if a log file becomes full and can no longer record events?

    A. Shut down the system

    B. Alert appropriate personnel

    C. Stop generating log entries

    D. Delete the log

Practice Question Answers

1. **D.** Senior management within a company is ultimately responsible for residual risk—the amount of risk that remains after mitigation steps have been taken. Administrators and security officers are responsible for informing management of threats and vulnerabilities and implementing risk management as directed. However, if management decides to allocate the necessary resources to mitigate a risk to a level they consider appropriate, administrators and security officers should not override management's decision and certainly aren't held responsible.

2. **A.** A quantitative risk assessment is based on the impact and asset value of a given risk. Using the impact of a risk as the only metric doesn't provide an adequate assessment. The purpose of risk management is to mitigate a risk to a level that the organization will accept, and a risk assessment is a part of risk management. Senior management is always ultimately responsible for the damage from a risk.

3. **A.** Nessus is a popular vulnerability assessment tool. Wireshark is a protocol analyzer used to capture and analyze packets. A honeypot is a server created to divert or attract attackers. RADIUS is used for authentication for RAS servers.

4. **B.** A vulnerability test or a penetration test could detect if the systems are vulnerable to known software bugs, but a vulnerability test would be the least intrusive. The penetration test would also try to exploit the vulnerability through an attack. A ping scan can determine if systems are online and answering pings. Wireshark can be used to capture and analyze packets.

5. **A, B.** Vulnerability scanners can check for open ports, weak passwords, and more. Revoked certificates are published on a certificate revocation list (CRL) and can be checked by normal applications such as a web browser. A vulnerability scanner can determine what services are running, but an administrator determines whether or not services are needed on a server.

6. **B.** After applying a patch that was discovered missing from a vulnerability scan, the vulnerability scan should be repeated. A penetration test differs from a vulnerability test in that the penetration test attacks and is considered intrusive. An upgrade is not necessary.

7. **B.** A penetration test will check for vulnerabilities and simulate or perform an actual attack on a network. A vulnerability test will check for vulnerabilities and provide a report; while a penetration test will start with a vulnerability test, the distinct difference is that the penetration test follows with an attack. A behavior-based NIDS requires a baseline, but it is not created by a penetration test. Antivirus software will detect and remove malware.

8. **D.** A protocol analyzer (such as Wireshark) can capture and display passwords sent across the network in clear text. John the Ripper and Cain and Abel are password crackers, but if the password is sent in clear text, a password cracker isn't needed. A port scanner can be used to detect open ports.

9. **B.** A protocol analyzer can capture and analyze packets on the network, including packets associated with specific protocols. An email filter can be used to filter spam and attachments on an email server or client. Antivirus software can be used to detect malware. Nmap is a port scanner that can be used to detect open ports.

10. **B.** A network scanner (sometimes called a network port scanner, or simply port scanner) can detect open ports on systems. A ping scanner uses ICMP to detect systems based on IP addresses. A malware scanner can detect malicious software. A pentest is used to perform penetration testing, which is a combination of a vulnerability test and an attack.

11. **B.** A ping scanner uses ICMP to detect systems on the network. A port scanner scans for open ports to determine what ports are open. A protocol analyzer captures and analyzes packets. ICMP uses UDP, not TCP.

12. **B.** Password crackers attempt to discover passwords and frequently use comparative analysis to do so. Passwords are rarely kept in simple password files anymore, and if so, they would be encrypted, preventing them from being read without some advanced analysis. A password cracker would not prevent passwords from working, and it wouldn't know the passwords of a system, but instead, attempts to discover them for the attacker.

13. **A, B, C.** John the Ripper and Cain and Abel are both well-known password-cracking tools. Rainbow tables are used by some password crackers to crack passwords. Wireshark is a protocol analyzer, or sniffer, used to capture and analyze packets on a network.

14. **A, B, C.** USB flash drives can be prevented from being used within systems by disabling the driver, disabling the USB hub within the operating system, or disabling the USB hub in the BIOS. PS2 ports are not used by USB devices.

15. **B.** A primary purpose of logging is to be able to reconstruct events, so the information needed to reconstruct events is needed; logs are stored on a disk, so the amount of disk space available (or the amount of disk space needed) is also a consideration. Since logs write directly to the disk, memory consumption isn't a significant factor. The TCP/IP configuration isn't a major consideration when planning logging.

16. **B.** The System log will record operating system events, such as when it was last shut down or when it was booted. The Application log will record events from applications or programs. The Security log will record auditable events. The Setup log is a newer log and includes events related to application setup.

17. **A, B, C, D.** You can secure logs by copying or saving them to a remote log server, storing the logs on a CD-R or DVD-R media, hashing the logs for file integrity auditing, or securing them with permissions.

18. **B.** File integrity auditing is the use of a hash function (such as MD5 or SHA1) to create a hash on the files; if the files are modified when the hash function is

later executed, the hash will be different, showing the file has been modified—it has lost integrity. Encryption uses cipher algorithms not hashing functions. If a log records who performed an action, it provides non-repudiation, but hashing doesn't provide non-repudiation. Digital signatures provide authentication, integrity, and non-repudiation but are not used with logs.

19. **B.** The step that is most often overlooked during the auditing process is reviewing the logs. Archiving the logs can be done if the logs are needed for long term, but this is often forced since the logs will fill up, requiring action. Logs should be stored on write-once, read-many media such as CD-R or DVD-R, not rewritable media. Files are often hashed for file integrity auditing but rarely encrypted.

20. **A.** The attacked computer's logs would hold information that may be useful to determine the source of the attack. Since you don't know which computer attacked, you can't check the attacking computer's logs. Since the attack was internal, it wouldn't go through the network firewall. DNS logs will hold information on name resolution traffic, such as zone transfers, but would not hold information from an internal attack.

21. **D.** The firewall log can be used to record normal traffic, such as the transfer of data from a specific computer at a specific time. Since auditing is not enabled, the Security log wouldn't include any data. The System log would not record normal network traffic. Anti-spyware software is used to detect malware, not employees who may be snooping like a spy.

22. **B.** Appropriate personnel should be notified if a log becomes full and events can no longer be recorded. Shutting down the system is not recommended, since attackers can use this as a denial-of-service attack by just filling up the log. If the log is full and can no longer record events, it has already stopped generating log entries. Deleting the log will delete all the recorded data.

Chapter 8

Preparing For and Preventing Disasters

CompTIA Security+ objectives covered in this chapter

6.1 Explain redundancy planning and its components.

- Hot site
- Cold site
- Warm site
- Backup generator
- Single point of failure
- RAID
- Spare parts
- Redundant servers
- Redundant ISP
- UPS
- Redundant connections

6.2 Implement disaster recovery procedures.

- Planning
- Disaster recovery exercises
- Backup techniques and practices—storage
- Schemes
- Restoration

6.5 Explain the importance of environmental controls.

- Fire suppression
- HVAC
- Shielding

* * *

Most companies don't want to experience disasters, but they still need to prepare for them. The first step is the creation of a disaster recovery plan.

While you can't prevent some disasters (such as hurricanes or floods), you can prevent catastrophic failures by taking other preventive steps. Single points of failure can be identified and protected with redundancy solutions; fire suppression systems can prevent a fire from destroying an entire location; HVAC systems can protect the equipment by controlling the environment; and effective shielding solutions can protect data from emanating beyond a defined footprint.

Disaster Recovery

Disaster recovery includes all the elements necessary to allow an organization to recover from a disaster and return to full operation. Disasters can take many forms, including:

- Natural disasters, such as hurricanes, floods, and earthquakes
- Fires
- Attacks
- Hardware and software failures
- Data loss from any cause

Disaster recovery planning takes a lot of time and effort to adequately predict the different types of disasters, the impact of each, and what should be protected.

Disaster Recovery Plans

A disaster recovery plan (DRP) is the single most important document a company can develop to prepare for potential disasters. A DRP is designed to allow an organization to plan for and recover from disasters.

An effective disaster recovery plan includes both redundancy solutions and backups.

- **Redundancy**. Redundant solutions, such as redundant hard drives, redundant servers, and redundant connections, provide high availability to systems and networks. When a fault occurs, the fault can be tolerated, and the system or network remains available.

- **Backups.** A backup is a separate copy of the data that can be used to restore the data in the event of data loss. An effective backup strategy includes some type of offsite storage of the backups. If a fire destroys a building and all the backups are in the building, the data is destroyed.

It's important to realize that disaster recovery includes both elements. Protecting data with a RAID-1 or RAID-5 does not negate the need for backups. If a fire destroys a server, the data on the RAID is destroyed. Without a backup, all of the data is gone.

Some of the basic steps involved in the creation of a disaster recovery plan include:

- Identify potential disasters.
- Identify assets to protect.
- Identify the scope of the plan.
    - o What assets will be included?
    - o What functions must continue to operate or be easily recovered?
- Identify utilities needed, such as water, heat, gas for generators, and so on.
- Identify alternate sites to support the plan.
- Identify backup strategies.

Disaster Recovery Testing

Disaster recovery strategies often include testing to ensure the plan works as desired. Testing can be done to verify redundancies work as desired and backups work as desired. Testing is normally done during off-peak times or in such a way that the primary services are either not impacted at all or minimally impacted.

Some of the common methods of testing are:

- **Server redundancy.** Servers are protected with failover clusters, where the cluster can be tested by taking a primary node offline and ensuring the inactive node takes over.
- **Redundant connections.** Sites can have redundant connections to ensure they retain connectivity in the event of a single failure. A T1 can be disconnected to ensure the secondary communication line is available.
- **Alternate sites.** An alternate site (hot, cold, or warm) can be tested by moving some of the functionality to the alternate site and ensuring the

alternate site works as desired. This is very simple with a hot site but extremely difficult with a cold site.

- **Backups**. Backups can be restored to alternate locations. If the backup cannot be restored, you know you have a problem with the backup strategy. The good news is that you know the problem and don't have a crisis since it was just a test.

Designing Redundancy

One of the constants with computers, subsystems, and networks is that they will fail. It's one of the few things you can count on. However, by designing redundancy into your systems and networks, you can increase the reliability of your systems even when they fail.

Redundancy adds duplication to critical system components and networks. If a critical component has a fault, the duplication provided by the redundancy allows the service to continue as if a fault never occurred.

This is referred to as adding fault tolerance. A system with fault tolerance can suffer a fault, but it can tolerate it and continue to operate.

Redundancy can be added at multiple levels:

- Disk redundancies using RAID
- Server redundancies by adding failover clusters
- Connection redundancies by adding additional connections
- Site redundancies by adding cold, warm, or hot sites

Redundancies are often added for subsystems that are determined to be a single point of failure.

Single Point of Failure

A single point of failure is a component within a system that can cause the entire system to fail if the component fails. When designing redundancies, different components are examined to determine if they are considered to be a single point of failure, and if so, steps are identified to provide a backup capability.

Some examples include:

- **Disk subsystem**. Disks can be upgraded to RAID, which can tolerate the failure of any single hard drive. If the system uses a single drive, the system will crash if the single drive fails. However, RAID can allow the system to continue to operate even if a single drive fails.

- **Server providing a critical service**. Servers can be protected in failover clusters, eliminating any single server from causing an entire process to fail. As an example, a single web server hosting a large e-commerce web site could access multiple back-end database servers. The single web server would be a single point of failure. If it fails, the entire e-commerce site fails.

- **Connections**. Additional connections can be used to prevent the failure of any single connection from causing an entire process to fail. This can be redundant NICs on a single server, redundant T1 lines from an ISP for WAN links, or even redundant ISPs.

Remember

Any single component within a system could represent a single point of failure if its failure could cause the entire system to fail. This could be a single critical server in a multiple-server system or a critical connection.

Disk Redundancies

Any workstation or server has four primary resources: processor, memory, disk, and network interface. Of these, the disk is the slowest and most susceptible to failure. Because of this, disk subsystems are frequently upgraded to improve their performance and redundancy.

Redundant Array of Independent (or Inexpensive) Disks (RAID) subsystems are frequently added to both workstations and servers to increase the performance and provide fault tolerance for disks. RAID systems are becoming much more affordable as the price of drives steadily falls and disk capacity steadily increases.

RAID-0

RAID-0 is somewhat of a misnomer since it doesn't provide any redundancy or fault tolerance. RAID-0 includes two or more physical disks and is often called striping. Files stored on a RAID-0 array will spread across each of the disks.

The benefit of a RAID-0 is increased reading and writing performance. Since a file is spread across multiple physical disks, the different pieces of the file can be read from or written to each of the disks at the same time.

If you have three 500 GB drives used in a RAID-0, you have 1500 GB (1.5 TB) of storage space.

RAID-1

RAID-1 uses two disks and is also called mirroring. Any data that is written to one disk is also written to the other disk. If one of the disks fails, the other disk still has all the data, so the system can continue to operate without any data loss.

An additional disk controller can be added to a RAID-1, removing the disk controller as a single point of failure. In other words, each of the disks also has its own disk controller. Adding a second disk controller to a mirror is called disk duplexing.

If you have two 500 GB drives used in a RAID-1, you have 500 GB of storage space. The other 500 GB of storage space is dedicated to the fault-tolerant, mirrored volume.

> ### Remember
> RAID-1 is also known as a mirror and includes two disks. RAID-5 is also known as striping with parity and includes three or more disks with the equivalent of one drive dedicated to parity. RAID-0 does not provide any fault tolerance. Hardware RAID solutions are more efficient than software RAID but generally cost more to implement.

RAID-5

A RAID-5 is three or more disks that are striped together similar to a RAID-0. However, the equivalent of one drive includes parity information. This parity information is striped across each of the drives in a RAID-5 and is used for fault tolerance.

If one of the drives fails, the system can read the information on the remaining drives and determine what the actual data should be. If two of the drives fail in a RAID-5, the data is lost.

If you have three 500 GB drives used in a RAID-5, you have 1000 GB of storage space and 500 GB of space dedicated to parity. The equivalent of one drive (500 GB in this example) is dedicated to fault tolerance. If you striped five 500 GB drives in a RAID-5, you'd have 2000 GB of data storage space and 500 GB of parity space.

RAID-10

A RAID-10 configuration combines the features of mirroring (RAID-1) and striping (RAID-0). RAID-10 is sometimes called RAID 1+0. A variation is RAID 01 or RAID 0+1 that also combines the features of mirroring and striping but implements the RAID in a different way.

Software vs. Hardware RAID

RAID configurations can be managed through software or hardware. Hardware RAID configurations are significantly better. Hardware RAID provides better overall performance for the system hosting the RAID and will typically include extra features.

For example, a hardware RAID may include five physical disks using three in an active RAID-5 configuration and two as online spares. If one of the active disks in the RAID-5 fails, the hardware RAID will continue, though it will be a little slower since the data has to be recalculated each time it's accessed.

However, a hardware RAID can logically take the failed disk out of the configuration, add one of the online spares into the configuration, and rebuild the drive. Hardware RAID systems are often hot swappable, allowing you to swap out the failed drive without powering the RAID down.

Server Redundancies

For some services, it's desirable to achieve 99.999 percent uptime. This is often referred to as five nines. That equates to less than six minutes of downtime a year: 60 * 24 * 365 *.00001.

While five nines is achievable, it's often expensive. The cost of the redundant technologies needs to be weighed against the cost of the lost service.

For example, some web sites generate a significant amount of revenue. Every minute a web site is unavailable represents lost money. High-capacity failover clusters are frequently used to ensure the service is always available.

On a lesser scale, the high cost of a failover cluster may not be justified, but if a failure occurs, you may still want to get it up and operational as quickly as possible. A bank of spare parts can be maintained so that you can quickly recover from a failure.

Failover Clusters

Failover clusters use two or more servers in a cluster configuration. The servers are referred to as nodes, and at least one server is active, and at least one is inactive. If an active node fails, the inactive node can take over the load.

Consider figure 8.1, which shows a two-node failover cluster. Both nodes are individual servers, and they both have access to external data storage used by the active server. One node is designated as the active node, and the other node is the inactive node ready to take over if the active node fails.

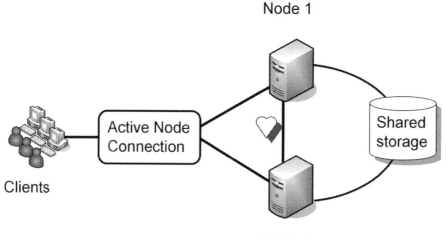

Figure 8.1: Failover Cluster

Node I could start off as the active node. When any of the clients connect, the cluster software (installed on both nodes) would ensure that the clients connect to the active node. The two nodes each have a monitoring connection to the other node used to check the health or heartbeat of each other.

If the active node fails, the inactive node senses the failure and configures itself as the active node. Since both nodes have access to the same shared storage, there is no loss of data for the client. Clients may notice a momentary hiccup or pause, but the service continues.

In figure 8.1, the shared storage represents a single point of failure. It's not uncommon for this to be a robust hardware RAID-5.

Cluster configurations can include many more nodes than just two. Nodes need to have close to identical hardware and are often quite expensive. If a company truly needs to achieve 99.999 percent uptime, it's worth the expense.

Spare Parts

A less expensive option than a failover cluster is a well-stocked bank of spare parts. Some parts are known to fail, and if they are readily available, the part can be quickly replaced to return the server to full operation.

As an example, hard drives are known to have relatively high failure rates. It's not uncommon to have spare hard drives that can be readily swapped out in the event of a failure.

Redundant Connections

Redundant connections are used to ensure that companies have backup connectivity to critical networks. For some companies, the critical network may be a remote site; for others, the critical network may be the Internet.

VPNs were covered in Chapter 4. Many companies use gateway-to-gateway connections to allow users in remote office locations to transparently connect over a VPN to a headquarters' connection.

Redundant connections are used if it is critical for a remote location to remain connected in the event of a failure of a primary connection. Redundant connections often come in the form of alternate paths. For example, a company's headquarters could be in Atlanta with other office locations in San Francisco, Chicago, San Diego, and Virginia Beach, as shown in figure 8.2.

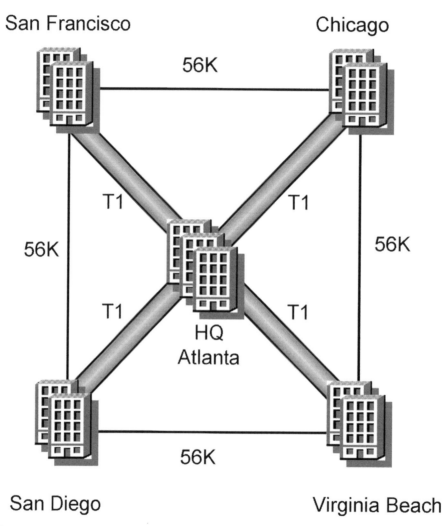

San Francisco   Chicago

56K

T1   T1

56K   56K

T1   T1

HQ
Atlanta

56K

San Diego   Virginia Beach

Figure 8.2: Redundant Connectivity

    The Atlanta headquarters site is connected to the outlying sites with T1 lines. Each site also has redundant connectivity to other remote sites. If the T1 line between San Francisco and Atlanta failed, San Francisco could still connect to headquarters via Chicago or San Diego. The redundant links are much slower at 56K, but they would still provide connectivity for critical needs.

    A T1 line can carry as much as 1.544 Mbps bandwidth. While this is slow compared to an internal network that is using 100 Mbps networking components, a T1 is quick for a wide area network (WAN) connection. If a company doesn't need a full T1, partial T1 lines, such as 256K, 128K, or 56K lines, are leased instead. It's also possible to lease higher bandwidth lines like a T3.

> ### Remember
> Failover clusters can be used to provide redundancy for servers. Redundant WAN links (such as T1 or partial T1 lines) can be used to provide redundant connections. A second ISP can be contracted to provide redundant connections to the Internet.

Telecommunications companies often lease lines to businesses and are often Internet Service Providers (ISPs), so it's not uncommon to lease a T1 line from an ISP. For added redundancy, a second ISP could be contracted to provide a second line.

Site Redundancies

Entire site operations can be considered important enough that redundant sites must be identified. A redundant site can take over the critical operations of a site in the event of some type of disaster or impending disaster.

In this context, a site is a location where services are provided. It could be a single building or a group of buildings. The three types of alternate sites are:

- Hot site
- Cold site
- Warm site

Hot Site

A hot site would be up and operational twenty-four hours a day, seven days a week and would be able to take over functionality from the primary site within minutes of a primary site failure. A hot site would include all the equipment, software, and communications capabilities of the primary site, and all the data would be up-to-date.

Clearly, a hot site is the most effective disaster recovery solution to provide site redundancy. However, a hot site is the most expensive to maintain and keep up-to-date.

> ### Remember
> A hot site includes the equipment, software, and communications capabilities of the primary site with all the data up-to-date. A hot site can take over for a failed primary site within minutes. It is the most effective disaster recovery solution for an alternate site, but it is also the most expensive to maintain. A cold site includes only the very basic utilities and is the hardest to test. A warm site is a compromise between a hot site and a cold site.

Cold Site

A cold site would have a roof, electricity, and running water, but not much else. All the equipment, software, and data needs to be brought to the site and enabled.

I often take my dogs for a walk at a local army base, which is sometimes used as an extreme example of a cold site. On some weekends, one or more of the fields are empty. Other weekends, a field has been transformed into a complete operational site with tents, antennas, cables, generators, and porta-potties.

Since the army has several buildings on the base, they don't need to operate in the middle of fields, but what they're really doing is testing their ability to stand up a cold site wherever they want. If they can do it in the field, they can do it in the middle of a desert.

A cold site is the cheapest to maintain, but it is also the most difficult to test.

Warm Site

A warm site is a compromise between a hot site, which is available 24/7, and a cold site, which may be nothing more than a roof, electricity, and running water. Clearly, there are a lot of different configurations between these two extremes.

After the Disaster

After the disaster has passed, you will want to return all the functions to the primary site. Only the least critical functions should be returned at first. Remember, the critical functions are operational at the alternate site and can stay there as long as necessary.

If a site has just gone through a disaster, it's very likely that all the problems haven't been discovered yet. By enabling the least critical functions first, undiscovered problems will appear and can be resolved without significantly impacting critical business functions.

Power Sources

Power is a critical utility to consider when reviewing any disaster preparedness plan. For highly critical systems, line filters, UPS, and generators could be used. When all three are used, they are used in this order:

- **Line filters.** Commercial power is received and filtered to ensure that power delivered to critical systems is clean. Dirty power is power that has excessive noise or interference such as EMI and RFI. Line filters are also referred to as line conditioners.

- **UPS.** An uninterruptible power supply (UPS) system is used to ensure that if the commercial power fails, the UPS can continue to provide power to the equipment for a short period of time. UPS would provide power to the equipment long enough to do a logical shutdown or long enough to allow backup generators to power up and stabilize.

- **Generators.** If power is lost, generators can be configured to automatically turn on. Once the generator power stabilizes, power can be switched from UPS to the generators. UPS provides short-term power, but generators provide interim long-term power.

> **Remember**
>
> The different methods used to ensure that clean power is consistently provided to critical equipment are line conditioners, UPS, and backup generators. A line conditioner is the first protection for commercial power. UPS is the next line of defense and will provide short-term battery power if commercial power fails, and generators can provide long-term power if commercial power is out for an extended period.

Line Filters

AC power is 120 VAC at 60 Hz in the U.S. and 240 VAC at 50 Hz in many countries around the world. Ideally, the power should arrive as a clean sine wave without any additional signals, noise, or modulation on it. Unfortunately, AC power sometimes arrives as dirty power with something more than just the clean sine wave.

Dirty power can be filtered with line filters. A line filter is often an external device that plugs into commercial power. The line filter will eliminate the interference or noise on the AC signal and provide clean power. Electrical devices would then plug into the line filter.

Line filters can be implemented on a small scale for just one or two electrical devices or on a large scale for an entire site. When implemented on a large scale, all site commercial power would first pass through the filter and then be passed to an internal power grid.

When needed, a line filter would be used before an UPS system. In other words, you would place the line filter between the AC power source and the UPS system.

UPS

An uninterruptible power supply (UPS) is nothing more than a battery or bank of batteries used as a backup in case of primary power failure. An UPS is not intended to provide power for very long. Common UPS systems provide power for ten to fifteen minutes.

The UPS is intended to provide power until:

- **The supported system has enough time to logically shut down**. For example, a ten-minute UPS may send a shutdown signal to a system after power has been lost for five minutes. The system now has five minutes to perform a logical shutdown.

- **Generators have enough time to power up and stabilize**. Critical systems are supported by both UPS and generators. The UPS provides short-term power, and the generator provides long-term power.

- **Commercial power returns**. If commercial power returns before the UPS has sent the shutdown signal to the system, the system will automatically switch back to using commercial power.

During normal operation, commercial power will provide power through the UPS. When commercial power fails, the UPS will provide the power.

Generators

For critical systems that need long-term power, generators can be used. Diesel generators are common.

It isn't reasonable to keep the generators running all the time; instead, they are only started when power fails. Since it will take time for a generator to rev up to full power and stabilize, it can't provide AC power immediately.

Critical systems will be powered by an UPS until the generators are stabilized, and then the power is switched over to generator power. Some systems exist that can sense when the generator is stabilized and automatically switch over to generator power. Other systems are manually monitored and switched over when someone determines that the generator is stable enough to switch over.

Protecting Data with Backups

Backups are copies of data created to ensure that if the original data is lost or corrupted, it can be restored. Maybe I should restate that. Backups are copies of data created to ensure that *when* the original data is lost or corrupted, it can be restored.

The truth is, if you work with computers long enough, you will lose data. The difference between a major catastrophe and a minor inconvenience is the existence of a backup. I often consider a pain factor. If I lost some data, how painful would it be? If it's more pain than I want, I ensure the data is backed up.

A Backup Horror Story

A friend of mine did consulting for small businesses and was once hired to help a small business owner recover some lost data. The owner had been growing his business for about five years and had just about everything related to his business (client lists, billing information, proposals, agreements, and more) on one system. This system crashed.

The consultant tried to restore information from the disk but couldn't get anything. The business owner panicked, knowing he simply needed the information. If he couldn't get this data back, his business might indeed fail. Although it's expensive, it is possible to have a "clean-room" facility take a hard drive apart and read the data at the bit level to restore at least some of the data. At this point, the owner was willing to try anything, so he paid the high price and the disk was sent off. Unfortunately, the disk suffered a catastrophic failure, and they weren't able to retrieve any meaningful data.

My friend visited the owner to relay this news. He said that when he left, the owner had his head in his hands and was literally crying. The business he had built for five years was close to ruins without much chance for recovery.

The sad part of this story is that it's repeated over and over with many different people in many different environments. Too many people don't recognize the importance of backups, until they've lost their data. But by then, it's too late.

Several different types of backups are possible with different backup programs. To fully understand the backups, you should understand the function of an archive bit. An archive bit is a property of any file that identifies if it has been changed since it was last backed up.

The different states of the archive bit related to backups are:

- **New file.** The archive bit will be set indicating the file is not backed up.
- **File backed up using a normal backup.** The archive bit is cleared indicating the file is backed up.
- **Modified file.** The archive bit is set indicating the file is not backed up in its current version.

Several different types of backups are supported by different backup utilities. While third-party backup programs can be quite sophisticated in what they do and how they do it, you should have a solid understanding of the basics.

- **Full backups.** A full (or normal backup) backs up all the selected data and clears the archive bit.
- **Differential backup.** Backs up all data that has changed since the last full backup. Does not modify the archive bit.
- **Incremental backup.** Backs up all data that has changed since the last full or incremental backup. Clears the archive bit.

Full Backups

A full backup will back up all data specified in the backup. For example, you could have several folders on the D: drive. If you specify these folders in the backup program, then all the data in these folders will be included.

While it's possible to do a full backup on a daily basis, this is only done in very small environments. Larger environments have two limiting factors:

- **Time.** A full backup can take several hours to complete, and frequently a system needs to be operational with only a limited amount of time dedicated to maintenance.
- **Money.** Backups need to be stored on some type of media, such as tape, optical media, or hard drives. Daily full backups require more media, often resulting in a prohibitive cost.

Instead, full backups are typically combined with differential or incremental backups. However, every backup strategy must start with a full backup.

Differential Backups

A differential backup strategy starts with a full backup. It then backs up any data that has changed, or is different since the last full backup. The differential backup doesn't modify the archive bit.

For example, a full/differential strategy could start with a full backup on Sunday night. The full backup would clear the archive bit of all the backed-up files, indicating that a good backup exists of the file.

On Monday night, a differential backup would back up all the files that changed since the last full backup. It knows what files have changed since the archive bit is set if a file is modified. The differential backup does not modify the archive bit.

On Tuesday night, the differential backup would again back up all the files that changed since the last full backup. Since the archive bit wasn't modified during the differential backup on Monday, files that were backed up on Monday would be included on Tuesday.

Similarly, the Wednesday night backup would back up all files that changed since the last full backup. As the week progresses, the differential backup steadily grows in size.

> ### Remember
> A differential backup will back up all files that have changed since the last full backup. It will steadily grow throughout the week. When recovering data, the full backup and only the last differential backup need to be recovered.

Restoring a Full/Differential Backup Set

Assume for a moment that each of the backups were stored on different tapes. If the system crashed on Thursday morning, how many tapes would be needed to recover the data?

The answer is two. You would first need to recover the full backup from Sunday. Since the differential backup on Wednesday night includes all the files that changed after the last full backup, you would restore that tape and have all the data up to Wednesday night.

Incremental Backups

An incremental backup strategy starts with a full backup. It then backs up any data that has changed, or is different since the last full backup or the last incremental backup if one has been done. The incremental backup clears the archive bit, indicating the file has been backed up.

As an example, a full/incremental strategy could start with a full backup on Sunday night. The full backup would clear the archive bit of all the backed-up files, indicating that a good backup exists of the file.

On Monday night, an incremental backup would back up all the files that changed since the last full backup. It knows what files have changed since the archive bit is set if a file is modified. The incremental backup clears the archive bit, indicating the files have been backed up.

On Tuesday night, the incremental backup would back up all the files that changed since the incremental backup on Monday night. Similarly, the Wednesday night backup would back up all files that changed since the last incremental backup on Tuesday night. As the week progresses, the incremental backups stay about the same size.

> ### Remember
> An incremental backup will back up all files that have changed since the last full backup or the last incremental backup. Incremental backups are about the same size throughout the week. When recovering data, the full backup and every incremental backup since the full backup must be recovered. Additionally, each of the incremental backups must be restored in the order they were backed up.

Restoring a Full/Incremental Backup Set

Assume for a moment that each of the backups were stored on different tapes. If the system crashed on Thursday morning, how many tapes would be needed to recover the data?

The answer is four. You would first need to recover the full backup from Sunday. Since the incremental backups would be backing up different data each day of the week, each of the incremental backups must be restored and in the right order.

Sometimes people mistakenly think the last incremental backup would have all the relevant data. This isn't true if more than one incremental backup was done.

For example, if you worked on a single file named Project.docx each day of the week, then the last incremental *would* hold the most recent copy of this file. However, what if you compiled a report named Report.docx every Monday but didn't touch it again until the following Monday? Only the incremental backup from Monday would include the most recent copy. An incremental backup from Tuesday or another day of the week wouldn't include the report.

Choosing Full/Incremental or Full/Differential

A logical question is, "Why are there so many choices for backups?" The answer is that there are many different needs in an organization.

For example, one organization may not have much time to perform maintenance throughout the week. The backup administrator is told to minimize the amount of time that backups take. Incremental backups stay relatively the same size and don't back up unchanged data that was backed up previously. In this instance, a full/incremental backup is the best choice.

In another organization, the backup administrator may be told that if a recovery is necessary, it should be performed as quickly as possible. Since a full/differential only requires the restoration of two backups (the full and the last differential), it would be much quicker than a full/incremental that can require the restoration of several different backups.

Test Restores

I've heard many horror stories where personnel are regularly performing backups thinking all is well. Ultimately, something happens, and a restore needs to be done, but suddenly, they find out that none of the tapes holds valid data. People have been going through the motions, but something in the process is flawed.

The only way to validate a backup is to do a test restore. Performing a test restore is nothing more than restoring the data from a backup. The test restore would most often be done to a different location than the live data but in such a way that the data could be validated.

As a simple example, a random tape could be retrieved that was recently used to back up data. An administrator would attempt to restore the data. There are two possible outcomes of this test, and both are good.

- **The test succeeds**. Excellent! You know that the backup process works. You don't necessarily know that every backup tape is valid, but at least you know that the process is sound and at least some of your backups work.

- **The test fails**. Excellent! You know there's a problem that you can fix before a crisis. If this was discovered after actual data loss, you wouldn't be able to fix it in time, but now you can.

An additional benefit of doing regular test restores is that it allows you to become familiar with the process. The first time you do a restore shouldn't be in the middle of a crisis with several high-level managers peering over your shoulder.

> **Remember**
> Test restores are the best way to test the integrity of a company's backup data. A test restore is simply an attempt to restore data from a backup. If the restore succeeds, you have verified the integrity of the backup.

Backup Policies

A backup policy is used to identify what data is included in the backups, how the backups are stored, and how long the data is retained.

Identifying the critical data to back up is no small feat. Often you have competing forces at work. One manager or department may want all their data backed up no matter how large, while the department responsible for backing up the data doesn't have the money or other resources to meet those desires. Compromises are often made and identified in the backup policy.

A copy of a backup should be stored in a separate geographical location. This protects against some type of disaster, such as a fire or flood. Even if the building is destroyed, a backup copy of the data exists and can be retrieved.

Data is often retained for specific periods of time based on legal issues or on monetary constraints. For example, some laws exist that require backups in some governmental institutions to be retained for twenty years or more.

Other environments that aren't constrained by laws may choose to keep backups for a single month. By limiting the backup to a month, they are able to control long-term storage costs.

Protecting Backups

If data is important enough to be backed up, it's important enough to protect. Backup media should be protected at the same level of protection as the data that it holds. In other words, if proprietary data protected at the highest level of protection within an organization is backed up, the backup also deserves the highest level of protection.

Protecting backups includes:

- **Storage**. Backups should be protected when stored. This includes clear labeling to identify the data and physical security protection to prevent others from easily accessing it.
- **Transfer**. Data should be protected any time it is transferred from location to location. This is especially true when transferring a copy of the backup to a separate geographical location.
- **Destruction**. When the backups are no longer needed, they should be adequately destroyed. This can be accomplished by degaussing the media,

shredding or burning the media, or scrubbing the media by repeatedly writing varying patterns of 1s and 0s onto the media.

Environmental Controls

Environmental controls primarily include fire-suppression and HVAC equipment. In some secure environments, a Faraday cage can be used to prevent data from emanating outside an enclosure.

While environmental controls may not seem security related, they can impact the availability of data. Remember, the security triad includes confidentiality, integrity, and availability. If adequate environmental controls aren't maintained, you will very likely lose availability of data and/or services.

Fire Suppression

Fires can be suppressed or fought with the use of individual fire extinguishers or through fixed systems. Fire extinguishers are used by individuals to suppress a small fire. A fixed system can detect a fire and automatically activate to extinguish the fire.

The different components of a fire are:

- Heat
- Oxygen
- Fuel
- Chain reaction creating the fire

The following are the primary methods of suppressing fires:

- **Remove the heat.** This is often done with water or other chemical agents.
- **Remove the oxygen.** This is often done by displacing the oxygen with another gas, such as carbon dioxide (CO_2). This is a common method of fighting electrical fires since it is harmless to electrical equipment.
- **Remove the fuel.** Remove what is burning. Fire-suppression methods don't fight a fire this way, but of course once the material is burned, the fire will extinguish.

- **Disrupt the chain reaction.** This is often done with a chemical. Halon is used in some countries to disrupt the chain reaction and is very effective at quickly extinguishing a fire. Another benefit of halon is that it leaves very little residue, providing added protection for electrical equipment.

Fire Classes

The class of fire often determines what element of the fire you will try to remove or disrupt. Fires are categorized in one of the following fire classes in the U.S.:

- **Class A – Ordinary combustibles.** This includes wood, paper, cloth, rubber, trash, and plastics.
- **Class B – Flammable liquids.** This includes gasoline, propane, solvents, oil, paint, lacquers, and other synthetics or oil-based products.
- **Class C – Electrical equipment.** This includes computers, wiring, controls, motors, and appliances. The CompTIA Security+ exam is computer-centric, so you should especially understand that a Class C fire is from electrical equipment.
  - Class C fires are often fought by either displacing the oxygen with a gas such as CO_2 or by disrupting the fire's chain reaction with a chemical such as halon. Both CO_2 and halon also serve to protect the equipment since very little residue remains after the fire is extinguished.
  - Class C fires should never be fought with water or water-based materials, such as foam, since the water is conductive and can pose significant risks to personnel.
- **Class D – Combustible metals.** This includes combustible metals, such as magnesium, lithium, titanium, and sodium.

A Class A fire is fought by using water to remove the heat. However, water will make things much worse if you use it on any of the other classes. For example, using water on live equipment will actually pose a risk since electricity can travel up the stream and shock you. Additionally, water will damage electrical equipment.

> **Remember**
>
> Electrical fires can be suppressed with carbon dioxide (CO2) and halon without damaging the equipment or leaving excessive residue. While halon is no longer manufactured, existing stockpiles are still being used in some countries.

Risks of Carbon Dioxide and Halon

Carbon dioxide and halon are both often used to fight electrical fires, but you should be aware of a couple of other issues.

If carbon dioxide is used in an enclosed space where people are present, it presents a risk of suffocation since it displaces oxygen in the room. People have been killed from carbon dioxide agents that have been released in enclosed spaces.

Carbon dioxide (CO_2) is sometimes confused with carbon monoxide (CO). Carbon dioxide is used in fire-suppression methods, while carbon monoxide is not. Carbon monoxide is produced from burning fossil fuels such as in an internal-combustion engine.

Halon presents two risks:

- **Danger to environment.** Halon is known to contribute to ozone depletion, and there are international agreements that have effectively ended the production of halon. However, there are significant amounts of halon still in existence, and these may still be used. As other effective measures are developed, the use of halon is being reduced.

- **Danger to personnel.** Exposure to halon is known to affect the central nervous system and cause dizziness and tingling in the extremities. Environments that have fixed halon systems typically have warning systems to notify people prior to activation.

The European Union banned the use of halon completely after 2003. Even though the production of halon has stopped worldwide, the use of halon in other countries is expected to continue for years to come. Most of the halon that existed in European countries was shipped to other countries around the world.

If you have choices other than halon, use them. However, you may still encounter the use of halon in different environments.

HVAC

Heating, ventilation, and air conditioning (HVAC) systems are important environmental control considerations when planning any computer environment. Quite simply, computers and other electronic equipment don't like to get too hot, too cold, or wet.

The temperature within computers is often as much as 10 degrees Fahrenheit warmer than the ambient temperature of a room. If computer and electronic components get too hot, they often simply burn up.

Many times, when I was working in environments that had an air-conditioning problem, we had a policy of shutting down all electronics when the room temperature reached a certain threshold. When this policy wasn't followed, the systems developed problems due to the heat and ended up out of commission for a lot longer than the AC.

Humidity controls ensure that there isn't too much moisture in the air. Just as computers and electronics don't like to get too hot, they don't like to get wet either.

Shielding

Shielding can be used to prevent electromagnetic interference (EMI) and radio frequency interference (RFI) from corrupting signals or protect against unwanted emissions. A Faraday cage can be used to prevent interference and emissions, and a TEMPEST survey can be accomplished to measure emissions and interference.

Faraday Cage

A Faraday cage is a room that prevents signals from emanating beyond the room. It includes electrical features that cause RF signals that reach the boundary of the room to be reflected back, preventing signal emanation outside the Faraday cage.

In addition to preventing signals from emanating outside the room, a Faraday cage also provides shielding to prevent outside interference such as EMI and RFI from entering the room.

At a very basic level, some elevators act as a Faraday cage (though I seriously doubt the designers were striving to do so). You may have stepped into an elevator and found that your cell phone stopped receiving and transmitting signals. The metal shielding around the elevator prevents signals from emanating out or signals such as the cell phone tower signal from entering the elevator.

> **Remember**
>
> A Faraday cage is a room or small enclosure primarily used to block electronic signals from emanating outside the controlled space. Elevators sometimes mimic the qualities of a Faraday cage by blocking signals such as cell phone or wireless device signals.

On a smaller scale, electrical devices such as computers are shielded to prevent signals from emanating out and interference from getting in.

TEMPEST

TEMPEST is a government program that has been around for several decades to measure emanations from different devices. Devices placed within Faraday cages or built with a Faraday-like enclosure cannot emanate signals outside the enclosure. TEMPEST measurements ensure that sensitive signals cannot be captured and exploited.

The word TEMPEST is not an acronym but instead a code name created by the U.S. government. However, I do like one of the acronyms that someone created and posted on the web—Tiny ElectroMagnetic Particles Emitting Secret Things.

Exam Topic Review

When preparing for the exam, make sure you understand these key concepts, which were covered in this chapter.

Disaster Recovery

The most important element to start with is a disaster recovery plan. This plan can identify all of the elements of a plan that will protect a company in the event of a disaster. Elements include both different types of redundancies and backup strategies.

Redundancies

Redundancies can be added at several different layers including:

- **Disks**. RAID-1 and RAID-5 can be used to provide fault tolerance for disks.
- **Servers**. Failover clusters can be used to provide fault tolerance for servers.
- **Connections**. Alternate connections such as alternate T1 or partial T1 lines and even alternate ISPs can be used to ensure multiple paths exist for critical connectivity issues.
- **Sites**. Alternate sites such as hot, cold, and warm sites can provide fault tolerance for locations. A hot site is the most expensive but is the most effective and provides the best level of protection. A cold site is often nothing more than a roof, electricity, and running water and is the hardest to test.
- **Power**. Redundant power solutions start with line filters to ensure that clean power is provided to internal systems. If commercial power sources fail, an UPS is used for short-term power, and generators are used for long-term power.
- **Backups**. Backups include full backups, differential backups, and incremental backups. Most solutions are combinations of full/differential or full/incremental. Differential backups back up all data that has changed since the last full backup. Incremental backups back up all data that has changed since the last full or incremental backup.

- **Backup policies.** A copy of a valid backup should be kept in a separate geographical location to prepare for different types of disasters that can destroy an entire location. Data should only be retained for a specified period.

Environmental Controls

- **Fire suppression.** Electrical fires should be fought with Class C fire extinguishers. Both carbon dioxide (CO_2) and halon can be used effectively on electronic equipment fires while leaving little residue. Halon is known to cause damage to the ozone and is no longer being manufactured, but some countries are using existing stockpiles.
- **HVAC.** Heating, ventilation, and air conditioning systems are used to ensure computing spaces have adequate environmental controls.
- **Shielding.** Faraday cages are used to prevent signals from emanating outside the room or interference from entering the room. Most electrical devices such as cell phones will not be able to communicate with anything outside of the Faraday cage. TEMPEST surveys are used to measure emissions from rooms or devices that are shielded.

Practice Questions

1. You are called in as a consultant to help a company set up a new location. The location is on the East Coast and is at risk for hurricanes during the hurricane season. What is most important to ensure that the company can recover in case of a direct hit from a severe hurricane or other natural disaster?

    A. Cold site

    B. Hot site

    C. Disaster recovery plan

    D. Failover clusters

    E. Offsite location for backups

2. Which of the following could provide fault tolerance for data stored on a server's disk subsystem? (Choose all that apply.)

    A. RAID-0

    B. RAID-1

    C. RAID-5

    D. Redundant ISP

3. Which of the following could provide fault tolerance for a failed T1 line?

    A. Failover cluster

    B. RAID-1

    C. RAID-5

    D. Redundant ISP

4. A company sells a large volume of books via a web site. This web site generates approximately $60,000 in revenue per hour. The web site is hosted on a web server within a DMZ, which accesses database servers in the internal network. What is a potential fault with this configuration?

    A. The web server represents a single point of failure.

    B. The database servers represent a single point of failure.

    C. The web server should be protected with a cold site.

    D. The web server should be protected with a hot site.

5. Of the following, what can be used to provide long-term backup power for critical systems?

    A. UPS

    B. Diesel generator

    C. TEMPEST

    D. Halon

6. You are designing a power continuity plan for a site that normally receives publicly provided power. You want to ensure that systems will continue to operate in the event of a long-term power loss and are consistently provided clean power. What redundant power systems should be used, and in what order should the power be provided?

    A. Generator, UPS

    B. UPS, generator, line filter

    C. UPS, line filter, generator

    D. Line filter, UPS, generator

7. The headquarters of a bank needs to plan for the possibility of a severe outage. In the event of a severe outage, they need to be able to ensure that they can become operational again within minutes without any loss of data. What should be implemented?

    A. Cold site

    B. Warm site

    C. Hot site

    D. Failover clusters

8. What type of disaster recovery site would take the most time to become operational after the loss of a primary site?

    A. Cold site

    B. Warm site

    C. Hot site

    D. Frigid site

9. What type of disaster recovery site would be the most effective at restoring functionality to a company's business after a disaster takes down a primary site?

    A. Cold site

    B. Warm site

    C. Hot site

    D. Remote site

10. Your company implemented disaster recovery plans and switched all functions over to a warm site prior to a hurricane. The primary site had power outages and minor flooding but is now ready to take back its original functions. What functions should be returned to the primary site first?

    A. Critical functions

    B. Least critical functions

    C. Internet-based functions

    D. Remote access functions

11. What backup type will back up files that have changed since the last full backup?

    A. Full

    B. Differential

    C. Incremental

    D. System State

12. Backups have been regularly performed on a key file server. How can you verify the integrity of these backups and ensure you are able to retrieve lost data?

    A. Perform test restores.

    B. Perform test backups.

    C. Run integrity checks when the backups are performed.

    D. Document the dates and times when the backups are performed.

13. A company regularly backs up all the data on their servers, and periodically checks the validity of this data by performing test restores. What else should be done to protect against a potential site disaster?

    A. Perform differential backups.

    B. Perform incremental backups.

    C. Copy the data to DVDs and store them in a fireproof safe.

    D. Store a copy of the tapes at an alternate location.

14. A file server has the following backups done throughout a week. Full backups are done every Saturday night at 11 p.m. Incremental backups are done every night during the week at 11 p.m. The server crashes on Wednesday morning. Assuming each of the backups are stored on a different tape, how many tapes must be restored?

    A. One

    B. Two

    C. Three

    D. Four

15. Your company maintains the entire third floor of a building in a large city. You complete backups of several key servers on a regular basis. You want to ensure that this data is still available even if the building suffers a catastrophic disaster. What should you do?

    A. Ensure that both full and differential backups are completed.

    B. Ensure that both full and incremental backups are completed.

    C. Ensure that a copy of the backup is stored at a separate geographical location.

    D. Ensure that the backup tapes are destroyed when no longer needed.

16. You are planning to install a fixed fire-suppression system to protect a computer room. You want to minimize the damage to equipment if the system is activated. What should you use?

    A. Water sprinklers

    B. CO_2

    C. Halogen

    D. Yellow cake

17. What would be used to prevent signals from emanating outside a room?

    A. TEMPEST survey

    B. Faraday cage

    C. Proximity card

    D. A WAP

Practice Question Answers

1. **C.** The most important thing to create is a disaster recovery plan. The disaster recovery plan (DRP) will define all the details that are used to plan for multiple environmental disasters such as hurricanes, floods, tornadoes, and more. A DRP will also provide plans for disasters such as a fire. While the DRP may include plans for cold sites, hot sites, failover clusters, and offsite locations for backups, none of these individually will adequately plan for every possible disaster.

2. **B, C.** A RAID-1 (mirror) and RAID-5 (striping with parity) both provide fault tolerance for disk subsystems. A RAID-0 can improve performance but does not provide fault tolerance. A redundant ISP can provide fault-tolerant connections for WAN links or to the Internet but not for disk subsystems.

3. **D.** A redundant Internet Service Provider (ISP) could provide fault tolerance for a failed T1 line. A T1 line is used for communications, such as over a WAN link, and could be leased through an ISP. A failover cluster would provide redundancy for a server. RAID-1 and RAID-5 would provide redundancy for disk subsystems.

4. **A.** The web site is hosted on one web server, which represents a single point of failure. If the web server fails, the company risks losing $1000 for every minute the server is down. Since multiple database servers are being used, it implies a redundancy with the database servers. Hot, warm, and cold sites are used to provide alternate locations for entire sites, not a single server.

5. **B.** Diesel generators or any type of backup generator can be used to provide long-term backup power for critical systems. UPS systems are only intended to provide short-term backup power. An UPS would provide power long enough for a system to perform a logical shutdown or to switch over to generator power after the generators have leveled off after starting. TEMPEST is a code name for a U.S. government program that measures emanations from electronic systems. Halon is a gas that is sometimes used to fight fires.

6. **D.** Power should be provided through the line filter first; line filters are also referred to as line conditioners. If the power source fails, an UPS should provide the power to the system until the generators have started and can provide smooth power. Once the generators are online and stable, power should be provided by the generators.

7. **C.** A hot site will include all the equipment, software, and data to allow it to become operational almost immediately in the event of a failure of a primary site. A cold site includes a roof, power, and water but couldn't become operational within minutes. A warm site is a cross between a cold site and a hot site. While a warm site would have the equipment, it would not have up-to-date data, so it could not become operational within minutes without any data loss. A failover cluster could provide redundancy for a server but not for an entire headquarters.

8. **A.** A cold site includes a roof, power, and water and would take the most time and energy to make it operational. A hot site can become operational in minutes, and a warm site is a compromise between a hot site and cold site. There is no such thing as a frigid site within the context of disaster recovery.

9. **C.** A hot site would be the most effective backup site for disaster recovery and can become operational within minutes of the outage. A cold site doesn't include equipment or data, so it would take much longer. A warm site has equipment, but the data isn't kept up-to-date, requiring more time to make it operational. A remote site wouldn't typically be able to restore functionality of a company's primary business unless it was designated as a hot site.

10. **B.** The least critical functions should be returned first from the backup facility to the primary facility. After a disaster, there are sure to be minor issues that haven't been resolved and aren't known yet. Moving the least critical functions first allows the site to test basic functionality. If the critical functions are returned first, it's possible the critical functions would fail due to problems that haven't been discovered yet. Internet-based functions or remote access functions would only matter based on the criticality of the functions.

11. **B.** Differential backup types back up all the files that have changes since the last full backup. Incremental backup types back up all the data that changed since the last full or incremental backup. A full backup will back up all the files specified regardless of what files have changed. System State backs up key system files such as boot files and the registry; on a domain controller, System State includes Active Directory.

12. **A.** The integrity of backups can be checked by performing test restores. A test restore simply attempts to restore the data from a backup tape. If it fails, it indicates at least some of the backups have lost data integrity and are not valid. If test restores are regularly done and always succeed, you have a higher level of confidence in the integrity of your backups. Test backups won't verify the data on the backups. Documenting the steps and using integrity checks on the backups are good steps but won't verify that data can be restored.

13. **D.** To fully protect backups from a site disaster, a copy of the backup should be kept in a separate geographical location. Neither differential nor incremental backups would protect against a site disaster. While fireproof safes can protect papers, the internal temperature will still get hot enough to melt DVDs.

14. **D.** Four tapes are needed—the full backup created on Saturday night and the incremental tapes from Sunday night, Monday night, and Tuesday night. All restores must start by restoring the full backup. When using incremental backups, each incremental backup performed after the full backup must be restored.

15. **C.** A copy of the backup should be stored in a separate geographical location to prepare for a catastrophic disaster at a single location. Using either full/differential or full/incremental strategies wouldn't impact the ability to recover from a significant disaster. While it's a good strategy to ensure that unneeded backup tapes are destroyed, this isn't relevant to the question.

16. **B.** Carbon dioxide (CO_2) is often used to fight Class C electrical fires. Water would cause additional damage to the equipment. Halogen is a type of lightbulb, and yellow cake is related to the processing of uranium ores.

17. **B.** A Faraday cage is a room designed to prevent signals from emanating outside the controlled space. A TEMPEST survey attempts to detect any unauthorized emanations. A proximity card is used for access control and activates when placed in close proximity to a reader. A WAP is intended to transmit and receive RF signals.

Chapter 9

Understanding Cryptography

CompTIA Security+ objectives covered in this chapter

5.1 Explain general cryptography concepts.

- Key management
- Steganography
- Symmetric key
- Asymmetric key
- Confidentiality
- Integrity and availability
- Non-repudiation
- Comparative strength of algorithms
- Digital signatures
- Whole disk encryption
- Trusted Platform Module (TPM)
- Single vs. Dual sided certificates
- Use of proven technologies

5.2 Explain basic hashing concepts and map various algorithms to appropriate applications.

- SHA
- MD5
- LANMAN
- NTLM

5.3 Explain basic encryption concepts and map various algorithms to appropriate applications.

- DES
- 3DES
- RSA
- PGP
- Elliptic curve

- AES
- AES256
- One time pad

5.4 Explain and implement protocols.

- SSL/TLS
- S/MIME
- HTTP vs. HTTPS vs. SHTTP
- IPSEC
- SSH

5.5 Explain core concepts of public key cryptography.

- Public Key Infrastructure (PKI)
- Recovery agent
- Public key
- Private keys
- Certificate Authority (CA)
- Registration
- Key escrow
- Certificate Revocation List (CRL)
- Trust models

5.6 Implement PKI and certificate management.

- Public Key Infrastructure (PKI)
- Recovery agent
- Public key
- Private keys
- Certificate Authority (CA)
- Registration
- Key escrow
- Certificate Revocation List (CRL)

* * *

While cryptography is only 15 percent of the exam, you may find that many of these topics aren't as familiar to you as other topics, and you may have to spend more than 15 percent of your study time here. When tackling these topics, don't lose sight of the basics outlined in the very first section of the chapter—Basic Cryptography Concepts.

Confidentiality is enforced with encryption and prevents the unauthorized disclosure of data. Integrity is enforced with hashing and provides assurances that the data has not been modified. This chapter covers many of the details of encryption and hashing and also presents some basics on a Public Key Infrastructure (PKI).

Basic Cryptography Concepts

Cryptography has several important concepts that you need to grasp, but they are often topics that are new to many IT professionals. Confidentiality and integrity were introduced as part of the security triad in Chapter 1—confidentiality, integrity, and availability.

> ### *Remember*
> Confidentiality (preventing unauthorized disclosure) is enforced with encryption. Integrity (ensuring that data is not modified or corrupted) is enforced with hashing. Non-repudiation and authentication can be enforced with digital signatures.

This chapter will cover the details of confidentiality and integrity along with some other important cryptography topics. The core cryptography concepts are:

- **Confidentiality**. Prevents the unauthorized disclosure of data. Confidentiality is enforced with encryption.
    - o **Encryption**. Encryption ciphers data to make it unreadable if intercepted. Encryption normally includes an algorithm and a key. The algorithm is usually well known, and the key is kept private and/or frequently changed.
    - o **Symmetric encryption**. Uses one key to both encrypt and decrypt data.
    - o **Asymmetric encryption**. Uses two keys—public and private. One key encrypts, and the other key decrypts.

- **Integrity**. Provides assurance that data is not modified, corrupted, or tampered with. Integrity is enforced with hashing.
  - o **Hash**. A hash is a number derived from performing a calculation on a message or file. If the message or file is the same (or remains unchanged), the hash will always be the same no matter how many times the hash is calculated.
  - o **Common hashing algorithms**: MD5 and SHA1.
- **Authentication**. Used to validate the sender is who she claims to be. Within the context of cryptography, authentication is enforced with digital signatures.
- **Non-repudiation**. Non-repudiation prevents a party from denying he took a specific action. Digital signatures are used to enforce non-repudiation.
- **Digital signature**. A digital signature is created by hashing a message and encrypting the hash with the private key. The hash can only be decrypted with the matching public key, providing authentication, non-repudiation, and integrity.

Encryption

Encryption is used to provide confidentiality and prevent the unauthorized disclosure of data. Encrypted data is in a cipher text format that is unreadable to anyone who receives it. Most encryption includes two elements:

- **Algorithm**. The algorithm performs a specific calculation on a message or file. The algorithm is always the same and is often well known.
- **Key**. The key is kept private and/or changed frequently. The key is used as a variable within the algorithm. A weak key allows the encryption to be broken more easily than a strong key.

> ### Remember
> Most encryptions are composed of an algorithm and a key. The algorithm is well known and tested. Weak keys allow attackers to crack the encryption quicker and easier.

Encryption Algorithm and Key

As a simple example, when I was a child, a friend and I used to pass encoded messages back and forth to each other. Our algorithm was:

- **Encryption algorithm**: Move _____ spaces forward to encrypt.
- **Decryption algorithm**: Move _____ spaces backward to decrypt.

On the way to school, we would identify the key we would use that day. For example, we may have used the key of three one day. Now we knew that if we wanted to encrypt a message, we would move each character three spaces forward, and if we wanted to decrypt a message, we would move each character three spaces backward.

Imagine the message "PASS" needs to be sent.

- Three characters past "P" is "S"—Start at P (Q, R, **S**)
- Three characters past "A" is "D"—Start at A (B, C, **D**)
- Three characters past "S" is "V"—Start at S (T, U, **V**)
- Three characters past "S" is "V"—Start at S (T, U, **V**)

The encrypted message is SDVV. It can be decrypted by moving backwards three spaces and learning that "PASS" is the original message.

While our code helps to demonstrate an algorithm and a key, it is admittedly simple. Most algorithms and keys are much more complex.

Weak Keys

Encryptions used today would never use a key as simple as "3," which can be represented by 2 bits. Symmetric encryption using a relatively small 56 bits may be cracked in less than five minutes with enough processing power. However, increasing the number of bits to 96 can increase this to as long as three million years with the same processing power. Clearly, attackers like it when weak keys are used.

Chapter 4 discussed wireless technologies including WEP. WEP had several weaknesses, and one of them was weak keys. Attackers were able to attack WEP keys to gain a foothold into breaking the encryption. Ultimately, WEP was scrapped completely in favor of WPA2.

Longer keys are used to provide better protection. Additionally, keys are changed frequently to prevent their discovery.

Symmetric Encryption

Symmetric encryption uses a single key for encryption and decryption. The algorithm always stays the same, and the key is frequently changed for security. Symmetric encryption is much more effective than asymmetric encryption at encrypting large amounts of data.

Symmetric encryption is also called:

- Secret-key encryption
- Session-key encryption

Remember
Symmetric encryption is also known as secret-key encryption or session-key encryption. Symmetric encryption is much more efficient at encrypting large amounts of data than asymmetric encryption.

When symmetric encryption ciphers data, it uses one of two methods: block cipher and stream cipher.

- **Block cipher**. Block cipher is a method used for encrypting data in specific sized blocks, such as 64 bits. A large message would be divided into several smaller blocks, and each individual block is then encrypted. Block cipher is stronger than stream cipher.
- **Stream cipher**. A stream cipher encrypts data bit-by-bit as opposed to encrypting it in blocks. Stream ciphers are vulnerable to attacks and aren't considered as secure as block ciphers.

The most popular current symmetric algorithm is AES. Other symmetric algorithms are:

- DES
- 3DES
- IDEA
- CAST
- RC

AES and AES256

The Advanced Encryption Standard (AES) is a strong encryption algorithm that is commonly used worldwide for the encryption of data. The AES algorithm uses an elegant mathematical formula, making it both strong and efficient.

AES can use key sizes of 128 bits, 192 bits, or 256 bits. When used with 256-bit key sizes, it is called AES256. It is currently considered the strongest encryption algorithm that uses mathematical evaluation techniques and has been identified as a successor to 3DES.

In order of their release, some of the popular symmetric algorithms have been:

- **DES**. Has been compromised. No longer considered secure.
- **3DES**. Replaced DES. Uses DES with three passes through the encryption algorithm and different keys for each pass.
- **AES**. Replaced 3DES. Considered the strongest standard of the three.

> *Remember*
> AES is considered a fast, highly secure encryption algorithm. It is significantly faster (using less processor and memory resources) than both DES and 3DES and can provide stronger encryption than both of these earlier algorithms. AES256 uses a key size of 256 bits.

AES was adopted from the Rijndael encryption algorithm after a lengthy evaluation of several different algorithms by the National Institute of Standards and Technology (NIST). NIST is a federal technology agency that develops and promotes standards, and it chose AES over several other strong encryption algorithms.

Some of the strengths of AES are:

- **Fast**. Uses mathematical formulas to require only one pass to encrypt the data.
- **Wide usage**. Performs quickly even when encrypting data on small devices such as smart cards, smart phones, and USB flash drives.

- **Conserves processing resources.** AES is less resource intensive than 3DES, which has to perform three passes on the same data. In other words, it has a lower processor and memory utilization.

DES

Data Encryption Standard (DES) was widely used for a period of time dating back to the 1970s. However, it uses a relatively small key of only 56 bits and can be broken with brute force attacks. In the '70s, the technology required to break 56 bits wasn't easily available, but with the advances of computers, a 56-bit key is considered small today.

> ### *Remember*
> While AES is the standard symmetric algorithm in use, other symmetric algorithms exist. They include: DES, 3DES, IDEA, CAST, and RC, RC5, and RC6. RC, RC5, and RC6 use block ciphers, which are stronger than stream ciphers

3DES

3DES (pronounced as Triple DES) improved the DES encryption by encrypting the data with DES three times with two, or sometimes three, keys. While 3DES is a significant improvement over DES, it does consume a lot of processor and memory resources in the process. AES is much less resource intensive and is intended to replace 3DES.

IDEA

The International Data Encryption Algorithm (IDEA) is a block cipher using a 128-bit key. IDEA is patented but is freely available for commercial use and is one of the encryption algorithms supported in Pretty Good Privacy (PGP).

CAST

CAST was invented by Carlisle Adams and Stafford Tavares, and its name is derived from the first letters of their names. It uses a 64-bit block cipher with key sizes up to 128 bits. CAST is another encryption algorithm supported by PGP.

RC

Ron Rivest invented several versions of RC (which is sometimes referred to as Ron's Code or Rivest's Cipher). Some of the different versions of RC are:

- **RC2.** A 64-bit block cipher created in 1987.
- **RC4.** Widely used stream cipher.
- **RC5.** Block cipher that can use 32-bit, 64-bit, or 128-bit blocks. Developed in 1994.
- **RC6.** A 128-bit block cipher based on RC5, developed in 1997. RC6 was one of the ciphers considered for AES.

One Time Pad

A one time pad is an algorithm that uses a key only once. It is used to encrypt data that is also intended to be used only once, such as a one-time password. As long as the key is random and only used once, it provides strong security.

As a common example, a fob or token used for authentication makes use of one time pads. Fob-based authentication was covered in Chapter 1. As a reminder, a user is issued a fob that will display a number on an LED display. This number changes every sixty seconds and is synchronized with a server that will know the displayed number at any point in time.

Users can enter their username and password, and also the number displayed on the fob. The number can be used to generate a key used one time to encrypt the credentials.

Asymmetric Encryption

Asymmetric encryption uses two keys—a public key and a private key. The two keys are created as a matched pair. Anything encrypted with a public key can be decrypted with the private key. Similarly, anything encrypted with a private key can be decrypted with the public key.

Asymmetric encryption depends on a Public Key Infrastructure (PKI). PKI will be described in more depth later in this chapter. A PKI allows certificates to be requested, issued, and revoked; certificates include embedded keys. Asymmetric encryption is also called:

- Public-key encryption
- Public/private-key encryption
- Public Key Infrastructure (PKI) encryption

While asymmetric encryption is very strong, it is also very resource intensive, taking a lot of processing power to encrypt and decrypt messages. Asymmetric encryption is commonly used to encrypt and decrypt small amounts of data. Symmetric encryption is used to encrypt large amounts of data.

Some protocols that use asymmetric cryptography include:

- SSL
- TLS
- RSA
- Diffie-Hellman
- Elliptic curve cryptography

Some of the more advanced topics related to PKI become much harder to understand if you don't understand the relationship of public and private keys. These are a matched pair—one key encrypts, and the other key decrypts. However, since these keys can't be seen, they are sometimes hard to grasp for some people. The Rayburn box demonstrates how physical keys can be used for the same purposes as these public and private keys.

The Rayburn Box

I often talk about the Rayburn box in the classroom to help people understand the usage of public and private keys. A Rayburn box is a lockbox that allows people to securely transfer items over long distances. It has two keys. One key can lock the box but can't unlock it. The other key can unlock the box but can't lock it.

Both keys are matched to one box and won't work with other boxes.

- Only one copy of one key exists—think of it as the private key.
- Multiple copies of the other key exist, and copies are freely made and distributed—think of this as the public key.

The box comes in two different versions. In one version, it's used to send secrets in a confidential manner to prevent unauthorized disclosure. In the other version, it's used to send messages with authentication so you know the sender actually sent the message.

The Rayburn Box Used to Send Secrets

Imagine that I wanted you to be able to send some proprietary information and a working model of a new invention to me. Obviously, we wouldn't want anyone else to be able to access the information or the working model. I could send you the empty open box with the key that can be used to lock it.

You place everything in the box and then lock it with the key I've sent with the box. This key can't unlock the box, so even if someone copied the key while the box was in transit, it wouldn't help him unlock it. When I receive the box back from you, I can unlock it with the only key that will unlock it.

This is the same way public and private keys are used to send encrypted data over the Internet to ensure confidentiality. Data is encrypted with the public key. Once encrypted with the public key, it can only be decrypted with the private key, and the private key always stays private. This process will be discussed in the SSL section later in this chapter.

The Rayburn Box Used for Authentication

With a little rekeying of the box, it can be used to send messages while giving assurances that the message was actually sent by me. In this context, the message isn't secret and doesn't need to be protected; it's only important that you know the message was sent by me.

When used this way, the Rayburn box is keyed so that the private key will lock the box but can't unlock it. Remember, there is only one private key, and it is highly protected. Multiple copies of the public key exist, and they are freely given out and available. The public key can unlock the box but can't lock it.

Imagine that we're allies in a battle. I want to give you a message of "SY0-201," which tells you to launch a specific attack at a specific time. We don't care if someone reads this message; instead, we want you to be assured the message came from me.

I can write the message, place it in the box, and lock it with my private key. When you receive it, you can unlock it with the public key. Since the public key opens it, you know this is my box and was locked with my private key—you know definitively the message was sent by me.

If someone intercepted the box and opened it with the public key, it couldn't be locked again with the public key, so you'd receive an open box. This doesn't prove it was sent by me. The only way you have assurances that it was sent by me is if it is locked when you receive it and you can unlock it with the public key.

This is similar to how public and private keys are used for digital signatures. Digital signatures are explained in more depth later in this chapter, but in short, I could send you a message digitally signed with my private key. If the digital signature can be opened with my matching public key, you know it has been signed with my private key. Since only one copy of the private key exists, you know it has been sent by me.

The Rayburn Box Demystified

Before you try to find a Rayburn box, let me clear something up. The Rayburn box is just a figment of my imagination. Rayburn is my middle name.

I haven't discovered a real-world example of how public/private keys work, so I've created the Rayburn box as a metaphor to help people visualize how public/private keys work. Feel free to build one if you want.

SSL

Secure Sockets Layer (SSL) is commonly used on the Internet to secure web traffic using both asymmetric and symmetric encryption. If you're able to grasp how SSL works, you'll have what you need to know for most protocols that use both asymmetric and symmetric encryptions.

Remember

SSL uses both asymmetric and symmetric encryption. Asymmetric encryption is used to privately share the session key, and symmetric encryption is used to encrypt the session data. SSL operates on the session layer of the OSI model to encrypt the data.

HTTPS (HTTP over SSL) uses SSL to encrypt the entire web session. SSL encrypts data on the Session layer of the OSI model. Users can easily tell if a session is encrypted with SSL using two methods:

- The URL includes HTTPS (instead of just HTTP).
- Most web browsers include an icon of a lock.

Since asymmetric encryption isn't efficient to encrypt large amounts of data, asymmetric encryption is only used to transmit the session key. The session key is then used with symmetric encryption to encrypt all the data in the HTTPS session. As you read through the SSL handshake process, try to keep these two concepts in mind:

- **SSL uses asymmetric encryption to securely share the session key.**
- **SSL uses symmetric encryption to encrypt the session data.**

Take a look at figure 9.1 for a simplified explanation of the SSL process. The numbered steps correlate to the circled numbers in the figure.

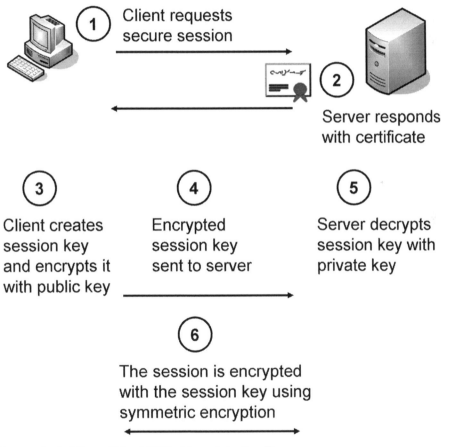

Figure 9.1: Simplified SSL Handshake Process

1. The client begins the process by requesting the HTTPS session. This could be by entering an HTTPS address in the URL or by clicking on an HTTPS link.

2. The server responds by sending the server's certificate. The certificate includes the server's public key, which is mapped to a private key that only the server can access.

3. The client creates a session key and then encrypts it with the private key. As a simple example, the session key may be 53 (though in reality it would be much more complex). The key of **53** is encrypted with the public key to create **UcaNP@$$.**

4. The encrypted session key (**UcaNP@$$**) is sent over the Internet. This encrypted session key can only be decrypted with the matched private key. The server (and no one else) has the private key, so the transmission is secure.

5. The server receives the encrypted session key and decrypts it with the private key. At this point, both the client and the server know the session key.

6. The rest of the session is encrypted with the session key using symmetric encryption.

The amazing thing to me is that this happens so quickly. If a web server takes as long as five seconds, we're frequently impatient. However, a lot is happening to establish this SSL session.

TLS

Transport Layer Security (TLS) was designed as a replacement for SSL. Similar to SSL, TLS also uses both asymmetric and symmetric encryption. It uses asymmetric encryption to privately share session keys and symmetric encryption to encrypt the session data.

Session keys are privately shared within TLS by using the Diffie-Hellman algorithm.

Remember

TLS is the designated replacement for SSL and works similarly. TLS uses the asymmetric Diffie-Hellman algorithm to privately share the session key. TLS operates on the Transport layer of the OSI model.

TLS operates on the transport layer. Remember, though, even though TLS was designed to replace SSL, SSL still operates on the Session layer.

Interestingly, TLS was approved as a standard in 1999 with the expectation that it would replace SSL. However, SSL usage is still strong. It's not that TLS isn't a good algorithm, but that SSL is still meeting many cryptography needs and the change to TLS hasn't been required.

RSA

RSA was developed by Ron Rivest, Adi Shamir, and Leonard Adleman and is named from the first letters of their last names. It is widely used on the Internet and uses the mathematical properties of prime numbers. Specifically, it relies on the fact that large prime numbers can't be factored.

> ### *Remember*
> RSA is widely used on the Internet. It relies on the mathematical properties of prime numbers for its strength. RSA uses sufficiently large prime numbers (1024 bits and 2048 bits) to create keys that can't be discovered easily or quickly.

Keys are created using sufficiently large enough prime numbers in RSA, making it technically infeasible to discover the private key. What is sufficiently large?

RSA uses at least 1024-bit public keys, and it's not uncommon to see RSA public keys 2048 bits long. RSA Laboratories (which has its roots in the RSA algorithm) published an interesting paper titled, "A cost-based security analysis of symmetric and asymmetric key lengths." They estimate that if someone spent ten million dollars to crack a key, it would take three million years to crack a 1024-bit RSA key.

RSA is used on the Internet as one of the protections for credit cards. It's safe to say that today's credit card information won't be of much value in a few million years.

On the weak side, it would take less than five minutes to crack a 430-bit key.

The goal isn't to make an encryption algorithm impossible to break. Instead, the goal is to make the key large enough that it will take too much money and too long to make cracking it worthwhile.

Diffie-Hellman

Diffie-Hellman is a key exchange algorithm where two parties are able to securely share the knowledge of a shared key (or session key) over a public network. Once the shared key is known, both sides can then use this single key to encrypt and decrypt data within the session.

> **Remember**
> Diffie-Hellman is used to privately share a session key over a public network. TLS uses Diffie-Hellman for the key exchange.

TLS uses the Diffie-Hellman algorithm for the key exchange. As a reminder, TLS was created as a replacement for SSL.

The Diffie-Hellman scheme was first published in 1976 by Whitfield Diffie and Martin Hellman. Interestingly, Malcolm J. Williamson secretly created a similar algorithm while working in a British intelligence agency. It is widely believed that the work of these three provided the basis for public-key cryptography.

Elliptic Curve Cryptography

Elliptic curve cryptography (ECC) is commonly used with small wireless devices since it doesn't take a lot of processing power to achieve the desired security. It uses mathematical equations to formulate an elliptical curve. It then graphs points on the curve to create keys. This is mathematically easier and requires less processing power, while also being more difficult to crack.

The math behind ECC is quite complex, but a simple fact helps to illustrate the strength of ECC. In 2005, the U.S. National Security Agency (NSA) announced that ECC was approved for digital signatures and Diffie-Hellman key agreements. If ECC is endorsed by the NSA, it is well tested and strong.

Steganography

Steganography hides data inside other data, or as some people have said, it hides data in plain sight. The goal is to hide the data in such a way that no one suspects a message is hidden within the file. It doesn't actually encrypt the data, so it can't be classified as either symmetric or asymmetric. However, it can effectively hide information, so it is included with encryption objectives and topics.

Some common examples of steganography are:

- **In images or sound files**. Bits can be manipulated to hide a message in a file. The sound file or image will sound or look normal, but the embedded message can be retrieved.

- **In writing**. A simplistic form of steganography uses every nth letter or every nth word to create a message. For example, **I will pass Security Plus** can be embedded in a message using every fourth word like this: **I** know that I **will** enjoy a free **pass** and will enjoy **security** with a substantial **plus** in my salary.

> **Remember**
>
> Steganography is the practice of hiding data inside data, or hiding a message within a file. It doesn't actually encrypt the data but hides it in a place where it's not expected. One method of steganography modifies the least significant bits of multiple bytes to hide a message within graphic files such as .jpg pictures.

One method of embedding data in large files is modifying the least significant bit in some bytes. Consider how colors are displayed in an image. Computers use red, green, and blue, and often colors are displayed by giving each of these colors a different intensity using numbers from 0 through 255.

Colors are represented as R, G, and B with different numbers between 0 and 255 for red, green, and blue.

- **Red**. Red is coded as 255, 0, 0 with red at maximum intensity and green and blue off.

- **Green**. Green is coded as 0, 255, 0 with green at maximum intensity and red and blue off.
- **Blue**. Blue is coded as 0, 0, 255 with blue at maximum intensity and red and green off.

In binary, a bit is coded as either a 0 or a 1. The binary equivalent of 255 is 1111 1111 (eight ones). However, the visual difference between 255 (1111 1111) and 254 (1111 1110) is hardly noticeable, and this is one method used by steganography. If the least significant bit of several bytes is modified, a complete message can be hidden within the file.

For example, the letter A could be hidden within a message. The capital letter A is represented in ASCII by the decimal number of 65. A decimal 65 is represented with 8 binary bits as 0100 0001. This is the number we want to hide in the file—0100 0001.

To hide the letter A in a file, you only need to modify the least significant bit in 8 bytes. Some of these least significant bits may not even be modified, depending on the original value as you can see in the following example.

The original data is shown in binary and decimal. The hidden message (0100 0001 representing an A) is added to the original data. The resulting values are shown in both binary and decimal.

Original Binary	Original Decimal	Hidden Message A (0100 0001)	Binary with Hidden Message	Decimal with Hidden Message
10100101	165	0	1010 0100	164
1001 0111	151	1	1001 0111	151
1011 0110	182	0	1011 0110	182
1101 1100	220	0	1101 1100	220
0001 0011	19	0	0001 0010	18
0101 1010	90	0	0101 1010	90
01100111	103	0	01100110	102
0001 1101	29	1	0001 1101	29

These 8 bytes now include the letter A hidden within them. Only three values actually changed when the message was added, and even these changes were minimal—165 changed to 164; 19 changed to 18; and 103 changed to 102.

Obviously, you'd need to change more than just 8 bytes to include a lengthy message, but image files are already quite large. It's nothing to have a file with over 1 million bytes (1 MB), allowing you to embed a message of one million letters.

Using Encryption Protocols

While many encryption protocols and their usage were covered in the symmetric and asymmetric sections, a few protocols have wider usage and deserve special mention. These include:

- IPSec
- SSH
- S/MIME
- PGP

IPSec

Internet Protocol Security (IPSec) is used to encrypt IP packets at the Network layer of the OSI model or to provide authentication between two hosts prior to transferring data. IPSec is built into IPv6, and it can be implemented in IPv4.

Tunneling protocols, including L2TP, were covered in Chapter 4. IPSec is commonly used with L2TP (L2TP/IPSec) for VPN connections. It can also be used to encrypt traffic between two hosts without L2TP. IPSec provides authentication, integrity, and confidentiality.

> **Remember**
> IPSec can provide authentication, integrity, and confidentiality. The Authentication Header (AH) is used to provide both authentication and integrity. AH uses protocol ID number 51, and ESP uses protocol ID number 50.

Authentication Header

An Authentication Header (AH) is used to provide authentication and integrity. AH can be used by itself to provide authentication and integrity. AH packets are identified with protocol ID number 51 embedded in the packet.

Integrity is provided by AH through the use of a hash. The entire packet is hashed. Authentication data is added to the hash and placed in an authentication data field. This hash is encrypted to prevent tampering.

Encapsulating Security Payload

Encapsulating Security Payload (ESP) is used to provide confidentiality by encrypting the data. ESP also includes the same integrity and authentication protections provided by AH.

ESP packets are identified with protocol ID number 50 embedded in the packet. The protocol IDs are used to uniquely identify the IPSec traffic. Routers and firewalls can be configured to explicitly allow IPSec traffic based on these protocol ID numbers and even explicitly deny anything but IPSec traffic to ensure that all the data is protected.

Security Associations

IPSec uses security associations (SAs) to establish a secure connection. A security association is a group of algorithms and parameters (such as encryption keys) used to create the secure connection. IPSec uses one security association for each direction of traffic.

The Internet Key Exchange (IKE) is used to create and manage security associations for IPSec. It has the capability of choosing the strongest protocol that is supported by both hosts in a connection. Busy VPNs may have multiple security associations managed by IKE at the same time.

SSH

Secure Shell (SSH) is a security protocol that can create a secure channel between two computers. A primary purpose of SSH is to encrypt traffic on the wire to prevent the effectiveness of sniffing attacks with a protocol analyzer.

SSH has been used in a wide variety of applications, including:

- To securely log in to a remote host
- To remotely execute a command
- To secure FTP traffic

The original version of SSH is known as SSH-1. SSH-1 is free but has several known flaws. SSH-2 is a replacement for SSH-1 and has been proposed as a formal standard.

PGP

Pretty Good Privacy (PGP) is commonly used to secure email communications between private individuals. It can be used to encrypt, decrypt, and digitally sign emails, and it is free for individual use. It was designed by Phillip Zimmerman in 1991 and has gone through a lot of changes and improvements over the years.

While PGP can be used commercially, it is most often used privately. S/MIME is most often used within corporate environments.

Normally, keys are embedded in certificates, and they are issued by a Certificate Authority (CA). While PGP still uses certificates to distribute keys, there is no CA to validate the certificates. Instead, PGP uses a Web-of-Trust.

> ### *Remember*
> Pretty Good Privacy (PGP) is used to encrypt, decrypt, and sign emails between private users. It has used a Web-of-Trust (also known as peer-to-peer CA) and can currently use a root CA for authentication; the major flaw with PGP authentication when using the Web-of-Trust is that users must trust keys that are received as valid without a guarantee of a third-party verification. PGP uses asymmetric RSA for digital signatures and symmetric IDEA, CAST, or 3DES for symmetric encryption of data.

Web-of-trust

The greatest flaw with early PGP authentication is that a user had to trust that the public key was received without any third-party validation. Instead of a root

CA validating a certificate, a Web-of-Trust, or peer-to-peer, trust model is used. Current versions of PGP can use either a Web-of-Trust or a hierarchical model.

A Web-of-Trust is a decentralized trust model with no root CA. Instead, multiple users introduce their certificates and keys so that they are available to others. Someone who receives these certificates and keys can indicate that the person who introduced these certificates and keys is a "trusted introducer" and considered trustworthy.

The idea is that if many people indicate a level of trust with a certificate, there's a better chance that it is trustworthy. While this would work if all the peers are known to be honest, this model can be circumvented by a hacker with many hacker friends.

PGP Encryption

PGP uses both asymmetric and symmetric cryptography to encrypt and sign data. Earlier, SSL was described and explained in great detail—how SSL uses the public and private keys in asymmetric encryption to privately share a session key. The session key is then used to encrypt the data in the session. PGP works similarly.

A difference is that with PGP, the encrypted session key is often sent with the encrypted data since the data is sent via email. SSL splits the sharing of the secret key and the session data into different transmissions.

PGP uses the asymmetric RSA algorithm for digital signatures and the secure transmission of a symmetric session key. PGP has used the following symmetric encryption methods for data encryption:

- IDEA
- CAST
- 3DES

S/MIME

Secure/Multipurpose Internet Mail Extensions (S/MIME) is commonly used in email messaging applications. S/MIME can provide several protections, including:

- **Confidentiality**. Data and attachments can be encrypted.
- **Integrity**. If the data or attachments are modified or corrupted, users will know.

- **Authentication.** A receiver has assurances that the sender is who she appears to be.
- **Non-repudiation.** A sender can't later deny sending the email.

> **Remember**
>
> S/MIME can be used to encrypt and digitally sign email messages. S/MIME provides confidentiality, integrity, authentication, and non-repudiation.

S/MIME uses certificates and depends on a Public Key Infrastructure. S/MIME also makes use of digital signatures, which are described in more detail later in this chapter.

Trusted Platform Module

A trusted platform module (TPM) is a combination of hardware and software used to provide encryption. A user is able to encrypt data (such as an entire hard drive) with the use of a pre-shared key (PSK). After the data is encrypted, the user must enter the PSK to access the data.

TPMs come as embedded chips on motherboards and can be activated with some operating systems such as Windows Vista. Windows Vista uses a TPM with its BitLocker technology to encrypt entire drives. When enabled, the user enters a password used by TPM as the pre-shared key to encrypt the entire drive.

The pre-shared key works like other symmetric keys. The same key used to encrypt the data is also used to decrypt the data.

Hashing

Integrity of data is provided through hashing. Hashing is an algorithm performed on a file or message to produce a number called a hash. The hash is used to verify that data is not modified, tampered with, or corrupted—or in other words, the data has maintained integrity.

A hash will be created on the file or message at the source and again at the destination. The two hashes are compared at the destination, and if they are different, integrity has been lost. If the hashes are the same, integrity has been maintained.

Hashes are also called message digests. A hash is created by digesting the message down to a number.

How a Hash Works

Take a look at figure 9.2 to see how a hash is used to provide integrity. One point to remember here is that the message is not secret, so encryption is not used. This explanation is focused only on hashing to provide integrity.

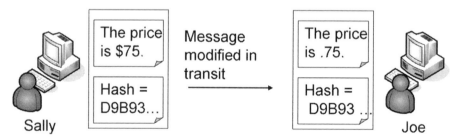

Figure 9.2: Simplified Hash Process

Sally is sending a message to Joe. The message is "The price is $75." A program on Sally's computer calculates the MD5 hash as D9B93C99B62646ABD06C887039053F56. In the figure, I've shortened the full hash down to just the first five characters of "D9B93." Both the message and the hash are sent to Joe.

The message is modified before it reaches Joe. When Joe receives the message and the original hash, the message is now "The price is .75." A program

on Joe's computer calculates the MD5 hash on the modified message as
`564294439E1617F5628A3E3EB75643FE`.

- Hash created on Sally's computer:
  `D9B93C99B62646ABD06C887039053F56`
- Hash created on Joe's computer:
  `564294439E1617F5628A3E3EB75643FE`

Clearly, the hashes are different, so you know the message has lost integrity. The program on Joe's computer would report the discrepancy. Joe doesn't know what caused the problem; it could have been a malicious attacker changing the message, or it could have been a technical problem. However, Joe does know the received message isn't the same as the sent message and he shouldn't trust it.

Encrypting the Hash

You may have noticed a problem in the explanation of the hashed message. If an attacker can change the message, why can't he change the hash too?

In other words, if the attacker changed the message to "The price is .75," he could also calculate the hash on the modified message and replace the original hash with the modified hash. Now, when Joe's computer calculates and compares the hash, it would be:

- Hash created on Sally's computer:
  `D9B93C99B62646ABD06C887039053F56`
- Modified hash inserted by attacker after the message has been modified:
  `564294439E1617F5628A3E3EB75643FE`
- Hash created on Joe's computer:
  `564294439E1617F5628A3E3EB75643FE`

The calculated hash on the modified message would be the same as the received hash. This would erroneously indicate that the message maintained integrity.

Confidentiality of the hash needs to be maintained. Encryption is used to enforce confidentiality. Take a look at figure 9.3 to see how this is accomplished.

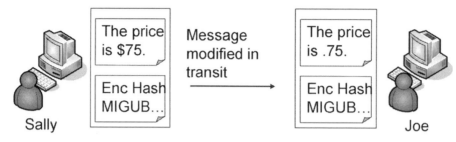

Figure 9.3: Encrypted Hash Process

Sally is still sending the same message. The MD5 hash is:

`D9B93C99B62646ABD06C887039053F56`. However, this hash is encrypted, and the result is:

`MIGUBgkrBgEEAYI3WAOggYYwgYMGCisGAQQBgjdYAwGgdTBzAg`
`MCAAAC`
`AmYDAgIAwAQIs3PZkd1hpLYEENChut928RblNwsif7gpnt`
`MESHEfuUH6UEU9`
`403ZPr6AUivXWuMKF+z6qq9a/HybJst0o/DA1bK2tJI+d8H0L`
`qrrxJqSE2Rwpe37Ok62/W4LwLJLfY+IrmLIrA==`

In figure 9.3, I've shortened this to only the first five characters: `MIGUB`. The message is modified in transit, but the attacker can't decrypt the hash, so he can't modify the hash.

A program on Joe's computer calculates the MD5 hash on the modified message as `564294439E1617F5628A3E3EB75643FE`. Joe's computer also decrypts the received encrypted hash to identify the original hash.

- Hash created on Sally's computer:
  `D9B93C99B62646ABD06C887039053F56`

- Hash created on Joe's computer:
  `564294439E1617F5628A3E3EB75643FE`

Again, we can see that the hashes are different and the message has lost integrity.

A common question is, "If we are encrypting the hash, why not just encrypt the message too?" The short answer is that it takes extra resources, such as the CPU and memory, to encrypt and decrypt, so data should only be encrypted when necessary.

When the 32-hexadecimal character MD5 hash was encrypted, it resulted in several lines of text. Imagine that instead of a one-line message, the transmitted data is all the written works of William Shakespeare. The resources necessary to encrypt and decrypt the data would be much greater.

Remember the basics:

- Encrypt to maintain confidentiality.
- Use hashing to maintain integrity.

Common Hash Algorithms

Several hashing algorithms are used and specifically mentioned in the exam objectives. MD5 and SHA1 are specific message-digest hashing algorithms. MD5 is susceptible to collision attacks, but SHA1 is still considered secure.

Older Microsoft systems used hashing algorithms to secure passwords. While the protocols were primarily used for authentication, they are relevant here due to how they used hashing. These are:

- **LANMAN**. Used with Windows 95, 98, and ME and included in many systems for backward compatibility. Passwords are easily cracked.
- **NTLM**. Improvement of LANMAN. Provided better protection but still vulnerable. NTLM is also called NTLMv1.
- **NTLMv2**. Improvement over NTLM. Best of the three.

> ### Remember
> SHA1 uses 160 bits and is more secure than MD5. NTLMv2 is the strongest hashing authentication mechanism when compared with LANMAN (the oldest and least secure) and NTLMv1.

MD5

MD5 (Message-Digest algorithm 5) is a one-way function that produces a 128-bit hash. The hash is often represented in hexadecimal format. Four bits are needed to represent a hexadecimal character, so MD5 hashes can be represented with 32-hex characters (128/4).

Previous versions (MD1–MD4) are considered compromised.

MD5 has known flaws. Specifically, it's possible to create another message that will result in the same hash. This is known as a collision and is considered a serious compromise. Collisions are discussed in more detail later in this chapter.

SHA

The Secure Hash Algorithm (SHA) algorithms are grouped into three families: SHA0, SHA1, and SHA2.

SHA1 is the most popular and creates a 160-bit message digest using a one-way function. SHA1 was designed by the U.S. National Security Agency and is commonly used by the U.S. military and other government institutions.

While the SHA2 family does provide better security, it isn't as widely used due to some incompatibility issues with other cryptographic functions. SHA3 is under development.

LANMAN

LAN Manager (LANMAN) is a very old authentication protocol used to provide backward compatibility to Windows 95, 98, and ME clients. LANMAN has significant weaknesses with how it stores the password.

Even though LANMAN is very old, some legacy services and software applications still use LANMAN. Additionally, some newer authentication protocols will still store passwords in the LANMAN format if the password is less than fifteen characters long.

LANMAN performs a hashing algorithm on passwords that makes it easy for password-cracking tools, such as L0phtCrack, to discover the actual password.

The LANMAN passwords are always stored as fourteen characters. If the password is less than fourteen characters, the password is padded with trailing spaces. The password is converted to all uppercase and then divided into two separate seven-character strings. A hash is created on each seven-character string, and the two hashes are stored locally as a single string.

If the password is only seven characters long, the resulting hash on the trailing seven spaces would always be: AAD3B435B51404EE. If the entire password is blank, the hash would be: AAD3B435B51404EE AAD3B435B51404EE.

However, even if the password is more than seven characters long, it doesn't take L0phtCrack long to successfully crack the password, because it only needs to work on seven characters at a time. L0phtCrack guesses different one to seven character combinations and compares the hash of the guessed password with the hash of the stored password.

If at all possible, LANMAN should be disabled on all computers within a network. It is disabled in Windows Vista and Windows Server 2008 by default.

NTLM

NT LAN Manager (NTLM) was introduced by Microsoft as an improvement over LANMAN. There are two versions of NTLM: NTLM (or NTLMv1) and NTLMv2.

NTLMv1 uses the LANMAN hash and a MD4 hash of the user's password. Both LANMAN and MD4 are considered compromised, resulting in known vulnerabilities with NTLMv1 today.

Microsoft improved NTLMv1 with NTLMv2. NTLMv2 changed the process completely and uses an MD5 type of hash. NTLMv2 is significantly complex, making it infeasible to crack using current technologies.

Even though NTMLv2 is a strong hashing algorithm, Kerberos is the preferred authentication mechanism within Microsoft domains.

While NTLMv1 and NTLMv2 are improvements over LANMAN, a significant vulnerability exists in systems before Windows Vista. LANMAN is still enabled by default, and when it is enabled, NTLMv1 will store a copy of the password in the LANMAN version, if the password is fourteen characters or less.

Many networks impose the requirement that administrator passwords must be at least fifteen characters or more. This fifteen-character requirement is specifically designed to overcome the LANMAN vulnerability.

Hashes Are One-Way

A hash is a one-way function. In other words, a hash can be used to create a number, but the resulting number cannot be used to accurately determine the message.

As an example, the MD5 hash from the message "I will pass the Security+ exam" is:

538412826 ICF2EEA6D90ADACE48CD41B

However, it's impossible to reverse the hashing process to accurately determine the original message. There are simply too many possible combinations that can create the same hash.

It is possible to create another message that will produce the same hash. That's what L0phtCrack and some other password-cracking tools do. They don't necessarily guess the correct password, but they guess some combination of characters that will produce the same hash result.

Hash Collisions

A hash collision occurs when two completely different messages or files produce the same hash when they are hashed using the same hashing algorithm.

For example, imagine that the following two messages created the hash as shown:

- I will pass CompTIA Security+.

    0ED343DDFBEAA40883B4EF1D5281F3D9

- I am CompTIA Security+ certified!

    0ED343DDFBEAA40883B4EF1D5281F3D9

Notice that the hash of the first message is the same as the hash of the second message, even though the messages are not the same. This is a collision.

Collision resistance is a hashing algorithm's ability to avoid producing the same hash from two different guessed inputs.

Remember

Collisions occur when the hash of two different messages or files are the same when using the same hashing algorithm. A birthday attack attempts to create two different messages that will produce the same hash. Strong algorithms (such as SHA1) are resistant to collisions; they have the ability to avoid producing the same hash from two different inputs.

Birthday Attack

In a birthday attack, an attacker is able to create two different messages that both produce the same hash or message digest. Clearly, the two different messages are different. However, if the two hashes are the same, it incorrectly indicates that the different messages have retained integrity.

A birthday attack is named after the birthday paradox in mathematical probability theory. The birthday paradox states that for any random group of twenty-three people, there is a 50 percent chance that two of them have the same birthday. This is not the same year, but instead one of the 365 days in any year.

Birthday attacks on hashes are thwarted by increasing the number of bits used in the hash to increase the number of possible hashes. For example, the MD5 hash uses 128 bits and has been cracked with a birthday-hash technique as a part of the MD5CRK project. SHA1 uses 160 bits and has not been cracked.

Preimage Attack

A preimage attack will attempt to discover a message that can replicate the hash of a given message. A preimage attack is much more serious than a birthday attack.

- **Birthday attack.** A birthday attack will attempt to find two hashes that are the same from different messages. This is similar to finding any two people with the same birthday from a random group of twenty-three.
- **Preimage attack.** A preimage attack can reproduce a hash that is the same as a known hash. This would be similar to you walking into any room of twenty-two other people and finding one of them has the same birthday as you. It's a 50 percent chance any two of the twenty-three people have the same birthday, but significantly less likely that you are one of these two people.

As an example of a preimage attack, LANMAN passwords were cracked by using L0phtCrack (as described earlier in this section). The hash was stored locally in a format L0phtCrack could read. L0phtCrack then produced another password that could produce the same hash.

L0phtCrack succeeded due to the different ways the password was simplified, resulting in fewer possible combinations. However, using strong and complex passwords makes a preimage attack significantly more difficult.

Remember, hashing is intended to be a one-way function. You shouldn't be able to use the hash to discover the original message. In other words, a secure hash cannot be reversed. If you can discover the original message from the hash, it indicates a serious flaw.

Rainbow Tables

Rainbow tables are commonly used in password attacks to speed up the calculation process. Rainbow tables use pre-calculated hashes stored in lookup tables.

It helps to review the process of how comparative analysis works in a password attack.

1. The hash of the original password is identified.
2. A password is guessed.
3. The guessed password is hashed.
4. The hashes of the original password and the guessed password are compared.
5. Steps 2 through 4 are repeated until a match occurs.

In a rainbow table attack, the hashes are calculated before the attack and stored in a lookup table. Now, the time-consuming and processor-intensive step of hashing a guessed password (step 3) can be skipped. Instead, the original password hash is compared against all the hashes in the lookup table. If a match occurs, the original password (or at least text that can reproduce the hash of the original password) is discovered.

Admittedly, this is a simplistic explanation of a rainbow table attack, but it's adequate if you don't plan on writing the algorithm to create your own rainbow table attack software.

Rainbow table attacks are successful against hashes of plain-text passwords. Passwords that are hashed with random bits, known as a salt, prevent this attack. Additionally, encrypting and then hashing the password will defeat a rainbow table attack.

Hashes and Files

The majority of the previous discussions were focused on messages and passwords, but hashes are often used to validate the integrity of data files, especially when files are being downloaded and there's a strong desire to ensure that integrity has been maintained.

Even though MD5 is subject to hash collisions, this isn't much of a risk with files. The primary integrity problem with a file is that it could be infected with a virus. However, the chance of an infected file resulting in the same hash as the original file is close to impossible. MD5 using 128 bits for the hash is commonly used with files such as patches, updates, and other downloaded files.

> ### Remember
> Hashes are often included with files available for download. The hash could be displayed, allowing the user to manually check the hash, or it could be available to the application to automate the integrity check. If the hashes are different, the file is considered suspect and should not be trusted as valid and should not be used.

Occasionally, the file will be listed with the hash number. The user can then manually compare the hash of the program file at the source with the hash of the file at the destination. Other times, the application used to download the file has the ability to read an associated file that includes the file's hash.

Either way, if the hashes are different, it indicates the file has lost integrity. Worse, if the file is an application and the hash is different, it strongly indicates the file has been infected with some type of malware. A downloaded executable with a modified hash should not be executed (unless you have a virtualized environment specifically set up to test malware).

Message Authentication Code

Another method used to provide integrity is a message authentication code (MAC). A message authentication code is a string of data created from the message using an algorithm and a shared key.

> **Remember**
>
> A message authentication code (MAC) is used to provide integrity for messages. It uses a secret key to encrypt the hash.

The word *authentication* in the name is misleading. A MAC will authenticate the message as valid (which is another way of saying integrity is maintained), but it does not authenticate the sender the way a digital signature can authenticate a sender. The primary purpose of the MAC is integrity.

A key difference between a MAC and a hashing algorithm is that a MAC is always encrypted as part of the process. While it's not uncommon to encrypt a hash, all hashes aren't encrypted, and all encrypted hashes aren't encrypted using symmetric encryption. However, a MAC is always encrypted.

Since a MAC provides integrity, it is sometimes referred to as a message integrity code (MIC) or even a message authentication and integrity code (MAIC).

Digital Signature

A digital signature is primarily used to authenticate a sender of a message over an insecure channel. The receiver is able to verify that the message was actually sent by the sender. Since it is relatively easy to spoof email, digital signatures can be quite valuable.

The three services provided by digital signatures are:

- **Authentication.** Validates to the receiver who sent the message.
- **Non-repudiation.** The sender can't later deny sending the message.
- **Integrity.** Validates that the received message has not been modified or corrupted.

> **Remember**
>
> Digital signatures are used for authentication, non-repudiation, and integrity. The message is hashed, and this hash provides integrity. The hash is encrypted with the sender's private key. The receiver decrypts the hash with the sender's public key; if successful, it provides authentication and non-repudiation.

Understanding digital signatures is much easier if you understand some other cryptography concepts discussed in this chapter.

- **Hashing**. Digital signatures start by creating a hash of the message. A hash is simply a number created by performing an algorithm on the data.
- **PKI**. Digital signatures need certificates, and certificates are supported by a Public Key Infrastructure (PKI). The PKI issues, manages, and revokes certificates.
- **Public/private keys**. These are a matched set. One key is used to encrypt, and one key is used to decrypt. Public/private key sets are used for both digital signatures and encryption.
  - o **Private key**. Individuals have access to a private key on their systems, which is matched to a public key. In a digital signature, the private key is used to encrypt the hash of the message.
  - o **Public key**. The public key is widely available to other users. In a domain environment, systems are able to automatically retrieve certificates holding the public key from network servers. The public key is used to decrypt the hash of the message.

Take a look at figure 9.4 for an explanation of the process used with a digital signature. In the figure, Sally is sending a message to Joe. It is being digitally signed so that Joe knows it was sent by Sally. Note that the message is not secret. If it was, it would be encrypted, which is a completely separate process. The focus in this explanation is only the digital signature.

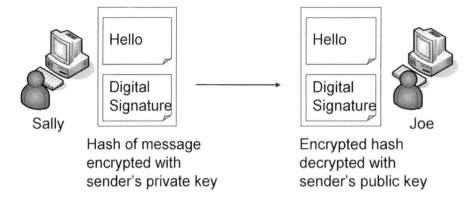

Figure 9.4: Digital Signature Process

Sally creates her message in an email program, such as Microsoft Outlook. Once Microsoft has been configured correctly, all she has to do is click a button to digitally sign the message. Here's what happens.

- The message is hashed. This hash provides integrity.
- The hash is encrypted with the private key. The private key provides both authentication and non-repudiation.
- The encrypted hash and the unencrypted message are sent to Joe.
- Joe's system will retrieve Sally's public key and perform the following actions:
    o Decrypt the encrypted hash with Sally's public key.
    o Calculate the hash on the received message.

If the calculated hash of the received message is the same as the unencrypted hash, then several things have been validated.

- **Authentication**. Since the public key can only decrypt something encrypted with the private key, and only Sally has the private key, this hash must have been encrypted with Sally's private key. Sally must have sent it.
- **Non-repudiation**. Sally cannot later deny sending the message. The hash was encrypted with her private key, which no one else can access.
- **Integrity**. Since the hash on the sent message matches the hash of the received message, the message has maintained integrity.

At this point, you might be thinking, if we do all of this, why not just encrypt the message too? The answer is resources. It doesn't take much to encrypt a 160-bit SHA1 hash used for the digital signature, but it would take quite a bit more to encrypt a lengthy email and its attachments.

Notice also that the processes of both digital signatures and public-key encryption are similar. The difference is in which key is used to encrypt and which is used to decrypt.

- **Digital signatures**
  - o The private key encrypts a hash of the message.
  - o The public key decrypts it.
- **Encryption**
  - o The public key encrypts the data.
  - o The private key decrypts it.

Non-Repudiation

Non-repudiation is used to prevent a party from denying he took a specific action. There are two primary methods used to provide non-repudiation:

- **Audit logs.** An audit log will record details, such as who, what, where, and when, of an event. If a valid authentication mechanism is used, a user can't deny the action since it is recorded. Audit logs were presented in Chapter 7.
- **Digital signatures.** A digital signature uses public and private keys. Messages signed with a private key provide non-repudiation. Digital signatures were discussed previously in this chapter.

> **Remember**
>
> Non-repudiation is provided by audit logs and digital signatures. When digital signatures are used, the private key provides non-repudiation, and the digital signature can also be used to validate a message's origin.

An indirect way of looking at non-repudiation with a digital signature is that it can be used to validate a message's origin.

Public Key Infrastructure

A Public Key Infrastructure (PKI) is a group of technologies used to request, create, manage, store, distribute, and revoke digital certificates. A PKI is based on the asymmetric encryption scheme using public and private keys and can also use public and private keys for digital signatures.

You aren't expected to know everything about a PKI, but you should have a basic understanding of the different elements.

In this section, you'll learn about:

- Certificate Authorities
- Certificates
- Key management

Certificate Authorities

A Certificate Authority (CA) is an organization that issues, manages, and signs certificates. Certificate Authorities can be very large, such as the public CA named Verisign. They can also be very small, such as a single service running on a server in a domain.

Large CAs are often public and make money by selling certificates. For this to work, the public CA must be trusted. Any certificates issued by the CA are trusted as long as the CA is trusted.

At a basic level, this is similar to how a driver's license is trusted because it was issued by a trusted government authority, such as the department of motor vehicles (DMV). If you want to cash a check, you may have to present your driver's license to prove your identity. Your driver's license is trusted as valid since it was issued by a trusted authority—the DMV.

Similarly, certificates issued by trusted CAs are trusted.

Trusted CAs

In order for issued certificates to be trusted, the CA issuing the certificate must be trusted. This trust relationship is often built into web browsers.

Public CAs will often negotiate with web browser developers to have their certificates included with the web browser. For example, Internet Explorer

includes about twenty certificates from public CAs. You can view these
certificates in Internet Explorer 7 by following these steps:

1. Open Internet Explorer.
2. Select the Tools drop-down menu. Select Internet Options.
3. In the Internet Options dialog box, select the Content tab.
4. Click the Certificates button.
5. Select the Trusted Root Certification Authorities tab.

    This is referred to as the Trusted Root Certification Authority store. Any
    certificates issued by companies that have certificates in the Trusted Root
    Certification Authority store are automatically trusted.
6. Select any certificate and click View. You will see three tabs.
    a. **General**. Provides information on the purpose of the certificate,
        who it is issued to, and validity dates.
    b. **Details**. Allows you to view the contents of the certificate, such
        as the serial number, validity dates, and public key.
    c. **Certificate Path**. Shows the path to the root CA.

It's also possible to add certificates to this store. If you add root CA
certificates to this store, certificates in the CA chain are also trusted.

Root CAs and a Trusted CA Model

The very first CA in a CA trust chain is referred to as the root CA. In large
CA organizations, the root CA will issue certificates to child CAs. The child CAs
can issue certificates to end users or to other child CAs that will ultimately issue
certificates to end users.

Even if there are multiple levels in the trust chain, as long as the root CA is
trusted, all certificates issued by any CA in the chain are also trusted.

Two of the common types of trusted CA models are:

- **Hierarchical**. A root CA is at the top. All certificates issued by the root
  CA or any child CAs are also trusted.
- **Web-of-Trust**. A Web-of-Trust is used with Pretty Good Privacy (PGP).
  Instead of a root CA, a Web-of-Trust uses a peer-to-peer model.

Private CAs

While most CAs are public and accessible via the Internet, some CAs are private. One of the reasons companies often create a private CA is to support Outlook Web Access (OWA).

OWA is used to allow employees to access company email via the Internet using a web browser. OWA requires a secure connection using SSL, so it must have a certificate issued. The private CA is used to issue a certificate to the OWA server.

Since a certificate from the company's private CA isn't in employees' home computers, the certificate won't be trusted. However, employees are often given instructions on how to bypass the warning or install the certificate.

Certificates

A certificate is a digital document that includes information on the owner of the certificate and the owner's public key. Remember, the public key is matched to a private key and is used in asymmetric encryption.

Certificates are used for a variety of purposes, including:

- Server authentication
- Client authentication
- Secure email
- Code signing
- Sending the public key for encryption

Users can have more than one certificate assigned to them in a process referred to as certificate mapping. Certificate mapping can be one-to-one or many-to-one.

- **One-to-one mapping**. One certificate is mapped to one user.
- **Many-to-one mapping**. Many certificates are mapped to one user. This is commonly done when users need different certificates, such as one for authentication and another for email.

The most popular certificate type is X.509 version 3. The exception is CRL certificates, which are version 2. Version 3 certificates include the following elements:

- **Signature.** The signature is used to identify the holder of the certificate and can be validated by the CA.
- **Public key.** The public key used by the RSA asymmetric encryption. This key is matched to the private key of the certificate holder.
- **Serial number.** The serial number is used to uniquely identify the certificate when the CA validates it.
- **Validity dates.** Certificates include "Valid From" and "Valid To" dates. This allows a certificate to expire.
- **Issuer name.** The name of the CA that can be contacted to validate the certificate.

Viewing Certificates

You can view a certificate anytime you have an SSL session within a web browser. Most browsers include a lock icon to indicate that the session is secure. If you right-click the lock, you usually have a View choice, which can be used to view the details of the certificate.

Similarly, you can view the details of a certificate as demonstrated in the steps in the trusted CAs section.

Revoking Certificates

It's possible for certificates to become compromised before the validity dates expire. If a certificate is compromised, the CA revokes it. Some of the reasons a CA will revoke a certificate are:

- The private key is compromised or is no longer held privately only by one entity.
- The CA discovers it was improperly issued.
- The certificate has been superseded.

> ### *Remember*
> Compromised keys are revoked. Revoked keys are published on a certificate revocation list (CRL).

Revoked certificates are published on a certificate revocation list (CRL, pronounced as "crill"). The CRL includes a list of revoked certificates identified by their serial numbers and is available for download by any entity trying to validate a certificate.

Validating Certificates

Clients need to be able to validate certificates when they are received. By validating the certificate through the CA, the client is able to verify that the certificate can be trusted and also verify that it hasn't been revoked.

Figure 9.5 shows the process of validating a certificate.

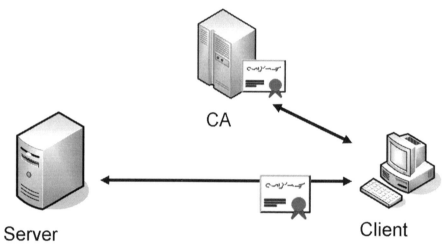

Figure 9.5: Validating a Certificate

You may remember from the SSL section that a client initiates the SSL session. The server responds by sending a certificate that holds the public key. When the client receives the certificate, it then queries the server to validate the certificate.

The validation can be done by one of two methods:

- **CRL.** The client requests a copy of the CRL and checks it to see if the received certificate is on the list and has been revoked.
- **OCSP.** The Online Certificate Status Protocol (OCSP) allows the client to query the CA with the serial number of the certificate. The CA then responds with an answer of "healthy," "revoked," or "unknown." A response of "unknown" could indicate the certificate is a forgery.

Single-sided vs. Dual-sided Certificates

Single-sided certificates are normally used in public-key cryptography where a server uses a certificate to validate its identity to clients. However, the clients don't validate their identity back to the server when single-sided certificates are used.

It is occasionally desirable to have both sides of a session validate their identities with each other using certificates. This is often referred to as mutual authentication, but it can be done with dual-sided certificates in public-key cryptography.

Dual-sided certificates are feasible when a small number of clients need to authenticate back to a server. When using dual-sided certificates, instead of just issuing the certificate for the server, a matching certificate needs to be issued to the client. If multiple clients are involved, this can quickly result in a large number of certificates that have to be issued.

However, if only a limited number of clients need to be authenticated back to the server, dual-sided certificates can be used.

Key Management

Key management includes all the elements used to generate, distribute, store, and protect cryptography keys. One of the primary considerations of keys is ensuring that they are of sufficient length and adequately protected, all of which has been discussed throughout this chapter.

Another consideration is how the keys are generated. This is important as part of key management, because keys must be kept secret. If they aren't controlled when they are generated, they can become compromised even before they are distributed. The possibilities are:

- **Centralized key generation**. Keys can be generated on a central server. A benefit of the central server model is better control of the keys.
- **Decentralized key generation**. Keys can be generated on individual computers. This model can be used when the computers have adequate protection for the keys.
- **Hybrid model**. Some keys can be generated on a central server, and other keys can be generated on individual computers.

Key Escrow

Key escrow is the process of placing an encryption key in a safe environment so that it can be used for recovery if needed. This is often done as a backup for private keys or to ensure that keys are available, even if employees leave the company.

One method of placing a key in key escrow is to divide it into multiple pieces. The different pieces of the key are distributed to escrow agents. None of the different escrow agents can use the key by themselves, but if the key is needed, all the escrow agents can work together to reproduce the key.

Recovery Agent

A key recovery agent is a designated individual who can recover or restore cryptographic keys. A single person can be designated as a recovery agent in some key storage systems. Or, multiple individuals can be designated to hold multiple portions of the key for recovery.

Exam Topic Review

When preparing for the exam, make sure you understand these key concepts covered in this chapter.

Cryptography Basics

- Confidentiality uses encryption to prevent the unauthorized disclosure of data.
- Integrity uses hashing to provide assurances that data has not been modified or corrupted.
- Digital signatures can provide authentication, integrity, and non-repudiation.

Encryption to Provide Confidentiality

- Encryption is accomplished by using an algorithm and one or more keys.
  - o Algorithms are usually well known. Protection is ensured by using strong keys and protecting them.
  - o Weak keys and poor key management make it easy for attackers to discover the confidential data.

- Symmetric encryption uses a single key, and asymmetric encryption uses two keys (public and private).
- Symmetric encryption (also known as secret-key encryption or session-key encryption) is much quicker than asymmetric encryption and is best for encrypting large amounts of data.
- AES is a strong, fast algorithm and is considered the current standard for symmetric encryption. AES256 uses 256 bits in the symmetric key.
- Other symmetric algorithms include DES (considered compromised), 3DES (which is considerably slower than AES), IDEA, CAST, and RC.

Asymmetric Encryption

- Asymmetric encryption (also known as public-key encryption and PKI encryption) uses two matched keys: public and private.
  - o If a public key encrypts something, only the matching private key can decrypt it.
    This is the process used for encryption of data such as when the session key in the SSL process is encrypted with the public key.
  - o If a private key encrypts something, only the matching public key can decrypt it.
    This is the process used for digital signatures when the hash of a message is encrypted with the private key.
- SSL uses both asymmetric and symmetric encryption with HTTPS sessions. SSL uses asymmetric encryption to privately share the session key and symmetric encryption to encrypt the session's data. SSL operates on the session layer to encrypt data.
- TLS is the designated replacement for SSL. TLS uses Diffie-Hellman to privately share the session key.
- RSA is widely used on the Internet for secure connections. RSA uses large prime numbers to create public and private keys.

Steganography

Steganography is a method of hiding information within a file. It is used to hide data within graphic images, sound files, and videos by modifying the least significant bit of bytes to embed a hidden message.

Using Encryption Protocols

- IPSec provides authentication, integrity, and confidentiality.
  - o IPSec uses an Authentication Header (AH) to provide integrity and authentication. AH is identified with protocol ID 51.
  - o IPSec uses Encapsulating Security Payload (ESP) to provide encryption. ESP is identified with protocol ID 50.
  - o IPSec creates a security association for each direction of secure traffic. Internet Key Exchange (IKE) is used to create and manage security associations for IPSec.
- Pretty Good Privacy (PGP) is used to encrypt, decrypt, and sign email between private individuals.
  - o PGP uses a Web-of-Trust (also known as peer-to-peer) instead of a root CA for authentication.
  - o The flaw with the Web-of-Trust is that users must trust keys that are received without a guarantee.
  - o PGP uses asymmetric RSA for digital signatures.
  - o PGP has used IDEA, CAST, and 3DES for symmetric encryption of data.
- S/MIME is used in email messaging applications in many corporate environments to encrypt and digitally sign email messages. S/MIME provides confidentiality, integrity, authentication, and non-repudiation.
- A trusted platform module (TPM) can be used for whole disk encryption. TPM systems use a pre-shared key (PSK).

Hashing to Provide Integrity

- Hashing is used to provide integrity and verify that data has not been modified or corrupted.
- A collision occurs when two different messages produce the same hash or message digest.
  - o Birthday attacks attempt to identify two messages that will produce the same hash using the birthday paradox (a mathematical puzzle).
  - o Strong hashing algorithms are collision resistant.

- o Rainbow tables use lookup tables to reduce processing time in collision attacks.
- MD5 and SHA1 are two common hashing algorithms.
  - o MD5 uses 128 bits and has been compromised but is still used.
  - o SHA1 uses 160 bits and is widely used, including by the U.S. military.
- NTLMv2 is a strong hashing algorithm used with authentication in Windows systems. LANMAN is a legacy hashing algorithm with significant weaknesses. LANMAN was superseded by NTLMv1, and NTLMv1 was superseded by NTLMv2.
- A secure hash is a one-way function. A message can be hashed producing a number, but the process cannot be reversed to reproduce the message from the hash in a secure hash. An insecure hash can be reversed to reproduce the original message, or said another way, is subject to hash collisions.
- Hashes are used to verify the integrity of files. If the hash of a downloaded file is different than the hash was when the file was posted, it indicates the file has been modified or corrupted and should not be used.
- A message authentication code (MAC) is used to provide integrity for messages. A MAC uses a hash encrypted with a symmetric key.

Digital Signature

- The primary purpose of a digital signature is to provide authentication of the sender. It provides assurances to the receiver of who sent the message.
- Digital signatures provide authentication, integrity, and non-repudiation.
  - o The message is hashed, providing integrity.
  - o The hash is encrypted with the private key of the sender.
  - o If the receiver can decrypt the hash with the matching public key, the receiver knows it was encrypted with the private key, providing authentication. The sender can't later deny sending the message, providing non-repudiation.

Non-repudiation

- Non-repudiation prevents a party from denying he took an action.
  - Audit logs record who, what, where, and when. The "who" provides non-repudiation.
  - Digital signatures use cryptography to provide non-repudiation.

Public Key Infrastructure

- A Public Key Infrastructure (PKI) is a group of technologies used to manage, store, distribute, and revoke digital signatures.
- Key pairs can be generated on a central server (centralized) or on individual computers (decentralized).
- When private keys are compromised, the PKI will revoke the associated certificate and publish revoked certificates on a certificate revocation list (CRL).
- Certificates can be mapped to users.
  - A one-to-one mapping is one certificate mapped to one user.
  - A many-to-one mapping is many certificates mapped to one user.
- Private keys can be stored in escrow to ensure that data encrypted with a private key can still be retrieved if the original key becomes unavailable (such as if an employee leaves the company).

Practice Questions

1. What do most encryption schemes use?

    A. Algorithm and key

    B. Algorithm and hash

    C. Hash and key

    D. Certificate and one time pad

2. Which of the following is considered the strongest symmetric algorithm?

    A. DES

    B. 3DES

    C. AES

    D. PGP

3. Which one of the following can encrypt data with the least processor utilization?

    A. DES

    B. 3DES

    C. AES

    D. MD5

4. What type of encryption would be best for large amounts of data?

    A. Symmetric

    B. Asymmetric

    C. Message digest

    D. Diffie-Hellman

5. Which of the following means the same as secret-key encryption? (Choose all that apply.)

    A. Symmetrical encryption

    B. Session-key encryption

    C. One-way function

    D. Asymmetrical encryption

6. A client is planning to make a purchase on an e-commerce site. She clicks the checkout icon, and an SSL session is started. What types of keys does SSL use? (Choose all that apply.)

A. Private key

B. Public key

C. Session key

D. Remote key

7. What type of encryption is used by a PKI?

A. Symmetric

B. Asymmetric

C. Steganography

D. MD5

8. What does TLS use to establish a session key?

A. SSL

B. AES

C. Diffie-Hellman

D. RSA

9. Which encryption algorithm uses the mathematical properties of prime numbers to create keys?

A. ECC

B. RSA

C. PKI

D. PGP

10. What is steganography?

A. A method of hiding information

B. A method of encrypting information

C. A method of hashing

D. A method of providing non-repudiation

11. What does IPSec use to provide authentication in the Authentication Header?

    A. A hash created from the computer name of the source computer

    B. A hash created from the computer name of the destination computer

    C. A hash created from the bytes in the packet

    D. A hash that will be different at the destination than the source

12. What has PGP used in place of a root Certificate Authority (CA)? (Choose all that apply.)

    A. Web-of-Trust

    B. Peer-to-peer

    C. Hierarchical

    D. Symmetric

13. A specific type of attack is able to identify two different messages that both produce the same message digest. What type of attack is this?

    A. Dictionary attack

    B. Brute force attack

    C. Birthday attack

    D. One-way function

14. A hash is used to identify a message. However, it is possible for a hashing algorithm to create the same hash from two different messages. What is this called?

    A. Collision

    B. Attack

    C. Rainbow table

    D. Birthday attack

15. An attacker is able to create two identical hashes using two different messages with MD5. However, an attacker has not been able to create two identical hashes using two different messages with SHA1. What can be said about SHA1?

    A. SHA1 has greater collision strength.

    B. SHA1 has greater collision resistance.

C. MD5 has greater collision strength.

D. MD5 has greater collision resistance.

16. What's the difference between a secure encryption and a secure hash? (Choose two.)

A. A secure encryption can be reversed.

B. A secure encryption cannot be reversed.

C. A secure hash can be reversed.

D. A secure hash cannot be reversed.

17. Your company is releasing a software patch for a product. You want to provide assurances to users that the patch has not been modified after it was posted to the download site. What would you do?

A. Use L2TP/IPSec to download the file.

B. Use an HTTPS session for the download.

C. Use an MD5 hash.

D. Post a notice on the web site.

18. What can a message authentication code be used for?

A. To provide integrity

B. To retrieve messages

C. To validate a message's origin

D. To encrypt a message

19. What is the first key that is used when providing non-repudiation using public-key cryptography?

A. Private key of the sender

B. Private key of the receiver

C. Session key

D. Public key

20. What would a PKI do if a key is considered compromised?

A. Cancel the key

B. Expire the key

    C. Revoke the key

    D. Reissue the key

21. Of the following, what are considered valid types of certificate mapping?

    A. Many-to-many mapping and one-to-one mapping

    B. Many-to-one mapping and one-to-one mapping

    C. One-to-many mapping and one-to-one mapping

    D. Symmetric and asymmetric mapping

22. A company wants to ensure they have access to an employee's data encrypted with public keys and decrypted with private keys, even if the employee leaves the company. What should be done?

    A. Ensure that users don't encrypt their data.

    B. Store the public keys in escrow.

    C. Store the private keys in escrow.

    D. Store the keys in a publicly accessible location.

Practice Question Answers

1. **A.** Most encryptions use an algorithm and a key. Hashing algorithms are used to enforce integrity, not encryption. One time pads are algorithms that use a key only once, but this isn't used by most encryption schemes.

2. **C.** Advanced Encryption Standard (AES) is considered the strongest symmetric algorithm of those presented. DES has been compromised. 3DES replaced DES, and AES replaced 3DES. PGP is used to encrypt and sign email, but it is not a symmetric algorithm.

3. **C.** Advanced Encryption Standard (AES) is considered the most secure symmetric algorithm of those listed and uses the least amount of CPU and memory resources. 3DES replaced DES and uses a significant amount of resources since it encrypts the data in three passes. MD5 is a hashing algorithm used for integrity.

4. **A.** Symmetric encryption uses one key for both encryption and decryption of data and is much more efficient than asymmetric encryption for encrypting large amounts of data. Message digest is another name for hashing algorithms that create a hash but do not encrypt data. Diffie-Hellman is an asymmetric algorithm used with TLS to privately share a session key.

5. **A, B.** Symmetrical encryption is also known as secret-key encryption or session-key encryption; it uses one key to encrypt and decrypt the data. A one-way function is used with hashing algorithms where the algorithm creates a number from the message, known as the hash, but the hash can't be used to recreate the message. Asymmetrical encryption uses two keys and is also known as public-key encryption or PKI encryption.

6. **A, B, C.** SSL uses asymmetric encryption to privately share the session key, and asymmetric encryption uses a private key and a public key. SSL uses symmetric encryption to encrypt the session data; symmetric encryption uses a session key. SSL does not use a remote key.

7. **B.** A PKI is based on an asymmetric encryption scheme using public and private keys. Symmetric encryption uses just a single key. Steganography is the practice of embedding a message within a message, such as by modifying the least significant bit of multiple bytes in an image file.

8. **C.** Transport Layer Security (TLS) uses the Diffie-Hellman algorithm to privately share a session key. TLS is intended to replace SSL. AES is a fast, secure symmetric algorithm, but it isn't used with TLS. RSA is an asymmetric algorithm that depends on the inability of large prime numbers to be successfully factored.

9. **B.** RSA relies on the inability to factor large prime numbers and uses sufficiently large prime numbers to create keys. ECC is used in smaller wireless devices and uses mathematical equations to create curves and identify points on the curves. PKI is a group of technologies used to issue, manage, and revoke certificates. PGP is used to encrypt email between individuals.

10. **A.** Steganography is a method of hiding information within a file. One method of steganography is to modify the least significant bit of many bytes to embed a message. Steganography doesn't actually encrypt the data, but just hides it. Hashing is used to enforce integrity. Non-repudiation prevents a party from denying an action.

11. **C.** Authentication Header (AH) uses a hash of the bytes in the packet, providing integrity, combined with other authentication data to provide authentication. AH does not use the computer names. Hashes should be the same at both the source and destination, and if they aren't, it indicates the data has lost integrity.

12. **A, B.** Pretty Good Privacy (PGP) has used a Web-of-Trust network instead of a root CA. The flaw with this is that users have to trust any public key that they receive. A hierarchical trust model includes a root CA and provides a level of assurance that certificates are what they appear to be. Symmetric encryption uses one key to encrypt and is not related to certificates.

13. **C.** A birthday attack allows an attacker to create two different messages that produce the same message digest. A dictionary attack uses a database or dictionary of words to try to guess a password. A brute force attack attempts to try all possible combinations to guess a password. Hashes are one-way functions, meaning the message can be used to create the hash, but the process can't be reversed to create the message from the hash.

14. **A.** A collision occurs when two completely different messages can produce the same hash when they are hashed using the same hashing algorithm. Attacks (such as birthday attacks and rainbow table attacks) attempt to discover collisions, but an attack doesn't always result in a collision. A rainbow table attack uses a lookup table to reduce processing time in the attack.

15. **B.** SHA1 has greater collision resistance than MD5. Collision resistance is the ability of a hashing algorithm to prevent collisions. A collision occurs when two completely different messages produce the same hash. A collision is a weakness and is not referred to as collision strength.

16. **A, D.** A secure encryption can be reversed through decryption to see the original data. A hash is intended to be a one-way function and cannot be reversed if it is secure. If it isn't secure, a hash is subject to collisions and can be reversed.

17. **C.** A hash (such as an MD5 hash) can be used to provide assurances to users that the file has not been modified and has not lost integrity. Using an encrypted session with L2TP/IPSec or HTTPS to download the file doesn't provide an assurance of integrity on the original file. A file could be modified after a notice has been posted.

18. **A.** A message authentication code (MAC) is used to provide integrity. It uses a secret key to encrypt the hash. It is not used to retrieve or encrypt a message. A digital signature can be used to validate a message's origin.

19. **A.** Non-repudiation is provided through a digital signature by encrypting a hash of the message with the private key of the sender. The encrypted hash

can be decrypted by the receiver using the sender's public key. Public-key cryptography doesn't use a session key.

20. **C.** A key that is compromised is revoked. Revoked keys are published on the CRL. Keys can't be cancelled. Keys will expire when the validity dates expire, but if a key is compromised, it should be revoked earlier. Expired keys can be reissued.

21. **B.** Many certificates can be mapped to a single user (many-to-one mapping), or a single certificate can be mapped to a single user (one-to-one mapping). One-to-many and many-to-many mappings aren't valid certificate mappings. Symmetric encryption uses one key and asymmetric encryption uses two keys, but neither is a term used with certificate mapping.

22. **C.** The private keys should be stored in escrow so that the data can be decrypted with them if necessary. A change in policy restricting users from encrypting data is not necessary. The public keys are already accessible, so they don't need to be placed in escrow. Private keys should stay private and not be stored in a publicly accessible location.

Chapter 10

Implementing Organizational Policies

CompTIA Security+ objectives covered in this chapter

3.1 Identify and apply industry best practices for access control methods.

- Least privilege
- Separation of duties
- Job rotation

4.7 Conduct periodic audits of system security settings.

- Storage and retention policies

6.3 Differentiate between and execute appropriate incident response procedures.

- Forensics
- Chain of custody
- First responders
- Damage and loss control
- Reporting—disclosure of

6.4 Identify and explain applicable legislation and organizational policies.

- Secure disposal of computers
- Acceptable use policies
- Password complexity
- Change management
- Classification of information
- Mandatory vacations
- Personally Identifiable Information (PII)
- Due care
- Due diligence
- Due process

- SLA
- Security-related HR policy
- User education and awareness training

* * *

This chapter covers many of the policies that are implemented within an organization and some of the guiding principles included in these policies. Topics include:

- Business policies
- Incident response policies
- Auditing

Business Policies

Businesses create organizational policies to address many of the normal functions of a business, and many of these policies can affect different elements of security. Some of the policy issues directly related to security include:

- Security policies
- Personnel policies

Security Policies

Security policies lay out a plan for security within a company. Security policies are created as a first step to mitigate risks, and when created early enough, they help ensure that security is considered and implemented throughout the life cycle of various systems in the company.

Policies are often brief, high-level statements that identify goals based on an organization's overall beliefs and principles. After the policy is identified, standards and guidelines are derived. While the policies are often high-level statements, the standards and guidelines provide details on implementation.

For example, a security policy could specify that "strong authentication mechanisms will be used for all personnel." This would be interpreted and implemented through standards and guidelines, perhaps by using smart cards and

PINs. Notice that the policy is broad and allows for interpretation and adaptation as technologies change.

A security policy can be a single large document or divided into several smaller documents, depending on the needs of the company. Some of the key driving factors of any security policy are:

- **Security goals.** The overall goals identify the end result after risks are identified and mitigated within the company.
- **Easy to understand.** An effective security policy includes clear language and omits technical jargon. Regular users should be able to read it and understand the overall goal.
- **Supports business objectives.** The goal of security is to enhance the company's objectives, not detract from them. In line with this, the security policy should support all legislation and regulations affecting the company.
- **Data management.** The handling of proprietary data and Personally Identifiable Information (PII) is addressed to ensure that data is adequately protected.
- **Change management.** Effective change management enhances the stability of an organization and reduces outages. This will normally include patch management.
- **Hardware management.** This will often outline overall hardening goals, such as eliminating defaults, removing unneeded services and protocols, and keeping systems up-to-date.
- **Account management.** This includes the basics of creation, deletion, and disabling of accounts for personnel.
- **Review element.** A security policy should be reviewed on a regular basis, such as once a year, to ensure it still meets the needs and objectives of the company. Additionally, auditing could be regularly performed to ensure the policy is being followed.

Even the best written security policy isn't useful if it isn't enforced. Security policies need support from management and should be created with management's input and support. Once personnel realize that a policy is not enforced, it can quickly become ignored.

> **Remember**
>
> Security policies must be enforced. If security problems exist within a company, one of the first things to check is the existence of a policy. If a policy exists and includes guidelines or procedures that can reduce or eliminate the problems, the policy should be enforced.

All personnel should have access to the sections of the security policy that affect them. HR personnel should be trained on the guidelines and enforcement of all policies that affect personnel, including the security policy.

Change Management

Change management is a growing field in IT. It requires that any changes go through a structured change-management process before being implemented. The process allows multiple experts to review the change for potential impact. It also ensures that all parties are aware of the change.

A significant amount of downtime and service outages are caused by well-intentioned technicians making changes without realizing the negative impact. Systems and networks are complex and intertwined. A change to one firewall, router, or server can cause another firewall, router, or server to no longer function as it once did.

For example, an engineer may be reviewing open ports on a firewall. He notices port 5678 is open and determines that this is a risk. He closes the port. Unfortunately, this port is used by an internally developed application that synchronizes payroll data twice a month. Payroll and paychecks are late.

The engineer had good intentions when closing the port. It wasn't a malicious action. However, for all the employees who didn't get their paycheck on time, the effect was the same. This is one example of thousands where a well-intentioned change negatively impacts the services on a network.

Documentation

Change management provides documentation of a change. Most change-management procedures start with a change request that can be reviewed by different experts. Once approved, the documentation is made available so that everyone knows what changes have occurred or will occur.

Documentation ensures that any changes are well known, can be easily reversed if necessary, and can be reproduced if a system needs to be rebuilt after an outage.

Hey! Who Moved My Changes?

In one environment where I worked, several technicians spent the weekend troubleshooting a problem that was negatively affecting services. They ultimately identified two servers that were configured incorrectly. Through a slow, painful process, they identified all the incorrect configurations and returned the services to 100 percent by the end of the weekend.

On Monday, another group of technicians came in and realized that the changes they made on Friday to two servers were all undone. The changes made on Friday weren't communicated to the technicians working on the weekend, and the changes weren't adequately tested, resulting in unintended service loss.

The Monday technicians were upset that their work was undone. The weekend technicians were upset that they wasted their time troubleshooting an undocumented change. The end users suffered through reduced services.

Effective change management ensures that changes have the least effect on services, are well documented, and all personnel are adequately informed of the changes.

Patch Management

Patch management is also included in a change-management process. Patch management ensures that needed patches are deployed after a testing and approval process.

Remember

Patch management uses a change-management process. Patches are reviewed and tested before being approved and deployed to minimize the negative impact on the business.

Sometimes it's useful to look at the worst-case scenario. The worst that can happen when a patch is applied is that systems will no longer function.

For example, one patch caused certain systems to constantly reboot. If you are patching a single system and it breaks, it's inconvenient. You'll have to troubleshoot to restore it. It may be time consuming, but it's possible. However, if a patch is deployed to five hundred systems and all five hundred systems break, it's more than inconvenient. It can cripple the business.

Patches included in the change-management process are reviewed, tested, and only deployed after being approved. This reduces the possible negative impact of deployed patches on the business.

Due Diligence and Due Care

Companies have a responsibility to exercise both due diligence and due care. These two concepts work together.

- **Due diligence**. Due diligence refers to a company's obligation to take a reasonable amount of time and effort to identify risks to data and systems it owns and manages. A company has a responsibility to understand and investigate risks it faces.
- **Due care**. Due care refers to the steps a company has taken to protect against the risks. If risks are known, a company needs to take a reasonable amount of action to protect its resources.

Need-to-know

Need-to-know is a principle that specifies that individuals are given enough information to adequately perform their jobs, but no more. The purpose is to prevent sensitive data from being given out to too many people.

A secret is easy to keep if only one person knows it—at least for some people. With each additional person who learns the secret, it becomes increasingly more difficult to keep the information secret. If you can limit the number of people who have access to secret or classified information, you can reduce the potential of the information being leaked to the wrong people.

> **Remember**
> Need-to-know specifies that individuals are given access to the data they need, but no more. For example, a user may be granted access to Secret data, but that doesn't mean she has the right to see all secret data. The difference between need-to-know and least privilege is that need-to-know focuses on data only, while least privilege includes rights and permissions.

For example, Sally is working on a project designing lasers used for defensive purposes, which is classified Secret and is granted a Secret clearance. She would have access to any Secret data that is directly related to her part of the project, but she wouldn't necessarily have access to all data on the project if she didn't need to know the information to succeed with her tasks.

Similarly, just because she has been granted a Secret clearance, she wouldn't be granted access to all secret data within the organization.

Least Privilege

The principle of least privilege specifies that individuals or processes are granted only the rights and permissions needed to perform assigned tasks or functions, but no more. For example, if Joe needs to print to a printer, you should grant him print permission for that printer but nothing else.

> **Remember**
> Least privilege specifies that individuals or processes are granted rights and permissions needed to perform their jobs, but no more. For example, if a person needs to print to a printer, he is granted print permission, instead of being added to the Administrators group, which would grant many more rights and permissions.

Notice the difference between need-to-know and least privilege—need-to-know focuses on data only, while least privilege includes rights and permissions.

- The need-to-know principle specifies that individuals are given access to the data they need, but no more. A Secret clearance does not automatically grant access to all secret data.
- The principle of least privilege specifies that individuals or processes are granted rights and permissions needed to perform their jobs, but no more.

A colleague shared an extreme example of how this principle was violated where he worked. He was the lone IT administrator, and no matter how much he asked for help, his boss was never able to get him additional manpower. The company grew, and he found he was fielding a lot of complaints because users didn't have the access they needed. He knew he needed to improve the administrative model with groups and roles, but he just didn't have enough time.

The users complained to his boss, who then put pressure on him. He was told, "Fix this problem!"

Ultimately, he put all the users into the Domain Admins group. In a Windows Active Directory domain, the Domain Admins group has full rights and permissions to do anything and everything in a domain; so suddenly, all the users had full privileges. This was the equivalent of lighting the fuse on a time bomb; it would only be a matter of time before users purposely or accidentally caused problems with their newfound permissions.

Ironically, his boss was happy because the users stopped complaining. I heard from him a couple of months later. One of the users found payroll data on the network and discovered how much other employees were getting paid. It spread through the company quickly and caused a significant amount of infighting. At that point, his boss's boss wasn't very happy.

Service Level Agreement

Companies often have service level agreements (SLAs) with vendors or service providers when services are contracted. The SLA will specify an expected level of performance often stated in the form of a guarantee. An SLA will often include:

- Performance expectations
- Roles and responsibilities of the customer and the vendor
- Problem resolution paths
- Maximum outage time frames
- Minimum uptime percentages

For example, a company may lease a T1 communications line from a telecommunications company. The telecommunications company (the vendor) may provide a performance guarantee providing the company with assurances that the line will be available for end-to-end traffic delivery.

Personnel Policies

Companies frequently develop polices to specifically define and clarify issues related to personnel. This includes personnel behavior, expectations, and possible consequences. Personnel are often indoctrinated on these policies when they are hired and as changes occur.

A human resources (HR) department will have a direct impact on the enforcement of policies related to employees within the company. HR personnel should be trained on any policies they are expected to enforce. However, HR personnel are not expected to understand or implement any technical aspects of the policies.

Some of the policies directly related to personnel are:

- Acceptable use
- Code of ethics
- Mandatory vacations
- Separation of duties
- Job rotation

Acceptable Use

The acceptable use of computers and networks is defined for employees in an acceptable use policy or document. This document will describe the purpose of the systems, how users can access them, and the responsibilities of users when accessing the systems.

> **Remember**
> Personnel are often required to read and acknowledge acceptable use policies. An acceptable use policy will define the purpose of IT systems, how users can access them, and the responsibilities of users when accessing the systems. They are sometimes reinforced with logon banners or other company communications.

Many companies require users to read and sign a document indicating they understand the acceptable use policy. Some companies require users to review and sign the document annually. Acceptable use is sometimes reinforced through other communications such as logon banners or emails.

An acceptable use policy may also include definitions and examples of unacceptable use. For example, users may be prohibited from using company resources for personal business such as shopping on the Internet or visiting web sites that are unrelated to their work.

Code of Ethics

Many companies include an ethics statement or code of ethics in company documents. In general, ethics are the moral standards that others use to judge behavior. However, all people's judgments aren't equal, and what constitutes good behavior is sometimes debated.

Within a company, a code of ethics is intended to serve as a guide for employees for daily professional conduct. It isn't intended to be a goal to aspire to, but instead it prescribes the minimum acceptable behavior.

A code of ethics is used to:

- Define or describe minimum acceptable behavior
- Promote high standards of practice
- Establish a framework for professional behavior
- Provide a standard for self-evaluation

Mandatory Vacations

Mandatory vacation policies are commonly implemented in some institutions to help detect when employees are involved in malicious activity such as fraud or embezzlement. As an example, employees in positions of fiscal trust are often required to take an annual vacation of at least five consecutive workdays.

For embezzlement actions of any substantial size to succeed, an employee would need to be constantly present in order to manipulate records and respond to different inquiries. On the other hand, if an employee is forced to be absent for at least five consecutive workdays, the likelihood of any illegal actions succeeding is reduced, since someone else would be required to answer the queries during the absence.

Of course, mandatory vacations by themselves won't prevent fraud. Most companies will implement the principle of defense in depth by using multiple layers of protection. Additional policies may include separation of duties and job rotation to provide as much protection as possible.

Separation of Duties

Separation of duties is a principle that prevents any one person or entity from being able to complete all the functions of a critical or sensitive process. It's designed to prevent fraud, theft, and errors.

The classic example is found in accounting. Accounting departments are frequently divided into two divisions: Accounts Receivable and Accounts Payable. Personnel in the Accounts Receivable division review and validate bills. Valid bills are then passed to the personnel in the Accounts Payable division, who then pay the bills.

If Joe was the only person doing both functions, it would be possible for him to create and approve a bill from Joe's Most Excellent Retirement Account. After approving the bill, Joe would then pay it. And if Joe doesn't go to jail, Joe may indeed retire early at the expense of the financial health of the company.

Job Rotation

Job rotation is a concept that has employees rotate through different jobs to learn the procedures and processes in each. From a security perspective, job rotation helps to prevent or expose dangerous shortcuts or even fraudulent activity. Knowledge is shared with multiple people, and no one person can retain explicit control of any process or data.

For example, your company could have an accounting department. As mentioned in the separation of duties section, you would separate accounting into two divisions—Accounts Receivable and Accounts Payable. Additionally, you could rotate personnel in and out of jobs in the two divisions. This would ensure more oversight over past transactions, ensure that rules and policies are being followed as expected, and reduce the possibility of collusion.

Collusion is where two or more people engage in a secret activity for the purpose of fraud. By rotating people to different jobs, the possibility of collusion is reduced because employees realize a different person could be in the job sometime in the future.

If a single person always performs the same function without any expectation of oversight, the temptation to go outside the bounds of established policy increases.

Classification of Information

Data within a company needs to be organized into different classifications so that the company knows what data to protect privately within the company and what data to share. Some data warrants a lot of resources to protect, and other data is freely shared.

Government entities often classify data with labels such as Top Secret, Secret, Confidential, and Unclassified. Rules are in place to specifically identify how data is classified and how classified data is protected.

While private companies may not use the same labels or the same rules, they do use similar concepts. Financial data, products in development, and customer and employee information could all be classified as private within the company and not released. Other information could be designated as public and made freely available.

I'll Go to Jail Before I Give You the Passwords!

The city of San Francisco allegedly had an extreme example of the dangers of a single person with too much explicit knowledge or power. A network administrator who held Cisco's highest certification of Cisco Certified Internetwork Expert (CCIE) allegedly made changes to the city's network, changing passwords that only he knew and ensuring that he was the only person with administrative access.

It could be that this CCIE was taking these actions to protect the network that he considered his "baby." He was the only CCIE, and it's possible he looked on others as simply not having the knowledge necessary to adequately maintain the network. Over the years, fewer and fewer people had access to what he was doing, and his knowledge became more and more proprietary. Instead of being malicious in nature, he may have simply been protective, even if overly protective.

However, someone internal to the city recognized that all the information eggs were in the basket of this lone CCIE; it was just too risky. What if he got hit by one of the trolleys in San Francisco? What would they do? They tried to get him to share some of the information, such as the passwords, and he allegedly refused even when faced with arrest. Later, he gave passwords that didn't work to law enforcement personnel.

Ultimately, he was charged with four counts of tampering with a computer network and kept in custody with a $5 million bail. The city of San Francisco had to bring in experts from Cisco, and they were anticipating costs as high as $250,000 to regain control of their network.

What's the lesson here? Internal controls such as creating and enforcing policies related to rotation of duties, separation of duties, and cross-training may have avoided this situation completely. If this CCIE truly did have good intentions toward what he perceived as his network, these internal controls might have prevented him from allegedly going over the line of overprotection and looking at the world through the bars of a jail cell.

Account Management

Personnel policies should also include account management. Users that need access to computers need an account. Considerations with accounts include both account creation and termination.

> **Remember**
> Account management will specify what to do with an account for employees on a leave of absence or terminated. Normally, accounts are disabled so that access to data can be maintained for a period of time.

Other considerations could include:

- **Initial passwords**. If an administrator must create the initial password, users should be forced to change their passwords when they first log on. If more than one person knows the credentials for an account, the credentials no longer uniquely identify the individual—someone else could log on with the same credentials, and even if the event is logged, you can't prove who did it.
- **Leave of absence**. If an employee will be absent for an extended period of time, the account should be disabled while she is away.
- **Terminated employee**. Accounts for ex-employees should be disabled or deleted. Often, a company will disable the account to ensure that data maintained by the employee can still be accessed if necessary. After a period of time, the account is deleted.

Education and Training

Training helps personnel understand their responsibilities related to security. While all personnel need to be trained, all personnel don't need the same training. Training is often targeted to different groups.

- **Management**. Management needs training on the policies and procedures they are expected to enforce.
- **Technical personnel**. Technical personnel need more targeted training than other groups on how to implement different security policies.

- **HR personnel.** HR personnel need training on the guidelines and enforcement of all policies affecting personnel.
- **All users.** End users need training on security elements that directly affect them, such as acceptable use and protection of passwords.

> ### Remember
> Training needs to be targeted to different groups within a company. For example, all personnel need training on the policies and procedures they are expected to follow, and HR personnel should know the guidelines and enforcement of the policies.

As an example of the different needs for training, a simple security principle such as password protection would need to be stressed to different types of users in different ways.

- **End users.** End users need to be told that they should NEVER give out their passwords, and if someone asks for their passwords, they should be highly suspicious. Phishing attempts and phone scams are successful because some users give out their passwords or privacy information.
- **Technical personnel.** Technical personnel need to know they shouldn't ask end users for their passwords. While it may make a job easier, if the end user makes an exception and gives out the password to a trusted person, he may mistakenly make an exception and give it out to an untrusted person.
- **Management.** Management needs to enforce the policies consistently. They need to understand the reasoning behind the policies, the risks that are being addressed, and consequences of these risks.

Computer Disposal

When computers reach the end of their life cycles, they are donated, recycled, or sometimes just thrown away. From a security perspective, you need to ensure that the computers don't include any data that may be useful to people outside your company or damaging to your company if it's released.

It's common for organizations to have a checklist to ensure that a system is sanitized prior to being released. This sanitization process ensures that data is not inadvertently released. The process could include:

- **Check all removable drives.** This includes CD/DVD and floppies if they exist. It's often possible for a user to forget a disk in a drive.
- **Sanitize internal disks**. Data contained on internal disks must be rendered unreadable before release.

The level of sanitization is often directly related to the type of data the computer held or processed. From a classification perspective, a computer processing unclassified data wouldn't require as much sanitization as a computer that processed Top Secret data.

Every company has secrets. Keeping these secrets can often make the difference between success and failure. Sometimes, the secrets come in the form of Personally Identifiable Information on customers or employees.

Personally Identifiable Information

Personally Identifiable Information (PII) is personal information about individuals. PII can be information used to trace an individual's identity besides the name, including:

- Social Security number
- Financial records
- Medical records
- Biometric data

A significant amount of PII has been lost or stolen by companies and government institutions in recent years. This has raised the awareness of the importance of protecting PII.

For example, a Veteran's Administration employee copied a database onto his laptop that contained PII on over twenty-six million U.S. veterans. He took the laptop home, which was later burglarized, and the laptop was stolen. The VA then went through the painful and expensive process of notifying all of the people who were vulnerable to identity theft, and the affected individuals spent countless hours scouring their records for incidents of identity theft.

This story is repeated time and time again. A laptop stolen from an investment company included PII on over 200,000 potential customers. Another laptop with data on over 215,000 customers and advisers disappeared from a car.

A question that can be asked in any of these scenarios is, "Did the company exercise due diligence to protect this data?" If not, the company can also face civil liabilities in the form of lawsuits.

Each of these instances resulted in potential identity theft and the loss of goodwill and public trust of the company. Both customers and employees were negatively impacted, and the companies were forced to spend time and energy discussing the incident and often dollars trying to repair their reputations.

> ### *Remember*
> The unauthorized transfer of Personally Identifiable Information (PII) represents a significant risk to a company. The capability of small storage devices such as USB flash drives or USB hard drives to store vast amounts of data represents the greatest risk associated with these devices. When data falls into the wrong hands, confidentiality is lost.

Protecting PII

Companies have a moral and legal obligation to protect PII. This includes protecting the data from being accessed within a network, protecting data that is accessible via the Internet, and protecting data that is controlled or transferred by employees.

Many laws have been passed requiring companies and government institutions to protect PII. These include:

- U.S. Health Insurance Portability and Accountability Act (HIPAA)
- U.S. Privacy Act of 2005
- EU Article 8 of the European Convention on Human Rights

One of the common reasons data seems to fall into the wrong hands is that employees don't understand the risks involved. They may not realize the value of the data on a laptop, or they may casually copy PII data onto a USB flash drive.

One of the goals of security professionals is to reinforce the risks of not protecting PII. When employees understand the risks, they are less likely to needlessly risk customers and other employees to identity theft.

Sanitizing Systems

Systems or drives that contain PII must be sanitized before being disposed of. The sanitization can mean different things depending on the importance of the data, but it's important to realize that simply formatting a disk drive won't erase the data.

Different methods of sanitizing a disk drive include:

- **Writing patterns of ones and zeros onto the drive**. Different programs are available that will write patterns of ones and zeroes a specific number of times to ensure that data originally on the disk is rendered unreadable.

- **Degauss the disks.** A degausser is a very powerful electronic magnet. Passing a disk through a degaussing field will render the data on the disk unreadable, and it will often destroy the motors of the disk. Degaussing of backup tapes is often done to sanitize a tape without destroying the tape.

- **Physical destruction**. Disk platters can be removed and sanded down to the bare metal.

Remember

Disk drives that have held Personally Identifiable Information (PII) or other classified material must be sanitized before being placed into use again.

This process is dependent on the data it contained. Simply formatting the drive won't make the data unreadable. A company may approve the use of a bit writing program that writes a series of ones and zeros for some drives, but they may require that other disks be degaussed or physically destroyed.

Incident Response Policies

Incident response policies are created to help personnel know how to react to incidents. An incident is commonly defined as a series of events that are significant enough that they either negatively affect the performance of the company or have the potential to do so.

A single event is usually not classified as an incident. If a user inserts a personal USB flash drive on his work computer, and the antivirus software detects and deletes a virus, this is an event, not an incident. However, if an attacker is able to retrieve credit information on over ten thousand customers, that would be considered an incident even though it may have occurred in a single event.

Several uncontrolled events typically are considered an incident. For example, if several computers are discovered to be zombies as part of a large botnet and have been sending several thousand spam emails a day, this is an incident.

Incidents could include attacks, compromises, policy violations, system failures, and much more.

An incident response policy will usually contain the following elements:

- Incident response team
- Response steps

Incident Response Team

An incident response team is usually a specific group of employees with expertise in different areas. Combined, they have the knowledge and skills to effectively respond to an incident. Team members may include:

- **Senior management**. Someone needs to be in charge with enough authority to get things done.
- **Network administrator/engineer**. A technical person needs to be included who can adequately understand the problem and relay the issue to other team personnel.
- **Communications expert**. If an incident needs to be relayed to the public, a public relations person should be the one to do so.

It's not uncommon for an incident response team to set up alternate methods of communications. This could be ensuring that each person is issued a cell phone or two-way radio. If the primary method of communication is email, and the email server goes down, the incident response team will have problems before they even start.

Additionally, the response team will likely set up a centralized location at which to gather and report on progress during the incident. This is sometimes referred to as a war room. All team members will know they can get up-to-date information from the war room, and they would also report progress there.

First responders are the first security-trained people who arrive on the scene. The term comes from the medical community, where the first medically trained person to arrive on the scene of an emergency or accident is a first responder. A first responder could be someone from the incident response team or someone with adequate training to know what the first response steps should be.

Response Steps

There are several possible ways to respond to an incident. While it's important to always ensure that the problem is contained or isolated, and evidence is preserved, other steps could also be included.

Response steps could include:

- **Identifying an incident**. Identifying an incident is referred to as escalating the status from an isolated event to an incident.
- **Containment**. The first response, once an incident is identified, should be to contain or isolate the problem. This may be done by personnel who escalate the event or by first responders on the incident response team, depending on the incident.
- **Gather evidence (while preserving evidence)**. Evidence is gathered without modifying it. Chain of custody documentation would be initiated here.
- **Investigate the incident**. Identify the scope and source of the incident. If possible, identify the cause and identify the damage that was sustained.
- **Eradicate the threat**. The threat should be removed from the environment. This could be done by removing the malware or disconnecting the attacker.

- **Recovery and repair**. Perform any repairs necessary and bring systems back online.
- **Adjust procedures**. Review the overall incident and determine if there are any lessons to be learned, anything that could be done better next time, or any flaws in procedures.

While different incident response policies could include different elements, there are two elements that are consistent within these policies:

- Containment
- Preservation of evidence

Containment

The first response to an incident is to contain or isolate the problem. Often, this can be done by simply disconnecting the CAT5 cable from the NIC or using another method to take a computer off the network. Networks can be isolated from the Internet by modifying ACLs on a router or a network firewall.

> ### Remember
> The first step to take for an incident is containment or isolation. An event is first investigated, and if it is determined to be an incident, then steps to prevent the problem from spreading or continuing should be taken. This is often as simple as disconnecting the cable from the NIC.

This is similar to a flood caused from an overflowing sink. You wouldn't start cleaning up the water until you first turned off the faucet. The goal of containment is to prevent the problem from spreading to other areas or other computers in your network, or to simply stop the attack.

Computer Forensics

What do you think of when you hear "forensics"? A lot of people think about the TV program *CSI* (short for Crime Scene Investigation) and all of its spin-offs. These shows demonstrate the phenomenal capabilities of science in crime investigations.

Computer forensics is used to analyze evidence from computers to determine details on computer incidents similar to how CSI personnel analyze evidence from crime scenes. It uses a variety of different tools to gather and analyze computer evidence. Computer forensics is a growing field, and many educational institutions have even launched degrees around the science.

While you may not be the computer forensic expert analyzing the evidence, you should know about some of the basic concepts related to gathering and preserving the evidence.

Preservation of Evidence

Preservation of evidence is achieved by ensuring that data is not modified during the collection process. Just as a rookie cop wouldn't walk through the blood at a crime scene (at least not more than once), employees shouldn't access systems that have been attacked or power them down.

Files have properties that show when they were last accessed, but if a curious user accesses the file, this property is modified. Now it can no longer be shown that an attacker accessed the file. Additionally, data in cache (the volatile RAM) can sometimes contain valuable evidence.

Remember
When collecting evidence for forensic analysis, steps should be taken to ensure that data is not modified. This is often done by first creating a bit copy of a disk.

Personnel on an incident response team will often have tools that allow them to retrieve data from volatile RAM or make binary copies of the disks. Binary copies are sometimes referred to as bit copies. As an example, dd (short for data definition) is a forensic tool that can be used to create a bit copy of a disk. It will create an exact copy without modifying the original.

In addition to preserving the evidence, chain of custody must be documented for any evidence that is collected.

Chain of Custody

A proper chain of custody ensures that evidence presented in a court of law is the same evidence that was collected. It does so by documenting who had custody of the evidence or where it was stored the entire time since it was collected. The chain of custody should be established when evidence is first collected.

> ### Remember
> A chain of custody should be established as soon as evidence is collected and maintained throughout the lifetime of the evidence. It could be documented on a chain of custody form or something else, but it must be documented. A properly documented chain of custody will prove that the evidence presented in a court of law is the same as the evidence that was collected.

If evidence is not controlled, it can be modified, tampered with, or otherwise corrupted. Evidence can be ruled inadmissible in court if there is a lack of adequate control or even a lack of documentation showing that adequate control was maintained.

A chain of custody is commonly documented on a chain of custody form.

Auditing

Auditing is the independent and objective examination of processes and procedures. The goal is to determine if standards and guidelines are being followed. In other words, a company has several policies in place, but are these policies being followed?

For example, an organization may have a policy that states that individuals with administrative accounts should use their normal accounts for regular work and only use the administrative account when doing administrative tasks. An audit of this policy would use some means to determine if users are following the policy.

Vulnerability assessments and penetration tests were covered in Chapter 7. These assessments and tests can be used in an audit to determine if the steps that a company has taken to mitigate risks were successful.

Many companies and industries are required to have specific audits done to comply with legislation. For example, banks and other financial institutions are regularly audited to ensure they are conforming to existing laws.

Any audit will result in a report. If discrepancies are identified during the audit, a company is expected to address and correct them.

Auditing in this context is different than auditing logs covered in Chapter 7. An audit log would be used to record events such as who did something to provide non-repudiation.

Exam Topic Review

When preparing for the exam, make sure you understand these key concepts, which were covered in this chapter.

Business Policies

- A company security policy lays out a plan for security within the company. It should be easy to understand and support business objectives. Additionally, it should address management of systems, changes, hardware, and accounts.

- If a security policy doesn't exist, it should be created. If it's not followed, it should be enforced.

- Change-management procedures should be followed to ensure all changes (including patches) go through a review and approval phase before being implemented.

- The principle of need-to-know ensures that users are granted access to only the data needed to perform their jobs, no more.

- The principle of least privilege ensures that users are granted the rights, permissions, and privileges they need to do their jobs and no more.

- A service level agreement (SLA) provides a company with a performance guarantee for services outsourced to a vendor.

- An acceptable use policy is used to ensure that personnel know the purpose of a company's IT structure and the methods used to access IT resources.

- A code of ethics is used to define and describe expected minimum behavior.

- Several policies are used to reduce collusion and incidents of fraud. A separation of duty policy separates job processes to prevent any single person or entity from controlling the entire process. A job rotation policy rotates personnel into different jobs on a regular basis. Mandatory vacations reduce the possibility that someone is involved in malicious activity.

- Accounts for ex-employees are often disabled instead of deleted to ensure that access to their data is not lost.

- Education and training should be targeted to different groups, such as all personnel, management, technical personnel, and HR personnel.

- Personally Identifiable Information (PII) needs to be protected from accidental disclosure. Data copied to portable systems and removable hard drives represents the biggest risk to PII. If not controlled, data confidentiality is lost.

- Drives that contain data must be sanitized before being reused. A company can approve a software program that overwrites existing data with repeating patterns of ones and zeros as an acceptable method of sanitizing a hard drive.

Incident Response Policies

- An incident is a series of events that are significant enough to negatively affect business functions, or a single event that is serious.

- Once an event is investigated and determined to be an incident, it is escalated to incident status.

- The first step in response to an incident is containment or isolation of the problem. This can be as simple as pulling the cable from the NIC.

- Computer forensics are used to collect data. Binary copying tools can copy a hard disk without modifying the data.

- A chain of custody should be used to ensure that the data presented later as evidence is the same data that was collected.

Auditing

Auditing is used to verify that a company is following their established procedures or the relevant laws. Vulnerability assessments are often a part of an audit.

Practice Questions

1. You are hired as a security consultant to help a company improve their security posture. After performing an audit, you determine that some servers still include default passwords, unneeded servicesare running, users have installed personal software on their systems, and antivirus definitions aren't being kept up-to-date. What should be done first?

    A. Remove unneeded services

    B. Remove the personal software

    C. Update antivirus software

    D. Enforce a security policy

2. A web server is being added to your company's DMZ. It will include access to a database that includes PII. The developers are asking that the server become operational before a required security review can be completed. What will this likely violate?

    A. Principle of least privilege

    B. Need-to-know

    C. Security policy

    D. Penetration assessment requirement

3. What should HR personnel be trained on related to security policies? (Choose two.)

    A. How to implement the policies

    B. How to enforce the policies

    C. Technical administration methods

    D. The policy guidelines

4. A patch has been released for a server. What process should be followed before the patch is deployed?

    A. Due diligence

    B. Due process

    C. Change management

    D. Disaster planning

5. Sally has been granted a Secret clearance. However, when she asks to view secret data that is unrelated to her job, she is denied. What policy is being followed?

    A. Least privilege

    B. Implicit deny

    C. Mandatory vacation

    D. Need-to-know

6. What can be used to provide a performance guarantee when a company outsources a service?

    A. SLA

    B. SLE

    C. L2TP

    D. DRP

7. A new employee has been trained on the purposes of the company's IT systems and methods of accessing the systems. What is this called?

    A. Privacy information

    B. Acceptable use

    C. Due diligence

    D. PII

8. A company's HR manual includes a section describing expected minimum behavior for employees. What is a possible subtitle for this section?

    A. Acceptable Use

    B. Code of Ethics

    C. Due Diligence

    D. Due Care

9. Of the following choices, what should be implemented to reduce the possibility that employees are involved in malicious activity against the company, or at least increase the possibility that these activities are discovered?

    A. Single sign-on

    B. Multifactor authentication

    C. Chain of custody

    D. Mandatory vacations

10. You want to provide more oversight of past transactions within your accounting department. What principle would you implement?

    A. Separation of duties

    B. Job rotation

    C. Confidentiality

    D. Least privilege

11. What should be done to a user's account and his data if he has been terminated? (Choose two.)

    A. Delete the user's account

    B. Disable the user's account

    C. Delete the user's data

    D. Hold the user's data for a specified period of time

12. A disk drive is removed from a computer before the computer is donated to a local school. The disk drive includes PII. What should be done with the disk drive before it is reused?

    A. Reformat it

    B. Sanitize it

    C. Destroy it

    D. It cannot be reused

13. An administrator has just discovered that a newly released virus has infected a computer on the network and appears to be part of a botnet. What should her first response be?

    A. Contact the command and control center of the botnet and tell them to release control.

    B. Contain the threat.

    C. Move the computer to another area of the network.

    D. Run antivirus software.

14. Which of the following steps could be found in an incident response procedure? (Choose three.)

    A. Containment

    B. Removal

    C. Repair

    D. Repudiation

15. A computer system has been attacked, and the incident response team has been called. An administrator on the incident response team wants to complete a forensic analysis of the system. What should be done?

    A. Run a malware scan.

    B. Check the firewall logs.

    C. Reboot the system.

    D. Get a bit copy of the disk.

16. A user is suspected of copying secret company data onto his computer. You are tasked with seizing his computer. What should be established as soon as you do so?

    A. Contents of cache

    B. Forensic evidence

    C. Chain of custody

    D. Chain of command

Practice Question Answers

1. **D.** All of these issues should be addressed in an overall security policy. It appears as if the policy is not being enforced. If a policy doesn't exist, it should be created. While unneeded services and personal software should be removed, and antivirus definitions should be updated, the first step should be to create or enforce a security policy.

2. **C.** Allowing a server to become operational without a security review would likely violate a corporate security policy, but it wouldn't violate any of the other possible answers; a corporate security policy would require systems to be reviewed, tested, and approved before deployment. The principle of least privilege specifies that individuals or processes are granted only the rights and permissions needed to perform their assigned tasks or functions. The need-to-know principle specifies that individuals are given access to the data they need, but no more. A penetration test would perform a vulnerability assessment and then perform an attack to exploit a vulnerability.

3. **B, D.** HR personnel should be trained on the guidelines and enforcement of policies. Security policies are often implemented through technical means; HR personnel aren't expected to implement security policies nor understand the technical methods of achieving them.

4. **C.** Change management will ensure that the patch is reviewed and tested before being approved. Due diligence refers to a company's obligation to take a reasonable amount of time and effort to identify risks to data and systems it owns and manages. Due care refers to the steps a company has taken to protect against the risks. Disaster planning is used to prepare for disasters such as fires and floods.

5. **D.** The need-to-know principle specifies that individuals are given access to the data they need, but no more. A Secret clearance does not automatically grant access to all secret data. The principle of least privilege specifies that individuals or processes are granted rights and permissions needed to perform

their jobs, but no more. Notice the difference between need-to-know and least privilege—need-to-know focuses on data only, while least privilege includes rights and permissions. Implicit deny is a principle often used with routers and firewalls where rules are created to allow traffic, but all other traffic is blocked or denied. Mandatory vacations force employees to take annual vacations to reduce the possibility that employees are involved in malicious activities such as embezzlement.

6. **A.** A service level agreement (SLA) can be used to provide a performance guarantee for services provided from an external service provider. SLE is used in risk management. L2TP is a tunneling protocol used with VPNs. A DRP is used to help a company prepare for potential disasters.

7. **B.** An acceptable use policy will describe the purposes of a company's IT systems and methods used to access them. Employees will often be required to sign a document indicating that they understand the policy. An acceptable use policy is not privacy information and wouldn't be called PII. Due diligence refers to a company's obligation to take a reasonable amount of time and effort to identify risks to data and systems it owns and manages.

8. **B.** A code of ethics would define and describe expected minimum behavior for employees. An acceptable use policy would describe the purpose of systems and how users can access them. Due diligence refers to a company's obligation to take a reasonable amount of time and effort to identify risks to data and systems it owns and manages.

9. **D.** Mandatory vacations force employees to take annual vacations to reduce the possibility that employees are involved in malicious activities such as embezzlement. If an employee is on vacation, other employees will perform her functions, and malicious activities are more likely to be discovered. Single sign-on allows individuals to present credentials only once, and these credentials are then used for an entire session. Multifactor authentication uses more than one method of authentication, such as combining biometrics with the use of a smart card. Chain of custody is an evidence maintenance practice used to ensure that evidence is always controlled and can't be modified.

10. **B.** Job rotation can provide more oversight of past transactions by rotating new personnel into the job. As a part of regular work, past transactions will be examined, and discrepancies will be discovered. Additionally, since a new person may be performing the job in the future, job rotation will minimize collusion between staff members. Separation of duties ensures that no single entity controls an entire process. However, even if the duties were separated into two different divisions, and job rotation wasn't implemented, the same person may always be doing the same job, increasing the potential for fraud. Confidentiality is used to prevent the unauthorized disclosure of information. The principle of least privilege specifies that individuals or processes are granted only the rights and permissions needed to perform their assigned tasks or functions.

11. **B, D.** Accounts for terminated employees are disabled so that they can't be used, and the data is kept for a specified period of time, such as sixty days or six months. If the data is protected, it can be enabled by an administrator, allowing another user to log on and access the data. If the account is deleted, the data may no longer be accessible. The data may be useful, so it shouldn't be deleted until someone has an opportunity to review it.

12. **B.** The disk should be sanitized before it is reused. Sanitization means different things depending on the data the drive contains. It may be possible to use software to write multiple patterns of ones and zeros to overwrite data, but other classified data may require the physical destruction of the disk. Reformatting a drive does not erase the data. Destroying it may not be necessary if a software program can adequately destroy the data.

13. **B.** The first response to an incident should be containment or isolation; containment is done after an event has been investigated and escalated to an incident. Containment can be done by disconnecting the NIC. Contacting the botnet command and control center will simply warn them they've been discovered and they need to modify their steps. Moving the computer won't help if it is still connected to the network. Antivirus software is a good idea but after the system has been contained.

14. **A, B, C.** Containment of the threat, removal or eradication of the threat, and repair or recovery of the system are all steps that could be in an incident response procedure. Repudiation is when someone denies or disclaims an action; while an attacker may try to repudiate claims that he attacked, this is not part of an incident response procedure.

15. **D.** When conducting forensic analysis, the data should be preserved, which can be done by first getting a bit copy, or binary copy, of the disk. Running a malware scan, checking any logs, or rebooting the system has the potential to modify the evidence.

16. **C.** A chain of custody should be established when seizing any evidence; the chain of custody verifies that evidence presented later is the same as the evidence that was collected. This is true for any evidence collected, including cache or any other computer forensic evidence. A chain of command identifies who's in charge, and that should already be established.

CompTIA Security+ Practice Exam

Use this practice exam as an additional study aid before taking the live exam. An answer key with explanation is available at the end of the practice exam.

1. You want to ensure that a user who sent an email cannot later claim that he did not send it. What should be used?
    A. Confidentiality
    B. Integrity
    C. Non-repudiation
    D. Access control

2. Which authentication model requires the use of a ticket-granting server?
    A. RADIUS
    B. Kerberos
    C. Smart cards
    D. Biometrics

3. What type of authentication is being used when both a server and a client authenticate each other prior to sending data?
    A. Multifactor authentication
    B. Mutual authentication
    C. Teaming authentication
    D. Smart card authentication

4. Of the following choices, what authentication mechanisms require something to be in your physical possession? (Choose two.)
    A. Fob
    B. Smart card
    C. Certificate
    D. Password
    E. PAP

5. A user is able to log on to multiple systems after only supplying credentials one time. What is this called?

    A. Multifactor authentication

    B. Fob-based authentication

    C. SSO

    D. SID

6. What's the difference between identification and authorization?

    A. Nothing. They are synonymous.

    B. Identification verifies the identity of a user prior to issuing credentials. Authentication verifies that the credentials provided by the user are the credentials issued or belonging to that user.

    C. Authentication verifies the identity of a user prior to issuing credentials. Identification verifies that the credentials provided by the user are the credentials issued to that particular user.

    D. Authentication is used in MAC models, and identification is used in DAC models.

7. What's a benefit of TACACS+ over RADIUS?

    A. TACACS+ is more efficient since it only encrypts the password, while RADIUS encrypts all of the credential information.

    B. TACACS+ encrypts the entire authentication process, while RADIUS only encrypts the password.

    C. TACACS+ provides encryption of the data.

    D. TACACS+ can be used with VPNs, but RADIUS can only be used with dial-up.

8. What port does Kerberos use by default?

    A. Port 22

    B. Port 80

    C. Port 88

    D. Port 143

9. Of the following, which one would provide the highest level of security control for a room that holds important servers?

A. Combination cipher lock and key lock

B. Cipher lock

C. Biometric reader and smart card

D. Smart card and proximity card

10. How are permissions to a file identified in the DAC model?

A. ACLs

B. Predefined

C. Role membership

D. Owner delegation

11. Which access control model uses predefined access privileges to identify the users who have permissions to a resource?

A. MAC

B. DAC

C. RBAC

D. DoS

12. Which access control model is Microsoft's NTFS primarily based on?

A. MAC

B. DAC

C. RBAC

D. WAP

13. What can be used to prevent tailgating?

A. Mantrap

B. DMZ

C. Time–of-day restrictions

D. Account expiration

14. Which one of the following protocols would be considered nonessential?

    A. ARP

    B. TCP

    C. UDP

    D. TFTP

15. Your network has several servers located in an area of the network between the Internet and the intranet. What is this area called?

    A. Router

    B. Firewall

    C. DMZ

    D. NIDS

16. What would be used to control the traffic that is allowed into or out of a network?

    A. Hub

    B. ARP

    C. ACL

    D. ALE

17. Which one of the following statements correctly refers to file sharing?

    A. A peer-to-peer connection is used when files are stored and shared among individual computers.

    B. FTP is used to share files from multiple individual computers.

    C. SSH is commonly used to encrypt P2P sessions.

    D. File sharing is not done over the Internet.

18. You are checking a firewall that is operating at the boundary between the Internet and your network. You notice that port 3389 is open. Why would port 3389 be open?

    A. To allow HTTPS traffic

    B. To allow SMTP traffic

    C. To allow Terminal Services traffic

    D. To allow LDAP traffic

19. What port does DNS use?

    A. 110

    B. 53

    C. 1701

    D. 443

20. An administrator is reviewing local firewall logs on a web server and sees the following entries.

Time	Source IP	Destination IP	Port
10:01	12.34.67.89	89.67.34.12	79
10:02	12.34.67.89	89.67.34.12	80
10:03	12.34.67.89	89.67.34.12	81
10:04	12.34.67.89	89.67.34.12	82

What is occurring?

    A. Port scanning

    B. Sniffing

    C. Rainbow table attack

    D. Brute force attack

21. What protocol is commonly used to determine the status of network devices?

    A. SNMP

    B. SMTP

    C. PPTP

    D. HTTPS

22. What is a primary risk of coaxial cable?

    A. Data emanation from the core

    B. Interference from EMI

    C. Interference from RFI

    D. Vampire taps that capture the light pulses

23. What's the easiest way to take down an entire Thicknet network?

    A. Remove a terminator

    B. Install a terminator

    C. Remove an RJ45 connector

    D. Insert malformed packets

24. What type of IDS uses a predefined model to determine an alert?

    A. Sniffer

    B. Anomaly

    C. Signature

    D. Active

25. Of the following choices, what can actively detect server or workstation anomalies? (Choose three.)

    A. HIDS

    B. NIDS

    C. Antivirus software

    D. Host-based firewall

26. What type of IDS is configured to generate an alert based on specific traffic patterns?

    A. Anomaly-based

    B. Behavior-based

    C. Signature-based

    D. Active response

27. An unauthorized WAP has been discovered connected to your network. What should be done?

    A. Change the SSID.

    B. Disable SSID broadcasting.

    C. Unplug the WAP from the network.

    D. Enable WPA2.

28. What encryption protocol is used by WPA2?

    A. SSL

    B. RC4

    C. AES

    D. WTLS

29. What is bluesnarfing?

    A. A Smurf attack launched by zombies

    B. The unauthorized access of an 802.11 wireless network

    C. The unauthorized sending of messages through someone else's Bluetooth device

    D. The unauthorized access to or theft of information from someone else's Bluetooth device

30. What is the best protection against bluesnarfing and bluejacking attacks?

    A. Ensuring the Bluetooth device is in discovery mode

    B. Ensuring the Bluetooth device is in non-discovery mode

    C. Using WPA2

    D. Using SSL

31. A network administrator is tasked with securing network devices that are maintained on the network infrastructure. What is this called?

    A. Removing unneeded services and protocols

    B. Hardening

    C. Increasing vulnerabilities

    D. Changing defaults

32. What could be changed in a computer's BIOS to prevent personnel from modifying BIOS settings?

    A. The jumper on the motherboard

    B. The boot drive

    C. The BIOS password

    D. NIDS

33. How does performance monitoring provide security protection?

    A. It can detect system degradation caused by attacks.

    B. It can detect when the disk subsystem needs to be upgraded.

    C. It can detect when the processor needs to be upgraded.

    D. It can detect when the memory needs to be upgraded.

34. Why do attackers like it when they find nonessential services running on a server?

    A. Because the services are often not managed and attacks are often noticed

    B. Because the services are often managed and attacks go unnoticed

    C. Because the services are correctly configured and attacks go unnoticed

    D. Because the services are often not managed or configured correctly and attacks go unnoticed

35. What has been used in applications for ease of administration but can result in undesired vulnerabilities?

    A. Buffer overflow

    B. Botnet

    C. Zombies

    D. Back doors

36. A system administrator is tasked with configuring a server for the first time. She wants to harden the server as part of the process. What should she do to harden the server? (Choose all that apply.)

    A. Disable unnecessary services

    B. Disable the firewall

    C. Remove unnecessary protocols

    D. Enable the Guest account

    E. Apply patches and hotfixes

37. You use patch-management software to deploy updates to clients within your network. After auditing for the successful application of the patches, you notice that while most of the systems are accepting the patches, some of the systems are not accepting the patches. What could be a reason why?

A. Cookies aren't enabled.

B. ActiveX controls are blocked.

C. The password used for the patch-management software has expired.

D. The local firewall is blocking the updates.

38. What can be used by spyware to collect and report a user's activities on the Internet?

    A. Tracking cookie

    B. Worm

    C. Patch

    D. Zombie

39. A software developer has identified a method that should significantly improve the performance of a web application. What process should be followed before implementing the modification?

    A. Change management

    B. Discovery mode

    C. Full/incremental backup

    D. Open relay

40. A buffer overflow vulnerability has recently been discovered. What is the best way to prevent a buffer overflow attack?

    A. Use configuration baselines

    B. Use security baselines

    C. Keep the servers up-to-date with current patches

    D. Disable peer-to-peer software

41. An attacker is attempting to access and manipulate internal heaps and stacks on a server. What type of attack is this?

    A. DLL injection

    B. Buffer overflow

    C. Rootkit

    D. Worm

42. A server is accepting more input than it expects, resulting in erratic behavior. What is this?
    A. Buffer overflow attack
    B. Password-cracking attack
    C. SYN Flood attack
    D. MAC flood attack

43. Every time a user tries to access google.com on her web browser, another search engine appears. What could cause this?
    A. Altered Hosts file
    B. Altered PTR records on DNS
    C. Bluejacking
    D. Kiting

44. Which one of the following items is an added feature of some web browsers?
    A. Proxy
    B. Local firewall
    C. WAP
    D. Pop-up blocker

45. Your email server is getting flooded with unwanted emails from the same email address. These emails are being sent to many of the email clients. What can be done to resolve this?
    A. Nothing. Spam can't be filtered.
    B. Install an anti-spam filter and filter the clients' email addresses.
    C. Install an anti-spam filter on the mail server and filter the spammer's email address.
    D. Implement firewall rules to block the spam.

46. Email servers have a specific vulnerability that can cause them to forward email to other email servers from anonymous clients. What is this called?
    A. SMTP relay
    B. Buffer overflow
    C. SYN Flood
    D. Sandbox

47. What is a weakness associated with virtualization?

A. Virtual servers can be isolated.

B. The host operating system can be isolated.

C. If an attack occurs on the host, it could disrupt multiple servers.

D. If one virtual server is attacked, all virtual servers will suffer from the same attack.

48. What can be used to isolate an operating system from security threats?

A. Virtualization

B. Bluetooth

C. Imaging

D. VPN

49. What problems can result from virus hoaxes? (Choose two.)

A. Users can inflict damage on their own systems.

B. Users can lose PII.

C. Help-desk staff workload can be increased.

D. Help-desk staff can be tricked into locking users out of their systems.

50. What type of malware travels across computer networks without user action?

A. Virus

B. Trojan horse

C. Worm

D. Logic bomb

51. After a user downloaded and installed a screen saver, he notes excessive disk activity and realizes some of his files have been deleted. What happened?

A. The user installed a worm.

B. The user installed a virus.

C. The user installed a Trojan horse.

D. The user installed a logic bomb.

52. What type of program would lie dormant until a specific program is launched, detect that the program has been run, and then delete files?

    A. Botnet

    B. Trojan horse

    C. Worm

    D. Logic bomb

53. Of the following choices, what would be best to prevent a virus from spreading through a network?

    A. Ensure that users only log on as administrators.

    B. Prevent users from downloading and installing screen savers.

    C. Block all spam from entering the network.

    D. Scan all email attachments.

54. What type of computer attack is launched from multiple zombies?

    A. DoS

    B. DDoS

    C. Botnet

    D. Birthday attack

55. What would a computer be called that is remotely controlled by a command and control center and can be involved in DDoS attacks?

    A. Botnet

    B. Worm

    C. SYN Flood

    D. Zombie

56. What type of attack exploits the TCP session initiation process?

    A. Smurf

    B. Rainbow attack

    C. SYN attack

    D. Kiting

57. An internal employee has installed a system that is being used to intercept SSL sessions. The system is able to decrypt the SSL session, view the content, and then reestablish an SSL session with the Internet server. What type of attack is this?

A. DLL injection

B. Man-in-the-middle

C. DoS

D. Smurf

58. What is eavesdropping, and which type of attack uses it?

A. Listening to or overhearing parts of a conversation; used by active interception

B. Listening to or overhearing parts of a conversation; used by MAC flooding

C. Looking through files; used by MAC flooding

D. Looking through files; used by active interception

59. An attacker is performing a malicious port scan on a system. What is the attacker seeking?

A. The IP address of the system

B. The name of the system

C. Credentials

D. The fingerprint of an operating system

60. What type of attack cannot be prevented or deterred solely through the use of technical measures?

A. Social engineering

B. DoS

C. DDoS

D. Replay

61. Multiple types of social engineering attacks are possible and are usually preventable through different security measures. What type of social engineering can be thwarted by the use of turnstiles or security guards?

A. Impersonation

B. Piggybacking

    C. Tailbacking

    D. Snooping

62. An attacker disguises himself as a repair technician for a reputable company and appears at a company. He explains that he is there to service their server. What is he doing?

    A. Normal service call

    B. Social engineering

    C. Kiting

    D. Phishing

63. What is the most effective tool to discover security holes in a network?

    A. NIDS

    B. HIDS

    C. Vulnerability assessment

    D. Antivirus software

64. Which of the following sometimes uses DLL injection?

    A. SQL injection

    B. Penetration testing

    C. Ping scanner

    D. Active interception

65. What is Wireshark?

    A. Protocol analyzer

    B. Port scanner

    C. Vulnerability assessment tool

    D. Password cracker

66. You suspect an attacker is launching a very slow SYN Flood attack that is getting past your NIDS. What can you use to analyze the packets in the TCP/IP handshake?

    A. Port scanner

    B. Ping scanner

C. Protocol analyzer

D. Password cracker

67. Which of the following is a protocol analyzer?

A. Pentest

B. LophtCrack

C. Wireshark

D. Rainbow table

68. You want a NIC to monitor all network traffic that reaches it, not just traffic addressed to the NIC. What mode should be used for this NIC?

A. All

B. Duplex

C. Promiscuous

D. Non-promiscuous

69. You are tasked with capturing all traffic that goes through a specific router. What tool would you use?

A. Protocol analyzer

B. Penetration assessment tool

C. Network mapper

D. Port scanner

70. An administrator is running John the Ripper on her network. What is she doing?

A. Antivirus scan

B. Anti-spyware scan

C. Creating a baseline

D. Password cracker

71. Which of the following attacks cannot occur through email? (Choose all that apply.)

A. Dictionary attack

B. Brute force attack

C. Trojan horse

D. Virus

72. Users in your company use company-issued cell phones that also function as PDAs. What security guidance should you pass on to cell phone users?

    A. Only turn the phone on when using it.

    B. Don't use the PDA functions.

    C. Don't use the phone for email.

    D. Password-protect the cell phone.

73. You suspect that someone has tried to guess passwords for the Administrator account on a server. Auditing has been enabled. Where will unauthorized usage attempts be logged?

    A. Application

    B. System

    C. Security

    D. Setup

74. What security information could be discovered by reviewing the logs on a DNS server?

    A. Rogue DHCP servers

    B. Port scanning attempts

    C. Unauthorized zone transfer attempts

    D. Intrusion detection logs

75. What can you do to secure log files? (Choose all that apply.)

    A. Copy the logs to a remote log server.

    B. Store the logs on USB flash disks.

    C. Store the logs on DVD-RW media.

    D. Only allow access to authenticated users.

76. You have discovered that the audit logs have been accessed and modified by users within the network. What can you do to protect the logs from being accessed or modified?

    A. Move the logs to a different area on the server.

    B. Protect the logs with a HIDS.

    C. Change the security groups that can access the logs.

    D. Hash the logs' files.

77. You are tasked with implementing procedures to secure log files. What can you do? (Choose all that apply.)

    A. Create hashing of the log files.

    B. Use file integrity auditing.

    C. Store them on USB drives.

    D. Store them on DVD-RW media.

78. A file server has the following backups done throughout a week. Full backups are done every Saturday night at 11 p.m. Differential backups are done every night during the week at 11 p.m. The server crashes on Wednesday morning. Assuming each of the backups are stored on a different tape, how many tapes must be restored?

    A. One

    B. Two

    C. Three

    D. Four

79. Of the following choices, what can be effectively used to combat an electrical fire while also preventing damage to equipment and protecting personnel?

    A. Foam

    B. Water

    C. CO_2

    D. Heat

80. You have walked into a Faraday cage. What will no longer work?

    A. Proximity cards

    B. Computers

    C. Flash drives

    D. Cell phones

81. What could be used to prevent radio frequency signals from emanating outside of an enclosure?

    A. TEMPEST

    B. Mantrap

C. EMI/RFI

D. Faraday cage

82. An attacker is trying to discover the contents of encrypted data. What would make his job easier?

A. Block cipher

B. Streaming cipher

C. Use of a public algorithm

D. Weak key

83. Which one of the following is considered a highly secure encryption algorithm for small hardware devices, and performs quicker than the others?

A. MD5

B. SHA1

C. 3DES

D. AES256

84. Which one of the following is a symmetric encryption algorithm?

A. MD5

B. RC5

C. RSA

D. SHA1

85. What uses public/private key combinations as part of the process when securing traffic on the Internet?

A. SSL

B. AES

C. DES

D. MD5

86. What is the Diffie-Hellman algorithm used for?

A. To privately exchange a key

B. To create strong keys from large prime numbers

C. To validate integrity

D. To improve the performance problems of 3DES

87. How does steganography hide data within a graphic or sound file?

    A. By replacing the most significant bit of many bytes

    B. By replacing the least significant bit of many bytes

    C. By modifying the least significant bit of the file header

    D. By converting the format of the file

88. PGP can be used to encrypt and sign email. What is a flaw related to authentication in PGP?

    A. The root CA has to be trusted.

    B. The root CA cannot be trusted.

    C. The user must trust the public key that is received.

    D. The user must trust the private key that is received.

89. What is a benefit of S/MIME?

    A. It can be used to encrypt HTTP traffic.

    B. It can be used to provide whole disk encryption.

    C. It can be used to encrypt and digitally sign email messages.

    D. It can be used to provide guaranteed delivery of email messages.

90. What can be used to provide an integrity check?

    A. Encryption

    B. Hash

    C. Public key

    D. Private key

91. What type of algorithm cannot be reversed resulting in the discovery of the original data?

    A. Symmetric encryption

    B. Public-key encryption

    C. Secret-key encryption

    D. One-way function

92. Which of the following is a tool that helps an attacker discover weak passwords?

    A. Rainbow table

    B. A hash generator

    C. Kiting

    D. Protocol analyzer

93. After downloading an executable file, you realize the calculated MD5 hash is different than the original MD5 hash posted on the download site. What should you do?

    A. Scan the file with antivirus software.

    B. Run the file since the MD5 algorithm is considered compromised.

    C. Run the file since the MD5 hash is supposed to be different after download.

    D. Avoid executing the file and contact the administrator of the web site.

94. A digital signature is being used for messages sent through an insecure channel. What would be used to encrypt the digital signature?

    A. Sender's private key

    B. Sender's public key

    C. Receiver's private key

    D. Session key

95. A certificate's private key has become compromised. What should be done?

    A. The user should revoke the certificate and publish it on the CRL.

    B. The CA should revoke the certificate and publish it on the CRL.

    C. The certificate should be cancelled.

    D. The certificate should be reissued.

96. You are accessing a secure web site and want to validate that the web page has a valid certificate. What should you do?

    A. Check the root Certificate Authority store to verify that the certificate is stored there.

    B. Go to the web page of the root CA and request the CRL.

C. Verify that the URL has HTTPS as part of the path.

D. Right-click the lock icon to view the certificate's details.

97. Your company wants to ensure that any user or group only has access to resources within the network that they need to do their jobs, but no more. What security principle is being implemented?

A. Least privilege

B. Implicit deny

C. Mandatory vacation

D. DAC

98. What is the biggest threat posed by USB flash drives and other external storage media in relation to PII?

A. Loss of PII

B. Destruction of PII

C. Introduction of PII

D. Modification of PII

99. You've learned that a newly released virus has infected a computer, but the antivirus software didn't detect the problem. What would be the first action to take?

A. Notify the CEO.

B. Install antivirus software.

C. Update the antivirus signature files.

D. Contain the problem.

100. What documentation is needed to verify that the evidence collected is the same evidence that is presented in court?

A. Evidence trail

B. Chain of custody

C. Affidavit of evidence

D. Lawyer's permission slip

Practice Exam Answers

When checking your answers, take the time to read the explanation given. Understanding the explanations will help ensure you're prepared for the live exam. The explanation also shows the chapter or chapters where you can get more detailed information on the topic.

1. **C.** Non-repudiation can be used to prevent someone from later denying an action. Non-repudiation is commonly enforced with digital signatures. Confidentiality is used to prevent the unauthorized disclosure of information, often by encrypting the data. Integrity is used to verify that data has not been modified and is enforced with hashing or message authentication codes. Access control is one of many methods used to grant access to resources after an entity has been authenticated.
See chapters 1 and 9.

2. **B.** Kerberos requires the use of a Key Distribution Center (KDC) server, which issues tickets. Remote Authentication Dial-In User Service (RADIUS) is a centralized method of authentication for remote access, but it does not use a ticket-granting server. Smart cards require certificates and a Public Key Infrastructure (PKI) but do not use tickets. Biometrics do not use a ticket-granting server.
See Chapter 1.

3. **B.** Mutual authentication is accomplished when both entities of a connection (a server and a client) authenticate with each other prior to sending data. Multifactor authentication is accomplished by combining two of the three factors (something you know, something you have, and something you are) in a single authentication session. There is no such thing as teaming authentication. Smart card authentication requires someone to have a smart card; while smart cards require certificates and a supporting PKI, they do not provide mutual authentication.
See Chapter 1.

4. **A, B.** Both fobs and smart cards fall into the authentication factor category of something you have. A fob (also called a token) and a smart card are both physical items you can touch and feel. A certificate is a digital file that is used for authentication, but you can't physically hold the certificate. Likewise, you can't hold a password. Password Authentication Protocol is an older remote access authentication that passes passwords in clear text and is rarely used today.
See Chapter 1.

5. **C.** Single sign-on (SSO) authentication is used to prevent users from having to enter credentials at each server or application for normal work. Instead, users would authenticate once, and the supplied credentials would be used throughout the session. Single sign-on would not be decentralized, but instead, it would use a central database (such as Active Directory) for authentication. Multifactor authentication uses more than one method of authentication. Fob-based authentication uses a fob or physical token. A security identifier (SID) is used to uniquely identify users and groups to determine permissions.
See Chapter 1.

6. **B.** Identification is used to verify the identity of the user (such as with a driver's license). Once a user is identified, credentials (such as username and password) are issued. These credentials can then be used to authenticate a user on a system or network. MAC and DAC are access control models and aren't restricted to the use of any specific identification or authentication methods.
See Chapter 1.

7. **B.** TACACS+ encrypts the entire client-server authentication process, while RADIUS only encrypts the password. Both are only used for authentication and will not encrypt the data. Both can be used with VPNs.
See Chapter 1.

8. **C.** Kerberos uses port 88 by default. Port 22 is used by Secure Shell (SSH). Port 80 is used by HTTP. Port 143 is used by IMAP with email.
See Chapter 1.

9. **C.** A biometric reader and smart card would provide two factors of authentication (biometrics for something the user is and a smart card for something the user has). Additionally, biometrics is considered the strongest method of authentication. Cipher locks and key locks provide physical security only. Combining a smart card and a proximity card would use one factor of authentication (something you have); even though the user has two things, they still only address one factor.
See chapters 1 and 2.

10. **A.** Permissions are identified in the Discretionary Access Control (DAC) model through the use of access control lists (ACLs), or more specifically, Discretionary Access Control Lists (DACLs). Permissions and privileges are predefined in the MAC model. RBAC uses roles. While every object has an owner in the DAC model, permissions aren't delegated to other users but are granted to other users by the owner.
See Chapter 2.

11. **A.** The Mandatory Access Control (MAC) model uses predefined access privileges and is relatively inflexible. In DAC, every object has an owner who can change access and permissions relatively easily. In RBAC, the privileges are based on the roles, and these privileges can be changed by the administrator. Denial-of-service (DoS) is an attack designed to disrupt a server or a service's normal operation.
See Chapter 2.

12. **B.** The Discretionary Access Control (DAC) model uses Discretionary Access Control Lists (DACLs) in NTFS. NTFS is the file system used in Microsoft environments to provide security to files and folders. NTFS is not based on either the MAC or the RBAC models. A wireless access point (WAP) is used as a central device to connect wireless devices to a wired network.
See Chapter 2.

13. **A.** A mantrap can be used to prevent tailgating or piggybacking, a social engineering tactic where an unauthorized person follows closely behind an

authorized person. A mantrap is used to control the access between a secure area and a nonsecure area by creating a buffer zone. A DMZ is a buffered area of a network between two firewalls used to host Internet-facing servers. Time-of-day restrictions can be used to prevent users from logging in during certain times of the day. Accounts can be set to expire to ensure the users, such as contractors, can't use the account after a certain period of time, such as after thirty days.
See Chapter 2.

14. **D.** Trivial File Transfer Protocol (TFTP) is considered nonessential and can be disabled on a server. It's a safe bet to consider any protocol with the name "trivial" in it as nonessential. ARP, TCP, and UDP are all essential for basic communication.
See Chapter 3.

15. **C.** A demilitarized zone (DMZ) is used to host Internet-facing servers and is an area located between the Internet and the internal network. A router is used to segment a network into multiple subnets. Two firewalls are often used to create the buffer zone of the DMZ, but servers can't be placed on a firewall. A network-based intrusion detection system (NIDS) is used to detect, and sometimes respond to, attacks.
See Chapter 3.

16. **C.** An access control list (ACL) is implemented to control inbound and outbound traffic on a network segment. A hub has no intelligence and will pass all traffic to all ports. Address Resolution Protocol (ARP) is used to resolve IP addresses to MAC addresses in a subnet. Annualized loss expectancy (ALE) is used to identify how much money is expected to be lost in a quantitative analysis.
See Chapter 3.

17. **A.** File sharing is also known as sharing files over peer-to-peer (P2P) networks. Files are shared by multiple systems over the Internet, and a significant risk is data leakage where users inadvertently share private or classified data. FTP uses an FTP server, which has the risk of sending and/or receiving data and

credentials in clear text unless the information is encrypted with a protocol such as Secure Shell (SSH). SSH is not used for P2P sessions.
See Chapter 3.

18. **C.** Port 3389 is used for Terminal Services traffic, such as Microsoft's Remote Assistance or Remote Desktop Protocol. HTTPS uses port 443. SMTP uses port 25. LDAP uses port 389.
See Chapter 3.

19. **B.** Domain Name System (DNS) uses port 53. POP3 uses port 110. L2TP uses port 1701. HTTPS and SSL use port 443.
See Chapter 3.

20. **A.** A port scan attack will scan the same destination IP from the same source IP, checking different port numbers. If port 80 was open, it would indicate HTTP is running and this IP may be hosting a web server. A protocol analyzer capturing packets is also known as a sniffer. Rainbow table and brute force attacks are methods used to crack passwords.
See Chapter 3.

21. **A.** The Simple Network Management Protocol (SNMP) is commonly used to manage network devices and determine their status. SMTP is used for email. PPTP is a tunneling protocol used with VPNs. HTTPS is used for secure web traffic on the Internet.
See Chapter 3.

22. **A.** A primary risk of coaxial cable is data emanation from the core. The shielding provides good protection against EMI and RFI. Vampire taps could be a concern, but coaxial cable does not use light pulses.
See Chapter 3.

23. **A.** Removing a terminator on a Thicknet (10Base5) network will prevent all computers on the network from communicating. Both Thinnet (10Base2) and Thicknet (10Base5) networks use coaxial and must be terminated on both ends.

RJ45 connectors are used on networks using twisted pairs. Malformed packets are used in denial-of-service (DoS) attacks but would attack a single server, not an entire network.

See Chapter 3.

24. **C.** A signature-based intrusion detection system (IDS) uses a database of predefined signatures. Traffic patterns are matched to the signature models to determine alerts. An anomaly-based IDS uses a performance baseline to compare current traffic patterns against, to determine an alert. A sniffer is a protocol analyzer used to capture and view traffic. An active IDS will respond by changing the environment, but it only takes action after the IDS determines the alert.

See Chapter 4.

25. **A, C, D.** A network-based intrusion detection system (NIDS) cannot actively detect server or workstation anomalies. Host-based IDSs and host-based firewalls can detect anomalies on a server or workstation, such as abnormal traffic. Antivirus software can detect abnormal behavior of malware on a server or workstation.

See Chapter 4.

26. **C.** A signature-based (or definition-based) IDS can create an alert based on specific traffic patterns that match patterns within the signature database. Anomaly-based (or behavior-based) traffic starts with a performance baseline and alerts based on significant deviations from the baseline. An IDS can respond either actively or passively, but not until an attack is detected; a response cannot generate an alert.

See Chapter 4.

27. **C.** If an unauthorized WAP is discovered, it should be disconnected. Basic security steps for authorized wireless access points (WAPs) include changing the SSID, disabling SSID broadcasting, and enabling WPA2; however, this is an unauthorized WAP.

See Chapter 4.

28. **C.** Advanced Encryption Standard (AES) is the encryption protocol used by WPA2. SSL is commonly used with HTTPS over port 443 and can also be used to encrypt other traffic. Wired Equivalent Privacy (WEP) uses RC4 stream cipher encryption. WTLS is used to encrypt traffic for smaller wireless devices but is not used by WEP.
See Chapter 4.

29. **D.** Bluesnarfing is the unauthorized access to or theft of information from a Bluetooth device. A Smurf attack sends a broadcast ping message with the source IP spoofed to cause the pings to attack the victim, but it doesn't use zombies. Bluesnarfing is done on a Bluetooth network, not an 802.11 wireless network. Bluejacking is the unauthorized sending of text messages from a Bluetooth device.
See Chapter 4.

30. **B.** Placing Bluetooth devices in non-discovery mode is the best protection against bluesnarfing and bluejacking attacks. When in discovery mode, Bluetooth devices can easily be exploited. WPA2 would be used to secure 802.11 wireless networks. SSL is used to encrypt data on wired networks and is most often used with HTTPS on port 443.
See Chapter 4.

31. **B.** The baseline process of securing network devices on a network is called hardening. Key steps include removing unneeded services and protocols and changing defaults, but the overall process is called hardening. Hardening a network device would reduce vulnerabilities, not increase them.
See Chapter 5.

32. **C.** The BIOS password can be set to prevent personnel from accessing the BIOS and changing settings. Most systems have a jumper on the motherboard that can be used to reset this (often to turn off the password protection). Modifying the boot drive settings wouldn't prevent access to the BIOS. A network-based intrusion detection system (NIDS) can monitor network traffic and network devices but would not protect the BIOS on an individual system.
See Chapter 5.

33. **A.** Performance monitoring can detect system degradation changes as the result of an attack. An anomaly-based IDS starts with a baseline and can measure current operations against the baseline to determine when the behavior has changed significantly. Performance monitoring is also done to determine when different system resources need to be upgraded, but this is normal maintenance unrelated to security.
See Chapter 5.

34. **D.** Attackers find nonessential services appealing because they are often not managed, not configured correctly, not secured, and attacks go unnoticed.
See Chapter 5.

35. **D.** Back doors have been included in applications for ease of administration, but if back doors are discovered by attackers, they can be exploited. A buffer overflow occurs when an attacker sends more information than the application expects and can result in malware being executed by the application. A botnet includes multiple zombies that can be remotely controlled for malicious purposes.
See Chapter 5.

36. **A, C, E.** Basic steps to harden a server or workstation include disabling unnecessary services, removing unnecessary protocols, and bringing the system up-to-date by applying patches and fixes. Additionally, defaults (such as default accounts and passwords) should be changed, and a firewall should be enabled. Since a Guest account may allow users to access the system without authenticating, a Guest account should remain disabled.
See Chapter 5.

37. **D.** A firewall could be blocking the patch updates. Cookies and Active X controls are related to web pages, not updates. If most systems are accepting patches, a password for the patch-management software can't be the problem.
See Chapter 5.

38. **A.** A tracking cookie is often used by spyware to track a user's activities. A worm is malware that travels over the network without needing a host application. A patch is a small piece of code intended to repair bugs. A zombie is a computer controlled by remote as part of a malicious botnet.
See Chapter 5.

39. **A.** A change-management process should be followed to ensure that changes to a system, network, or software application do not have unintended negative consequences. Discovery mode is a Bluetooth mode used to allow Bluetooth devices to become paired and is a vulnerability if left on. Depending on what is being modified, a backup may be desirable, but nothing requires it to be a full/incremental backup, and following a change-management process should still be the first step. Anonymous open relay is a vulnerability for mail servers and should be disabled.
See Chapter 5.

40. **C.** The single best step to prevent buffer overflow attacks after the software has been released is to keep the systems up-to-date. Before the software is released, extensive testing and code review may discover the vulnerability. Baselines won't protect against the vulnerability, unless the vulnerability was discovered before the baselines were created. Peer-to-peer (P2P) software can result in data leakage, so it may be disabled, but this is unrelated to buffer overflow problems.
See Chapter 5.

41. **B.** A buffer overflow allows an attacker to access internal memory locations referred to as heaps and stacks. The attacker can load malicious code, overwrite a return address, and cause the malicious code to run. DLL injection is associated with penetration testing. A rootkit is a program that modifies operating system processes to hide itself. A worm is malware that travels autonomously over the network.
See Chapter 5.

42. **A.** Buffer overflow attacks are common on web servers where an application receives more data than is expected, allowing malicious code to be delivered and executed by the application. Password cracking attempts to discover passwords. A SYN Flood attack holds back the third packet of a three-way handshake. A MAC flood attack attempts to overwhelm a switch so that it acts like a hub. See Chapter 5.

43. **A.** The Hosts file can be modified (and is often modified by malware) to bypass DNS name resolution. If the Hosts file includes an entry for a host name, then the IP address in the Hosts file will be used and DNS will not be queried. PTR records are used for reverse lookup (IP address to host name, not name to IP address). Bluejacking is the practice of sending text messages over someone else's Bluetooth device without her permission or knowledge. Domain name kiting is the practice of repeatedly registering a domain name, and then deleting it before five days have passed to avoid paying for it. See Chapter 5.

44. **D.** Most web browsers include pop-up blockers to prevent additional windows from opening up. Web browsers may connect through a proxy or a firewall, but these features would not be included in the browser. A browser could not also be a wireless access point (WAP). See Chapter 5.

45. **C.** An anti-spam filter can be installed on a mail server, and the spammer's email address can be filtered. It is possible to filter some spam. You wouldn't want to filter internal clients' email addresses. Firewalls aren't as effective at blocking email as an anti-spam filter installed on an email server. See Chapter 5.

46. **A.** SMTP relay allows a server to forward email to other email servers. When SMTP relay (or anonymous SMTP relay) is enabled, anonymous clients can use this feature to forward spam through the email server. Buffer overflow is when an application receives more input than expected and allows the attacker to install malware. A SYN Flood attack can be used against any server using TCP/IP.

A sandbox is a restricted space in memory where scripts or Java applets will run without having access to local data.
See Chapter 5.

47. **C.** A weakness associated with virtualization is that if an attack occurs, it could potentially disrupt multiple servers. A primary benefit of virtualization is that the virtual servers and the host operating system can be isolated from each other.
See Chapter 5.

48. **A.** Virtualization can be used to isolate an operating system from different security threats. For example, malware could be released on a virtual server that is isolated from the host operating system, and the malware could be observed on the virtual server, but its actions would not impact the host. Bluetooth is a wireless technology used in personal area networks (PANs). Imaging can be used to create baselines. A VPN is used to access a private network over a public network.
See Chapter 5.

49. **A, C.** A virus hoax can trick users into changing their system configurations or deleting files and damaging their systems, and help-desk staff workload can be increased due to the damaged systems or due to the staff answering many questions about the hoax. Users won't lose Personally Identifiable Information (PII), and a hoax wouldn't trick help-desk staff into locking users out of systems.
See Chapter 6.

50. **C.** A worm doesn't need to be executed, doesn't have a host application, and can autonomously travel over the network. Viruses and Trojan horses have host applications that must be executed. A logic bomb executes in response to an event, such as on a specific date or when a specific program is run.
See Chapter 6.

51. **C.** A Trojan horse is a program that looks like one thing (such as a screen saver) but is actually something else and malicious. A worm is malware that travels over the network without the need for a host application. A virus is executed by running an application, but viruses add themselves onto existing host

applications; they don't masquerade as something else. A logic bomb executes in response to an event, such as a date.
See Chapter 6.

52. **D.** A logic bomb executes in response to an event, such as when a specific program is run or on a specific date. A botnet is a group of computers controlled by a central console computer. A Trojan horse appears to be one thing (such as a screen saver) but includes other malicious code. A worm is malware that doesn't have a host application and can autonomously travel over the network, regardless of events.
See Chapter 6.

53. **D.** Scanning email attachments and stripping off suspicious files is one of the most effective methods of preventing malware from entering an organization. Malware frequently comes in as attachments to spam, but it's impossible to block all spam. Users should only log on as administrators when doing administrative work. Screen savers often include hidden Trojan horses, but just blocking screen savers would not stop the majority of the viruses delivered through email.
See Chapter 6.

54. **B.** A DDoS attack is launched from multiple computers (commonly called zombies) against a single organization. The zombies are remotely controlled in a botnet from a command and control center. A birthday attack attempts to use a hash function to get an identical message digest or hash from a different message.
See Chapter 6.

55. **D.** Zombies are remotely controlled in a botnet from a command and control center. Worms are malware that replicate over a network. SYN Flood attacks disrupt a system by withholding the third packet of the TCP handshake.
See Chapter 6.

56. **C.** A SYN Flood attack (also called a SYN attack) withholds the third packet of the TCP three-way handshake process started at the beginning of any TCP session. A Smurf attack is where a single computer sends out a broadcast ping

with the source address spoofed with a victim's IP; ping uses UDP, not TCP. A rainbow table is used as a tool to crack passwords. Domain name kiting is the practice of repeatedly registering a domain name, and then deleting it before five days have passed so that the domain does not have to be purchased.
See Chapter 6.

57. **B.** A man-in-the-middle attack can act as a proxy to create two separate SSL sessions, which mimic a single SSL session and allow the attacker to view all the data sent in the SSL session. DLL injection is used by attackers to inject code into a process and can be used by security professionals as part of penetration testing. A DoS attack attempts to stop a server from providing a service. A Smurf attack is a broadcast ping with a spoofed source IP address.
See Chapter 6.

58. **A.** Eavesdropping is listening to or overhearing parts of a conversation. It is used by active interception (also known as a man-in-the-middle attack). MAC flooding attempts to cause a switch to act like a hub. Looking through files would be called snooping.
See Chapter 6.

59. **D.** Fingerprinting is part of a reconnaissance attack where an attacker queries an IP address with different protocols to determine details about the operating system. The port scan can tell what services or protocols are running, but how the operating system responds provides details about the operating system. The IP address must already be known to do a port scan. The name of the system can be learned in other ways and isn't as important as the IP address. Credentials can't be determined with a port scan.
See chapters 3 and 6.

60. **A.** Social engineering attacks don't require the use of any technical means but rely instead on conning and trickery, and a lack of security awareness on the part of the victim. DoS, DDoS, and replay attacks are all technical attacks that can be thwarted with technical measures.
See Chapter 6.

61. **B.** Piggybacking or tailgating occurs when one user follows closely behind another user without using valid credentials, and it can be thwarted through the use of turnstiles, double entry doors, and security guards. Impersonation is when an attacker masquerades as someone else. Tailgating is the same as piggybacking, but a tailback is related to football. Snooping is the process of looking through files.
See Chapter 6.

62. **B.** Impersonation is a social engineering tactic where an attacker masquerades as someone else, such as a repair technician. An attacker would not be doing a normal service call. Domain name kiting is the practice of repeatedly registering a domain name and then deleting it before five days have passed to avoid having to pay for it. Phishing is the practice of sending unwanted email to users with the purpose of tricking them into revealing personal information.
See Chapter 6.

63. **C.** A vulnerability assessment tool would be the most effective to discover security holes in a network. Intrusion detection systems (IDSs) are intended to detect attacks after they've been launched. Antivirus software will detect malware.
See Chapter 7.

64. **B.** DLL injection is sometimes used with penetration testing, where a security professional simulates an attack by injecting DLL code into a process and forcing the process to run the code. Web servers that don't use input validation are susceptible to SQL injection attacks. A ping scanner uses ICMP to ping IP addresses and locate systems that are operational. A man-in-the-middle attack uses active interception, where a computer is placed between a sender and receiver.
See Chapter 7.

65. **A.** Wireshark is a popular protocol analyzer (sometimes referred to as a sniffer) that can be used to capture and analyze packets sent across a network. Nessus is a popular vulnerability assessment tool. Nmap is a popular port

scanner that can be used to detect open ports. John the Ripper and Cain and Abel are password crackers.

See Chapter 7.

66. **C.** A protocol analyzer can be used to analyze TCP/IP traffic. The SYN Flood attack would include packets with the SYN flag set, and then the SYN/ACK flags would be sent, but it would withhold the third packet in the handshake.
A port scanner can detect open ports. A ping scanner can detect if systems are operational and responding to pings.

See Chapter 7.

67. **C.** Wireshark is a protocol analyzer used to capture and analyze packets. Pentest is short for penetration test, which starts with a vulnerability assessment and follows with an attack. LophtCrack and rainbow tables are used to crack passwords.

See Chapter 7.

68. **C.** A NIC will be able to monitor and process all traffic when it is placed in promiscuous mode. Duplex (including full duplex and half duplex) indicates how many wires are on the line and how they are used to send and/or receive data. Non-promiscuous indicates that the NIC will only capture data addressed to the NIC or coming from the NIC.

See Chapter 7.

69. **A.** A protocol analyzer can capture traffic. While a penetration assessment tool can also capture traffic, it will also launch an attack. A network mapper is also known as a port scanner and can be used to detect open ports.

See Chapter 7.

70. **D.** John the Ripper is a password cracker and can be used as part of a vulnerability scan. John the Ripper won't detect malware or help in the creation of a baseline.

See Chapter 7.

536 | CompTIA Security+: Get Certified Get Ahead

71. **A, B.** Dictionary attacks and brute force attacks are used in password-cracking attempts. Malware (including Trojan horses and viruses) is frequently sent through email. See Chapter 7.

72. **D.** Cell phones (especially those that include personal digital assistant [PDA] features) should be password protected, requiring the user to enter a password after a period of inactivity. If the phone is only turned on when using it, incoming calls will be missed. PDA functions (including the use of email) are useful features and can be used. See Chapter 7.

73. **C.** The Security log will record auditable events. The System log will record operating system events, such as when it was last shut down or when it was booted. The Application log will record events from applications or programs. The Setup log is a newer log and includes events related to application setup. See Chapter 7.

74. **C.** DNS logging could include unauthorized zone transfer attempts (which would occur if an unauthorized party attempted to download DNS zone records). DHCP logs would help to identify a rogue DHCP server. Port scan attempts could be identified in firewall or intrusion detection logs. An unauthorized zone transfer attempt can be done using the command line tool NSLookup and is not detectable by an intrusion detection system. See chapters 5 and 7.

75. **A.** You can secure logs by copying or saving them to a remote log server. Storing them on write-once, read-many (WORM) media such as CD-R would be secure, but USB flash drives or rewritable media (DVD-RW) would make them easily accessible and allow them to be changed. Securing them with permissions is a good idea, but not if they are accessible to all authenticated users. See Chapter 7.

76. **C.** You can control who can access the logs by changing the security groups that access them—in effect changing the permissions. Moving the logs won't necessarily protect them if the same users have access. A host-based intrusion

detection system (HIDS) can detect unauthorized intrusions, but not files that users have access to normally. Hashing the log files can detect if they are modified, but it won't prevent the logs from being accessed.
See Chapter 7.

77. **A, B.** File integrity auditing is the process of creating hashes of log files that can be used to later determine if the files have been modified. If files are stored on USB drives or rewritable media (such as DVD-RW), they can be modified, losing data integrity.
See Chapter 7.

78. **B.** Two tapes are needed—the full backup created on Saturday night and the differential tape from Tuesday night. All restores must start by restoring the full backup. When using differential backups, only the most recent differential backup must be restored.
See Chapter 8.

79. **C.** Carbon dioxide (CO_2) is the best choice of those listed to combat an electrical fire while also preventing damage to equipment and protecting personnel. Foam (and other water-based) agents is conductive and may damage the equipment or pose electrical shock hazards to personnel. Heat is an element of fire, so adding heat won't help put it out.
See Chapter 8.

80. **D.** A Faraday cage is designed to prevent signals from emanating outside the enclosure and also prevents signals from entering the enclosure, so cell phones would not work within a Faraday cage. Proximity cards, computers, and flash drives all work locally without requiring signals to transmit outside the room, so they would work.
See Chapter 8.

81. **D.** A Faraday cage is designed to mitigate data emanation and also prevents EMI/RFI from entering the enclosure. TEMPEST is a government program designed to measure emanations. A mantrap is used to prevent piggybacking. EMI and RFI are types of interference.
See Chapter 8.

82. **D.** Attackers can break encryptions easier when weak keys are used. A block cipher is stronger than a stream cipher, but cryptography doesn't include something called a steaming cipher. Most algorithms are public, which allows them to be tested. Weak algorithms fall into disuse.
See Chapter 9.

83. **D.** AES256 is a fast, highly secure encryption algorithm. It performs better than both DES and 3DES. MD5 and SHA1 are hashing algorithms used for integrity checking.
See Chapter 9.

84. **B.** RC5 is a symmetric encryption algorithm. MD5 and SHA1 are hashing algorithms. RSA is an asymmetric algorithm.
See Chapter 9.

85. **A.** HTTPS uses Secure Sockets Layer (SSL) to secure traffic on the Internet; SSL uses public and private keys for asymmetric encryption and a session key for symmetric encryption. AES is a fast, strong, symmetric encryption. DES is a weak symmetric encryption that was replaced with 3DES, and then AES. MD5 is a message-digest algorithm used to create a hash to verify integrity.
See Chapter 9.

86. **A.** The Diffie-Hellman encryption algorithm is used for secure-key exchange. RSA uses keys from large prime numbers that can't be factored. Hashing algorithms (such as MD5 and SHA1) are used to validate integrity. AES is the selected standard after 3DES and does perform better than 3DES.
See Chapter 9.

87. **B.** One method of steganography is to modify the least significant bit of many or all of the bytes to embed a message in the file. If the most significant byte was modified, the modification would be much more apparent. Modifying only a single bit in the file header wouldn't allow a message to be included. Steganography does not change the format of the file.
See Chapter 9.

88. **C.** A flaw related to early implementations of Pretty Good Privacy (PGP) is that the user had to trust the public key that was received. PGP uses of Web-of-Trust instead of a hierarchical model with a root CA; current versions of PGP can use a hierarchical model.
See Chapter 9.

89. **C.** Secure/Multipurpose Internet Mail Extensions (S/MIME) is used in email messaging applications to encrypt and digitally sign email messages; S/MIME provides confidentiality, integrity, authentication, and non-repudiation. SSL is used to encrypt HTTP traffic. TPM uses a pre-shared key to provide whole disk encryption. Return receipts can be used to provide proof of email delivery.
See Chapter 9.

90. **B.** Hashing is used to provide integrity. Encryption is used to provide confidentiality. Public and private keys are used for asymmetric encryption.
See Chapter 9.

91. **D.** A one-way function cannot be reversed to decode the original data. Secure hash algorithms are one-way functions. Encryption includes the ability to decrypt the data.
See Chapter 9.

92. **A.** A rainbow table is a table of calculations performed separately and then used as a lookup table during the password-cracking process to discover weak passwords. A hash generator will perform a calculation on a message or file to produce a number called the hash. Domain name kiting is the practice of repeatedly registering a domain name, and then deleting it before five days have passed. A protocol analyzer is used to capture and analyze traffic on a network.
See Chapters 7 and 9.

93. **D.** The MD5 hash provides assurances of integrity, but since the hashes are different, it indicates the file is no longer the same as the original file. It is likely infected with a virus, but even if the virus scan passes without an error, you should still consider the file suspect and notify the web site administrator. While

MD5 is susceptible to collision attacks, this is not an issue when used to validate the integrity of files.
See Chapter 9.

94. **A.** A digital signature is created by encrypting a hash of the message with the private key of the sender. The encrypted hash can be decrypted by the receiver using the sender's public key (which is matched to the sender's private key). Public key (or asymmetric) cryptography doesn't use a session key.
See Chapter 9.

95. **B.** If a private key becomes compromised, it should be revoked by the CA and published on the CRL. Users can't revoke a certificate. A certificate can't be cancelled. Reissuing a certificate won't revoke the compromised certificate.
See Chapter 9.

96. **D.** Most browsers include a lock icon that can be clicked to view details of the certificate. A certificate used for a secure web site would not be in the root Certificate Authority store. CRLs are requested by the application, not by visiting a web page. If HTTPS is in the path, it indicates a certificate has been used to create the connection, but it doesn't validate the certificate.
See Chapter 9.

97. **A.** The principle of least privilege specifies that individuals or processes are granted rights and permissions needed to perform their jobs, but no more. If need-to-know was a possible answer, both answers could be correct since the question doesn't specify whether the access includes rights and permissions to perform functions or merely permissions to access data. Implicit deny is a principle often used with routers and firewalls where rules are created to allow traffic, but all other traffic is blocked or denied. Mandatory vacations force employees to take annual vacations to reduce the possibility that employees are involved in malicious activities such as embezzlement. Discretionary Access Control (DAC) is an access control model where every object (such as files and folders) has an owner, and the owner has exclusive control of the object.
See Chapter 10.

98. **A.** One of the threats posed by USB flash drives is that Personally Identifiable Information (PII) can easily be transferred to a USB drive and lost to an attacker. PII wouldn't be destroyed or modified by a USB flash drive, and copying PII from a USB flash drive to a system isn't a threat. While USB flash drives also pose the threat of spreading malware from system to system, this is not directly related to PII, and it's highly unlikely that malware from a USB would destroy or modify PII on a system; if anything, it would attempt to steal the data.
See Chapter 10.

99. **D.** The first step in response to an incident is to contain or isolate the problem. This can often be done by simply disconnecting the cable on the NIC. Notification should be done after containment, but policy would often dictate the notification of someone on an incident response team. You should ensure that a system has antivirus software and updated signature files installed; however, the first step should be to contain the problem to the single system before installing the software and updating definitions.
See Chapter 10.

100. **B.** A chain of custody verifies that evidence presented in court is the same evidence that was collected; a chain of custody should be established when seizing any evidence. The other documents listed won't take the place of chain of custody documentation.
See Chapter 10.

Appendix A - Acronym List

This acronym list is intended to provide you with a quick reminder of what the acronym represents along with a short explanation to jog your memory. Where appropriate, the concepts are explained in greater depth within the book. You can use the index to identify the specific pages on which the topics are covered.

3DES – Triple Digital Encryption Standard. A symmetric algorithm used to encrypt data. Today, AES is commonly used instead of 3DES.

ACE – Access Control Entry. Identifies a user or group that is granted permission to a resource. ACEs are contained within a DACL in NTFS.

ACL – Access control list. A list of rules used to grant access to a resource. In NTFS, a list of ACEs makes up the ACL for a resource. In a firewall, an ACL identifies traffic that is allowed or blocked.

AES – Advanced Encryption Standard. A symmetric algorithm used to encrypt data. AES is quick and highly secure.

AES256 – Advanced Encryption Standard 256-bit. AES using 256-bit encryption keys.

AH – Authentication Header. IPSec includes both AH and ESP. AH provides authentication, and ESP provides encryption. AH is identified with protocol ID number 51.

ALE – Annualized loss expectancy. Used to measure risk with ARO and SLE. Identifies total amount of loss expected for a given risk. SLE * ARO = ALE.

ARO – Annualized Rate of Occurrence. Used to measure risk with ALE and SLE. Identifies how many times a loss is expected to occur in a year. SLE * ARO = ALE.

ARP – Address Resolution Protocol. Resolves IP addresses to MAC addresses.

AUP – Acceptable Use Policy. Used to ensure that personnel know the purpose of a company's IT structure and the methods used to access it.

BGP – Border Gateway Protocol. Protocol used by routers on the Internet to share routing information.

BIOS – Basic Input/Output System. A computer's firmware used to manipulate different settings such as the date/time, boot drive, and access password.

BOTS – Network Robots. An automated program or system used to perform one or more tasks. A network of bots is referred to as a botnet. (Bots is not truly an acronym but often expressed as though it is.)

CA – Certificate Authority. An organization that manages, issues, and signs certificates. CAs can be public or private.

CCTV – Closed-circuit television. Use of video cameras to monitor a specific location.

CHAP – Challenge Handshake Authentication Protocol. Authentication mechanism where a server challenges a client.

CRL – Certification Revocation List. A list of certificates that have been revoked. A CRL is published by a CA.

DAC – Discretionary Access Control. An access control model where all objects have owners and owners can modify permissions for the objects (files and folders). Other access control models are MAC and RBAC.

DACL – Discretionary Access Control List. List of Access Control Entries (ACEs) in NTFS. Each ACE includes a security identifier (SID) and a permission.

DDoS – Distributed denial-of-service. An attack on a system launched from multiple sources intended to make a computer's resources or services unavailable to users. DDoS attacks are often launched from zombies in botnets.

DES – Digital Encryption Standard. Symmetric encryption standard. Uses 56 bits and is considered cracked.

DHCP – Dynamic Host Configuration Protocol. A service used to dynamically assign TCP/IP configuration information to clients. DHCP is often used to assign IP addresses, subnet masks, default gateways, DNS server addresses, and much more.

DLL – Dynamic Link Library. A compiled set of code that can be called from other programs.

DMZ – Demilitarized zone. Area between two firewalls separating the Internet and an intranet. Provides a layer of protection for Internet-facing servers.

DNS – Domain Name System. Used to resolve host names to IP addresses. DNS is the primary name resolution service used on the Internet and is also used on internal clients. DNS uses port 53.

DoS – Denial-of-service. An attack on a system intended to make a computer's resources or services unavailable to users.

DRP – Disaster recovery plan. A comprehensive document designed to help a company predict and plan for possible disasters, such as hurricanes, floods, and fires.

ECC – Elliptic curve cryptography. An asymmetric encryption algorithm commonly used with smaller wireless devices.

EMI – Electromagnetic interference. Interference caused by motors, power lines, and fluorescent lights. Cables can be shielded to protect signals from EMI.

ESP – Encapsulating Security Protocol. IPSec includes both AH and ESP. AH provides authentication, and ESP provides encryption. ESP is identified with protocol ID number 50.

FTP – File Transfer Protocol. Used to upload and download files to an FTP server. FTP uses ports 20 and 21.

GPO – Group policy object. Group Policy is used within Microsoft Windows to manage users and computers within a domain. GPOs can be created, configured, and linked to a site, domain, or Organizational Unit to quickly configure and manage many users and computers.

HIDS – Host-based intrusion detection system. An IDS used to monitor an individual server or workstation.

HIPS – Host-Based Intrusion Prevention System. An extension of a host-based IDS. Designed to react in real time to catch an attack in action.

HTML – HyperText Markup Language. Language used to create web pages served on the Internet. HTML documents are displayed by web browsers and delivered over the Internet using HTTP or HTTPS.

HTTP – Hypertext Transfer Protocol. Used for web traffic on the Internet and in intranets. HTTP uses port 80.

HTTPS – Hypertext Transfer Protocol over SSL. Secure (encrypted) HTTP traffic. HTTPS uses port 443.

HVAC – Heating, ventilation, and air conditioning. Systems within a building used for climate control. Climate control is important for both people and equipment.

ICMP – Internet Control Message Protocol. Used for diagnostics such as ping. Many DoS attacks use ICMP.

IGMP – Internet Group Management Protocol. Used for multicasting. Computers belonging to a multicasting group have a multicasting IP address in addition to a standard unicast IP address.

IDS – Intrusion detection system. System designed to detect attacks. An IDS can be either host-based (HIDS) or network-based (NIDS).

IEEE – Institute of Electrical and Electronic Engineers. International organization with a focus on electrical, electronics, and information technology topics. IEEE standards are well respected and followed by vendors around the world.

IIS – Internet Information Services. A Microsoft Windows web server. IIS comes free with Microsoft Windows Server products.

IMAP4 – Internet Message Access Protocol v4. Used to store email on servers and allow clients to manage their email on the server. IMAP4 uses port 143.

IP – Internet Protocol. Identifies hosts using an IP address. IPv4 uses 32 bits for the IP address, and IPv6 uses 128 bits for the IP address.

IPX/SPX – Internetwork Packet Exchange/Sequenced Packet Exchange. Used by Novell in earlier implementations of Novell Netware. Replaced with TCP/IP in current implementations.

IPSec – Internet Protocol Security. Used to encrypt traffic on the wire. IPSec includes both AH and ESP. AH provides authentication, and ESP provides encryption.

ISA – Internet Security Accelerator. Microsoft server product that is used as a firewall, a proxy server, or both.

ISP – Internet Service Provider. Company that provides Internet access to customers.

JVM – Java Virtual Machine. An application that runs Java applets in an isolated virtual environment. The JVM is sometimes referred to as a sandbox.

KDC – Key Distribution Center. Part of the Kerberos protocol used for authentication. The KDC issues tickets and ticket-granting tickets to clients that have been authenticated.

L2F – Layer 2 Forwarding. Previously used by Cisco for VPNs. L2F was combined with PPTP to create L2TP.

L2TP – Layer 2 Tunneling Protocol. Tunneling protocol used with VPNs. L2TP is commonly used with IPSec (L2TP/IPSec). L2TP uses port 1701.

LAN – Local area network. Group of hosts connected within a network.

LANMAN – Local Area Network Manager. Older authentication protocol used to provide backward compatibility to Windows 9x clients. LANMAN passwords are easily cracked due to how they are stored.

LDAP – Lightweight Directory Access Protocol. Language used to communicate with directories such as Microsoft's Active Directory. LDAP uses port 389 when unencrypted and port 636 when encrypted.

MAC – Mandatory Access Control. Access control model that uses sensitivity labels assigned to objects (files and folders) and subjects (users). Other access control models are DAC and RBAC.

MAC – Media access control. A 48-bit address used to uniquely identify network interface cards. Commonly displayed as six pairs of hexadecimal characters.

MAC – Message authentication code. Method used to provide integrity for messages. A MAC uses a secret key to encrypt the hash.

MBSA – Microsoft Baseline Security Analyzer. A free tool provided by Microsoft to check systems for updates and common vulnerabilities.

MD5 – Message-Digest 5. A hashing function used to provide integrity. MD5 uses 128 bits.

MS-CHAP – Microsoft Challenge Handshake Authentication Protocol. Microsoft's implementation of CHAP. MS-CHAPv2 provides mutual authentication.

NAS – Network Access Service. A service used to provide access to an internal network from an outside location. Also known as Remote Access Service provided by a Remote Access Server.

NAT – Network Address Translation. A service that translates public IP addresses to private and private IP addresses to public. Static NAT uses one-to-one mapping, and dynamic NAT uses multiple public IP addresses.

NetBEUI – NetBIOS Extended User Interface. Legacy networking protocol. Does not support routing and largely replaced with TCP/IP.

NIDS – Network-based intrusion detection system. IDS used to monitor a network.

NIPS – Network-Based Intrusion Prevention System. An extension of a network-based IDS. Designed to react in real time to catch an attack in action.

NNTP – Network News Transfer Protocol. Used to host newsgroups where users share information with each other. NNTP uses port 119.

NTFS – New Technology File System. A file system used in Microsoft operating systems that provides security.

NTLM – New Technology LANMAN. Authentication protocol intended to improve LANMAN. NTLMv1 stores the password in LANMAN format for backward compatibility, making the password easy to crack. NTLMv2 is significantly improved.

OSPF – Open Shortest Path First. Protocol used by routers in larger networks to share routing information.

OVAL – Open Vulnerability Assessment Language. International standard proposed for vulnerability assessment scanners to follow.

P2P – Peer-to-peer. Virtual networks used for file sharing. P2P networks are highly susceptible to data leakage problems where files are unintentionally shared.

PAP – Password Authentication Protocol. An older authentication protocol where passwords were sent across the network in clear text.

PDA – Personal digital assistant. Small, handheld computing device such as an iPhone or a BlackBerry.

PGP – Pretty Good Privacy. Commonly used to secure email communications between two private individuals. Instead of a public CA, PGP often uses a Web-of-Trust, or a peer-to-peer CA.

PII – Personally Identifiable Information. Information about individuals that can be used to trace a person's identity.

PKI – Public Key Infrastructure. Group of technologies used to request, create, manage, store, distribute, and revoke digital certificates.

PIN – Personal identification number. A number known by a user and entered for authentication. PINs are often combined with smart cards to provide two-factor authentication.

POP3 – Post Office Protocol v3. Used to transfer email from mail servers to clients. POP3 uses port 110.

PPP – Point-to-Point Protocol. Used to create dial-up connections.

PPTP – Point-to-Point Tunneling Protocol. Tunneling protocol used with VPNs. PPTP uses UDP port 1723.

RADIUS – Remote Authentication Dial-In User Service. Provides central authentication for remote access clients.

RAID – Redundant Array of Inexpensive (or Independent) Disks. Multiple disks added together to increase performance or provide protection against faults.

RAID-0 – Disk striping. RAID-0 improves performance but does not provide fault tolerance.

RAID-1 – Disk mirroring. RAID-1 uses two disks and provides fault tolerance.

RAID-5 – Disk striping with parity. RAID-5 uses three or more disks and provides fault tolerance.

RAS – Remote Access Service. A server used to provide access to an internal network from an outside location. RAS is also known as Remote Access Server and sometimes referred to as Network Access Service (NAS).

RBAC – Role Based Access Control. An access control model that uses roles to define access. When a user is placed into a role, he is granted all the access provided to the role. Other access control models are MAC and DAC.

RBAC – Rule Based Access Control. An access control model that uses rules to define access. Rules are created by the administrator to grant or deny access. Other access control models are MAC and DAC.

RIPv2 – Routing Information Protocol version 2. Protocol used by routers in smaller networks to share routing information.

RC – Ron's Code or Rivest's Cipher. Symmetric encryption algorithm that includes versions RC2, RC4, RC5, and RC6. RC4 was a less secure stream cipher, and RC5 and RC6 use the more secure block cipher method.

RFI – Radio frequency interference. Interference from RF sources such as AM or FM transmitters. RFI can be filtered to prevent data interference, and cables can be shielded to protect signals from RFI.

RSA – Rivest, Shamir, and Adleman. An asymmetric algorithm used to encrypt data and digitally sign transmissions. Relies on the fact that large prime numbers can't be factored. Named after its creators. RSA is also the name of the company they founded together.

S/MIME – Secure/Multipurpose Internet Mail Extensions. Used to secure email. S/MIME provides confidentiality, integrity, authentication, and non-repudiation.

SCCM – System Center Configuration Manager. Microsoft's replacement product for Systems Management Server (SMS). Includes patch management, operating system deployment, hardware and software inventory, and remote control capabilities.

SCSI – Small Computer System Interface. Set of standards used to connect peripherals to computers. Commonly used for SCSI hard disks and/or tape drives.

SHA – Secure Hash Algorithm. A hashing function used to provide integrity. SHA1 uses 160 bits.

SHTTP – Secure Hypertext Transfer Protocol. An alternative to HTTPS. Infrequently used.

SID – Security identifier. Unique set of numbers and letters used to identify each user and each group in Microsoft environments.

SLA – Service level agreement. An agreement between a company and a vendor that stipulates performance expectations, such as minimum uptime and maximum downtime levels.

SLE – Single loss expectancy. Used to measure risk with ALE and ARO. Identifies the expected dollar amount for a single event resulting in a loss. SLE * ARO = ALE.

SLIP – Serial Line Interface Protocol. An older protocol used to provide connections to remote computers using serial ports, modems, and phone lines.

SMS – Systems Management Server. Used to manage large numbers of computers. Includes patch management, operating system deployment, hardware and software inventory, and remote control capabilities.

SMTP – Simple Mail Transfer Protocol. Used to transfer email between clients and servers and between email servers and other email servers. SMTP uses port 25.

SNMP – Simple Network Management Protocol. Used to manage network devices such as routers or switches. The original SNMP had vulnerabilities, but SNMP v2 and v3 are more secure.

SSID – Security Set Identifier. Identifies the name of a wireless network.

SSH – Secure Shell. Used to encrypt traffic such as telnet and FTP on the wire. SSH uses port 22.

SSL – Secure Sockets Layer. Used to encrypt traffic on the wire. SSL is used with HTTPS to encrypt HTTP traffic on the Internet with both symmetric and asymmetric encryption algorithms. SSL operates on the Session layer and uses port 443 when encrypting HTTPS traffic.

SSO – Single sign-on. Authentication method where users can access multiple resources on a network using a single account.

STP – Shielded twisted pair. Cable type used in networks that includes shielding to prevent interference from EMI and RFI, and reduce the risk of a signal passing from one cable to another through cross talk.

SUS – Software Update Services. A free Microsoft Windows Server product that can be used to deploy updates. Superseded by WSUS.

TACACS+ – Terminal Access Controller Access-Control System+. Provides central authentication for remote access clients. Used as an alternative to RADIUS. TACACS+ uses port 49.

TCO – Total cost of ownership. A factor considered when purchasing new products and services. TCO attempts to identify the cost of a product or service over its lifetime.

TCP – Transmission Control Protocol. Provides guaranteed delivery of IP traffic using a three-way handshake. Operates on the Transmission layer.

TCP/IP – Transmission Control Protocol / Internet Protocol. Represents the full suite of protocols.

TFTP – Trivial File Transfer Protocol. Used to transfer small amounts of data with UDP. FTP is used to transfer larger files using TCP for guaranteed delivery.

TKIP – Temporal Key Integrity Protocol. Wireless security protocol introduced to address the problems with WEP. TKIP was used with WPA.

TLS – Transport Layer Security. Used to encrypt traffic on the wire. TLS is identified as the replacement for SSL and operates on the Transport layer.

TPM – Trusted platform module. Combination of hardware and software used to encrypt an entire hard drive. TPMs often use a pre-shared key (PSK).

UDP – User Datagram Protocol. Used instead of TCP when guaranteed delivery of each packet isn't necessary. Operates on the Transmission layer.

UPS – Uninterruptible power supply. A battery backup intended to provide power to a system when commercial power fails. UPS is intended to last a short period of time for the system to shut down smoothly or to transfer to generator power.

URL – Universal Resource Locator. Address used to access web resources, such as http://www.sy0-201.com.

USB – Universal Serial Bus. A serial connection used to connect peripherals such as printers, flash drives, and external hard disk drives.

UTP – Unshielded twisted pair. Cable type used in networks that do not have any concerns over EMI, RFI, or cross talk. If these are a concern, STP is used.

VLAN – Virtual local area network. LAN that uses a switch to connect multiple computers.

VPN – Virtual private network. Provides access to a private network over a public network such as the Internet.

WAN – Wireless Area Network. Two or more LANs connected over a distance using slower connections, such as a T1 or 56 Kbps.

WEP – Wired Equivalent Privacy. Original wireless security protocol. Had significant security flaws and was replaced with WPA, and ultimately WPA2.

WLAN – Wireless local area network. Network connected wirelessly.

WPA – Wi-Fi Protected Access. Replaced WEP as a wireless security protocol. Superseded by WPA2.

WPA2 – Wi-Fi Protected Access version 2. Newer security protocol used to protect wireless transmissions.

WSUS – Windows Server Update Services. A free Microsoft Windows Server product that can be used to deploy updates.

WTLS – Wireless Transport Layer Security. Used to encrypt traffic for smaller wireless devices.

Index

Bolded page numbers indicate the main discussion of a topic

W